THE EMERGENCE OF EU CRIMINAL LAW

Criminal law can no longer be neatly categorised as the product and responsibility of domestic law. That this is true is emphasised by the ever-increasing amount of legislation stemming from the European Union (EU) which impacts, both directly and indirectly, on the criminal law. The involvement of the EU institutions in the substantive criminal laws of its Member States is of considerable legal and political significance. This book deals with the emerging EU framework for creating, harmonising and ensuring the application of EU criminal law.

This book aims to highlight some of the consequences of EU involvement in the criminal law by examining the provisions which have been adopted in the field of information and communications technology. It provides an overview of the criminal law competence of the EU and evaluates the impact of these developments on the criminal laws of the Member States. It then goes on to consider the EU legislation which requires Member States to regulate matters such as data protection, e-security, intellectual property and various types of illegal content. In the course of this evaluation, particular consideration is given to issues such as the basis on which the EU institutions establish the need for criminal sanctions, the liability of service providers and the extent to which the Member States have adhered to, or departed from, the legislation in the course of implementation.

Volume 14 in the series Studies in International and Comparative Criminal Law

Studies in International and Comparative Criminal Law
General Editor: Michael Bohlander

Criminal law had long been regarded as the preserve of national legal systems, and comparative research in criminal law for a long time had something of an academic ivory tower quality. However, in the past 15 years it has been transformed into an increasingly, and moreover practically, relevant subject of study for international and comparative lawyers. This can be attributed to numerous factors, such as the establishment of ad hoc international criminal tribunals and the International Criminal Court, as well as to developments within the EU, the UN and other international organisations. There is a myriad of initiatives related to tackling terrorism, money laundering, organised crime, people trafficking and the drugs trade, and the international 'war' on terror. Criminal law is being used to address global or regional problems, often across the borders of fundamentally different legal systems, only one of which is the traditional divide between common and civil law approaches. It is therefore no longer solely a matter for domestic lawyers. The need exists for a global approach which encompasses comparative and international law.

Responding to this development this new series will include books on a wide range of topics, including studies of international law, EU law, the work of specific international tribunals, and comparative studies of national systems of criminal law. Given that the different systems to a large extent operate based on the idiosyncracies of the peoples and states that have created them, the series will also welcome pertinent historical, criminological and socio-legal research into these issues.

Recent titles in this series:

Hybrid and Internationalised Criminal Tribunals
Sarah Williams

The Defendant in International Criminal Proceedings:
Between Law and Historiography
Björn Elberling

Counsel Misconduct before the International Criminal Court
Professional Responsibility in International Criminal Defence
Till Gut

The Concept of Mens Rea in International Criminal Law:
The Case for a Unified Approach
Mohamed Elewa Badar

Genocide and Crimes Against Humanity: Misconceptions and
Confusion in French Law and Practice
Caroline Fournet

The Emergence of EU Criminal Law

Cybercrime and the Regulation of the Information Society

Sarah Summers
Christian Schwarzenegger
Gian Ege
and
Finlay Young

·HART·
PUBLISHING
OXFORD AND PORTLAND, OREGON
2014

Published in the United Kingdom by Hart Publishing Ltd
16C Worcester Place, Oxford, OX1 2JW
Telephone: +44 (0)1865 517530
Fax: +44 (0)1865 510710
E-mail: mail@hartpub.co.uk
Website: http://www.hartpub.co.uk

Published in North America (US and Canada) by
Hart Publishing
c/o International Specialized Book Services
920 NE 58th Avenue, Suite 300
Portland, OR 97213-3786
USA
Tel: +1 503 287 3093 or toll-free: (1) 800 944 6190
Fax: +1 503 280 8832
E-mail: orders@isbs.com
Website: http://www.isbs.com

Hart Publishing is an imprint of Bloomsbury Publishing plc.

British Library Cataloguing in Publication Data
Data Available

ISBN: 978-1-84946-727-8

Typeset by Hope Services, Abingdon
Printed and bound in Great Britain by
CPI Group (UK) Ltd, Croydon CR0 4YY

TABLE OF CONTENTS

LIST OF ABBREVIATIONS

ACTA	Anti-Counterfeiting Trade Agreement of 1 October 2011
AFSJ	Area of freedom, security and justice
All ER	All England Law Reports
Art	Article
BEREC	Body of European Regulators of Electronic Communications
Berne Convention	Berne Convention for the Protection of Literary and Artistic Works of 9 September 1886
bn	billion
CEPOL	European Police College
cf	confer
ch	chapter
CIA	Central Intelligence Agency
CIIs	critical information infrastructures
CJEU	Court of Justice of the European Union
CMLR	Common Market Law Review
COE	Council of Europe
Commission	European Commission
Convention on Cybercrime	Convention on Cybercrime signed in Budapest on 23 November 2001, ETS 185
CP	French Criminal Code
CPPA	United States' Child Pornography Prevention Act 1996
CPS	Crown Prosecution Service
Corruption Protocol	Protocol drawn up on the basis of Article K.3 of the Treaty on European Union to the Convention on the Protection of the European Communities' Financial Interests [1996] OJ C313/2
DE	Germany
DR	Decisions and Reports
EAW	European Arrest Warrant
ECB	European Central Bank
ECHR	European Convention on Human Rights of 4 November 1950; 213 UNTS 221, ETS No 5
ECJ	European Court of Justice
ECR	European Court Reports
ECSC	Treaty establishing the European Coal and Steel Community of 18 April 1951
ECtHR	European Court of Human Rights

EC Treaty	Treaty of the establishment of a European Economic Community (TEC), signed at Rome on 25 March 1957 and entered into force on 1 October 1958
EC3	European Cybercrime Centre
ed/eds	Editor(s)
edn	Edition
EEC	The Treaty establishing the European Economic Community of 25 March 1957
eg	exempli gratia
EHRR	European Human Rights Reports
EL Rev	European Law Review
EP	European Parliament
EPPO	European Public Prosecutor's Office
E-Privacy Directive	Directive 2002/58/EC of the European Parliament and of the Council of 12 July 2002 concerning the processing of personal data and the protection of privacy in the electronic communications sector [2002] OJ L201/37
ERA	Academy of European Law
et al	et alii
etc	etcetera
ETS	European Treaty Series
et seq	et sequens
EU	European Union
Euratom	The Treaty establishing the European Atomic Energy Community of 25 March 1957
EU Treaty	The Treaty on European Union, signed at Maastricht on 7 February 1992, entered into force 1 November 1993, [1992] OJ C191/1 (Maastricht Treaty)
EUR	Euro
Europol	European Police Office
EWCA Crim	England and Wales Court of Appeal (Criminal Division) Decisions
FATF	Financial Action Taskforce
FD	Framework Decision
fn	footnote
GBP	Pound sterling
GDP	Gross Domestic Product
HRRS	Höchstrichterliche Rechtsprechung im Strafrecht
Ibid	ibidem
ICC	International Criminal Court
ICCLR	International Company and Commercial Law Review
ICCPR	International Covenant on Civil and Political Rights of 16 December 1966, 999 UNTS 171

ICT	Information and communications technology
ID	Identity document
ie	id est
ILC	International Review of Intellectual Property and Competition Law
IMF	International Monetary Fund
Int J Law Info Tech	*International Journal of Law* and *Information Technology*
IPRs	Intellectual property rights
IPRED	Directive 2004/48/EC of the European Parliament and of the Council of 29 April 2004 on the enforcement of intellectual property rights (OJ L157, 30 April 2004) [2004] OJ L195/15 (Enforcement Directive)
IPRED2	Directive on criminal measures aimed at ensuring the enforcement of intellectual property rights
ISPs	Internet service providers
IT	Information technology
ITU	International Telecommunication Union
JCMS	Journal of Common Market Studies
JHA	Justice and home affairs
JIBLR	Journal of International Banking Law and Regulation
LQR	Law Quarterly Review
MEP	Members of the European Parliament
MMS	Multimedia Messaging Service
MP	Members of Parliament
n	note
NGO	Non-governmental organizations
NJW	Neue Juristische Wochenschrift
No	Number
OECD	Organisation for Economic Co-operation and Development
OLAF	European Anti-Fraud Office
OJ	Official Journal of the European Union
Ö-StGB	Austrian Criminal Code
para	paragraph
PIF Convention	Convention drawn up on the basis of Article K.3 of the Treaty on European Union, on the protection of the European Communities' financial interests [1995] OJ C316/49
PJCC	Police and judicial cooperation in criminal matters
P2P	peer to peer
QC	Queen's Counsel
QMV	qualified majority voting
RabelsZ	Rabels Zeitschrift für ausländisches und internationales Privatrecht
Reg	Regulation

Rome Convention	International Convention for the Protection of Performers, Producers of Phonograms and Broadcasting Organizations, Rome on 26 October 1961
S Ct	Supreme Court Reporter
SMS	Short Message Service
SOCA	Serious Organized Crime Agency
StGB	German Criminal Code
Suffolk UL Rev	Suffolk University Law Review
TEU	Treaty on European Union
TFEU	Treaty on the Functioning of the European Union; Treaty of Lisbon amending the Treaty on European Union and the Treaty establishing the European Community, signed at Lisbon on 13 December 2007, entered into force on 1 December 2009 [2007] OJ C306/1 (Treaty of Lisbon)
TMG	German Telemedia Act
TRIPS Agreement	Agreement on Trade-Related Aspects of Intellectual Property Rights, annex 1C of the Marrakesh Agreement Establishing the World Trade Organization, signed in Marrakesh, Morocco on 15 April 1994
UCE	Unsolicited Commercial Email
UDHR	Universal Declaration of Human Rights of 10 December 1948
UK	United Kingdom
UKHL	United Kingdom House of Lords Decisions
UN	United Nation
UNESCO	United Nations Educational, Scientific and Cultural Organization
UNODC	United Nations Office on Drugs and Crime
UNTS	United Nation Treaty Series
US	United States
USA	United States of America
USC	United States Code
Util Law Rev	Utilities Law Review
UWG	German Unfair Competition Act
vol	volume
WCT	WIPO Copyright Treaty adopted in Geneva on 20 December 1996
WLR	Weekly Law Reports
WTO	World Trade Organisation
WIPO	World Intellectual Property Organisation
WPPT	WIPO Performances and Phonograms adopted in Geneva on 20 December 1996
YEL	Yearbook of European Law
ZERP	Zentrum für Europäische Rechtspolitik der Universität Bremen
ZEuS	Die Zeitschrift für Europarechtliche Studien

ZIS	Zeitschrift für Internationale Strafrechtsdogmatik
ZSR	Zeitschrift für Schweizerisches Recht
ZStrR	Schweizerische Zeitschrift für Strafrecht

Introduction

I EU Criminal Law

The involvement of the European Union (EU) in the field of criminal law has occurred gradually and at several different levels. There are a number of reasons for the adoption of this rather guarded and piecemeal approach. Undoubtedly, the most significant of these is the reticence of Member States to relinquish control of their criminal justice systems. The criminal law is often, and has traditionally been, regarded as being tied to the community in which it is applied; its character as being inextricably connected to the particular distinctiveness of the nation state. This is reflected in the fact that several provisions of the Treaty establishing the European Community expressly stated that the measures were not to impinge on the application of national criminal law or the national administration of justice.[1]

Recognition of the 'exceptional' character of the criminal law was also implied by the 'pillar' structure enshrined in the Treaty on European Union (TEU).[2] This structure was created to accommodate the possibility of inter-governmental regulation of certain areas, including police and judicial cooperation in criminal matters, which were deemed too sensitive to be suitable subjects for supra-national regulation. The complexity of the EU's involvement can be seen, in part, to have been a consequence of the pillar structure as the different institutions of the EU sought to establish their responsibility for, and indeed competency in relation to, matters involving the criminal law. Although the criminal law was traditionally treated as falling firmly within the third pillar, various developments, most clearly evidenced by the famous ruling of the European Court of Justice in the environmental crime case,[3] suggested that the first pillar institutions and legislation in relation to the criminal law could not be disregarded. These indications were confirmed

[1] See eg Art 135 EC Treaty (Customs cooperation) and Art 280 EC Treaty (Fraud against the EU Budget).

[2] The TEU was signed in Maastricht on 7 February 1992 and entered into force on 1 November 1993. The TEU was amended by the Treaty of Amsterdam, which was signed on 2 October 1997 and came into force on 1 May 1999 and by the Treaty of Nice, which was signed on 26 February 2001 and which entered into forced on 1 February 2003.

[3] Case C-176/03 *Commission of the European Communities v Council of the European Union* [2005] ECR I-7879; see further ch 1.

with the coming into force of the Treaty of Lisbon which led to the collapse of the pillar structure and to direct EU competence for the criminal law.[4]

Before embarking on an examination of the involvement of the EU institutions in the field of criminal law, it is important to reflect on the nature of the developments which have emanated from the EU in the context of the creation of 'European criminal law'. The majority of provisions affecting the substantive criminal law have ostensibly been created to further the aims of the creation of an area of freedom justice and security through the harmonisation of the criminal laws of the Member States. Many provisions were created under the auspices of the third pillar and required Member States to criminalise everything from the 'fraudulent making or altering of currency'[5] and 'the intentional accessing without right of the whole or any part of an information system',[6] to 'the intentional acquisition or possession of child pornography, whether undertaken by means of a computer system or not, without right'.[7] Typically these provisions were characterised by their relatively vague nature and Member States were left with considerable discretion in determining the sentences to be applied, although maximum sentences were sometimes stipulated. The potential lack of competence of the first pillar institutions in the field of criminal law meant that considerable care was taken not to refer to the criminal law as such in the context of the first pillar legislation. Nevertheless, as we shall see, even though the sanctions and penalties imposed as a result of contraventions of the provisions of first pillar instruments were not expressly referred to as criminal in nature, but merely had to be 'effective, proportionate and dissuasive', the Member States frequently responded by creating criminal law provisions. This meant that the criminal law was afforded de facto importance.

There is now a clear legal basis in the Lisbon Treaty for the creation of criminal law. Article 83(1) TFEU provides for the creation of 'minimum rules concerning the definition of criminal offences and sanctions in the area of particularly serious crime with a cross-border dimension', while Article 83(2) TFEU makes provision for the creation of criminal law for the purposes of approximation and ensuring the effective implementation of EU policy. The Commission frequently highlights the need to harmonise the criminal law and this objective is now clearly set out in Article 83 TFEU. The reasons behind, and the success of, the EU's harmonisation of the criminal law will be considered in the course of this book.

[4] See further ch 2.

[5] Council Framework Decision of 29 May 2000 on increasing penalties and other sanctions against counterfeiting in connection with the introduction of the Euro (2000/383/JHA) [2000] OJ L140/1, Art 3(1)(a).

[6] Council Framework Decision 2005/222/JHA of 24 February 2005 on attacks against information systems [2005] OJ L69/67, Art 2(1).

[7] Council framework Decision 2004/68/JHA of 22 December 2003 on combating the sexual exploitation of children and child pornography [2004] OJ L13/44, Art 3 (1)(d).

II The Importance of the Information Society

Globalisation and the dawn of the information era have meant that computers and information technology have become an essential part of modern society. Individuals, companies, governments and economies are heavily dependent on computer systems and the possibilities which they offer in terms of the transfer of information and facilitation of communication. This dependency calls, in turn, for regulation in order to maintain and safeguard these technologies. Criminal law is just one aspect of such regulation,[8] but it is nevertheless of considerable significance. The EU institutions frequently refer to the cross-border nature of crime as facilitated by advances in information and communications technology to justify the need for the harmonisation of the criminal law.

It is precisely the nature of the information society which has provided the most significant challenges for those seeking to regulate criminal behaviour in this field. Traditional approaches to the criminal law whereby the national state is responsible for detecting, investigating and prosecuting crime is complicated in cases in which crimes committed are in one country, while the victim lives in another. This has led the EU, and the Commission in particular, to characterise an internationally coordinated approach to judicial cooperation in criminal matters as being not simply desirable but also essential.

Different problems are associated with regulating the different types of crime. In relation to old types of crime committed with new tools (eg child pornography or racism),[9] many of the definitions of the crimes already exist, but the crimes are committed using modern technology which requires that countries adapt their laws to deal with the challenges of modern technology. There may therefore be a need for harmonisation to facilitate international cooperation in investigating and prosecuting crimes which involves the creation of common definitions of crimes, determination of the applicable jurisdiction, and attention to procedural issues such as preventing double jeopardy. With regard to new crimes committed with recourse to new tools (such as denial of service attacks),[10] difficulties include framing effective legislation to regulate criminal liability, but once the laws are enacted, they pose similar issues to the old crimes. Consideration of the EU's approach in the context of the information society allows analysis of the scope and limits of criminalisation and harmonisation under the auspices of Article 83(1) and (2) TEFU.

[8] See further ch 3.
[9] See further ch 5.
[10] See further ch 7.

III Criminalisation, Harmonisation, Europeanisation

The EU has become increasingly involved in the process of criminalisation and harmonisation of the criminal law. In this book we will examine these developments by focusing on its criminal law regulation with relevance for information and communications technology. In the first few chapters, we will trace the development of the EU's involvement in the criminal law by considering its law-making competence before and after the coming into force of the Treaty of Lisbon (chapters 1 and 2), before going on to consider how the EU's criminal law provisions fit into its broader regulatory approach to information and communications technology (chapter 3). This will provide the basis in the following chapters for an assessment of the process of criminalisation and harmonisation of the substantive criminal law in the context of the information society.

Chapter 4 focuses on the attempt to introduce criminal law provisions designed to enforce intellectual property rights and the considerations of the limits of criminalisation in an area of law in which there is little consensus between the Member States about the extent of, or indeed the need for, criminal liability. In chapters 5 and 6 we consider whether the EU's goal of harmonising the criminal law can be said to have been a success by considering the nature of the implementation of the provisions in the Member States. Chapter 5 focuses on content regulation by way of the criminal law (previously regulated in the third pillar and now falling within Article 83(1) TFEU), while the focus of chapter 6 is on the protection of privacy through the criminal law (previously a first pillar matter, now falling within the scope of Article 83(2) TFEU). Chapter 7 then goes on to set out the EU's approach to cybercrime and considers whether harmonisation of the substantive criminal law is possible in the absence of detailed guidance on the definition of 'general part' principles such as intention or principles guiding participation in crime. These chapters provide the basis, in the concluding part, for a critique of the EU's approach to criminal law in the information society and for some broader thoughts on the future of EU criminal law.

1

The Development of EU Criminal Law

I Introduction

The criminal law, once considered the preserve of the nation state, has increasingly become subject to 'outside' involvement. This is particularly evident in Europe, where the competence of the institutions of the European Union (EU) for the criminal law has steadily increased. Initially, the European Community had no formal role in relation to justice and home affairs policy.[1] It was clearly established that these areas fell outside the remit of the EC Treaty.[2] This position changed dramatically following the establishment at Maastricht of the Treaty on European Union (EU Treaty) which led to the dismantling of the previous treaty structure.[3] The inability of the EU Member States to agree to surrender national sovereignty in the spheres of justice and home affairs and foreign and security policy resulted in the establishment of the EU as 'founded on the European Communities, supplemented by policies and forms of co-operation established by this Treaty'.[4]

The EU was most commonly portrayed as resting on three metaphorical pillars, each with a separate institutional and regulatory structure: the first pillar (also known as the Community pillar) comprised, broadly, the European Communities, while the second and third pillars encompassed common foreign and security policy and justice and home affairs, respectively.[5] Although the establishment of the third pillar prevented the Member States from having to relinquish national sovereignty over justice and home affairs (JHA) matters to the European Community, it nevertheless meant that JHA policy, including the criminal law, could no longer be classed solely as a matter of national concern.[6]

[1] See S Peers, *EU Justice and Home Affairs Law*, 3rd edn (Oxford, Oxford University Press, 2011) 9.

[2] Treaty of the establishment of a European Economic Community (EEC), signed at Rome on 25 March 1957 and entered into force on 1 January 1958 (EC Treaty).

[3] The Treaty on European Union, signed at Maastricht on 7 February 1992, entered into force 1 November 1993, [1992] OJ C191/1 (Maastricht Treaty).

[4] *Ibid*, Art A.

[5] *Ibid*, Titles V and VI respectively.

[6] The third pillar was sometimes referred to as intergovernmental which some have argued was misleading, see eg A Arnull, A Dashwood, M Dougan, M Ross, E Spaventa and D Wyatt, *Wyatt and Dashwood's European Union Law*, 6th edn (Oxford, Hart, 2011) 329.

This clear allocation of criminal law competence to the third pillar and not the first pillar came under increasing strain as the European Commission argued that the EC Treaty allowed the Community to require the Member States to create criminal law. This position was subsequently endorsed by the European Court of Justice (ECJ), thereby setting the stage for further developments brought about by the creation of the Lisbon Treaty. The Lisbon Treaty dismantled the pillar structure and enabled the Union to replace and succeed the European Community. The Lisbon framework consists principally in two treaties: the Treaty on European Union (TEU) and the Treaty on the Functioning of the European Union (TFEU) which are designed to provide a unified legal structure for the EU.[7] The consequence of the Lisbon reforms is the qualified *communautarisation* of matters previously regulated in the third pillar including the criminal law.[8]

In this chapter, the development of the EU's involvement in the substantive criminal law in the context of both the third and first pillars will be traced. By considering the manner in which EU criminal law has developed, it should be possible to get a better idea of why cooperation between the Member States in the criminal law context was deemed to be so important. This in turn should provide some insight into the extent of the EU's involvement in the criminal law and will provide the basis for examining developments in the wake of the Lisbon reforms.

II Substantive Criminal Law in the Third Pillar

A Criminal Law within an 'Area of Freedom, Security and Justice'

Cooperation in the field of justice and home affairs had been under discussion long before the establishment of the EU Treaty, but the developments at Maastricht marked a turning point for EU involvement in the criminal law. The Member States expressly signalled their intention to 'develop close cooperation on Justice and Home Affairs'[9] and various policy areas were identified as being of common interest, including asylum policy, rules governing the crossing of the external borders of the Member States, immigration policy, combating drug addiction, combating international fraud, civil judicial cooperation, criminal judicial cooperation, customs cooperation, and police cooperation.[10] With regard to the criminal law, judicial cooperation was understood as principally requiring enhanced procedural cooperation between the Member States. The relevance of the substantive criminal law was only deemed evident in the context of exceptions

[7] Treaty of Lisbon amending the Treaty on European Union and the Treaty establishing the European Community, signed at Lisbon on 13 December 2007, entered into force on 1 December 2009, [2007] OJ C306/1 (Treaty of Lisbon).

[8] See further ch 2.

[9] Maastricht Treaty, Art B.

[10] *Ibid*, Arts K–K.9 (Title VI).

to the double criminality rule which were seen as requiring a degree of standardisation of the laws of the Member States. The EU's involvement in the substantive criminal law was at this stage tentative and, it is fair to say, of limited significance for national criminal law.[11]

The developments at Maastricht must now be seen as a precursor to considerably more important developments brought about by the revisions to the EU Treaty at Amsterdam, which led to many 'third pillar' areas, including civil legal matters and asylum and immigration, being transferred to the 'first pillar'.[12] Police and judicial cooperation in criminal matters (PJCC) was the only area to be left within the third pillar.[13] Following these reforms, the objective of the third pillar was no longer simply to promote cooperation between Member States on matters involving JHA but rather to enable the creation of an 'area of freedom, security and justice' (AFSJ) by improving police and judicial cooperation in criminal matters and by preventing racism and xenophobia.[14] This was to be achieved through 'preventing and combating crime', through 'closer cooperation between police forces, customs authorities and other competent authorities . . . and judicial and other competent authorities' and through the 'approximation, where necessary, of rules on criminal matters in the Member States'.[15] Although it was generally accepted that these provisions could not be construed as providing a general mandate for the harmonisation of the criminal law within the EU, they nevertheless provided for considerable inroads to be made into the national sovereignty of the Member States in respect of their criminal laws.[16]

The revisions to the EU Treaty at Amsterdam were of considerable relevance, not least because they emphasised the transfer of responsibility for the substantive criminal law away from the individual Member States and towards the institutions of the EU. The establishment of the AFSJ can be seen as an attempt by the

[11] See eg Joint Action 97/154/JHA of 24 February 1997 adopted by the Council on the basis of Article K.3 of the Treaty on European Union concerning action to combat trafficking in human beings and sexual exploitation of children [1997] OJ L63/2; Joint action/96/443/JHA of 15 July 1996 adopted by the Council on the basis of Article K.3 of the Treaty on European Union, concerning action to combat racism and xenophobia [1996] OJ L185/5; Joint Action 96/750/JHA of 17 December 1996 adopted by the Council on the basis of Article K.3 of the Treaty on European Union concerning the approximation of the laws and practices of the Member States of the European Union to combat drug addiction and to prevent and combat illegal drug trafficking [1996] OJ L342/6; Council Recommendation of 27 September 1996 on combating the illegal employment of third-country nationals [1996] OJ C304/1.

[12] Title IV of the EC Treaty.

[13] Treaty of Amsterdam amending the Treaty on European Union, The Treaties Establishing the European Communities and Certain Related Acts [1997] OJ C340/1, signed in Amsterdam on 2 October 1997, entered into force 1 May 1999 (Treaty of Amsterdam).

[14] Art 29 (ex Art K1) EU Treaty: 'Without prejudice to the powers of the European Community, the Union's objective shall be to provide citizens with a high level of safety within an area of freedom, security and justice by developing common action among the Member States in the fields of police and judicial cooperation in criminal matters and by preventing and combating racism and xenophobia'.

[15] *Ibid.*

[16] See eg P de Hert, 'Division of Competences between National and European Levels with regard to Justice and Home Affairs' in J Apap (ed), *Justice and Home Affairs in the EU: Liberty and Security Issues after Enlargement* (Cheltenham, Edward Elgar, 2004) 80: 'A harmonisation of criminal law, for instance, per se is not envisaged'.

EU to mark out its own legal territory, thereby enabling it to claim authority over the criminal law.[17] These revisions, together with developments brought about by the European Court of Justice (ECJ),[18] can be seen to have prepared the ground for the introduction of Treaty of Lisbon, which came into force in December 2009 and which was, from the perspective of the criminal law, ground breaking.[19]

In order to properly understand these developments, which will be considered in detail in chapter 2, it is instructive to examine the third pillar provisions impacting on the criminal law and the nature of the evolution of the EU's involvement in the substantive criminal law. The legal effects of the third pillar legislation will be preserved until it is repealed, annulled or amended in the implementation of the Treaties[20] and there are signs, as Baker and Harding have suggested, that 'the heritage of complicated and obscure method represented by the third pillar approach may be still resilient and influential'.[21] Further, the third pillar legislation provides some insight into the preoccupations of the European institutions and of course to some extent those of the Member States. It is also important to bear in mind that several of the issues of relevance in the context of the third pillar will continue to be of relevance in the future. Many questions remain unanswered, particularly in relation to the usefulness of the concepts of 'approximation' or mutual recognition as objectives for criminal law reform, the coherence of national criminal law in the light of the piecemeal approach to the creation or restatement of the definitions of crime, the principles and values underpinning the criminal law reform and fundamental issues involving the legitimacy of the involvement of the EU.

B The Legislative Instruments and Processes of the Third Pillar

(i) Third Pillar Legislative Instruments and their Legal Effect

Before the judgments of the ECJ in the cases involving the institutional competence of the EU institutions in the context of the criminal law[22] and the coming into force of the Lisbon Treaty,[23] it was commonly thought that Articles 29–42 of the EU Treaty (the third pillar) were the principal, if not the sole, legal bases for the creation

[17] See eg C Harding, 'The Identity of European Law: Mapping Out the European Legal Space' (2000) 6 *European Law Journal* 128.

[18] Notably Case C-176/03 *Commission v Council* [2005] ECR I-7879, [2005] 3 CMLR 20 and Case 440/05 *Commission v Council* [2007] ECR I-9097. For an overview of developments following the judgments of the ECJ in these cases, see section III D below.

[19] See also E Baker and C Harding, 'From Past Imperfect to Future Perfect? A Longitudinal Study of the Third Pillar' (2009) 34 *EL Rev* 25, 26 referring to these developments as 'momentous'. See further ch 2.

[20] Protocol on Transitional Provisions, Art 9. See also V Mitsilegas, *EU Criminal Law* (Oxford, Hart, 2009) 41.

[21] Baker and Harding, 'From Past Imperfect to Future Perfect? (n 19) 26

[22] Case C-176/03 *Commission v Council* (n 18); Case 440/05, *Commission v Council* (n 18). See further section III D, below.

[23] See further ch 2.

of EU law involving the imposition of criminal liability. The EU Treaty set out four separate legislative instruments to assist in 'the pursuit of the objectives of the Union': framework decisions, decisions, common positions and conventions.[24] Decisions were binding, did not entail direct effect and could be adopted by the Council of Europe for any purpose except the approximation of the laws and regulations of the Member States.[25] Common positions, on the other hand, embodied the approach of the Union in relation to a particular matter, while conventions could be adopted by the Member States on the recommendation of the Council. These instruments were of limited importance in the substantive criminal law-making context, which was almost entirely dominated by framework decisions.[26] The framework decision proved popular within the third pillar law-making context, particularly as Member States were required to implement them within a relatively short period of time (usually around two years) and because they did not require ratification by the national parliaments.

According to the EU Treaty, framework decisions were designed to enable the approximation of the laws of the Member States. They had a similar character to directives in that while they were binding on the Member States, the manner in which they were to be implemented in domestic law was left to the Member States.[27] They differed fundamentally from directives, however, in that they did not have direct effect and thus did not give rise to rights or obligations which individuals could enforce before their national courts.[28] Prior to the ECJ's judgment in *Pupino*, it was assumed that framework decisions were not capable of giving rise to indirect effects. In *Pupino*, however, the ECJ held that 'the principle of conforming legislation' was 'binding in relation to framework decisions adopted in the context of Title VI of the Treaty on European Union'.[29] In view of this the national courts were required to 'take consideration of all the rules of national law and to interpret them, so far as possible, in the light of the wording and purpose of the Framework Decision'.[30] This ruling had limited implications

[24] Art 34(2) EU Treaty.

[25] Art 34(2)(c) EU Treaty.

[26] See eg Peers, *EU Justice and Home Affairs Law* (n 1) 25 who writes that: 'in practice, the use of Conventions was phased out after the Treaty of Amsterdam provisions entered into force'.

[27] Art 34(2)(b) EU Treaty: 'The Council shall take measures and promote cooperation, using the appropriate form and procedures as set out in this title, contributing to the pursuit of the objectives of the Union. To that end, acting unanimously on the initiative of any Member State or of the Commission, the Council may: . . . (b) adopt framework decisions for the purpose of approximation of the laws and regulations of the Member States. Framework decisions shall be binding upon the Member States as to the result to be achieved but shall leave to the national authorities the choice of form and methods. They shall not entail direct effect'.

[28] *Ibid.* See J Steiner, L Woods and C Twigg-Flesner, *EU Law*, 10th edn (Oxford, Oxford University Press, 2009) 5.2 for an overview of the principle of direct effect.

[29] Case C-105/3 *Pupino* [2005] ECR I-4135, para 43.

[30] *Ibid*, para 62. For commentary, see M Fletcher, 'Extending "Indirect Effect" to the Third Pillar: The Significance of Pupino' (2005) 30 *EL Rev* 862–77; S Prechal, 'Direct Effect, Indirect Effect, Supremacy and the Evolving Constitution of the European Union' in Bernard (ed), *The Fundamentals of EU Law Revisited: Assessing the Impact of the Constitutional Debate* (Oxford, Oxford University Press, 2007) 35–70; S Peers, 'Salvation Outside the Church: Judicial Protection in the Third Pillar After the Pupino and Segi Judgments' (2007) 44 *CMLR* 883–929.

for the substantive criminal law, as the ECJ chose to expressly exclude the application of the indirect effects principle to provisions giving rise to the imposition of criminal liability. In almost identical terms to its line of authority preventing directives from directly imposing criminal liability in the absence of implementing legislation, it held that:

> [T]he obligation on the national court to refer to the content of a framework decision when interpreting the relevant rules of its national law is limited by general principles of law, particularly those of legal certainty and non-retroactivity. In particular, those principles prevent that obligation from leading to the criminal liability of persons who contravene the provisions of a framework decision from being determined or aggravated on the basis of such a decision alone, independently of an implementing law.[31]

It is clear therefore that the provisions of the various framework decisions imposing criminal liability did not give rise to either direct or indirect effect. They only attained legal effect or applicability through their implementation in the national law of the individual Member States. This was of importance not least because of the requirements that criminal laws be generally applicable, certain and non-retrospective.[32] The lack of independent legal effect of the framework decisions could be seen to lessen the need for them to comply, or indeed to free them altogether from compliance, with the general principles which the law is generally seen to depend upon for its legitimacy. To some extent this also seems implicit in the suggestion in the *Pupino* ruling that constraints such as legal certainty are to be guaranteed by national and not by EU law.

(ii) Law Making in the Third Pillar (PJCC)

There can be little doubt that the desire to prevent the transfer of criminal law making competence to the Community meant that the clear problems associated with law making in the third pillar were played down. In spite of widespread recognition of the lack of accountability and transparency in relation to police and judicial cooperation in the third pillar,[33] the deficiencies of the third pillar were perceived as being 'less visible' than the deficit in legitimacy and democracy which would accompany any transfer of the criminal law into the competence of the Community.[34]

[31] Case C-105/3 *Pupino* (n 29), paras 44–45.

[32] See eg R Unger, *Law in Modern Society: Towards a Criticism of Social Theory* (New York, Free Press, 1976) 176, referring to the rule of law as defined 'in its broadest sense' 'by the interrelated notions of neutrality, uniformity, and predictability'. See also L Fuller, *The Morality of Law* (New Haven, Yale University Press, 1963) 33–94, who outlines eight requirements to which legal norms must adhere: generality, promulgation, non-retroactivity, clarity, freedom from contradictions, the possibility that the law can be upheld, constancy and congruence. With regard to criminal laws, the requirements of certainty and non-retrospectivity have attained constitutional status and are guaranteed inter alia by Art 7(1) of the European Convention on Human Rights.

[33] S Douglas-Scott, 'The Rule of Law in the European Union – Putting the Security into the Area of Freedom, Security and Justice' (2004) 29 *EL Rev* 219.

[34] E Herlin-Karnell, 'Commission v Council: Some Reflections on Criminal Law in the First Pillar' (2007) 13 *European Public Law* 69, 73.

Doubts about the legitimacy of the European institutions' law-making role were especially pronounced in the context of the third pillar legislative process, and in particular, in relation to the so-called 'democratic deficit'. The Council acting unanimously (except in relation to procedural matters) had responsibility for adopting measures on the basis of an initiative either from the Commission or a Member State. The Commission made considerable use of its right of initiative and was responsible for instigating the vast majority of framework decisions relating to the substantive criminal law.[35] The third pillar legislative process was especially notable for the limited role afforded to the European Parliament. Initially, under the Maastricht Treaty, the views of the Parliament only had to be 'taken into consideration'. Its role was enhanced by the Treaty of Amsterdam, but only to the extent that it was granted 'consultative status' in relation to all measures, except common positions.[36] According to Peers, the opinions of the Parliament 'had limited if any impact upon the Council third pillar'.[37]

The deficiencies of the third pillar legislative process were widely acknowledged. Dominated by the Council of Ministers, a permanent institution that met, and often passed legislation, behind closed doors, it was not infrequently compared with the North Korean legislature, said to be 'the only other body in the world which passes legislation in secret'.[38] The Council of Ministers operated by way of a large number of committees – the most important of which was the rotating Article 36 Committee – comprised of one official from each of the Member States and a representative of the Commission and described as being both the 'engine of third-pillar policy-making'[39] and 'notorious and secretive'.[40] The strictly marginal role afforded both the national and European parliaments coupled with the secrecy surrounding the adoption of legislation led to criticism of 'a deplorable lack of scrutiny and transparency, suggesting that the rule of law is scarcely observed in this area of EU activity'.[41]

[35] See Peers, *EU Justice and Home Affairs Law* (n 1) 25.

[36] Art 39 EU Treaty.

[37] Peers, *EU Justice and Home Affairs Law* (n 1) 25.

[38] The United Kingdom Parliament Select Committee on European Scrutiny, *Democracy and Accountability in the EU and the Role of National Parliaments*, 33rd Report, HC 152 (London, 2002).

[39] C Harlow, *Accountability in the European Union* (Oxford, Oxford University Press, 2002) 42.

[40] P Craig and G de Búrca, *EU Law*, 5th edn (Oxford, Oxford University Press, 2011) 18 referring to the K4 committee. On issues relating to difficulties accessing Council documents, see eg Case T-188/98 *Aldo Kuijer v Council* [2000] ECR 2000 II-01959 and the cases brought by the NGO Statewatch to the Ombudsman: Complaint 1055/25 Statewatch against the Council (25 November 1996), Annual Report for 1998, 256–59; Complaint 1053/25STATEWATCH/United Kingdom/IJH against the Council, Annual Report for 1996, 232–33.

[41] Douglas-Scott, 'The Rule of Law in the European Union – Putting the Security into the Area of Freedom, Security and Justice', 221. See also S Skinner, 'The Third Pillar Treaty Provisions on Police Cooperation: Has the EU Bitten off More than it Can Chew?' (2002) 8 *Columbia Journal of European Law* 203, 215–19.

(iii) The Role of the ECJ in the Third Pillar

The ECJ traditionally had a markedly more restricted role in the context of the third pillar than in relation to the first pillar, although an important revision precipitated by the Amsterdam Treaty provided for the introduction of a preliminary reference procedure, similar to that set out in Article 234 EC Treaty.[42] The ECJ was given jurisdiction, subject to certain specified conditions, to give preliminary rulings 'on the validity and interpretation of framework decisions and decisions, on the interpretation of conventions established under this Title and on the validity and interpretation of the measures implementing them'.[43] This jurisdiction was subject to a number of caveats, notably the stipulation in Article 35(2) of the EU Treaty that only the courts of Member States which had made a declaration accepting the jurisdiction of the court could make a reference. Several Member States including the UK, Ireland and Denmark did not accept the jurisdiction of the ECJ pursuant to Title VI EU Treaty.[44] Another restriction on the jurisdiction of the ECJ was contained in Article 35(5) of the EU Treaty, which prevented the ECJ from reviewing 'the validity or proportionality of operations carried out by the police or other law enforcement services of a Member State or the exercise of the responsibilities incumbent upon Member States with regard to the maintenance of law and order and the safeguarding of internal security'. According to Arnull this posed 'a serious threat to the uniform application of the law in the Member States to which they apply'.[45]

Following the Amsterdam revisions, the ECJ was also provided with the authority to rule in an action brought by the Commission or a Member State on the legality of a framework decision with regard to 'lack of competence, infringement of an essential procedural requirement, or infringement of the Treaty or any rule of law relating to its application, or misuse of powers'.[46] In view of the fact that the provisions of the various framework decisions, which set out to harmonise the laws of the Member States, were relatively basic, judicial control and interpretation represented one way of ensuring their uniform and coherent application. In view of the restricted remit of the ECJ, coupled with the refusal of several Member States to accept its jurisdiction, it was unlikely, however, that the ECJ would have

[42] See generally A Arnull, 'Taming the Beast? The Treaty of Amsterdam and the Court of Justice' in D O'Keefe and P Twomey (eds), *Legal Issues of the Amsterdam Treaty* (Oxford, Hart, 2007) 153–92.

[43] Art 35 EU Treaty. See K Lenaerts and L Jadoul, 'Quelle contribution de la Cour de justice des Communautés européennes au développement de l'espace de liberté, de sécurité et de justice?' in G de Kerchove and A Weyembergh (eds), *L'espace pénal européen: enjeux et perspectives* (Bruxelles, Editions de l'Université de Bruxelles, 2002) 201.

[44] See A Albors-Llorens, 'Changes in the Jurisdiction of the European Court of Justice after the Treaty of Amsterdam' (1998) 35 *CMLR* 1273; A Arnull, *The European Union and its Court of Justice* (Oxford, Oxford University Press, 2006) 72–74. The Czech Republic and Hungary have however accepted the ECJ's jurisdiction, [2005] OJ L327/19.

[45] Arnull, *The European Union and its Court of Justice* (n 44) 72.

[46] Art 36(5) EU Treaty.

been able to contribute significantly to the harmonisation of the criminal laws of the Member States.[47]

C Criminal Laws Created to Protect the Interests of the EU

The first substantive criminal law provisions to be created under the auspices of the third pillar were designed to address conduct deemed to threaten the institutions and specific interests of the EU. The European Community was in the relatively unusual position of having responsibility for its budget, but having to rely on the Member States to investigate and prosecute acts of fraud or other illegal conduct with regard to the budget. The Commission attempted to address this by imposing punitive sanctions (to be administered through the authorities of the Member States) and establishing various regulatory measures. This response proved only partially successful, however, and the focus shifted towards ways of ensuring increased cooperation between the Member States.[48]

In 1995 the Member States agreed a Convention on the Protection of the European Communities' Financial Interests (PIF or Fraud Convention),[49] which originated in 'the growing alarm at the fraud committed against the Community budget'.[50] Despite the opinion of the majority of Member States that their criminal laws were adequate to 'effectively' protect the Community's financial interests, studies carried out by the Commission emphasised the need in the 'fight against fraud' for a 'stronger and homogeneous enforcement policy in the Union'.[51] According to the Explanatory Report on the PIF Convention, an EU response was required, despite the fact that the Member States already had criminal law

[47] Cases considered by the ECJ in this capacity included Case C-105/03 *Pupino* (n 29) (concerning the Framework Decision on the standing of victims in criminal proceedings). It also ruled in several references concerning the application of the *ne bis in idem* principle in the context of the implementation of Art 54 of the Convention implementing the Schengen Agreement of 14 June 1985 between the Governments of the States of the Benelux Economic Union, the Federal Republic of Germany and the French Republic on the gradual abolition of checks at their common borders, signed on 19 June 1990 [2000] OJ L239/19, including notably in Joined Cases C-187/01 and C-385/01 *Hüseyn Gözütok and Klaus Brügge* [2003] ECR I-1345; for an informative comment, see M Fletcher, 'Some Developments to the ne bis in idem Principle in the European Union: Criminal Proceedings Against Hüseyn Gözütok and Klaus Brügge' (2003) 66 *Modern Law Review* 769–80. For criticism by the Commission in respect of the Member States' implementation of third pillar measures, see eg Communication from the Commission to the Council and the European Parliament Report on Implementation of the Hague Programme for 2007, Brussels, 2 July 2008, COM (2008) 373 final.

[48] For a useful overview of these developments, see A Posadas, 'Combating Corruption under International Law (2000) 10 *Duke Journal of Comparative and International Law* 345, 395–400.

[49] Convention drawn up on the basis of Article K.3 of the Treaty on European Union, on the protection of the European Communities' financial interests [1995] OJ C316/49. The Convention came into force on 17 October 2002.

[50] Explanatory Report on the Convention on the protection of the European Communities' financial interests [1997] OJ C191/1, 1.

[51] Protection of the Community's Financial Interests, Synthesis Document of the comparative analysis of the reports supplied by the Member States on national measures taken to combat wastefulness and the misuse of Community resources, Brussels, 14 November 1995, COM (95) 556 final, A 6 and A 25. See also Commission Staff Working Paper, 16 July 1993, SEC (93) 1172.

provisions 'to protect the Communities' financial interests in many areas', because various comparative studies had uncovered 'loopholes and incompatibilities' which were considered to be 'prejudicial to the punishment of fraud and to judicial cooperation in criminal matters between Member States'. The aim of the Convention was thus to 'ensure greater compatibility between Member States criminal law provisions by establishing minimum rules in criminal law, in order to make the fight against fraud affecting the Communities' financial interests more effective and even more dissuasive and to strengthen cooperation in criminal matters between the Member States'.[52]

In 1996 a Protocol (known as the Corruption Protocol)[53] was added to the Convention in order, principally, to tackle 'acts of corruption which involve national and Community officials and damage, or are likely to damage, the European Communities' financial interests'.[54] The Corruption Protocol was followed in 1999 by a Second Protocol which required Member States to establish money laundering provisions related to the proceeds of 'serious' fraud, as defined in Council Directive 91/308/EEC, and to active and passive corruption as a criminal offence.[55]

The principal factor uniting these legislative instruments was their shared goal of using the criminal law to protect the Communities' financial interests, but this changed with the establishment of a Convention against Corruption.[56] Buoyed by their success in reaching agreement on the PIF Convention, the Member States approved the Convention on Corruption despite the fact that it was not just limited to corruption involving the financial interests of the Communities but also extended to all acts of corruption. The agreement on the establishment of this Convention clearly indicated a willingness on the part of the Member States to progress beyond the limited remit of protecting the Communities' interests in relation to cooperation on the criminal law.[57] This readiness was confirmed in the Treaty of Amsterdam which set out cooperation in criminal matters as an objective of the EU and which

[52] Explanatory Report on the Convention on the Protection of the European Communities' Financial Interests [1997] OJ C191/1.

[53] Protocol drawn up on the basis of Article K.3 of the Treaty on European Union to the Convention on the Protection of the European Communities' Financial Interests [1996] OJ C313/2 (Corruption Protocol).

[54] Explanatory Report on the Second Protocol to the Convention on the Protection of the European Communities' Financial Interests [1999] OJ C91/8. See also L Ferola, 'Anti-Bribery Measures in the European Union: A Comparison with the Italian Legal Order' (2000) 28 *International Journal of Legal Information* 512, 521–25.

[55] Second Protocol, drawn up on the basis of Article K.3 of the Treaty on European Union, to the Convention on the Protection of the European Communities' Financial Interests [1997] OJ C221/12, Art 2.

[56] Council Act of 26 May 1997 drawing up, on the basis of Article K.3(2)(c) of the Treaty on European Union, the Convention on the fight against corruption involving officials of the European Union or officials of Member States of the European Union [1997] OJ C195/2.

[57] This is also highlighted by the various Joint Actions which were agreed around this time, eg Joint Action 98/699/JHA of 3 December 1998 adopted by the Council on the basis of Article K.3 of the Treaty on European Union, on money laundering, the identification, tracing, freezing, seizing and confiscation of instrumentalities and the proceeds from crime [1998] OJ C333/1.

provided new legal instruments, notably the framework decision, to assist in the achievement of this goal.

D 'Approximation' of the Criminal Law and its Legal Basis in the EU Treaty

As a consequence of the revisions at Amsterdam, the EU Treaty provided the EU Council with a mandate to progressively adopt measures establishing minimum rules relating to the constituent elements of certain criminal acts and penalties through the creation of framework decisions and a considerable body of legislation was created with the aim of 'approximating' or harmonising the substantive criminal laws of the Member States.[58] This notion of approximation pervades the legislation and policy in the field of JHA but was never precisely defined.[59] Weyembergh suggests that it 'constitutes a stronger model of legal integration than coordination and cooperation', but 'a weaker means of legal integration than unification'.[60] That approximation was not to be understood as complete unification is underlined by the nature of the legal instrument by which it was to occur. According to Article 34(2)(b) of the EU Treaty, framework decisions which are binding upon the Member States as to the results to be achieved, but which leave the national authorities the choice of form and methods to be used, were to be used for the purposes of approximating the laws of the Member States.[61] Member States were thus left with a certain margin of appreciation in relation to the implementation of the provisions. As a result of this, much of the legislation created to approximate the criminal law contains vague definitions of criminal conduct and even vaguer guidance on the sentences to be imposed through the prescription of so-called minimum maximum sentences.[62]

It should come as little surprise that the Council, or perhaps more accurately the Commission as the principal initiator of the majority of these framework decisions, took advantage of the opportunity to establish legislation in the criminal legal sphere. Less predictable though is the extent to which this drive towards 'approximation' of the criminal laws of the Member States exceeded the mandate extended by the EU Treaty. The legal basis for approximation of the criminal law was set out in Articles 29 and 31(e) of the EU Treaty. According to Article 29 of the EU Treaty the 'area of freedom, security and justice' was to be achieved through closer police

[58] See Art 29 EU Treaty read in conjunction with Arts 31(e) and 34.2(b) EU Treaty.

[59] See eg Communication from the Commission to the Council and the European Parliament, Area of Freedom, Security and Justice: Assessment of the Tampere Programme and Future Orientations, Brussels 2.6.2004, COM (2004) 401 final, 12; Council of the European, Draft Multiannual Programme: The Hague Programme; strengthening freedom, security and justice in the European Union, Brussels, 15 October 2004, JAI 370, 26.

[60] A Weyembergh, 'Approximation of Criminal Laws, the Constitutional Treaty and the Hague Programme' (2005) 42 *CMLR* 1567, 1567.

[61] For a comparison of the various legislative instruments and law-making processes and the implications of these for the criminal law, see ch 2.

[62] For discussion of this point, see ch 7.

and judicial cooperation and 'where necessary, through the approximation of rules on criminal matters in the Member States, in accordance with the provisions of Article 31(e)'.[63]

Although Article 31(c) of the EU Treaty, which allowed for action to be taken to ensure 'compatibility in rules applicable in the Member States, as may be necessary to improve such cooperation', was interpreted as providing a broad basis for approximation of the criminal law,[64] the specific reference in Article 31(e) of the EU Treaty to the establishment of minimum criminal laws and penalties in the fields of 'organised crime, terrorism and illicit drug trafficking', seemed to call into question any role for Article 31(c) of the EU Treaty as a legal basis for approximation.[65] A strict interpretation of Article 31(e) of the EU Treaty would have implied that 'approximation' ought to be restricted to, or at least primarily focused on, the substantive criminal law fields of terrorism, organised crime and drug trafficking. The seemingly restrictive nature of this list did not prove to be an obstacle to the approximation of criminal laws not referred to in Article 31(e) of the EU Treaty. Indeed it is clear that such a restrictive interpretation was wholly ignored in practice. At the European Council meeting in Tampere, for instance, the Council stated that 'with regard to national criminal law, efforts to agree on common definitions, incriminations and sanctions should be focused *in the first instance* on a limited number of sectors of particular relevance, such as financial crime (money laundering, corruption, Euro counterfeiting), drugs trafficking, trafficking in human beings, particularly exploitation of women, sexual exploitation of children, high tech crime and environmental crime'.[66] Following Tampere, several framework decisions were proposed or adopted in areas of substantive criminal law which were not referred to in the EU Treaty, nor even in the Tampere Presidency Conclusions or the Millennium Strategy.[67] Moreover, it is notable that some of the most important developments, such as the establishment of the European Arrest Warrant, were undertaken despite the fact that procedural issues,

[63] Art 31(1)(e): 'Common action on judicial cooperation in criminal matters shall include: progressively adopting measures establishing minimum rules relating to the constituent elements of criminal acts and to penalties in the fields of organised crime, terrorism and illicit drug trafficking'.

[64] See eg Framework Decision 2005/212/JHA of 24 February 2005 on confiscation of crime-related proceeds, instrumentalities and property [2005] OJ L68/49.

[65] See eg Weyembergh, 'Approximation of Criminal Laws' (n 60) 1569, who writes that 'the narrow wording of Article 31(e) creates a certain ambiguity'.

[66] Presidency Conclusions of the Tampere European Council, 15–16 October 1999, para 48 (emphasis added).

[67] See G Vermeulen, 'Where Do We Currently Stand with Harmonisation in Europe?' in A Klip and H Van der Wilt (eds), *Harmonisation and Harmonising Measures in Criminal Law* (Amsterdam, Royal Netherlands Academy of Science, 2002) 70, who writes: 'In practice . . . the number of subject areas in which approximation has been completed or is underway has quietly been extended beyond the limits indicated in the EU Treaty, and even beyond the limits of the list of subject areas indicated in the Tampere conclusions or the Millennium Strategy on organised crime, which itself was already significantly expanded in order to remain compatible with the Treaty (terrorism, illicit drug trafficking and organised crime itself)'. See also Weyembergh, 'Approximation of Criminal Laws' (n 60) 1569 et seq.

jurisdiction and extradition seemed to be excluded from the ambit of Article 31(e) of the EU Treaty.[68]

Framework decisions were created in the following areas with the aim of standardising the criminal laws of the Member States: counterfeiting of the Euro,[69] fraud and counterfeiting of non-cash means of payment instruments,[70] money laundering,[71] terrorism,[72] trafficking in human beings,[73] unauthorised entry, transit and residence,[74] corruption in the private sector, [75] sexual exploitation of children and child pornography,[76] illicit drug trafficking, [77] attacks against information systems,[78] protection of the environment through the criminal law,[79] ship source pollution,[80] organised crime,[81] and racism and xenophobia.[82] According to

[68] Council Framework Decision of 13 June 2002 on the European arrest warrant and the surrender procedure between Member States (2002/584/JHA) [2000] OJ L190/1. See eg H Satzger and T Pohl, 'The German Constitutional Court and the European Arrest Warrant: Cryptic Signals from Karlsruhe' (2006) 4 *Journal of International Criminal Justice* 686; A Alegre and M Leaf, *European Arrest Warrant* (London, Justice, 2003).

[69] Council Framework decision of 29 May 2000 on increasing protection by criminal penalties and other sanctions against counterfeiting in connection with the introduction of the euro (2000/383/JHA) [2000] OJ L140/1, amended by Council Framework Decision 2001/888/JHA of 6 December 2001 amending Framework Decision 2000/383/JHA on increasing protection by criminal penalties and other sanctions against counterfeiting in connection with the introduction of the euro [2001] OJ L329/3.

[70] Council Framework Decision 2001/413/JHA of 28 May 2001 on combating fraud and counterfeiting of non-cash means of payment [2001] OJ L149/1.

[71] Council Framework Decision of 26 June 2001 on money laundering, the identification, tracing, freezing, seizing and confiscation of instrumentalities and the proceeds of crime (2001/500/JHA) [2001] OJ L182/1.

[72] Council Framework Decision of 13 June 2002 on combating terrorism (2002/475/JHA) [2001] OJ L164/3; Council Framework Decision 2008/919/JHA of 28 November 2008 amending Framework Decision 2002/475/JHA on combating terrorism [2008] OJ L330/21.

[73] Council Framework Decision of 19 July 2002 on combating trafficking in human beings (2002/629/JHA) [2002] OJ L203/1.

[74] Council Framework Decision of 28 November 2002 on the strengthening of the penal framework to prevent the facilitation of unauthorised entry, transit and residence (2002/946/JHA) [2002] OJ L328/1.

[75] Council Framework Decision of 22 July 2003 on combating corruption in the private sector (2003/568/JHA) [2003] OJ L192/54.

[76] Council Framework Decision 2004/68/JHA of 22 December 2003 on combating the sexual exploitation of children and child pornography [2004] OJ L13/44.

[77] Council Framework Decision 2004/757/JHA of 25 October 2004 laying down minimum provisions on the constituent elements of criminal acts and penalties in the field of illicit drug trafficking [2004] OJ L335/8, see, in particular, Recital 3.

[78] Council Framework Decision 2005/222/JHA of 24 February 2005 on attacks against information systems [2005] OJ L69/67, Art 1.

[79] Council Framework Decision 2003/80/JHA of 27 January 2003 on the protection of the environment through the criminal law [2003] OJ L29/55. The Framework Decision was annulled following the judgment in Case 176/03 *Commission v Council* (n 18).

[80] Council Framework Decision 2005/667/JHA of 12 July 2005 to strengthen the criminal-law framework for the enforcement of the law against ship-source pollution [2005] OJ L255/164 annulled in Case 440/05 *Commission v Council* (n 18).

[81] Council Framework Decision 2008/841/JHA of 24 October 2008 on the fight against organised crime [2008] OJ L300/42, Art 2(a).

[82] Council Framework Decision 2008/913/JHA of 28 November 2008 on combating certain forms and expressions of racism and xenophobia by means of criminal law [2008] OJ L328/55.

the Treaty of Lisbon, these provisions maintain their legal effect until such time as they are amended.[83] As we shall see in chapter 2, the Commission has begun the process of converting the various framework decisions into directives. The abolition of the third pillar took place following the coming into force of the Treaty of Lisbon, but its demise was, as we shall see, far from a sudden occurrence; rather it was a consequence of the developing confidence on the part of the Commission in the Community's role in the criminal law.

III The Criminal Law Competence of the European Community

A Introduction

For many years it was largely taken for granted that the Treaty Establishing the European Community (EC Treaty) did not provide a legal basis for defining crimes or prescribing criminal sanctions. The involvement of the EU in criminal matters was thought to be possible only by way of Title VI of the Treaty on European Union (EU Treaty).[84] Although there was no express reference in the EC Treaty to this effect, various different factors seemed to support this view. First, in several Articles of the EC Treaty, including Articles 135 and 280 EC Treaty,[85] it was expressly stated that matters concerning the application of the criminal law and the administration of justice were to be reserved to the Member States.[86] Secondly, and perhaps more importantly, express competence for judicial cooperation in criminal matters was conferred on the EU by the Member States in Articles 29, 30, and 31(e) of the EU Treaty. This arrangement was of considerable legal and political significance as it allowed Member States to retain control over the power to impose criminal penalties, while constraining EU involvement by necessitating unanimous intergovernmental agreement for the proposed legislation.[87]

[83] Art 9 of the Transitional Protocol to the Treaty of Lisbon.

[84] Police and Judicial Cooperation in Criminal Matters (PJCC) – commonly referred to as the 'third pillar', see section II, above.

[85] For an alternative interpretation, see M Wasmeier and N Thwaites, 'The Battle of the Pillars: Does the European Community Have the Power to Approximate National Criminal Laws?' (2004) 29 *EL Rev* 613, 624–25.

[86] According to Art 280(4) EC Treaty on fraud against the financial interests of the Community: 'The Council, acting in accordance with the procedure referred to in Article 251, after consulting the Court of Auditors, shall adopt the necessary measures in the fields of the prevention of and fight against fraud affecting the financial interests of the Community with a view to affording effective and equivalent protection in the Member States. *These measures shall not concern the application of national criminal law or the national administration of justice*' (emphasis added).

[87] See section II, above.

If the Member States can be said to have been satisfied with the consequences of restricting EU competence by tying criminal legal developments to the third pillar, the Commission did not attempt to disguise its impatience. It complained that the 'third pillar method', particularly the principle of unanimity and the limited role of the ECJ, meant that it proved 'very difficult to move forward in areas such as mutual recognition in criminal matters and police cooperation'.[88] In 2004 it mounted a direct and high-profile challenge to the status quo by making an application for the annulment of a Framework Decision designed to harmonise the laws of Member States in relation to serious environmental offences, arguing that the Community legislature was competent to require Member States to prescribe criminal penalties for infringements of Community law designed to protect the environment.[89] It claimed that Article 175(1) EC Treaty – and not Articles 29, 31 and 34(2)(b) EU Treaty – was the correct legal basis for creating provisions aimed at protecting the environment through the criminal law.

The ECJ upheld the Commission's arguments and in doing so posed its own challenge to both the pillar structure and to the conventional view of the distribution of criminal law competency within the EU.[90] It was widely acknowledged that the ruling had considerable implications, extending far beyond the confines of environmental protection.[91] The scope of the Community's criminal law competence was subsequently further clarified in proceedings before the ECJ in which the Commission successfully challenged the legal basis of the EU Framework Decision on Ship Source Pollution[92] and the claims of the Council, supported by a large number of the Member States, that the earlier environmental protection case dealt 'exclusively with environmental matters and can only apply to environmental matters'.[93]

It should come as little surprise that the Council's and the Member States' reaction to these developments was decidedly sceptical. In a speech published in a German newspaper in January 2006, the then President of the European Council,

[88] Communication from the Commission to the Council and the European Parliament, Implementing the Hague Programme: the way forward, Brussels, 28 June 2006, COM (2006) 331, 3.1.

[89] Case C-176/03 *Commission v Council* (n 18).

[90] *Ibid*, para 47 referring to Case C-226/97 *Lemmens* [1998] ECR I-3711, para 19.

[91] Eg Communication from the Commission to the European Parliament and the Council on the implications of the Court's judgment of 13 September 2005 (Case C-176/03 *Commission v Council*), Brussels, 24 January 2005, COM (2005) 583 final: the principles expounded in the case 'go far beyond the case in question'; European Union Committee of the House of Lords, *The Criminal Law Competence of the European Community*, 42nd Report of Session 2005–06 (London, The Stationary Office, 2006), para 46: 'Whether the principles and approach set out in the Court's judgment are limited to environmental protection is far from clear'. But see the evidence of JP Puissochet, judge at the ECJ, to the French Sénat, Réunion de la délégation pour l'Union européenne du mercredi 22 février 2006, arguing that the principles in the Court's judgment are focused on the issue of environnemental protection.

[92] Case C-440/05 *Commission v Council* (n 18). See also I Christodoulou-Varotsi, 'Recent Developments in the EC Legal Framework on Ship-Source Pollution: The Ambivalence of the EC's Penal Approach' (2006) *Transportation Law Journal* 371.

[93] See European Union Committee of the House of Lords, *The Criminal Law Competence of the European Community*, para 44, see also the evidence of Mr P Lachmann, Chief Adviser EU Law and Constitutional Law, Danish Ministry of Foreign Affairs, attached to the Report.

Austrian Chancellor Wolfgang Schüssel, criticised the ECJ on the basis that 'in the last couple of years' it had 'systematically expanded European Competences, even in areas, where there is decidedly no [European] Community law'.[94] Similarly, Danish Prime Minister Anders Fogh Rasmussen accused the ECJ of 'assuming over-inflated authority'[95] and called for European cooperation to be 'put back on a democratic basis'.[96] The response of the Member States underlined just how significant the development of the Community's competence in relation to the criminal law was perceived to be. Despite these concerns, the adoption of the Treaty of Lisbon – according to which the EC Treaty becomes part of the Treaty on the Functioning of the European Union (TFEU) – has served to bring EU criminal law within the core area of the Union and within the scope of the Court of Justice's jurisdiction.[97]

In order to appreciate the significance of these developments, it is important to have an understanding of the role of the European Community in relation to the criminal law. In this section the legislative instruments and law-making processes of the first pillar will first be described. This will be followed by an examination of the Community's criminal law competence, as it was understood prior to and following the ECJ's rulings in the environmental protection and ship source cases. A comprehensive understanding of the Community's competence in this regard will provide a basis in chapter 2 for an examination of the implications for EU criminal law following the entry into force of the Treaty of Lisbon.

B The Legislative Instruments and Law-Making Processes of the First Pillar

(i) Community Laws and their Legal Effect

The laws of the first pillar stemmed from a number of sources, including, most importantly, the Treaties[98] and the secondary legislation deriving from the EC Treaty. The principal types of secondary legislation were set out in Article 249 EC Treaty which stated that in order to carry out their tasks and in accordance with the provisions of the Treaty, 'the European Parliament acting jointly with the Council, the Council and the Commission shall make regulations, issue directives,

[94] Interview with W Schüssel, President of the European Council, *Die Süddeutsche Zeitung*, 1 January 2006.

[95] '[C]ompétences trop étendues', see T Ferenczi, 'La Cour de justice est accusée d'outrepasser ses compétences', *Le Monde*, 13 January 2006.

[96] *Ibid*, 'sur des décisions démocratiques'.

[97] E Herlin-Karnell, 'The Lisbon Treaty and the Area of Criminal Law and Justice' (2008) 3 *European Policy Analysis* 1, 3. On the criminal law consequences of the Treaty of Lisbon, see ch 3.

[98] Including the Treaties establishing the European Communities: the Treaty establishing the European Coal and Steel Community (ECSC) of 18 April 1951; the Treaty establishing the European Economic Community (EEC) of 25 March 1957; and the Treaty establishing the European Atomic Energy Community (Euratom) of 25 March 1957. For an overview of the other sources, see Arnull et al, *Wyatt and Dashwood's European Union Law* (n 6) 126–27.

take decisions, make recommendations or deliver opinions'. Article 249 EC Treaty is now reproduced in Article 288 TFEU and thus these instruments continue to be of relevance. Only the first three types of legislation (regulations, directive and decisions) are binding. Although recommendations and opinions do not have binding force, they can nevertheless be the subject of a reference to the ECJ, seeking to challenge their interpretation or legality.

Regulations apply to all Member States, and automatically become part of the law of each Member State without the State having to incorporate the measure into its domestic law: they are thus 'binding' in their entirety and 'directly applicable'. They do not therefore need any additional implementation in order to take effect, although in some cases it may be necessary for the Member States to take measures in order to ensure their implementation.[99] The character of regulations means that it is very likely (although not to be automatically assumed) that they have direct effect.[100] If the regulation meets the criteria to be considered directly effective, it can be applied both vertically (ie in the context of the relationship between the state and an individual) or horizontally (ie enabling the law to be enforced by one individual against another).[101]

Decisions, on the other hand, are binding in their entirety only on those to whom they are addressed. Their extent was outlined by the ECJ in *Grad v Finanzamt Traunstein* where it held that:

> Although the effects of a decision may not be identical with those of a provision contained in a regulation, this difference does not exclude the possibility that the end result, namely the right of the individual to invoke the measure before the courts, may be the same as that of a directly applicable provision of a regulation.[102]

In the context of the criminal law, the most important first pillar legislative instrument is unquestionably the directive. Following the judgment of the ECJ in the environmental crime case,[103] the Commission proposed the introduction of several directives which required Member States to criminalise a variety of conduct.[104] Directives differ from regulations in that they do not have to be addressed

[99] In Case 93/71 *Leonesio v Ministerio dell'Agricoltura e delle Foreste* [1972] ECR 00287 it was held that it was unacceptable for implementing provisions to differ from those set out in the regulation.

[100] In order to have direct effect a provision must be sufficiently clear and precise, it must be unconditional and it must leave no room for the Member States to exercise discretion in its implementation. As such it is possible that a regulation, which fails to meet one or more of these criteria, will not give rise to direct effect.

[101] See eg Case C-253/00 *Antonio Munoz Cia SA v Frumar Ltd* [2002] ECR I-07289. On vertical and horizontal direct effect, see Steiner, Woors and Twigg-Flesner, *EU Law* (n 28) 92 et seq.

[102] Case 9/70 *Franz Grad v Finanzamt Traunstein* [1970] ECR 825, para. 5: 'It would be incompatible with the binding effect attributed to Decisions by Article 189 [now 249] to exclude in principle the possibility that persons affected may invoke the obligation imposed by a Decision . . . the effectiveness of such a measure would be weakened if the nationals of that State could not invoke it in the courts and the national courts could not take it into consideration as part of Community law'.

[103] Case C-176/03 *Commission v Council* (n 18).

[104] See eg the Proposal for a European Parliament and Council Directive on criminal measures aimed at ensuring the enforcement of intellectual property rights, Brussels, 12 July 2005, COM (2005) 276 final.

to every State and while they are binding as to the result to be achieved, they leave the Member States scope to determine the form and the method of their implementation in national law.[105] Consequently, they offer more flexibility than regulations in that they do not need to be drafted in such a way as to be exactly compatible with each legal system. Directives have been described as being 'particularly useful when the aim is to harmonize the laws within a certain area or to introduce complex legislative change'[106] and 'perfect instruments for harmonizing national legislations'.[107] It is therefore of little surprise that the Commission chose the directive as its legislative instrument of choice in the development of Community criminal law.[108]

In ensuring that the terms of a directive are applied, the Member States are 'obliged to enact implementing measures rather than rely on the fact that pre-existing law or administrative practice complied with the requirements of the directive'.[109] The implementing legislation of the Member State does not have to use the same words as the directive but the provisions have to be clear and the ECJ has held that, 'in order to satisfy the requirement of legal certainty' it is important 'that individuals should have the benefit of a clear and precise legal situation enabling them to ascertain the full extent of their rights, and where appropriate, to rely on them before the national courts'.[110] The Member States are further bound to abide by and apply the provisions of Community law and the secondary legislation made under its auspices and to organise their legal systems in such a way as to ensure that the principles of the supremacy of Community law and of direct effect are recognised.[111] The notion of the supremacy of Community law means that 'no appeal to provisions of internal law of any kind whatever can prevail' over Community law[112] and that 'every national court must, in a case within its jurisdiction, apply Community law in its entirety and must accordingly set aside any provision of national law which may conflict with it, whether prior or subsequent to the Community law'.[113]

The application of the principle of direct effect to directives means that they are capable of being exercised by a natural or legal person against another natural or legal person or against the authorities of a Member State and can be enforced by way of the national court process. As there was no express reference in Article 249

[105] Art 249 TEC, see also Case 163/82 *Commission v Italy* [1983] ECR 3723, 3286–287.

[106] Craig and De Burcà, *EU Law* (n 40) 85.

[107] G Corstens and J Pradel, *European Criminal Law* (The Hague, Kluwer Law International, 2002).

[108] It is equally unsurprising that this continues to be the case following the adoption of the Lisbon Treaty. According to Art 83(1) TFEU: The European Parliament and the Council may, by means of directives adopted in accordance with the ordinary legislative procedure, establish minimum rules concerning the definition of criminal offences and sanctions in the areas of particularly serious crime with a cross-border dimension resulting from the nature or impact of such offences or from a special need to combat them on a common basis.

[109] Steiner, Woods and Twigg-Flesner, *EU Law* (n 28).

[110] Case C-236/95 *Commission v Greece* [1996] ECR I-4459.

[111] Eg Case 6/64 *Costa v Ente Nazionale per l'Energia Elettrica (ENEL)* [1964] ECR 585.

[112] Case 48/71 *Commission v Italy* [1972] ECR 527, 535.

[113] Case 106/77 *Simmenthal* [1978] ECR 629, 643.

EC Treaty to the 'direct applicability' of directives, it was originally thought that they could not have direct effect. In Case 41/74 *Van Duyn v Home Office*, however, the ECJ came to a different conclusion, holding not only that the directive in question could be invoked directly in the national courts, but also that the matter could be referred to the ECJ under Article 234 EC Treaty.[114] It held that in order to confer direct effect, the provision in the directive must be clear and precise, unconditional and must not provide the authorities of the Member States discretion in its implementation.[115] Although directives can have vertical direct effect, allowing individuals to rely on them directly in proceedings against the authorities of the Member States in the domestic courts,[116] the ECJ has rejected on several occasions arguments that they should also be interpreted as having horizontal direct effect.[117]

Although, the principles of direct and indirect effect often apply to directives, the ECJ has established, in a constant line of authority, an exception to these principles in relation to criminal liability. It has consistently ruled that 'the obligation of the national court to refer to the content of the directive when interpreting the relevant rules of its own national law reaches a limit where such an interpretation leads to the imposition on an individual of an obligation laid down by a directive which has not been transposed'[118] and further that a directive cannot 'of itself and independently of a national law adopted by a member state for its implementation, have the effect of determining or aggravating the liability in criminal law of persons who act in contravention of the provisions of that directive'.[119] This means that in a case where a directive has either been incorrectly implemented or

[114] Eg Case 41/74 *Van Duyn v Home Office* [1974] ECR 1337, para 12 where the ECJ held in relation to Directive 64/221 'It would be incompatible with the binding effect attributed to a directive by Article 189 to exclude, in principle, the possibility that the obligation which it imposes may be invoked by those concerned . . . It is necessary to examine, in every case, whether the nature, general scheme and wording of the provision in question are capable of having direct effects on the relations between Member States and individuals'. See also Case 148/78 *Pubblico Ministero v Tullio Ratti* [1979] ECR 1629.

[115] On the controversy associated with direct effect, see eg J Steiner 'Direct applicability in EEC law – A Chameleon Concept' (1982) 98 *LQR* 229; A Dashwood, 'The Principle of Direct Effect in European Community Law' (1978) 16 *JCMS* 229.

[116] See eg Case 26/62 *van Gend en Loos* [1963] ECR 1.

[117] See eg Case 152/84 *Marshall v Southampton & South West Hampshirpse Area Health Authority (Teaching)* [1986] ECR 00723; Case C-91/22 *Dori v Recreb Srl* [1994] ECR I-3325. Horizontal direct effect means that the provisions are enforceable against individuals or companies, see eg Case 127/73 *SABAM* [1974] ECR 51, 62 where the ECJ commented in relation to Arts 81(1) and 82 TEC that the relevant provisions tended 'by their very nature to produce direct effects in relations between individuals' and to 'create direct rights in respect of the individuals concerned which the national courts must safeguard'. See also Case 43/75 *Defrenne v Sabena* [1976] ECR 455. Not all provisions with vertical direct effect will also be horizontally effective; in determining whether a directly effective treaty provision is horizontally effective 'everything depends on an interpretation of the relevant provision – including its specific objective and broader context – to determine whether horizontal effect would actually be appropriate', see Arnull et al, *Wyatt and Dashwood's European Union Law* (n 6) 154.

[118] Case C-168/95 *Luciano Arcaro* [1996] ECR I-4705, para 42.

[119] Case 14/86 *Pretore di Salò* [1987] ECR 2545, para 20. See also Case 80/86 *Kolpnghuis Nijmegen BV* [1987] ECR 3969, para 13; Case C-60/02 *X* [2004] ECR I-651, para 16; Case C-384/02 *Knud Grøngaard & Allan Bang* [2005] ECR I-9939; Joined cases C-387/02, C-391/02 and C-403/02 *Berlusconi and others* [2005] ECR I-3565.

not implemented at all, the prosecuting authorities of the Member States cannot rely directly on the provisions of the directive in order to establish, or aggravate, the criminal liability of an accused person.

In explaining the basis for this exception from the general application of the principles of direct and indirect effect, the ECJ has referred to the general principle that a Member State should be prevented from 'taking advantage of its own failure to comply with Community law'[120] and to restrictions imposed by 'the general principles of law which form part of community law and in particular the principles of legal certainty and non-retroactivity'.[121] In *Berlusconi and others*, the ECJ expressly added the 'retroactive application of the more lenient penalty' to the list of principles deemed to form part of the general principles of Community law.[122]

There is some ambiguity surrounding the extent to which directives have to comply with the general principles to which laws are must adhere and from which they derive their legitimacy. As with framework decisions, the ECJ's emphasis on the implementing measures of national law seems to divert attention away from the potential legitimacy deficit in relation to the directives. The implementing measures are relied on to confer legitimacy, despite the fact that the Member States' discretion in implementation is strictly limited. This means that while requirements such as non-retrospectivity have to be guaranteed, those such as consistency, or even potentially legal certainty, may be neglected. Furthermore any restrictions generally applying in domestic law on the content of the law, on what could be considered criminal, such as for instance the *ultima ratio* principle, which demands that criminal sanctions can only be imposed as a last resort and cannot be applied to Community legislation. Where a directive has been decided at the EU level, the Member States are compelled to implement it, even if it would not have passed the *ultima ratio* test in domestic law. There thus seems to be something of a gap between the expectations placed on national law to uphold the requirements normally associated with laws and the competence of the national legislature to influence these laws.

(ii) The Community Method: Law Making under the First Pillar

The EC Treaty provided a variety of procedures for creating EC legislation. Each method set out a distinct arrangement for the interaction of the Commission, the

[120] See eg Case C-168/95 *Luciano Arcaro* [1996] ECR I-4705, para 36 referring to Case C-91/22 *Dori v Recreb Srl* [1994] ECR I-3325.

[121] See eg Case 80/86 *Kolpnghuis Nijmegen BV* [1987] ECR 3969, para 13.

[122] Joined cases C-387/02, C-391/02 and C-403/02 *Berlusconi and others* [2005] ECR I-3565, paras 66–69: 'The principle of the retroactive application of the more lenient penalty forms part of the constitutional traditions common to the Member States. It follows that this principle must be regarded as forming part of the general principles of Community law which the national courts must respect when applying the national legislation adopted for the purpose of implementing Community law and, more particularly in the present cases, the directives on company law'. *Cf* the opinion of the Advocate General of 14 October 2004.

Council and the European Parliament. Laws could be made by way of the Commission acting alone, the Council and Commission acting alone, the Council and Commission acting with the consultative input of the Parliament, the Council and the Commission acting in the context of the cooperation procedure with the Parliament and finally in the context of the Article 251 EC Treaty 'co-decision' procedure involving the Council, Commission and the Parliament. The principal factor in determining which procedure was to be used was procedural rather than substantive in that it was contingent on the directions specified in the relevant Treaty article. The Commission's monopoly with regard to initiating legislation was a particularly important aspect of the Community legislative process, leading to 'an inbuilt bias towards a text formulated (in principle) independently of particular national or sectoral interests, to further the wider interests of the Community as a whole'.[123]

The principal legislative procedures were the consultation and the 'co-decision' procedures.[124] The main difference between these procedures was the weight afforded to the role of the European Parliament, which despite increasing with each treaty revision was nevertheless restricted. Under the consultation procedure, the Commission initiated a proposal on which the European Parliament was consulted.[125] The Council then had the power of final decision, which meant that its assent was essential before legislation could be enacted. Although the Council was not bound by European Parliament's opinion, it had to wait for the opinion before determining whether to accept the proposal; failure to do so resulted in the measure being annulled. Although the Parliament's power was strictly limited, it nonetheless reflected at 'Community level the fundamental democratic principle that the people should take part in the exercise of power through the intermediary of a representative assembly'.[126] This obligation to the consult the Parliament did not extend however either to a duty to take account of, or to give reasons for its decision to ignore, the Parliament's views.[127]

According to the co-decision procedure the Commission simultaneously submitted its proposal to the Council and to the Parliament.[128] After it had taken into account the opinion of the Parliament, the Council could either approve the amendments suggested by the Parliament and adopt the act or adopt a common position on the proposal. If the Parliament approved the common position, the Council could then adopt it on the basis of a qualified majority vote. Alternatively, if the Parliament rejected the common position or proposed new amendments, it was then returned to the Commission, which then prepared a new draft which

[123] Arnull et al, *Wyatt and Dashwood's European Union Law* (n 6) 57.

[124] For an overview of the various other procedures, see Craig and de Búrca, *EU Law* (n 40) 109 et seq.

[125] Art 252 EC Treaty.

[126] Case 138/79 *Roquette Frères SA v Council* [1980] ECR 3333; see also Case 156-/93 *European Parliament v Commission (Re Genetically Modified Micro-organisms in Organic Products)* [1995] 3 CMLR 707.

[127] Case 138/79 *Roquette Frères SA v Council* [1980] ECR 3333, *ibid.*

[128] Art 251(2) EC Treaty.

could include all, some or none of the Parliament's amendments. This draft was then submitted to the Council, which could approve the amendments proposed by the Commission and adopt the proposal by way of a qualified majority vote. It was permitted to 'resurrect' Parliamentary amendments deleted by the Commission, but had to do by acting unanimously.[129] If the Council did not accept the proposal, then the Conciliation Committee (comprised of an equal number of representatives from the Council and the Commission) could be convened (albeit in camera) and could approve a joint text which had then to be adopted by both institutions.[130] While this model, which increasingly became the 'standard' legislative mechanism,[131] was criticised for being lengthy, complex and, particularly when the conciliation committee was involved, insufficiently transparent, there can be little doubt that it afforded the Parliament considerably more influence in the decision-making process than in the context of the third pillar and that it thus represented 'a great constitutional gain, in terms of both simplifying and helping to legitimate the process of Community law-making'.[132]

(iii) The Judicial Role in the First Pillar

In the context of the EC Treaty, the Community Courts were responsible for ensuring that 'in the interpretation and the application of this Treaty' the law was 'observed'.[133] Provision was made both for direct actions against the Community Institutions[134] and the Member States[135] and for indirect challenges through the national courts by way of the Article 234 EC Treaty reference procedure. Both direct and indirect actions were of considerable relevance in the context of the enforcing of provisions relating to the criminal law. Direct actions included actions for annulment,[136] for failure to act,[137] and infringement proceedings. Article 226 EC Treaty provided the Commission not just with the power to oversee the compliance of the Member States with their Treaty obligations, but also provided the Commission with standing to bring infringement proceedings before the Court of Justice against a Member State in the event of non-compliance with their obligations.[138] A considerable number of infringement actions involved

[129] Art 251(3) EC Treaty.

[130] Art 251(4) EC Treaty.

[131] Arnull et al, *Wyatt and Dashwood's European Union Law* (n 6) 66 and 62 for a useful pictorial overview of the Art 251 co-decision procedure.

[132] *Ibid*, 66.

[133] Art 220 EC Treaty.

[134] Including actions to 'review the legality of acts of the Council and the Commission other than recommendations and opinions', Arts 230 and 241 EC Treaty.

[135] Eg Art 226 EC Treaty, action by the Commission against a Member State for failing to 'fulfil an obligation under this Treaty'; Art 227 EC Treaty, action by a Member States against another Member States for failing to 'fulfil an obligation under this Treaty'.

[136] Art 230 EC Treaty.

[137] Art 232 EC Treaty.

[138] Art 227 EC Treaty allows a Member State which considers that another Member State has failed to fulfil an obligation under the Treaty to bring the matter before the ECJ.

cases taken by the Commission against the Member States for their failure to implement directives.[139] It is no defence, for instance, for a Member State to claim that their national provisions were better than the Community provisions concerned and that the national provisions were therefore 'better able to ensure that the objective pursued by the directive is achieved'.[140]

Indirect actions were also of considerable importance. Article 234 EC Treaty provided the ECJ with jurisdiction to give preliminary rulings, where national courts were unsure of how to properly implement Community law, concerning the interpretation of the Treaty, the validity and interpretation of the acts of the institutions of the Community and the European Central Bank (ECB), and the interpretation of the statutes and bodies established by an act of the Council, where those statutes so provided. The national courts could refer questions involving EC law to the ECJ at any stage in the proceedings. This Article served as an important link between national and community legal systems, enabling the ECJ to clarify and interpret the law. The Court referred to it as 'the veritable cornerstone of the operation of the internal market', since it played a 'fundamental role' in ensuring that the law established by the Treaties retained its 'Community character with a view to guaranteeing that the law has the same effect in all circumstances in all the Member States of the European Union'.[141]

C The Development of EC Criminal Law Competence: The Position Prior to the Environmental Crime Case

Just as the task of defining criminal behaviour was customarily understood to be the sole concern of national law, so too was punishment, or perhaps more accurately the monopoly on the right to punish, commonly regarded as 'the most prominent mark of national sovereignty',[142] as 'a core element of national sovereignty'[143] and as belonging to the '"hard core" of internal state legislation'.[144] Although various European developments in the last 50 years, not least the creation of the European Convention on Human Rights and the establishment of the international criminal tribunals in The Hague, have interfered with the certainty of this understanding of criminal law as principally a matter for national law, they have had little concrete impact on the main body of substantive criminal law of

[139] Arnull et al, *Wyatt and Dashwood's European Union Law* (n 6) 416 et seq; Steiner, Woods and Twigg-Flesner, *EU Law* (n 28) 150 et seq.

[140] Case C-194/01 *Commission v Austria* [2004] ECR I-4579, para 39.

[141] The ECJ's report on the application of the TEU in 'The Proceedings of the Court of Justice and Court of First Instance of the European Communities', May 22–26, 1995 (No 15/95), para 11.

[142] M Delmas-Marty, 'The European Union and Penal Law' (1998) 4 *European Law Journal* 87, 87.

[143] Wasmeier and Thwaites, 'The Battle of the Pillars: Does the European Community have the Power to Approximate National Criminal Laws' (n 85) 613.

[144] M Kaiafa-Gband, 'The Development towards Harmonization with Criminal Law in the European Union – A Citizen's Perspective' (2001) 9 *European Journal of Crime, Criminal Law and Criminal Justice* 239, 239.

the European countries.[145] It should come as little surprise therefore that the EU Member States jealously guarded their competence in this area and proved reluctant to cede responsibility for creating and defining criminal law to the European Community. The inclusion by the Maastricht Treaty of JHA in the TEU and the creation by the Amsterdam Treaty of 'an area of freedom, security and justice', while illustrating increased EU interest in the criminal law, nevertheless indicated that its regulation was principally a matter for the third pillar rather than the first pillar.

The decision of the ECJ in Case C-176/03 *Commission v Council* which outlined express Community competence in relation to the criminal law, a position later confirmed in the ship source pollution case, provoked considerable controversy.[146] Some even suggested that the ruling suggesting that the 'Member States, or at least a majority of them, had seemingly been labouring under a misapprehension as to what they had agreed in the Treaties';[147] yet it would be wrong to assume that prior to the ECJ's judgment, the Community was entirely detached from matters concerning the criminal law. Indeed the Community's developing involvement in the criminal law has been promoted, as we shall see, both by the judiciary and by the Community legislature.

(i) Judicial Developments concerning the Community's Competence to Establish Penalties Prior to the Judgment in Case C-176/03 Commission v Council

The ECJ continually stressed that, '[a]s a general rule, neither criminal law nor the rules of criminal procedure fall within the Community's competence'.[148] Although this emphasises the fact that the Community's involvement in the criminal law

[145] Although that is not to say that these developments have not been influential. The ECHR, for instance, has impacted on national substantive criminal law in three different ways. First, the Strasbourg authorities have restricted the imposition of criminal sanctions where these would interfere with the rights and freedoms set out in the Convention; secondly, they have compelled Member States to adequately investigate crimes and ensure that these are effectively punished; and finally, they have, in their interpretation of the notion of 'criminal charge' in Art 6(1), taken some responsibility for determining whether the proceedings are to be considered as criminal in nature, irrespective of the nature of the classification of the proceedings in national law, see S Trechsel, *Human Rights in Criminal Proceedings* (Oxford, Oxford University Press, 2005) 14 et seq.

[146] For comment on this judgment, see KM Apps, 'Case C-176/03, Commission v Council: "Pillars Askew: Criminal Law EC-Style"' (2006) 12 *Columbia Journal of European Law* 625; M Böse, 'Die Zuständigkeit der Europäsichen Gemeinschaft für das Strafrecht: Zugleich Besprechung von EuGH, Urteil vom 13.9.2005' (2006) 153 *Goltdammer's Archiv für Strafrecht* 211; KF Gärditz and C Gusy, 'Zur Wirkung europäischer Rahmenbeschlüsse im innerstaatlichen Recht: Zugleich Besprechung von EuGH, Urteil vom 16.6.2005' (2006) 153 *Goltdammers Archiv für Strafrecht* 225; S White, 'Harmonisation of Criminal Law under the First Pillar' (2006) 31 *EL Rev* 81.

[147] European Union Committee of the House of Lords, *The Criminal Law Competence of the European Community*, para 3.

[148] See eg Case C-176/03 *Commission v Council* (n 18), para 47, referring to Case C-226/97 *Lemmens* (n 90), para 19. See also Case 8/77 *Germany v Sagulo* [1977] ECR 1495; Case C-203/80 *Casati* [1981] ECR 2595; Case C-186/87 *Cowan v Trésor Public* [1989] ECR 195; B Hecker, *Europäisches Strafrecht*, 4th edn (Berlin, Springer, 2012) 146.

was of an extraordinary nature, it also demonstrates that even before the environmental protection case this general principle was subject to qualification. In those cases where the ECJ determined that the Member States were under an obligation to impose or indeed refrain from imposing criminal sanctions, this was generally formulated with reference to the principle of subsidiarity and through recourse to Article 10 [ex Article 5] of the EC Treaty, which was charged with ensuring the effectiveness of the Community legal order.[149] Article 10 EC Treaty was interpreted by the Court as obliging Member States to ensure both that they did not create criminal laws, which would 'disproportionately' interfere with the exercise of the freedoms set out in the Treaty and that they considered the use of criminal sanctions where this was necessary in order to ensure the effectiveness of Community law.

(a) The Obligation on Member States to Refrain from Imposing Criminal Sanctions

The ECJ held that Member States were not to apply rules that disproportionately interfered with the exercise of the free movement of capital, goods, workers, services or the freedom of establishment as protected by the EC Treaty. Moreover, in line with the principles of direct effect and the supremacy of Community law, Member States were obliged, in the event of a conflict between the provisions of domestic and Community law, to give precedence to Community law. This was famously enunciated in the *Costa ENEL* case, in which the ECJ ruled that:

> The law stemming from the Treaty, an independent source of law, could not, because of its special and original nature, be overridden by domestic legal provisions, however framed, without being deprived of its character as Community law and without the legal basis of the Community itself being called into question.
>
> The transfer, by Member States, from their national orders in favour of the Community order of the rights and obligations arising from the Treaty, carries with it a clear limitation of their sovereign rights upon which a subsequent unilateral law, incompatible with the aims of the Community, cannot prevail.[150]

This had considerable implications for the criminal law. In essence where provisions of national criminal law were deemed to interfere disproportionately with one of the fundamental freedoms, the national judge was obliged to respect the primacy of Community law and 'decriminalise' the conduct which was, according to national law, criminal.[151] While the Member States were to be presumed to be responsible for creating criminal law and the rules of criminal procedure, they were nevertheless obliged by Community law to ensure that any criminal sanctions imposed in areas regulated by the Treaty were 'strictly necessary', that they

[149] Art 10 EC Treaty requires Member States to 'take all appropriate measures whether general or particular, to ensure fulfilment of the obligations arising out of this Treaty or resulting from action taken by the institutions of the Community'.

[150] Case 6/64 *Costa v Ente Nazionale per l'Energia Elettrica (ENEL)* (n 111).

[151] M Jaeger, 'Les rapports entre le droit communautaire et le droit pénal: l'institution d'une communauté de droit' (2004) 84 *Revue de Droit Pénal et de Criminologie* 1099, 1107.

were not conceived in such a way as to interfere with the freedoms required by the Treaty and that they were not so disproportionate as to become an obstacle to the exercise of these freedoms.[152]

The impact of Community law on the domestic criminal laws of the Member States is clearly illustrated in cases such as *Schonenberg* and *Tymen*. In *Schonenberg* the masters of several Dutch trawlers were prosecuted in Ireland for breaching fisheries restrictions aimed at protecting the environment. In response to a reference from the Irish courts, the ECJ ruled that the Irish provisions were incompatible with Community law and held that 'where criminal proceedings are brought by virtue of a national legislative measure which is held to be contrary to community law, a conviction in those proceedings is also incompatible with that law'.[153] The ECJ reached the same conclusion in *Tymen* which involved a French fisherman prosecuted in Wales for infringing similar provisions.[154] These cases underline the fact that the Member States were expected to take particular care in relation to areas where the Community had already introduced measures towards harmonisation. Member States were not permitted to apply provisions unilaterally in areas for which they no longer had unilateral competence.

Similarly, a number of cases involved attempts by Member States to impose their own vehicle and driving restrictions, despite the existence of Community provisions in this area. In *van Lent* a Belgian national was prosecuted in Belgium, for driving a motor vehicle with a Luxembourg registration plate, which had not been registered in Belgium on a public road. According to Belgian law only those motor vehicles and trailers, which had been first entered in the register of motor vehicle and trailers on application by, and in the name of, their owner could legally be driven on public roads. The ECJ held that this restriction represented an unacceptable restriction on the freedom of movement for workers and was thus incompatible with Article 39 EC Treaty.[155] Likewise in *Kapper*, where a German national, in possession of a valid Dutch driving licence, was prosecuted in Germany for driving without a driving licence, the ECJ held that, taking into account all the circumstances of the case, Germany was precluded by Articles 1 (2) and 8 (4) of Directive 91/439 from refusing to recognise the validity of a driving licence issued by another Member State. The rules relating to the issue and mutual recognition of driving licences by the Member States were held to exert an influence, both direct and indirect, on the exercise of the rights guarantees by the provisions of the Treaty relating to freedom of movement for workers, freedom of establishment and to the freedom to provide services.[156]

[152] Case C-203/80 *Casati* (n 148), para 27.

[153] Case 88/77 *Minister for Fisheries v CA Schonenberg and others* [1978] ECR 473, para 16.

[154] Case 269/80 *R v Robert Tymen* [1981] ECR 3079.

[155] Case C-232/01 *Hans van Lent* [2003] ECR I-11525.

[156] Case C-476/01 *Kapper* [2004] ECR I-05205, para 78. Similarly in Case C-408/02 *Criminal Proceedings against José Antonio da Silva Carvalho* 2003, the ECJ held that a prohibition on using a diving licence issued in a different country from the one in which the holder resides could not be considered compatible with Community law.

Many of the cases which have been considered by the ECJ, concerned provisions 'enacted by Member States which are capable of hindering, directly or indirectly, actually or potentially, intra-community trade' and which fall to be considered as 'measures having an effect equivalent to quantitative restrictions'.[157] A wide variety of provisions imposing criminal sanctions for such diverse conduct as failing to comply with prior packaging regulations applying to partly-baked bread and the organised smuggling of an alcoholic substance were found to be incompatible with Community law, principally because they were deemed to constitute protectionist measures designed to favour nationals.[158]

In *Gambelli*, the ECJ had to consider the compatibility of Italian laws restricting the provision of licences to organise and carrying on betting with Community law.[159] Mr Gambelli, together with several others, had been prosecuted by Italian authorities for collaborating in Italy with a bookmaker abroad in collecting bets; their activities were deemed to be incompatible with the State monopoly on sporting bets and thus with Italian law. After establishing that the Italian legislation on betting constituted a restriction on the freedom of establishment and the freedom to provide services, the ECJ turned its consideration to the question whether these restrictions could be justified through recourse to reasons of overriding general interest. Referring to the cases of *Schindler, Läräa* and *Zenatti*,[160] it noted that 'moral, religious and cultural factors, and the morally and financially harmful consequences for the individual and society associated with gaming and betting, could serve to justify the existence on the part of the national authorities of a margin of appreciation sufficient to enable them to determine what consumer protection and the preservation of public order require'. The Court thus accepted that:

> [R]estrictions on gaming activities may be justified by imperative requirements in the general interest, such as consumer protection and the prevention of both fraud and incitement to squander on gaming, restrictions based on such grounds and on the need to preserve public order must also be suitable for achieving these objectives, inasmuch as they must serve to limit betting activities in a consistent and systematic manner.[161]

[157] Case 8/74 *Procureur du Roi* v *Dassonville* [1974] ECR 837. For a good overview of quantitative restrictions, measures having equivalent effect and the post-*Dassonville* jurisprudence, see especially *Cassis de Dijon* (Case 120/78 *Rewe-Zentral AG v Bundesmonopolverwaltung für Branntwein* [1979] ECR 649) and *Keck* (Joined cases C-267 and C-268/91 *Keck and Mithouard* [1993] ECR I-6097), Arnull et al, *Wyatt and Dashwood's European Union Law* (n 6) ch 16. In *Keck* the ECJ ruled that national provisions restricting or prohibiting certain selling arrangements are not likely to hinder directly or indirectly, actually or potentially, trade between Member States within the meaning of the judgment in *Dassonville*, so long as those provisions apply to all relevant traders operating within national territory and so long as they affect in the same manner, in law and in fact, the marketing of domestic products and of those from other Member States, para 16.

[158] See Case C-416/00 *Tommaso Morellato* [2003] ECR I-09343 and Case 434/04 *Jan-Erik Anders Ahokainen, Mati Leppik v Virallinen syyttäjä* [2006] ECR I-09171, opinion of the Advocate General Poiares Maduro of 13 July 2006 (check ECJ) respectively.

[159] Case C-243/01 *Piergiorgio Gambelli* [2003] ECR I-13031.

[160] Case C-275/92 *Schindler* [1994] ECR I-1039; Case C-124/97 *Läärä and Others* [1999] ECR I-6067 and Case C-67/98 *Zenatti* [1999] ECR I-7289.

[161] Case C-243/01 *Piergiorgio Gambelli* [2003] ECR I-13031, para 63.

In the case at issue, however, not only were the Italian authorities pursuing a policy of expanding betting and gaming at the national level, they were also doing so in a discriminatory manner and were not – as required by Community law – making licences available 'in the same way and under the same conditions to operators established in Italy and to those from other Member States alike'. Finally, the ECJ seemed sceptical as to whether the restrictions imposed by the Italian authorities, which also imposed criminal penalties on any person who used the Internet at home to connect to a bookmaker established in another Member State, could be said to fulfil the proportionality requirement.[162]

As is clearly illustrated in the reasoning in *Gambelli*, criminal laws which interfered with one of the freedoms set out in Community law could nevertheless be deemed to be compatible with Community law providing that they could be justified by a public-interest objective, such as the protection of the health and life of humans within the meaning of Article 36 of the EC Treaty, taking precedence over the freedom at issue.[163] This was the case in *Greenham*, which involved a prosecution for offences relating to the sale of foodstuffs.[164] The accused were charged with having displayed and put on sale adulterated foodstuffs and with having misled consumers, in particular as to the material quality of the products. The accused argued that the marketing restrictions constituted a measure having equivalent effect to a quantitative restriction and that the French authorities had not proven that the national legislation was necessary in order to avoid a serious risk to public health. The ECJ was unconvinced holding instead that it was for the Member States, in the absence of harmonisation and to the extent that there could be said to be uncertainty in the current state of research, to decide on the level of protection of human health and life that they wished to ensure and whether to require prior authorisation for the marketing of foodstuffs, taking into account the requirements of free movement of goods within the Community.[165] Similarly in *Schwarz*, provisions that required chewing gum put up for sale in vending machines to be packaged were found to constitute an adequate and proportionate measure for the protection of public health.[166] Other grounds, which were held to constitute legitimate public interest objectives, include consumer protection, the 'maintenance of order in society', the prevention of fraud,[167] and the 'fight' against illegal activities such as tax evasion, money laundering, drug trafficking and terrorism.[168]

[162] See also Case C-360/04 Placanica [2007] ECR I-1891; but see Case C-42/07 *Liga Portuguesa de Futebol Profissional and Bwin International Limited (formerly Baw International Ltd) v Departamento de Jogos da Santa Casa da Misericórdia de Lisboa* [2009] ECR I-07633.

[163] Eg Case C-416/00 *Tommaso Morellato* [2003] ECR I-09343, paras 37–38.

[164] Case C-95/01 *John Greenham and Léonard Abel* [2004] ECR I-01333.

[165] *Ibid*, para 37.

[166] Case C-366/04 *Georg Schwarz v Bürgermeister des Landeshauptstadt Salzburg* ECR [2005] I-10139.

[167] Case C-275/92 *Schindler* (n 160), para 58; see also the judgments in Joined Cases 110 and 111/78 *Ministère Public v Van Wesemael* [1979] ECR 35, para 28; Case 220/83 *Commission v France* [1986] ECR 3663, para 20; Case 15/78 *Société Générale Alsacienne de Banque v Koestler* [1978] ECR 1971, para 5.

[168] These were invoked (albeit unsuccessfully) in Joined Cases C-358/93 and C-416/93 *Criminal proceedings against Aldo Bordessa, Vicente Marí Mellado and Concepción Barbero Maestre* [1995] ECR I-0361, para 20 – the ECJ did however refer to them in its judgment however as 'interests which those States are entitled to protect'.

(b) Obligation to Impose Criminal Sanctions

The ECJ's judgment in case C-176/03 *Commission v Council* confirmed another aspect of Community competence in relation to the criminal law, namely that in certain circumstances Article 10 EC Treaty required Member States to 'punish conduct which threatens that order'.[169] In order to understand this requirement it is useful to consider the nature of its development. Initially there was no suggestion that the Member States were required to criminalise violations of Community law, rather the ECJ simply observed that this would be a legitimate course of action, should States wish to do so. In its judgment in *Amsterdam Bulb* the ECJ ruled that, 'in the absence of any provision in Community rules providing for specific sanctions to be imposed on individuals for a failure to observe those rules, the Member States are competent to adopt such sanctions as appear to them appropriate'.[170]

This issue was further developed in the *Greek Maize* case in which the ECJ held that Member States were under a duty to ensure the effectiveness of Community law, stating that:

> [W]here Community legislation does not specifically provide any penalty for an infringement or refers for that purpose to national laws, regulations and administrative provisions, Article 5 [now Article 10] of the Treaty requires Member States to take all measures necessary to guarantee the application and effectiveness of Community law.[171]

In this case it went a step further arguing that it was essential that Community law be treated equally with domestic law and holding that while the choice of penalties was to remain within the discretion of the Member States, they were duty bound 'to ensure in particular that infringements of Community law' were 'penalised under conditions, both procedural and substantive, which are analogous to those applicable to infringements of national law of a similar nature and importance and which, in any event, make the penalty effective, proportionate and dissuasive'.[172] The essence of these cases was expanded in *Zwartveld and others* where the ECJ held that Member States were required 'to take all the measures necessary to guarantee the application and effectiveness of Community law, if necessary by instituting criminal proceedings'.[173]

[169] Opinion of the Advocate General Ruiz Jarabo Colomer in Case C-176/03 *Commission v Council* [2005] ECR I-7879 delivered on 26 May 2005.

[170] Case C-50/76 *Amsterdam Bulb BV v Produktschap voor Siergewassen* [1977] ECR 137, para 33.

[171] Case C-68/88 *Commission v Greece* [1989] ECR 2965.

[172] *Ibid*, para 24. Paras 23–25 read: 'where Community legislation does not specifically provide any penalty for an infringement or refers for that purpose to national laws, regulations and administrative provisions . . . Member States [are required] to take all measures necessary to guarantee the application and effectiveness of Community law. For that purpose, whilst the choice of penalties remains within their discretion, they must ensure in particular that infringements of Community law are penalized under conditions, both procedural and substantive, which are analogous to those applicable to infringements of national law of a similar nature and importance and which, in any event, make the penalty effective, proportionate and dissuasive. Moreover, the national authorities must proceed, with respect to infringements of Community law, with the same diligence as that which they bring to bear in implementing corresponding national laws'. See also Case C-326/88 *Hansen & Soen I/S* [1990] ECR I-2911.

[173] Case C-2/88 *Imm, Zwartveld and others* [1990] ECR I-3365, para 17.

With the passing of time, the ECJ became noticeably bolder. In the *Österreichische Unilever* case it had to consider the extent of a Directive on the approximation of the laws relating to cosmetic products, which required Member States to take all measures necessary to ensure that, 'in the labelling, putting up for sale and advertising of cosmetic products, texts, names, trade marks, pictures and figurative or other signs are not used to imply that these products have characteristics which they do not have'.[174] Unilever sought an injunction restraining a competitor, Smithkline, from making statements in television advertisements and on tubes of toothpaste which Unilever claimed were inaccurate and misleading. Smithkline responded by arguing that the provisions of national law, which were more stringent than those set out in the Directive, were incompatible with Community law. Although the ECJ held that the provisions of national law were incompatible with Article 6(3) of the Directive it also held that where private persons infringed the provisions of the Directive, the Member State was under a duty to ensure that this behaviour 'constitute[s] a breach of the law and, in particular, a criminal offence punishable by penalties having a deterrent effect'.[175] This judgment, which was described by commentators as 'astonishing',[176] received considerable attention not only because it went further than the question that was raised in the case at issue, but also because it showed that the Court did not 'regard criminal law as an isolated area of law that would generally fall out of the scope of Community law and competence'.[177]

(ii) Legislative Developments: Penalties Prescribed by Community Legislation

The increasing European Community competence in relation to the criminal law was not just to be found in the jurisprudence of the ECJ, but also become increasingly apparent in secondary community legislation. Prior to the judgment in the environmental crime case,[178] it was thought that the Community legislature had no express competence to require Member States to impose criminal penalties. In spite of this, a substantial body of secondary community legislation was established, which not only required Member States to 'prohibit' a variety of acts, but which also required that they do so under threat of sanctions. Particularly interesting is the way in which the language used became more prescriptive, reflecting in turn the developing confidence of the Community. Member States were initially required simply to insure compliance with the provisions of Community law. Council Directive 91/477/EEC on the control of the acquisition and posses-

[174] Council Directive 76/768 on the approximation of the laws relating to cosmetic products [1976] OJ L262/169, Art 6(3).

[175] Case C-77/97 *Österreichische Unilever GmbH v Smithkline Beecham Markenartikel GmbH* [1999] ECR I-431, para 36.

[176] Wasmeier and Thwaites, 'The Battle of the Pillars' (n 85) 622.

[177] *Ibid*, 623.

[178] Case C-176/03 *Commission v Council* (n 18).

sion of weapons,[179] for instance, requires inter alia that 'the acquisition and the possession of the firearms and ammunition classified in category A' be prohibited[180] and that Member States prohibit entry into their territory various types of firearms.[181] Member States were required to 'introduce penalties for failure to comply with the provisions adopted pursuant to this Directive' which were 'sufficient' to promote compliance with the provisions.[182]

Provisions of this nature are also to be found in a Council Regulation on the harmonization of certain social legislation relating to road transport, containing various restrictions on lorry drivers' hours[183] and in an earlier data protection directive requiring Member States to provide for the application of sanctions in the event that the rights set out in the directive were infringed.[184] Similarly, Directive 91/308/EEC on the prevention of the use of the financial system for the purpose of money laundering, was concerned principally with prohibiting the laundering of the proceeds of drug-related activities through the financial sector, requires that, '[e]ach Member State shall take appropriate measures to ensure full application of all the provisions of this Directive and shall in particular determine the penalties to be applied for infringement of the measures adopted pursuant to this Directive'.[185]

[179] Council Directive 91/477/EEC of 18 June 1991 on control of the acquisition and possession of weapons [1991] OJ L256/51: This Directive was created on the basis that the completion of the internal market was contingent on the abolition of controls on the safety of objects transported, which in turn was deemed to require inter alia 'the approximation of weapons legislation'. For discussion of the legislative passage of the directive and the final provisions, see LP Leme, 'The Council Directive on Control of the Acquisition and Possession of Weapons and its Categorization of Firearms: A Rational Approach to Public Safety?' (1996) 37 *Harvard International Law Journal* 568; C Eigel, 'Internal Security in an Open Market: The European Union Addresses the Need for Community Gun Control' (1995) 18 *British International & Comparative Law Review* 429.

[180] Council Directive 91/477/EEC of 18 June 1991 on control of the acquisition and possession of weapons [1991] OJ L256/51, Art 6.

[181] *Ibid*, Art 14.

[182] *Ibid*, Art 16.

[183] Council Regulation 3820/85 of 20 December 1985 on the harmonization of certain social legislation relating to road transport [1985] OJ L370/1 (earlier regulations included Regulation 543/69). This Regulation required Member States to adopt such laws 'as may be necessary' for the implementation of the Regulation According to Art 17: 'Such measures shall cover, *inter alia*, the organization of, procedure for and means of control and the penalties to be imposed in case of breach'.

[184] Directive 95/46/EC of 24 October 1995 on the protection of individuals with regard to the processing of personal data and on the free movement of such data [1995] OJ L281/31; Directive 97/66/EC of the European Parliament and of the Council of 15 December 1997 concerning the processing of personal data and the protection of privacy in the telecommunications sector [1998] OJ L24/1.

[185] Directive 91/308/EEC of 10 June 1991 on prevention of the use of the financial system for the purpose of money laundering [1991] OJ L166/77, Art 14. The Directive was amended in 2001 by another directive (Directive 2001/97/EC of 4 December 2001 amending Council Directive 91/308/EEC, on the prevention of the use of the financial system for the purpose of money laundering' [2001] OJ L344/76) which sought to expand the scope of the provisions to include proceeds derived from a broader range of 'serious crimes' including those offences defined in Art 3(1)(a) of the Vienna Convention, fraud against the Communities' financial interests, corruption and offences which generate substantial proceeds and which would be punished by a 'severe sentence of imprisonment' in the Member State. The 2001 Directive also extended the scope of the provision by bringing a number of other professions, including lawyers, notaries, auditors, real estate agents and dealers in high-value goods, within its remit. For comment on this Directive, see E Akindemowo, 'The Pervasive Influence of

In subsequent legislation it is not unusual to find a more exacting test obliging Member States to implement a system of 'effective, proportionate and dissuasive penalties' for failure to comply with secondary community legislation. Directive 2002/15/EC, for instance, on the organisation of the working time of persons performing mobile road transport activities[186] requires Member States to lay down a system of 'effective, proportional and dissuasive' penalties for breaches of the national provisions adopted pursuant to this Directive and to ensure that all measures are taken to ensure that the penalties are applied. Similarly, Directive 2001/29/EC on the harmonisation of certain aspects of copyright and related rights,[187] designed to develop and expand on the existing provisions in the field[188] in order to provide for 'a rigorous, effective system for the protection of copyright and related rights', requires Member States to ensure that 'effective, proportionate and dissuasive' sanctions are in place in order to deal with any infringements of the rights and obligations set out in the Directive.[189]

Notably absent from the 'effective, proportionate and dissuasive' sanctions test is any express reference to criminal sanctions. In spite of this, however, Member States often implemented the test in such a way as to criminalise the conduct prohibited in the various directives. A good example of this is provided by the Conditional Access Directive, which seeks to proscribe the 'de-scrambling' of subscription-only Internet and broadcasting services.[190] The Directive requires that Member States prohibit 'the manufacture, import, distribution, sale, rental or possession for commercial purposes of any illicit devices'.[191] An illicit device is defined as being any equipment or software designed or adapted to give access to a protected service in an intelligible form without the authorisation of the service provider.[192] Also prohibited is 'the installation, maintenance or replacement for

Anti Terrorist Financing Policy: Post 9/11 Non Bank Electronic Money Issuance' (2004) 19 *JIBLR* 289; P Brindle and F Guelar, 'About the New Money Laundering EU Directive: Legal Analysis' (2004) 25 *ICCLR* 125.

[186] Directive 2002/15/EC of 11 March 2002 on the organisation of the working time of persons performing mobile road transport activities [2002] OJ L80/35.

[187] Directive 2001/29/EC of 22 May 2001 on the harmonisation of certain aspects of copyright and related rights in the information society [2001] OJ L167/10 created in order to realise a harmonised legal framework on *copyright and related rights* in order to promote the smooth functioning of the internal market and the proper development of the information society.

[188] Directive 91/250/EEC of 14 May 1991 on the legal protection of computer programs [1991] OJ L122/42; Directive 92/100/EEC of 19 November 1992 on rental right and lending right and on certain rights related to copyright in the field of intellectual property [1992] OJ L346/61, as amended by Directive 93/98/EEC; Directive 93/83/EEC of 27 September 1993 on the coordination of certain rules concerning copyright and rights related to copyright applicable to satellite broadcasting and cable retransmission [1993] OJ L248/15; Directive 93/98/EEC of 29 October 1993 harmonising the term of protection of copyright and certain related rights [1993] OJ L290/9; Directive 96/9/EC of 11 March 1996 on the legal protection of databases [1996] OJ L77/20.

[189] Directive 2001/29/EC of 22 May 2001 on the harmonisation of certain aspects of copyright and related rights in the information society [2001] OJ L167/10, Art 8.

[190] Directive 98/84/EC of 20 Nov 1998 on the legal protection of services based on, or consisting of, conditional access [1998] OJ L320/54.

[191] *Ibid*, Art 4(a).

[192] *Ibid*, Art 2(e).

commercial purposes' of such a device and 'the use of commercial communications to promote illicit devices'.[193] Although it is expressly stated in Recital 23 that Member States are 'not obliged to provide criminal sanctions' for the activities set out in the Directive, there can be little doubt that criminal sanctions are envisaged, not least because Recital 22 states that Member States may restrict the imposition of sanctions to those cases where the activities were carried out 'in the knowledge that the devices in question were illicit'. This 'knowledge requirement', has obvious parallels to the *mens rea* requirement of the criminal law and is a clear indication that the provisions were intended for application within the scope of the criminal laws of the Member States. Article 5 meanwhile rehearses the familiar requirement that the sanctions be 'effective, dissuasive and proportionate to the potential impact of the infringing activity'.

Further evidence of the connection between this Directive and the criminal law can be found in the 2003 Report of the Commission on its implementation.[194] According to this report the fact that 'knowledge-based economies of the 21st century' are expected to rely increasingly on pervasive electronic pay services, means that piracy will have the 'same detrimental effects in the knowledge society as white-collar crime and counterfeiting of goods in the 20th century'. The report specifically observes that pirating electronic pay services (and presumably also other types of piracy) constitutes criminal activity. There is also an attempt in the report to justify the imposition of criminal sanctions; at one point it is noted that, '[a]udio visual piracy is not a "victimless-crime". Most pay-TV broadcasters operate within narrow financial margins'. Parallels are drawn between piracy and burglary and theft, which in turn are deemed 'unacceptable in any civilised society because they attack the heart of our system of values'. Consequently, the 'cyber equivalents of these offences and the damage done to the public interest should be seen in the same light'.[195]

The de facto 'criminal' nature of the penalties envisaged by the Directive is best illustrated, however, by the fact according to the 2003 Report (see Figure 1) that all but two countries (Italy and Portugal) imposed criminal sanctions for the main infringing activities in the form of imprisonment and/or fines.[196]

[193] *Ibid*, Art 4(b) and Art 4(c), respectively.

[194] Report from the Commission to the Council, the European Parliament and the European Economic and Social Committee on the implementation of Directive 98/84/EC of the European Parliament and of the Council of 20 November 1998 on the legal protection of services based on, and consisting of, conditional access, Brussels, 24 April 2003, COM (2003) 198 final. See also the Second Report on the implementation of Directive 98/84/EC of the European Parliament and of the Council of 20 November 1998 on the legal protection of services based on, or consisting of, conditional access, Brussels, 30 September 2008, COM (2008) 593 final.

[195] *Ibid*, para 4.2.

[196] *Ibid*, para 3.2.

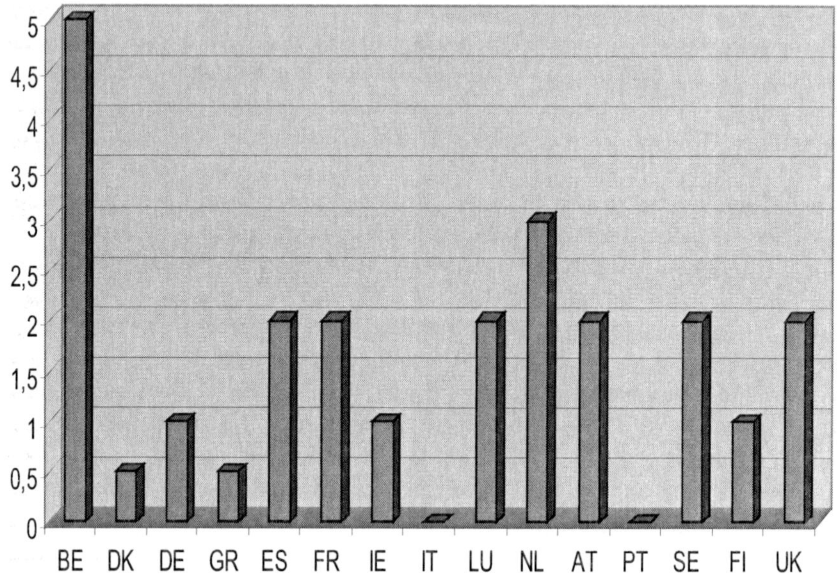

Figure 1: Maximum term of imprisonment in years for the main infringing activities[197]

D EC Legislative Competence to Determine that Certain Acts be Construed as Criminal

(i) Defining Offences: The Judgment of the ECJ in the Environmental Crime Case

In spite of the previous involvement of the Community in the criminal law, the judgment of the ECJ in the environmental crime case was extremely significant.[198] At the heart of this case lay important questions regarding the extent of Community competence in relation to the criminal law and the nature of the division of competences between the first and third pillar institutions. The case concerned legal provisions designed to protect the environment through the criminal law. Following the Presidency Conclusions of the Tampere Council meeting in 1999, which called for agreement in reaching common definitions, incriminations and sanctions in relation, inter alia, to environmental crime, the Council introduced a proposal for a Council Framework Decision designed to combat serious environmental based on Article 34(1)(b) EU Treaty in conjunction with Article 31(1)(e) EU Treaty.[199]

[197] This diagram is from the implementation report, 12 (n 194).

[198] Case C-176/03 *Commission v Council* (n 18).

[199] The initial proposal for a Framework Decision was based on an initiative of the Kingdom of Denmark, Council initiative of the Kingdom of Denmark with a view to adopting a Council Framework Decision on combating serious environmental crime [2000] OJ L/39/4. For a good summary of the legislative history, see White, 'Harmonisation of Criminal Law under the First Pillar' (n 146) 82–85.

Around this time, the Commission brought forward its own proposal for a Directive on the protection of Environment through the Criminal Law based on Article 175(1) EC Treaty.[200] The purpose of the Directive was to further Community law on the protection of the environment by requiring Member States to establish a 'minimum set of criminal offences'.[201] The Council rejected this Directive on the basis that in its opinion the EC Treaty did not provide a legal basis for requiring Member States to impose criminal sanctions. Instead it proceeded with the Framework Decision, framing it in almost identical terms to the Directive.[202]

The Commission countered by reiterating its view that the correct legal basis for such provisions was Article 175 EC Treaty and stating that in the event that the Council were to adopt the proposed Framework Decision, it would take proceedings at the ECJ to have it annulled. The Council rejected the Commission's analysis of the situation and adopted the Framework Decision arguing instead that Article 34 of the EU Treaty was the only legitimate legislative basis for requiring that Member States impose criminal sanctions.[203] The Commission subsequently brought proceedings in the ECJ to have the Framework Decision annulled.[204] The ECJ was thus faced with determining both the correct legal basis for criminal law provisions designed to protect the environment and, as a consequence of this, establishing the extent of the Community's competence to insist that Member States impose criminal penalties for infringements of community law.

The Commission's position, which was supported by the European Parliament, was clear:

> The Commission takes the view that the Framework Decision is not the appropriate legal instrument by which to require Member States to introduce sanctions of a criminal nature at national level in the case of offences detrimental to the environment.
>
> As the Commission pointed out on several occasions within Council bodies, it considers that in the context of the competences conferred on it for the purpose of attaining the objectives states in Article 2 of the Treaty establishing the European Community, the Community is competent to require the Member States to impose sanctions at national level – including criminal sanctions if appropriate – where that proves necessary in order to attain a Community objective.[205]

[200] Proposal for a Directive of the European Parliament and the Council on the protection of the environment through the criminal law, Brussels, 13 March 2001, COM (2001) 139 Final [2001] OJ C180/238; amended by Amended proposal for a Directive of the European Parliament and the Council on the protection of the environment through criminal law, Brussels, 30 September 2002, COM (2002) 544 final [2003] OJ C20E/284.

[201] *Ibid*, Art 1.

[202] According to the fifth Recital: 'The Council considered it appropriate to incorporate into the present Framework decision a number of substantive provisions contained in the proposed Directive, in particular those defining the conduct which Member States have to establish as criminal offences under their domestic law'.

[203] Council Framework Decision 2003/80/JHA of 27 January 2003 on the protection of the environment through the criminal law [2003] OJ L29/55.

[204] For a summary of the application, see [2003] OJ C/135/31.

[205] See Council of the European Union, Note from Secretariat to Coeper/ Council, Brussels, 13 November 2002, 13743/02, DROIPEN 77, ENV 624, 4.

Before the ECJ it argued that, in view of the fact that the 'purpose and content' of the Framework Decision fell within the Community's competence, the correct legal basis for the legislation were Article 3(1) and Articles 174–176 EC Treaty and not Article 34 TEU in conjunction with Articles 29 EU Treaty and Article 31(e) EU Treaty. Relying on secondary Community legislation which required Member States 'to introduce penalties which are necessarily criminal in nature, although that qualification has not previously been employed'[206] and on the jurisprudence of the ECJ in cases such as *Amsterdam Bulb* and *Zwartweld and others*,[207] it argued that the Community legislature was competent to require Member State to impose criminal penalties for infringements of Community law when this was essential to ensuring the effectiveness of the legislation.[208]

The Council was joined by eleven Member States in rejecting the Commission's claims.[209] It disputed the Community's assertion that it was competent to insist that Member States impose criminal penalties for the conduct set out in the Framework Decision. It argued that no express power in this regard had been conferred on the Community, citing in support the fact that Articles 135 and 280 of the EC Treaty expressly reserved matters concerning the application of the criminal law to the Member States and the fact that a specific title in the EU Treaty was directed towards judicial cooperation in criminal matters (Articles 29, 30 and 31(e) of the EU Treaty).[210]

The ECJ found for the Commission, ruling that the whole Framework Decision was unlawful. It based this finding on Article 47 EU Treaty according to which 'nothing in this treaty shall affect the Treaties establishing the Communities or the subsequent Treaties and Acts modifying or supplementing them' and Article 29 EU Treaty which provides that the third pillar is to operate 'without prejudice to the powers of the Community'.[211] While upholding 'as a general rule' the principle that 'neither the criminal law nor the rules of criminal procedure fall within the Community's competence', the Court nevertheless determined that this did not impede the Community legislature in requiring that Member States ensure 'the application of effective, proportionate and dissuasive criminal penalties by the national authorities' if this is deemed to be 'necessary' in order to combat serious environmental offences and to ensure that the Community rules on environ-

[206] See Case C-176/03 *Commission v Council* (n 18), paras 18–21. In this regard it referred expressly to Art 14 of Council Directive 91/308/EEC of 10 June 1991 on prevention of the use of the financial system for the purpose of money laundering [1991] OJ L/166/77 and Arts 1–3 of Council Directive 2002/90/EC of 28 November 2002 defining the facilitation of unauthorised entry, transit and residence [2002] OJ L328/17.

[207] See C) i) b) above.

[208] See Case C-176/03 *Commission v Council* (n 18), paras 18–21.

[209] Kingdom of Denmark, Federal Republic of Germany, Hellenic Republic, Kingdom of Spain, French Republic, Ireland, Kingdom of the Netherlands, Portuguese Republic, Republic of Finland, Kingdom of Sweden, and the United Kingdom of Great Britain and Northern Ireland. Although the Netherlands supported the Council's argument, it adopted different reasoning.

[210] Case C-176/03 *Commission v Council* (n 18), paras 26–30.

[211] This is the first case in which it has been held that Art 47 TEU invalidates legislation under the others pillars of the EU. See Apps, 'Case C-176/03, Commission v Council' (n 146) 628.

mental protection were fully effective.[212] Consequently, it held that the provisions of the Framework Decision could have been properly adopted on the basis of Article 175 EC Treaty.

The scope of the Community's criminal law competence was further clarified following the ECJ's judgment in the ship source pollution case.[213] Again, the Commission challenged the legality of the adoption of a framework decision, arguing that the measure should have been adopted under the auspices of the first pillar on the basis of Article 80(2) of the EC Treaty.[214] The ECJ agreed, ruling that several provisions of the Framework Decision on ship source pollution were 'designed to ensure the efficacy of the rules adopted in the field of maritime safety, non compliance with which may have serious environmental consequences, by requiring Member States to apply criminal penalties to certain forms of conduct' and that as they involved both environmental protection and maritime safety they could be validly adopted on the basis of Article 80(2) of the EC Treaty.[215]

(ii) Community's Competence to Prescribe Specific Criminal Penalties

Although the environmental crime judgment established at least some Community competence for defining criminal acts, it was considerably less clear whether it provided a basis on which the EC legislature could claim to be competent to prescribe specific criminal penalties. The ECJ was not called upon to determine this point as it held the whole Framework Decision to be invalid. In their evidence to the UK House of Lords Select Committee on the European Union, several commentators cast doubt on whether the judgment could be construed as providing a basis for allowing the Community to prescribe penalties. According to Peers, for instance:

> The further you get out from that core question of defining the offence, the less likely it is that on this judgment you could justify Community action, particularly because of paragraph 49 of the judgment, which does seem to lay some stress on the fact that the Framework Decision does not specify the exact criminal penalties which must be applied.[216]

The representatives of the Member States were also far from convinced. Richard Plender QC, counsel for the UK in the case before the ECJ, stated that it would be, 'inapt to confer on [the Community] legislature the power to prescribe maximum, minimum or guideline sentences for offences: the more so as the nature

[212] Case C-176/03 *Commission v Council* (n 18), para 48.

[213] Case C-440/05 *Commission v Council* (n 18). For commentary, see S Peers, 'The European Community's Criminal Law Competence: The Plot Thickens' (2008) 33 *EL Rev* 399–410.

[214] Council Framework Decision 2005/667/JHA of 12 July 2005 on the strengthening of the criminal law framework for the enforcement of the law against ship-source pollution [2005] OJ L255/164.

[215] Case C-440/05 *Commission v Council* (n 18), para 69. The Council and European Parliament have since adopted Directive 2009/123/EC of 21 October 2009 on ship-source pollution and on the introduction of penalties for infringements [2009] OJ L280/52.

[216] Evidence to the House of Lords' Select Committee on the European Union, Question 52.

and duration of any sentence is intimately linked to the treatment of offenders, which is a matter for national law and procedure'.[217] At a meeting of the JHA Council in Vienna, the Member States agreed several principles for considering the impact of the ECJ's case law, including the fact that:

> The Community legislature must leave to the Member States the choice of the criminal penalties to apply, as long as they are effective, proportionate and dissuasive. Consequently, Community acts cannot determine in detail and exclusively the level of penalties to be introduced. This should be left to the discretion of the Member States.[218]

The Commission, on the other hand, interpreted the ECJ's judgment as signifying that the Community legislature could not only define criminal offences, but was also entitled 'where appropriate' to determine the 'level of the criminal penalties applicable'.[219] This view was shared by the European Parliament, which in its report on the consequences of the judgment stated that, 'in certain cases it is appropriate to buttress the action taken by Member States by specifically stating (a) what type of conduct should incur criminal changes and/ or (b) what type of penalties should be applied and/ or (c) other measures relating to criminal law which are applicable in the relevant context'.[220] Clear indications that the Commission intended to push strongly for recognition of its competence to oblige Member States to impose specific sanctions were subsequently to be found in the amended proposal for a directive on criminal measures aimed at ensuring the enforcement of intellectual property rights.[221] In addition to proposing a wide definition of intellectual property crime – 'all infringements of an intellectual property right on a commercial scale, and attempting, aiding or abetting and inciting such infringements' – the Directive also set out detailed sanctions for both natural and legal persons.[222] Again, the ship source case provided some clarification. In the course of its ruling, the ECJ held that Community competence did not extend to cover the determination of the type and level of criminal sanctions.[223] This issue has been settled by the entrance into force of the Treaty of Lisbon.

[217] European Union Committee of the House of Lords, *The Criminal Law Competence of the European Community*, Evidence of Richard Plender, QC, para 39.

[218] JHA Council Meeting of 22 February 2006, document 6466/06 JAI 62. See also the Communication from the Presidency of the Council of the European Union to the Council of 22 September 2006 on the Amended proposal for a Directive of the European Parliament and of the Council on criminal measures aimed at ensuring the enforcement of intellectual property rights, 2005/0127 (COD).

[219] Communication from the Commission to the European Council and the Parliament on the implications of the Court's judgment of 13 September 2005 (Case C-176/03 *Commission v Council*), Brussels, 24 November 2005, COM (2005) 583 final, para 10.

[220] European Parliament, Report on the consequences of the judgment of the Court of 13 September 2005 (C-176/03 Commission/ Council), 8 May 2006, A6-0172/2006 (Gargani Report), para 15.

[221] Amended proposal for a Directive of the European Parliament and of the Council on criminal measures aimed at ensuring the enforcement of intellectual property rights, Brussels, 26 April 2006, COM (2006) 128 final.

[222] *Ibid*, Art 3. See further ch 4.

[223] Case C-440/05 *Commission v Council* (n 18), paras 70–71.

IV Beyond Environmental Protection: Community Involvement in the Criminal Law

The Member States deliberately eschewed codification of the criminal law in favour of a more gradual – and politically acceptable – encroachment into their criminal laws.[224] The gradual 'approximation' of some areas of the criminal law was seen as preferable to other interferences with the criminal laws of the Member States, such as for instance the creation of a unified EU criminal code, principally because it appeared to allow the Member States to retain considerably more sovereignty over their criminal laws. In spite of this, however, the emphasis on both the creation of a single 'area' of freedom, security and justice and on the principle of mutual recognition significantly interfered with traditional conception of criminal law as a matter for national law. Although mutual recognition seems to imply cooperation between distinct Member States, it is impossible to overlook the establishment of autonomous EU investigation and prosecution authorities such as Europol[225] and Eurojust.[226] There can be little doubt that developments concerning the approximation of the substantive criminal law, notwithstanding their tentative and perhaps even contradictory character, assisted in laying the foundations for more significant EU involvement in the prosecution of crime not just by simplifying the legal basis of the rules to be implemented, but also by facilitating broader acceptance among those living in the Member States of the increasing EU competence in the field of the criminal law.[227]

While the ECJ's judgment in the environmental crime case indicated a bigger role for the Community legislature in criminal matters, it also seemed to raise more questions than it answered.[228] One of the biggest issues involved clarification of the extent of the judgment outside the scope of environmental policy. While some commentators suggested that it could be read as being specific to measures

[224] This approach was in contrast to more radical approaches such as those embodied by the Corpus Juris project, see M Delmas-Marty and J Vervaele, *The Implementation of the Corpus Juris in the Member States*, vol 1 (Antwerp, Intersenia, 2000) or the draft Model European Penal Code U Sieber, 'Memorandum on a Model European Penal Code' (1998/99) *European Journal of Law Reform* 445–71.

[225] Convention of 26 July 1995 on the establishment of a European Police Office [1995] OJ C316/2.

[226] Council Decision of 28 February 2002 setting up Eurojust with a view to reinforcing the fight against serious crime (2002/187/JHA) [2002] OJ L63/1. See also Joint Action of 29 June 1998 on the creation of a European Judicial Network [1998] OJ L191/4 and Council Framework Decision of 13 June 2002 on joint investigation teams (2002/465/JHA) [2002] OJ L162/1.

[227] On the relationship between national identity and the criminal law in the context of the EU, see especially M Hildebrandt, 'European Criminal Law and European Identity (2007) 1 *Criminal Law and Philosophy* 57. See also M Verdussen, *Contours et enjeux du droit constitutionnel pénal* (Brussels, Bruyant, 1995) 695.

[228] White suggests that it adds 'new but unpredictable dynamic' to the relationship between national and European criminal law: S White, 'Harmonisation of Criminal Law Under the First Pillar', (2006) 31 *European Law Review* 81, 92. According to R Hefendehl, 'Europäischer Umweltschutz: Demokratiespritze für Europa oder Brüsseler Putsch' (2006) 4 *Zeitschrift für Internationale Strafrechtsdogmatik* 161, 164: '*[Die Entscheidung] enttäuscht nicht nur vom Ergebnis, sondern auch von der Begründung her auf ganzer Linie*'.

required to protect the environment, the fact that the ECJ did not explain why the protection of the environment in particular required the imposition of criminal sanctions seemed to call this interpretation into question.[229] There was no express reference in the judgment to the notion that it was restricted to policy involving the protection of the environment and the only reasoning offered in the judgment seemed rather to support the view that the principles of the judgment may well apply to other areas of Community policy.[230] Peers, in his evidence to the UK House of Lords Select Committee on the European Union, stated that following this judgment he was 'quite sure that there are at least some areas, and perhaps even all areas of Community law, where the Community has, in principles, a substantive criminal law competence'.[231] Similarly, the UK House of Lords Select Committee noted in its report that 'the fact that the Court did not expressly limit its judgment, that it described the environmental protection as "one of the essential objectives of the Community" and that the reasoning applied by the Court to the environment would seem to be equally well capable of application to other areas of Community policy and action if they met the test of being "essential objectives"'.[232] This opinion was subsequently confirmed as being the case in the ship source judgment.[233]

Even though the reaction of many commentators and national legislatures to these developments was cautious if not hostile, the Commission seized the opportunity to push for a broad interpretation of the judgment. Although conceding that the judgment was only concerned with Community environmental policy, it stated that 'the judgment lays down principles going far beyond the case in question. The same arguments can be applied in their entirety to the other common policies and to the four freedoms (freedom of movement of persons, goods, services and capital)'.[234] Consequently, it stated that it believed that the Court's reasoning could be applied to 'all Community policies and freedoms which involve binding legislation with which criminal penalties should be associated in order to ensure their effectiveness'. It also set out in the Communication a list of acts which it deemed following the judgment to be entirely or partly incorrect 'since

[229] See Apps, 'Case C-176/03, Commission v Council' (n 146) 629: 'what is crucially missing in the Court's judgment is an analysis of what makes environmental protection particularly and unusually specific in that it urges the use of criminal penalties. Without such an explanation the formulation of this test potentially could have ramification into many other areas of Community competence'.

[230] Reference is made to the fact that 'the protection of the environment constitutes one of the essential objectives of the Community', para 41 referring to Case 240/83 *ADBHU* [1985] ECR 531, para 13; Case 302/86 *Commission v Denmark* [1988] ECR 4607, para 8 and Case C-213/96 *Outokumpu* [1998] ECR I-1777, para 32; led commentators to suggest that 'the reasoning applied by the Court to the environment would seem to be equally well capable of application to other areas of Community policy and action if they met the test of being 'essential objectives'.

[231] European Union Committee of the House of Lords, *The Criminal Law Competence of the European Community*, see Peers's answer to Question 48 attached to the report.

[232] *Ibid*, para 40.

[233] Case C-440/05 *Commission v Council* (n 18).

[234] Communication from the Commission to the European Parliament and the Council on the implications of the Court's judgment of 13 September 2005 (Case C-176/03 *Commission v Council*) Brussels, 24 January 2005, COM (2005) 583 final, 1.2.6.

some or all of their provisions were adopted on the wrong legal basis' including framework decisions on increasing protection by criminal penalties and other sanctions against counterfeiting in connection with the introduction of the euro;[235] on increasing protection by criminal penalties and other sanctions against counterfeiting in connection with the introduction of the euro;[236] on combating fraud and counterfeiting of non-cash means of payment;[237] on prevention of the use of the financial system for the purpose of money laundering;[238] on money laundering, the identification, tracing, freezing, seizing and confiscation of instrumentalities and proceeds of crime;[239] on the strengthening of the penal framework to prevent the facilitation of unauthorised entry, transit and residence;[240] on combating corruption in the private sector;[241] on attacks against information systems;[242] and on the enforcement of the law against ship-source pollution.[243] It also proposed new acts including a proposal for a Directive on the criminal law protection of the Community's financial interests (PIF);[244] and a proposal for a Directive on criminal measures aimed at ensuring the enforcement of intellectual property rights and for a Council Framework Decision to strengthen the criminal law framework to combat intellectual property offences.[245]

The issue of the competence of the EU institutions for the substantive criminal law has now been settled by the entry into force of the Treaty of Lisbon. The Treaty as we will see in chapter 2 constitutes a continuation of these developments with the various third pillar framework decisions being converted into directives.

[235] Council Framework Decision of 29 May 2000 on increasing protection by criminal penalties and other sanctions against counterfeiting in connection with the introduction of the euro (2000/383/JHA) [2000] OJ L/140/1.

[236] Council Framework Decision 2001/888/JHA of 6 December 2001 amending Framework Decision 2000/383/JHA on increasing protection by criminal penalties and other sanctions against counterfeiting in connection with the introduction of the euro [2001] OJ L329/3.

[237] Council Framework Decision 2001/413/JHA of 28 May 2001 on combating fraud and counterfeiting of non-cash means of payment [2001] OJ L149/1.

[238] Directive 91/308/EEC of 10 June 1991 on prevention of the use of the financial system for the purpose of money laundering [1991] OJ L166/77.

[239] Council Framework Decision of 26 June 2001 on money laundering, the identification, tracing, freezing, seizing and confiscation of instrumentalities and the proceeds of crime (2001/500/JHA) [2001] OJ L182/1.

[240] Council Framework Decision of 28 November 2002 on the strengthening of the penal framework to prevent the facilitation of unauthorised entry, transit and residence (2002/946/JHA) [2002] OJ L328/1; Council Directive 2002/90/EC of 28 November 2002 defining the facilitation of unauthorised entry, transit and residence [2002] OJ L328/17.

[241] Council Framework Decision of 22 July 2003 on combating corruption in the private sector (2003/568/JHA) [2003] OJ L192/54.

[242] Council Framework Decision 2005/222/JHA of 24 February 2005 on attacks against information systems [2005] OJ L69/67.

[243] Directive 2005/35/EC of the European Parliament and of the Council of 7 September 2005 on ship-source pollution and on the introduction of penalties for infringements [2005] OJ L255/11 and Council Framework Decision 2005/667/JHA of 12 July 2005 to strengthen the criminal-law framework for the enforcement of the law against ship-source pollution [2005] OJ L255/164.

[244] Proposal for a Directive of the European Parliament and of the Council on the criminal law protection of the Community's financial interests, COM (2001) 272 final [2001] OJ C240E/125.

[245] Proposal for a European Parliament and Council Directive on criminal measures aimed at ensuring the enforcement of intellectual property rights, Brussels, 12 July 2005, COM (2005) 276 final.

2

EU Criminal Law after Lisbon

I Introduction

The Treaty of Lisbon entered into force in 2009 and led to the European Union (EU) replacing and succeeding the European Community.[1] The Lisbon framework, which consists of two distinct treaties, the Treaty on European Union (TEU) and the Treaty on the Functioning of the EU (TFEU), has resulted in significant changes to the legal regulation of justice and home affairs matters and thus to the regulation of the substantive criminal law. The legal effect of acts adopted before the Treaty of Lisbon came into force, is 'preserved until those acts are repealed, annulled or amended in implementation of the Treaties'.[2] This means that the framework decisions created prior to the coming into force of the Treaty of Lisbon continue to exist until such time as they are repealed and their lack of direct effect is preserved.[3] The Treaty of Lisbon provides for the conversion of framework decisions into directives; this process is, as we shall see, already well underway. This chapter aims to provide a broad overview of the Lisbon reforms and their implications for the regulation of the substantive criminal law. In this context, regard will be had both to the general law-making process and to the specific pieces of legislation which have been created. This will provide a basis for consideration of the policies underpinning the EU's involvement in the criminal law.

[1] Treaty of Lisbon amending the Treaty on European Union and the Treaty establishing the European Community, signed at Lisbon on 13 December 2007, entered into force 1 December 2009 [2007] OJ C306 (Treaty of Lisbon).

[2] Transitional Protocol, Art 9.

[3] S Peers, *EU Justice and Home Affairs Law*, 3rd edn (Oxford, Oxford University Press, 2011) 63. On the legal effect of these measures, see ch 1 above.

II Criminal Law Competence according to the Lisbon Treaty

A The Scope of Legislative Competence

The Lisbon Treaty consolidates and extends the legislative competence of the EU in the criminal law context. The main principle guiding criminal legislative competence post-Lisbon is that of 'shared competence' between the EU and the Member States for matters falling within the area of freedom, security and justice (AFSJ).[4] Article 69 TFEU expressly directs national parliaments to ensure that all legislative proposals and initiatives comply with the principles of subsidiarity and proportionality.[5] In addition, the Subsidiarity and Proportionality Protocol annexed to the Lisbon Treaty requires that wide consultations be undertaken before legislative acts are proposed.[6] The AFSJ is regulated in Title V of the TFEU; according to Article 67(1) TFEU the Union shall constitute an area of freedom and security and justice with respect for fundamental rights and the different legal systems and traditions of the Member States. In the context of ensuring 'a high level of security' the Union is obliged to take measures 'to prevent and combat crime, racism and xenophobia', to provide for 'coordination and cooperation between police and judicial authorities and other competent authorities', and to enable the 'mutual recognition of judgments in criminal matters' and, if necessary, the 'approximation of criminal laws'.[7] Judicial cooperation and procedural matters are regulated in Article 82 TFEU, while matters concerning the substantive criminal law are addressed in Article 83 TFEU. There are two distinct legal bases for the creation of criminal law in Article 83.

(i) Criminalisation of Serious Crime with a Cross-Border Dimension

According to Article 83(1) TFEU, the Parliament and the Council of Europe are entitled to 'establish minimum rules concerning the definition of criminal offences and sanctions in the areas of particularly serious crime with a cross-border dimension resulting from the nature or impact of such offences or from a special need to combat them on a common basis'. This suggests that the EU would

[4] Art 4(2)(j) TFEU.

[5] See E Herlin-Karnell, 'Subsidiarity in the Area of EU Justice and Home Affairs – A Lost Cause?' (2009) 15 *European Law Journal* 351. See too A Meuwese, *Impact Assessment in EU Lawmaking* (The Hague, Kluwer Law, 2008) 126; M Nolan, 'Law Reform, beyond Mere Opinion Polling and Penal Populism' in A Norrie et al (eds), *Regulating Device* (Oxford, Hart, 2009) 165.

[6] Protocol on Application of Principles of Subsidiarity and Proportionality, Art 2.

[7] Art 67(3) TFEU. The ECJ has held that Art 67(2) TFEU is only addressed to the Union and is thus not binding on the Member States – see Joined Cases C-188/10 and C-189/10 *Melki and Abdeli* [2010] ECR I-05667, para 62. This principle is likely to apply to all paragraphs of the provision.

be entitled to set out definitions of 'general part' terms such as intent or aiding and abetting.[8] It also provides the EU with the basis to set not just minimum maximum sentences, but also the potentially more prescriptive minimum sentences. The provision sets out an exhaustive list of areas for which the EU has criminal law competence: 'terrorism, trafficking in human beings and sexual exploitation of women and children, illicit drug trafficking, illicit arms trafficking, money laundering, corruption, counterfeiting of means of payment, computer crime and organised crime'.[9] It is no coincidence that these areas broadly correspond to the areas which were the subject of third pillar legislation, although the omission of any reference to racism and xenophobia is notable and seems to call into question the future of the provisions of the framework decision.[10]

Article 83(1) TFEU also makes provision for 'other areas of crime that meet the criteria specified in the paragraph', ie those crimes which have a cross-border dimension and are considered to be of a sufficiently serious nature, to be brought within the competence of the EU, but makes this contingent on unanimity and the consent of the European Parliament. The provision makes it clear that these laws are to be created only by directives, in accordance with the ordinary legislative procedure,[11] which is in marked contrast to the pre-Lisbon situation.[12] The Council is no longer entitled to decide alone, but must do so together with the Parliament in accordance with the procedure set out in Article 294 TFEU. This goes someway to addressing concerns about the democratic legitimacy of EU criminal law,[13] but expectations that this might reduce its punitive character have not (yet) been met.[14] The essence of this provision is that the EU is permitted to take action in relation to 'serious' crime with a cross-border dimension.

(ii) Criminalisation to Ensure the Effective Implementation of EU Policy

The EU also has competence in accordance with Article 83(2) TFEU to create laws in order to ensure the effectiveness of its policies. This competence can be understood in the context of the judgments of the European Court of Justice (ECJ) in the environmental crime and ship-source pollution cases.[15] The Commission had interpreted these judgments as affording it criminal law-making competence in

[8] See too J Vogel, 'Strafgesetzgebungskompetenzen der Europäischen Union' in K Ambos (ed), *Europäisches Strafrecht post-Lissabon* (Göttingen, Universitätsverlag Göttingen, 2011) 45. This matter is considered further in ch 7.

[9] Art 83(1) TFEU.

[10] See C Ladenburger, 'Police and Criminal Law in the Treaty of Lisbon' (2008) 4 *European Constitutional Law Review* 20. In view of the fact that racial discrimination is a EU policy area, Art 19(1) TFEU, there is likely to be competence for criminal law action here in the context of Art 83(2) TEFU.

[11] As regulated in Art 294 TFEU (ex Art 251 TEC), see further ch 1.

[12] See ch 1.

[13] See Peers, *EU Justice and Home Affairs Law* (n 3) 120–21.

[14] On this point, referring to the Directive on combating trafficking in human beings, Vogel, 'Strafgesetzgebungskompetenzen der Europäischen Union' (n 8) 44.

[15] See further ch 1.

any area of the law if this was necessary to ensure the effective implementation of EU law.[16] This competence is now expressly outlined in the Lisbon Treaty. Directives may be adopted in order to establish minimum rules concerning the definition of criminal offences and sanctions in an 'area which has been subject to harmonisation measures' providing that the 'approximation of criminal laws and regulations of the Member States' is 'essential to ensure the effective implementation of a Union policy' in such an area.

The extent of this competence remains unclear. The German Constitutional Court has referred to it as a serious extension of the EU's criminal law competence, but others have suggested that it is broadly in line with the law prior to the introduction of the Lisbon Treaty and that it is in fact more restrictive in view of the fact that it is subject to the emergency brake procedure.[17] The definition of terms such as 'effectiveness' and 'essential' will have to be determined and will necessarily define the scope of the provision. Further, some uncertainty surrounds the notion of an 'area which has been subject to harmonisation'. It is clear that this does not correspond to criminal law harmonisation – which would essentially restrict the scope of the provision to environmental crime – but there is no suggestion that 'full harmonisation' would be required.[18] Finally, it remains to be seen whether Article 83(2) TFEU will be considered to be a 'sufficient, self-standing legal basis for the adoption of criminal law' or whether a dual legal basis – Article 83(2) TFEU in conjunction with a 'specific EU sectoral provision' – will be required.[19] It is notable in this regard that the Commission's proposal for a directive on insider dealing relies on Article 83(2) TFEU as the sole legal basis. Directives created under the auspices of this provision are to be adopted by the same ordinary or special legislative procedure as was followed for the adoption of the harmonisation measures in question.[20]

(iii) Other Legal Bases for Creating Criminal Law

Article 83 TFEU is clearly the principal basis for EU criminal law making, but it has been suggested that various other Treaty provisions may also provide a basis for the creation of substantive criminal law. There is some overlap between Article 67 TFEU, which outlines the general criminal law competence in the AFSJ, and Article 83 TFEU which sets out detailed rules. It seems clear that Article 83 TFEU ought to be understood as the *lex specialis* and that Article 67 TFEU should not be

[16] Communication from the Commission to the European Parliament and the Council on the implications of the Court's judgment of 13 September 2005 (Case C 176/03 Commission v Council), Brussels, 24 November 2005, COM (2005) 583 final/2 and subsequently confirmed in the ship source case and in Case C-301/06 *Ireland v Parliament and Council* [2009] ECR I-593 (trade disparities).

[17] Vogel, 'Strafgesetzgebungskompetenzen der Europäischen Union' (n 8) 46.

[18] S Peers, 'EU Criminal Law and the Treaty of Lisbon' (2008) 33 *EL Rev* 507, 519.

[19] V Mitsilegas, *EU Criminal Law* (Oxford, Hart, 2009) 108. It is notable that the Commission's proposal for a directive on insider dealing relies on Art 83(2) TFEU as the sole legal basis.

[20] Art 83(2) TEFU.

relied on as a basis for creating law. Another provision which may provide a specific basis on which to create criminal law is Article 75 TFEU which gives the EU competence to adopt measures necessary to 'achieve the objectives set out in Article 67 as regards preventing and combating terrorism and related activities' by defining 'a framework for administrative measures with regard to capital movements and payments, such as the freezing of funds, financial assets or economic gains belonging to, or owned or held by, natural or legal persons, groups or non-State entities'.[21] Terrorism is specifically referred to in Article 83 TEFU, but there also seems to be scope for some measures, such as money laundering and financing of terrorism, to be adopted under Article 75 TFEU.[22]

Other provisions which have the potential to be used as the legislative basis for action in the criminal law context include Article 325(4) TFEU and Article 33 TFEU. Prior to the Lisbon reforms the corresponding provisions, which regulated the imposition of measures to combat fraud[23] and to strengthen customs cooperation[24] respectively, expressly ruled out criminal law measures: 'These measures shall not concern the application of national criminal law or the national administration of justice'. This sentence limiting the criminal law competence has been dropped in Article 325(4) TFEU and Article 33 TFEU. This gives rise to the question whether criminal laws can be adopted under these provisions without reference to, or indeed reliance on, Article 83(2) TFEU.[25] Some have suggested that the EU does in fact have competence under Article 325(4) TFEU to create criminal laws to tackle fraud against the EU budget without relying on Article 83 TFEU. This is important as it would allow the emergency brake procedure to be bypassed.[26] Others have argued that although the ECJ interpreted these provisions as conferring a criminal law competence on the EU in its earlier case law, the Treaty of Lisbon alters this situation by creating a distinct legal basis for regulating the EU's criminal law competence. According to this position, in the absence of any direct reference in the other provisions to the substantive criminal law, Article 83 TFEU must be understood as the *lex specialis* and the sole basis for creating EU criminal law.[27] It is interesting to note in this regard that in its proposal for a directive on the fight against fraud in connection with the EU's budget, the Commission expressly refers to Article 325(4) TFEU as the legal basis for the proposal; there is no mention of Article 83(2) TFEU. The Commission notes that the term fraud in the provision 'must be understood in the broad sense, including

[21] Art 75 (ex Art 60 TEU).

[22] On this point, see E Herlin-Karnell, 'EU Competence after Lisbon' in A Biondi, P Eeckhout and S Ripley (eds), *EU Law after Lisbon* (Oxford, Oxford University Press, 2012) 341.

[23] Art 280(4) EC Treaty.

[24] Art 135 EC Treaty.

[25] Mitsilegas, *EU Criminal Law* (n 19) 109; V Mitsilegas, 'The Competence Question: The European Community and Criminal Law' in E Guild and F Geyer (eds), *Security versus Justice: Police and Judicial Cooperation in the European Union* (Aldershot, Ashgate, 2008) 167.

[26] See Vogel, 'Strafgesetzgebungskompetenzen der Europäischen Union' (n 8) 48; H Satzger, *Internationales und Europäisches Strafrecht*, 6th edn (Baden-Baden, Nomos, 2013) para 9, Rdn 53.

[27] See eg Peers, 'EU Criminal Law and the Treaty of Lisbon' (n 18) 518.

also certain fraud-related criminal offences'.[28] This indicates clearly that the Commission does not consider that Article 83 TFEU is the sole legal basis for the creation of criminal law. Finally questions remain regarding the relevance of Article 114 TFEU (ex Article 95 EC Treaty) which provides a legal basis for the approximation of laws 'which have as their object the establishment and proper functioning of the internal market'.[29] In view, however, of the broad scope of Article 83(2) TFEU, reliance on this provision is unlikely to be necessary.

B Legislative Instruments and the Law-Making Process

The Treaty of Lisbon provides that regulations and directives are to be used to regulate police and criminal law matters; consequently the principles of supremacy and direct effect also apply.[30] According to Article 83 TFEU, only directives may be used to harmonise the substantive criminal law.[31] A directive is binding as to the result to be achieved upon each Member State to which it is addressed, but it leaves to the national authorities the choice of form and methods.[32] Directives aimed at harmonising the criminal law are to be adopted either on the basis of a proposal from the Commission or on the initiative of a quarter of the Member States.[33] This means that, unlike under the third pillar, Member States are no longer entitled to make legislative proposals unilaterally, but it also means that the Commission no longer has the sole competence to issue legislative proposals in the field of the criminal law for the purposes of protecting EU policy.

The power to create criminal law in the sense of Article 83(1) TFEU is subject to qualified majority voting (QMV) in the Council and co-decision with the European Parliament, a procedure known as ordinary legislative procedure.[34] This represents a considerable difference from the situation prior to the introduction of the Lisbon Treaty whereby unanimity in the Council and consultation with the European Parliament was required.[35] The fact that the Council can adopt a directive by way of qualified majority means that States which vote against the proposal may nevertheless be forced to adopt the legislation. Directives created to harmonise the criminal law in order to ensure the effective implementation of EU policy, in accordance with Article 83(2) TFEU are to be adopted by the same ordinary or special procedure as was followed for adoption of the harmonisation measures in question. This means that in some areas special legislative procedure

[28] Proposal for a Directive of the European Parliament and of the Council, on the fight against fraud to the Union's financial interests by means of the criminal law, Brussels, 11 July 2012, COM (2012) 363 final, at 6, para 3.1.

[29] See eg Herlin-Karnell, 'EU Competence after Lisbon' (n 22) 342–44. The same considerations apply in the context of Art 352 TFEU (ex Art 308 EC Treaty).

[30] Peers, *EU Justice and Home Affairs Law* (n 3) 42.

[31] See Art 83(1) and 83(2) EU Treaty.

[32] Art 288 TFEU (ex Art 249 EC).

[33] Art 76 TFEU.

[34] Art 294 TFEU (same in substance as ex Art 251 EC).

[35] See ch 1.

must be followed. In the context of tax fraud, for instance, Article 113 TFEU requires that the Council acts unanimously after consulting the European Parliament and the Economic and Social Committee. This means that the adoption of any criminal law provisions in this area would also require unanimous agreement in the Council. Special rules govern the position in the event that a country exercises its right to opt-out. Should a country decide not to opt in, unanimity of the members of the Council, with the exception of the representatives of the governments of the countries opting out, shall be necessary for decisions of the Council which must be adopted unanimously.[36] A qualified majority is to be defined in accordance with Article 238(3) TFEU.

C Emergency Brake

Article 83(1) and 83(2) TFEU gives the EU broad competence in the field of substantive criminal law, but this competence is subject to the emergency brake mechanism. The emergency brake procedure was designed to allay Member States concerns about the loss of their national sovereignty in the criminal law context. It remains to be seen whether the mechanism will be used broadly – thereby calling into question the potential for harmonisation – or if it will work by providing a basis for dissenting Member States to achieve concessions from the majority in Council.[37] If a Member State considers that a draft directive would 'affect fundamental aspects of its criminal justice system' it is entitled to request that the draft directive be referred to the European Council. Such a referral then results in the suspension of the ordinary legislative procedure. The Council is obliged 'in the event of consensus' to refer the draft back to the Council within a period of four months which will then 'terminate the suspension of the ordinary legislative procedure'. If consensus cannot be reached, a group of 'at least nine Member States' may establish enhanced cooperation on the basis of the draft directive. This group is entitled to proceed on the 'fast track' without being required to comply with normal substantive and procedural requirements, including the requirement of a proposal from the Commission, the consent of the European Parliament and the agreement of a qualified majority of all of the Member States: 'In such a case, the authorisation to proceed with enhanced cooperation referred to in Article 20(2) of the Treaty on European Union and Article 329(1) of this Treaty shall be deemed to be granted and the provisions on enhanced cooperation shall apply'.[38]

[36] Protocol (No 21).

[37] Herlin-Karnell, 'EU Competence after Lisbon' (n 22) 336; Peers, 'EU Criminal Law and the Treaty of Lisbon' (n 18) 528.

[38] Art 83(3) TFEU. For discussion of the emergency brake procedure, see Peers, 'EU Criminal Law and the Treaty of Lisbon' (n 18) 522–27.

D Jurisdiction of the Court of Justice

One of the most important developments brought about by the Lisbon Treaty concerns the jurisdiction of the Court of Justice (CJEU) for those areas which were previously regulated in the third pillar.[39] Previously, the Member States were entitled to decide whether or not to make a voluntary declaration accepting the jurisdiction of the CJEU in those areas.[40] Following the coming into force of the Lisbon Treaty, the CJEU is now afforded jurisdiction for matters concerning the AFSJ which is now fully integrated into the TFEU.[41] This is one of the most significant changes brought about by the Lisbon reforms, not least because it provides the CJEU with the authority to rule in the context of implementation proceedings brought against Member States which have not, or not fully, implemented the criminal law provisions of the EU instruments. A Member State may be sanctioned by the CJEU if it has failed to correctly transpose or implement an EU police or criminal justice measure. In addition, the courts in the Member States are able to seek a ruling from the CJEU on how the measure should be interpreted and applied. There is one limitation on the CJEU's jurisdiction; it does not have the competence to review 'the validity or proportionality of operations carried out by the police or other law-enforcement services of a Member State or the exercise of responsibilities incumbent upon Member States with regard to the maintenance of law and order and the safeguarding of internal security'.[42]

The Protocol to the Treaty provides for a five-year transitional period with regard to acts in the field of police cooperation and judicial cooperation in criminal matters which were adopted before the entry into force of the Treaty of Lisbon.[43] During this period[44] the jurisdiction of the CJEU remains the same for the pre-existing pillar measures as it was before the Treaty of Lisbon.[45] The consequence of this is that, during the five-year transitional period, the CJEU only has jurisdiction to adjudicate references from national courts in the context of pre-Lisbon third pillar legislation if the Member States chose to accept the jurisdiction of the Court in that regard. The UK, Ireland, Denmark, Poland, Bulgaria, Slovakia,

[39] S Peers, 'Finally "Fit for Purpose"? The Treaty of Lisbon and the End of the Third Pillar Order' (2008) *YEL* 47.

[40] Art 35 TEU. See further ch 1.

[41] The CJEU's competence is set out in Art 19 TEU (revised) and Arts 251–281 TFEU. See ch 1 for consideration of the competence of the Court of Justice in the third pillar.

[42] Art 276 TFEU. On the jurisdiction of the ECJ more broadly, see F Jacobs, 'The Lisbon Treaty and the Court of Justice' in A Biondi, P Eeckhout and S Ripley (eds), *EU Law after Lisbon* (Oxford, Oxford University Press, 2012) 197.

[43] Protocol No 36 on Transitional Provisions attached to the Lisbon Treaty, Art 10(1): 'the powers of the ECJ under Title VI of the Treaty on European Union in the version in force before the entry into force of the Treaty of Lisbon, shall remain the same, including where they have been accepted under Article 35(2) of the said Treaty on European Union'.

[44] The Lisbon Treaty entered into force on 1 December 2009; the transitional period will end on 1 December 2014.

[45] See ch 1.

Malta and Estonia refused to do so. In addition, it means that the CJEU has no jurisdiction over infringement actions brought by the Commission against Member States for non-compliance with third pillar acts created before the coming into force of the Treaty of Lisbon until the expiry of the transitional period.

The Protocol on Transitional Provisions qualifies the limitation on the CJEU's jurisdiction by providing that once a pre-existing third pillar Act has been amended, the CJEU will have jurisdiction in respect of those Member States to which the amended Act applies.[46] On expiry of the five year transitional period the CJEU will have jurisdiction over all third pillar Acts, irrespective of whether they have been amended or not.[47] The definition of 'amendment' takes on considerable importance. In the absence of any further guidance, it seems likely that even a minor amendment to a third pillar act would be sufficient to trigger the jurisdiction of the CJEU.[48]

In the criminal law context, the CJEU has competence to adjudicate in relation to trafficking in human beings and sexual abuse of children, as these are now regulated in directives which have replaced the earlier third pillar framework decisions. There can be little doubt that Court of Justice has played a considerable role in promoting legal integration within the single market and it remains to be seen what kind of role it will take on in the context of the criminal law.[49]

E Opt-Out/ Opt-In Provisions

These ground breaking changes in EU competence for police and criminal law measures were viewed in the UK in particular, but also in Ireland and Denmark, with some alarm, particularly as regards the increased jurisdiction of the CJEU. An important aspect of the Lisbon Treaty is the potential for the UK and Ireland to opt out of EU policing and criminal law measures adopted before the Treaty of Lisbon came into force.[50] According to the Protocol on Transitional Provisions, the UK may at any time before June 2014 notify the Council that it no longer wants to apply a range of EU measures concerning police and criminal law which were adopted prior to the entry into force of the Treaty of Lisbon.[51] The opt-out would take effect as of 1 December 2014. The opt-out is a block opt-out – the UK is not permitted to choose to 'pick and choose'.[52] The UK is entitled 'at any time afterwards' to request that it be permitted to opt back in to any acts which it pre-

[46] Protocol on Transitional Provisions, Art 10(2).

[47] *Ibid*, Art 10(3).

[48] See Peers, *EU Justice and Home Affairs* (n 3) para 2.2.3.3 at 64.

[49] For consideration of this point, see A Hinarejos, 'Integration in Criminal Matters and the Role of the Court of Justice' (2011) 36 *EL Rev* 420.

[50] See further A Hinarejos, S Peers and JR Spencer, 'Opting Out of EU Criminal Law: What is Actually Involved?', CELS Working Paper, New Series No 1, Cambridge, September 2012, available at www.cels.law.cam.ac.uk/publications/working_papers.php.

[51] Protocol (No 36) on Transitional Provisions to the Treaty on European Union, *Official Journal 115, 09/05/2008 P. 0322 – 0326, Art 10(4).*

[52] J Spencer, 'Opting out of EU Criminal Justice' (2012) 7 *Archbold Review* 6, 6.

viously opted out of, subject to the agreement of the Commission or in some cases Council.[53] The right to opt out is qualified in that it only applies to acts which have not been amended after the entry into force of the Treaty of Lisbon.[54] This gives rise to questions about the definition of 'amendment'. This could be of importance in that the amendment of acts before the expiry of the transitional period would impact on the UK's right to opt out. In relation to the substantive criminal law this is less relevant as the framework decisions have not been 'amended', but have instead been 'replaced' by directives.[55] In addition, the opt-out does not apply to legislation adopted following the entry into force of the Lisbon Treaty.

The consequence of the block opt-out would be that as of December 2014, the measures would no longer apply to the UK. The UK Government intimated in 2012 that it intended to opt out and immediately start negotiations on opting back in to various measures.[56] Of the approximately 130 pre-Lisbon police and criminal justice measures, the UK Government identified 35 measures which it intended to re-join.[57] This list is not binding or definitive; the UK Parliament will have the opportunity to vote on the number and content of any measures which the Government seeks to opt into.[58] The Government has intimated that it does not intend to re-join the measures establishing minimum requirements for the constituent elements of criminal offences in the field of fraud against the EU budget, trafficking in drugs and drug precursors, facilitating the unlawful entry of illegal immigrants, counterfeiting of currencies and of non cash means of payment, public and private sector corruption, participation in a criminal organisation, and racism and xenophobia.[59]

The UK and Ireland are entitled to decide not to take part in adoption of measures proposed pursuant to Title V of Part Three of the TFEU.[60] This essentially gives them the right to refuse to opt in to all new justice and home affairs legislation, including in the fields of policing and criminal law. Ireland is not entitled to

[53] Protocol (No 36) on Transitional Provisions to the Treaty on European Union (n 51), Art 10(5).

[54] *Ibid*, Art 10(4): This subparagraph shall not apply with respect to the amended acts which are applicable to the United Kingdom as referred to in para 2.

[55] See House of Commons European Scrutiny Committee, 'The UK's Block Opt-out of pre-Lisbon Criminal Law and Policing Measures', 21st Report of Session 2013–14, HC 683 (London, 2013) 23. See, however, Peers who suggests that the repeal of the framework decision might also constitute an amendment: S Peers, 'The Mother of All Opt-Outs? The UK's Possible Opt-Out from Prior Third Pillar Measures in June 2014' (2012) *Statewatch Analysis*, at 7.

[56] Oral statement in the House of Commons by the Home Secretary on Justice and Home Affairs Powers, 15 October 2012, available at www.homeoffice.gov.uk/media-centre/speeches/home-sec-eu-justice-statement.

[57] HM Government, Decision pursuant to Article 10 of Protocol 36 to the Treaty on the Functioning of the European Union, July 2013, Command Paper 8671.

[58] See House of Commons European Scrutiny Committee, 'The UK's Block Opt-out of pre-Lisbon Criminal Law and Policing Measures', 21st Report of Session 2013–14, HC 683 (London, 2013) 10.

[59] *Ibid*, 119, with criticism of the Government's reasoning.

[60] See Art 1 and Art 3 of Protocol (No 21) on the Position of the United Kingdom and Ireland in respect of the Area of Freedom, Security and Justice [2012] OJ C83/295. This protocol does not apply to measures adopted in the context of the Schengen *acquis* which are subject to different rules. See on this point Case C-77 *UK v Council* [2007] ECR I-11459.

opt out of the anti-terrorism measures set out in Article 75 TFEU. The UK, while entitled to do so, has made a unilateral declaration stating that it will opt in to these measures.[61] The UK is not permitted to opt out of other parts of the Treaty, which have criminal law implications, such as for instance Article 325 TFEU. Denmark is exempt from all policy and criminal law measures adopted after the entry into force of the Treaty of Lisbon. Unlike the UK and Ireland, it is not permitted to opt in to specific individual measures either at the time of adoption or a later date.[62] The UK and Ireland must inform the Council within three months of receipt of the proposal whether they intend to opt in. If agreement cannot be achieved, the other Member States are entitled to continue and adopt the measure. The UK and Ireland are permitted to adopt the measure at a later date, subject to the conditions set out in the Treaties.[63]

A number of directives have been introduced since the Lisbon Treaty came into force. The UK is bound by those measures which it has agreed to take part in. In the context of the substantive criminal law, the UK has exercised its right pursuant to Article 3 of Protocol No 21 to the Lisbon Treaty to take part in the adoption and application of the directives replacing the framework decisions on trafficking in human beings and child sexual abuse and pornography and the proposal for a directive on attacks against information systems.[64] It has not opted in to the proposal for a directive on criminal sanctions for insider dealing and market manipulation, although it 'hope[s] to be in a position to do so in the future',[65] nor has it opted in to the directive on the employment of illegal migrants.

III EU Criminal Offences: Areas of the Substantive Criminal Law Subjected to 'Approximation'

A Overview

Article 83(1) TFEU gives the EU competence to legislate to tackle serious cross-border crime in the context of terrorism, trafficking in human beings and sexual exploitation of women and children, illicit drug trafficking, illicit arms trafficking, money laundering, corruption, counterfeiting of means of payment, computer crime and organised crime. Prior to the coming into force of the Lisbon Treaty,

[61] Declaration of the United Kingdom of Great Britain and Northern Ireland on Art 61 H of the TFEU, Declaration no 65 annexed to the Final act [2007] OJ C306/271.

[62] See Art 1 of the Protocol (No 22) on the Position of Denmark [2010] OJ C83/299. Denmark is entitled to replace these rules with rules which are identical to those apply to the UK and Irish opt outs, but has not yet done so.

[63] See on this Peers, *EU Justice and Home Affairs Law* (n 3) para 2.2.5.1.2 at 75.

[64] The UK initially opted out of the Directive on Trafficking, but subsequently opted in.

[65] See the written statement of the Financial Secretary to the Treasury (Mr Mark Hoban), Hansard, Commons Debates, 20 February 2012: Column 58WS.

the EU had adopted third pillar framework decisions in all of those areas except illicit arms trafficking. Following the entry into force of the Lisbon Treaty, some of these measures have now been converted into directives. Various areas which previously fell within the third pillar and which were regulated by way of framework decisions – notably racism and xenophobia, illegal entry and residence, environmental crime and protection of the Union's financial interests – now fall within the ambit of Article 83(2) as they are deemed to be essential to the effective implementation of EU policy.

B EU Criminal Legislation within the Scope of Article 83(1) TEFU

(i) Terrorism

Terrorism has been described as a catalyst for the emergence, harmonisation and reform of the criminal law.[66] In the wake of September 11, the Member States adopted a number of instruments designed to address terrorism, including most significantly a framework decision to 'combat' terrorism.[67] Although consultations on the creation of a framework decision were in progress prior to September 11, there can be little doubt that these events contributed decisively not just to the speed with which the Commission tabled its proposal, but also to the relatively short period of time which the Member States required to agree to implement provisions which in other circumstances would likely have been viewed as extremely controversial.[68] Alegre and Leaf suggest that the process of reaching consensus on a definition of terrorism among the 15 Member States would 'under normal circumstances' have 'taken years' and not months.[69] This claim is lent

[66] K Nuotio, 'Terrorism as a Catalyst for the Emergence, Harmonisation and Reform of Criminal Law' (2006) 4 *Journal of International Criminal Justice* 998.

[67] Council Framework Decision 2002/475/JHA of 13 June 2002 on combating terrorism [2002] OJ L164/3. See Conclusions adopted by the Council (Justice and Home Affairs), SN 3926/6/01 REV 6. This was, however, by no means the only important piece of legislation produced by the EU. Common Position 2001/931, for instance, includes an annex in which 'persons, groups and entities' are listed which can be subject to restrictions. As there is no procedure listed which enables such a person or group to challenge this listing, a number of people turned to the courts in an attempt to have their names removed from the list. The applications of the Basque groups SEGI and Gestora were held by the European Court of Human Rights to be inadmissible on the basis that as the provisions were not directly applicable in the Member States, the applicants could not claim to be victims of the provisions, App no 6422702 *SEGI and Others v 15 Member States of the EU* and App no 9916/02 *Gestoras pro-Amnistia v The 15 Member States of the EU*. The CFI had already dismissed the cases of several people seeking to have their names removed from the list (Case T-338/02 [2003] OJ C7/48. See eg Case T-306/01 *Aden* [2002] ECR II-2387; T-315/01 *Kadi* [2002] OJ C56/15 and T-318/01 *Othman* [2002] OJ C68/13). An anti-terrorism 'roadmap' and an 'action plan on terrorism' were also produced, SN 4019/1/01.

[68] The Commission tabled its proposal for a Framework Decision on combating terrorism on 19 September 2001 together with its proposal for a European Arrest Warrant. The Framework Decision was adopted less than a year later on 13 June 2002. See further S Douglas-Scott, 'The Rule of Law in the European Union – Putting the Security into the Area of Freedom, Security and Justice' (2004) 29 *EL Rev* 219, 228–29.

[69] S Alegre and M Leaf, 'Criminal Law and Fundamental Rights in the European Union: Moving Towards Closer Cooperation' (2003) *European Human Rights Law Review* 326, 328.

weight by the fact that the Framework Decision was the first international agreement to set out a definition of 'terrorism'. Difficulties in agreeing how best to characterise terrorism have meant that international instruments have eschewed broad definitions and have instead focused on particular acts, such as hijacking aircraft or hostage taking.[70]

The definition of terrorism in the Framework Decision demonstrates a particular reliance on the criminal law and in doing so reflects a more general shift in the international response to terrorism away from 'the amorphous paradigm of a social problem to that of a narrowly construed problem of security and justice'.[71] Article 1 outlines a long list of 'traditional' crimes which includes not only violent crimes against the person such as 'attacks upon a person's life which may cause death' and 'attacks upon the physical integrity of a person', but also crimes against property, as is illustrated by the reference to acts which cause 'extensive destruction to a Government or public facility, a transport system, an infrastructure facility, including an information system, a fixed platform located on the continental shelf, a public place or private property likely to endanger human life or result in major economic loss'.[72] These offences are to be defined as terrorist offences if they were intentionally committed with the aim of 'seriously intimidating a population', 'unduly compelling a Government or international organisation to perform or abstain from performing any act', or 'seriously destabilising or destroying the fundamental political, constitutional, economic or social structures of a country or an international organisation'.[73] Member States are required not just to ensure that these acts are criminal, but must make certain that they are classed as 'terrorist offences'.

The Framework Decision also requires the directing of and participating in the activities of a terrorist group to be prohibited, while further provisions concern a variety of associated offences, including aggravated theft, extortion or drawing up false administrative documents with a view to committing one of the acts set out in Article 1, which are deemed to be related to terrorist activities and which thus

[70] See eg Hague Convention for the Suppression of Unlawful Seizure of Aircraft, 16 December 1970; Montreal Convention for the Suppression of Unlawful Acts against the Safety of Civil Aviation, 23 September 1971; International Convention against the Taking of Hostages, New York, 17 December 1979. See further G Guillaume, 'Terrorism and International Law' (2004) 53 *International and Comparative Law Quarterly* 537, 538–39.

[71] Nuotio, 'Terrorism as a Catalyst for the Emergence, Harmonisation and Reform of Criminal Law' (n 66) 998.

[72] Council Framework Decision 2002/475/JHA of 13 June 2002 on combating terrorism [2002] OJ L164/3, Art 1. The other crimes which are to be capable of being construed as terrorist offences are: 'kidnapping or hostage taking'; 'causing extensive destruction to a Government'; 'seizure of aircraft, ships or other means of public or goods transport'; 'manufacture, possession, acquisition, transport, supply or use of weapons, explosives or of nuclear, biological or chemical weapons, as well as research into, and development of, biological and chemical weapons'; 'release of dangerous substances, or causing fires, floods or explosions the effect of which is to endanger human life'; 'interfering with or disrupting the supply of water, power or any other fundamental natural resource the effect of which is to endanger human life'; as well as threats to commit any of these acts.

[73] *Ibid*, Art 1.

fall to be prohibited.[74] Member States are also required to criminalise incitement, aiding and abetting and attempts to commit any of the offences in Articles 1, 2 or 3. The Commission implementation report, published in 2004, suggested that many Member States struggled to implement several of the provisions, particularly those in Article 3.[75] In 2008, a second Framework Decision was adopted for the purposes of amending and extending the scope of the earlier Framework Decision.[76] In particular, the amending legislation replaces Article 3 with a provision designed to cover the public provocation to commit a terrorist offence, the recruitment and the training of terrorists.[77]

The definition of terrorism in the Framework Decision has been criticised as 'unacceptably broad', as 'likely to infringe the requirement of lawfulness under Art 7 ECHR' and as potentially capable of being used to suppress 'legitimate' political expression such as protest marches, demonstrations or dissent.[78] In addition, some have questioned whether there is sufficient differentiation in the legislation between 'an absolute prohibition on political violence in democratic societies and a more qualified prohibition relating to non-democratic states'.[79]

(ii) Trafficking in Human Beings

The Framework Decision on combating trafficking in human beings adopted in 2002 was one of the first third pillar acts to be repealed and replaced by a directive following the coming into force of the Treaty of Lisbon.[80] The Framework Decision took a comparatively broad approach to the question of trafficking, in that, unlike the 1949 Convention, it did not insist on associating trafficking in

[74] *Ibid*, Arts 2 and 3.

[75] Report from the Commission based on Article 11 of the Council Framework Decision of 13 June 2002 on combating terrorism, Brussels, 8 June 2004, COM (2004) 409 final.

[76] Council Framework Decision 2008/919/JHA of 28 November 2008 amending Framework Decision 2002/475/JHA on combating terrorism [2008] OJ L330/21. The Member States had until December 2010 to implement the legislation.

[77] *Ibid*, Art 3. These provisions are discussed in more detail in ch 5.

[78] See Douglas-Scott, 'The Rule of Law in the European Union' (n 68) 230–31; and Alegre and Leaf, 'Criminal Law and Fundamental Rights in the European Union: Moving Towards Closer Cooperation' 327. See also L Turano, 'Spain: Banning Political Parties as a Response to Basque Terrorism' (2003) 1 *International Journal of Constitutional Law* 730, 736 who notes that 'the EU definition of terrorism is broad enough to include organizations like Batasuna that give public and financial support to other groups that actually commit the violence'.

[79] Peers, *EU Justice and Home Affairs Law* (n 3) para 10.5.1.2 at 786.

[80] Directive 2011/36/EU of the European Parliament and of the Council of 5 Apr 2011 on preventing and combating trafficking in human beings and protecting its victims, and replacing Council Framework Decision 2002/629/JHA [2011] OJ L101/1. On trafficking in human beings, see T Obokata, '"Trafficking" and "Smuggling" of Human Beings in Europe: Protection of Individual Rights or State Interests?' (2001) 5 *Web Journal of Current Legal Interests* 1; T Obokata, 'EU Council Framework Decision on Combating Trafficking in Human Beings: A Critical Appraisal' (2003) 40 *CMLR* 917; I Staiger, 'Trafficking in Children for the Purposes of Sexual Exploitation in the EU: the Council Framework Decision of 19 July 2002 on combating trafficking in human beings and its implementation into German law' (2005) 13 *European Journal of Crime, Criminal Law and Criminal Justice* 603; M Lehti and K Aromaa, 'Trafficking for Sexual Exploitation' (2006) 34 *Crime and Justice* 133.

human beings with prostitution.[81] This continues to be the approach followed in the Directive. This is in line both with the position of the UN Protocol to prevent, suppress and punish trafficking in persons, especially women and children and with the opinion of the UN High Commissioner for Human Rights that 'the definition of the term "trafficking" in laws, policies and programmes should not be restricted to sexual exploitation'.[82] It has been suggested, however, that despite this broader notion of trafficking, the specific reference in the UN Protocol to 'sexual exploitation' alongside more general notions of forced labour, an approach also adopted by the Framework Decision, is 'duplicitous' in that it reflects a 'contradictory narrative which maintains a close conceptual link between trafficking and prostitution'.[83] According to the Commission's implementation report, the majority of Member States successfully transposed the provisions of the Framework Decision into their criminal laws.[84] In spite of this the Commission determined that in view of the low number of criminal proceedings and in order to combat trafficking in human beings, 'additional efforts' were required. It proposed that new legislation be created to clarify the definition of offences related to human trafficking and to define aggravating circumstances and penalties.[85] These recommendations have been incorporated into the Directive.

Article 2(1) of the Directive directs Member States to punish a wide range of intentional conduct relating to trafficking, namely 'the recruitment, transportation, transfer, harbouring or reception of persons, including the exchange or transfer of control over those persons, by means of the threat or use of force of other forms of coercion, of abduction, of fraud, of deception, of the abuse of power or of a position of vulnerability[86] or of the giving or receiving of payments or benefits to achieve the consent of a person having control over another person, for the purposes of exploitation'. Exploitation is defined as including 'the exploitation of the prostitution of others or other forms of sexual exploitation, forced labour or services, including begging, slavery or practices similar to slavery, servi-

[81] Council Framework Decision of 19 July 2002 on combating trafficking in human beings (2002/629/JHA) [2002] OJ L203/1. Contrast the Convention for the Suppression of the Traffic in Persons and the Exploitation of the Prostitution of Others 1949 (1949 Convention) 96 UNTS 271.

[82] See VE Munro, 'A Comparative Study of Responses to the Trafficking of Women for Prostitution' (2006) 46 *British Journal of Criminology* 318, 330.

[83] *Ibid*, 326.

[84] Report from the Commission to the Council and the European Parliament, Based on Article 10 of the Council Framework Decision of 19 July 2002 on combating trafficking in human beings, Brussels, 2 May 2006, COM (2006) 187 final.

[85] Proposal for a Council Framework Decision on preventing and combating trafficking in human beings, and protecting victims, repealing Framework Decision 2002/629/JHA, Brussels, 25 March 2009, COM (2009) 136 final, Arts 1–3. See too the subsequent Proposal for a Directive on preventing and combating trafficking in human beings, Brussels, 29 March 2010, COM (2010) 95 and Communication from the Commission, The EU Strategy towards the Eradication of Trafficking in Human Beings 2012–2016, Brussels, 19 June 2012, COM (2012) 286 final.

[86] Defined in Art 2(2) as 'a situation in which the person concerned has no real or acceptable alternative but to submit to the abuse involved'.

tude, or the exploitation of criminal activities of the removal of organs'.[87] The Directive, like the UN Protocol, makes it clear that 'the consent of a victim of trafficking in human beings to the exploitation, intended or actual, shall be irrelevant where any of the means set forth in paragraph 1 have been used'.[88]

This type of provision has, however, been criticised as leaving 'considerable scope for interpretation' and thereby leaving some people outside the protection of. criminal law.[89] Only in relation to children, defined as people below the age of 18, will the conduct referred to be considered to constitute trafficking regardless of whether any of the means set out Article 1 have been used.[90] Member States must ensure that an offence as defined in Article 2 is punishable by a maximum penalty of at least five years of imprisonment.[91] In addition, the Directive sets out a number of aggravating circumstances and requires Member States to ensure that in such cases the offence is punishable 'by a maximum penalty of at least 10 years of imprisonment'.[92]

(iii) Sexual Abuse and Exploitation of Children

The enactment of the Framework Decision on combating the sexual exploitation of children and child pornography followed a number of policy and legislative initiatives including European Parliament resolutions, a Council Joint Action and a Council Decision.[93] In its implementation report the Commission noted that most

[87] Directive 2011/36/EU of the European Parliament and of the Council of 5 April 2011 on preventing and combating trafficking in human beings and protecting its victims, and replacing Council Framework Decision 2002/629/JHA [2011] OJ L101/1, Art 2(3).

[88] *Ibid*, Art 2(4).

[89] Munro, 'A Comparative Study of Responses to the Trafficking of Women for Prostitution' (n 82) 326: 'It allows domestic countries to impose a narrow conception within which famllial pressures, emotional attachment to a "boyfriend" figure, or simply lack of employment opportunity in the country of origin, may be insufficient to constitute vulnerability. In turn, this runs the risk that consent to trafficking activity given under these conditions will fall outside the remit of Art 3b, remaining relevant in relegating the offence from trafficking to smuggling and thereby obviating the need to provide victim support'.

[90] Council Framework Decision of 19 July 2002 on combating trafficking in human beings (2002/629/JHA) [2002] OJ L203/1, Art 1(3).

[91] *Ibid*, Art 4(1).

[92] *Ibid*, Art 4(2): Aggravating circumstance are when the offence: 'was committed against a victim who was particularly vulnerable, which in the context of this Directive, shall include at least child victims'; 'was committed within the framework of a criminal organisation'; 'deliberately or by gross negligence endangered the life of the victim'; or 'was committed by use of serious violence or has caused particularly serious harm to the victim'.

[93] Resolution of the European Parliament of 11 April 2000; Resolution of the European Parliament of 30 March 2000 on the Commission Communication on the implementation of measures to combat child sex tourism; Joint Action 97/154/JHA of 24 February 1997 adopted by the Council on the basis of Article K.3 of the Treaty on European Union concerning action to combat trafficking in human beings and sexual exploitation of children [1997] OJ L63/2; Council Decision of 29 May 2000 to combat child pornography on the Internet (2000/375/JHA) [2000] OJ L138/1; Council Framework Decision 2004/68/JHA of 22 December 2003 on combating the sexual exploitation of children and child pornography [2004] OJ L13/44.

Member States had met the requirements set out in the Framework Decision.[94] In 2009, it nevertheless introduced a proposal for the purposes of inter alia criminalising forms of child sex abuse and exploitation not covered by the EU legislation, including the organisation of travel arrangements for the purpose of committing child abuse.[95] In 2011, the Framework Decision was repealed and replaced by a Directive on combating sexual abuse and exploitation of children.[96] The Directive defines a 'child' as 'any person below the age of 18 years' and requires Member States to ensure that various intentional acts of exploiting a child are 'punishable'.[97] These include offences concerning sexual abuse, sexual exploitation, child pornography and solicitation of children for sexual purposes.[98]

The Directive also stipulates that measures must be put in place to ensure that the instigation or aiding or abetting of the offences are also considered to be criminal offences, while attempts to commit some of the offences mentioned in these articles are also to be criminalised.[99] Member States are required to impose various minimum maximum penalties for the offences of between one and ten years of imprisonment[100] and higher sentences if there are 'aggravating circumstances'.[101] The Directive also instructs Member States to ensure that legal persons can be held liable for the various offences.[102]

(iv) Drug Trafficking

The Framework Decision on illicit drug trafficking requires Member States to adopt minimum rules relating to the constituent elements of the offences of illicit trafficking in drugs.[103] The conduct which must be criminalised is extremely broad and includes 'the production, manufacture, extraction, preparation, offering, offering for sale, distribution, sale, delivery on any terms whatsoever, brokerage, dispatch, dispatch in transit, transport, importation or exportation of drugs'.[104]

[94] Report from the Commission Based on Article 12 of the Council Framework Decision of 22 December 2003 on combating the sexual exploitation of children and child pornography, Brussels, 16 November 2007, COM (2007) 716 final, 4.

[95] Proposal for a Council Framework Decision on combating the sexual abuse, sexual exploitation of children and child pornography, repealing Framework Decision 2004/68/JHA, Brussels, 25 March 2009, COM (2009) 135 final.

[96] Directive 2011/92/EU of the European Parliament and of the Council of 13 December 2011 on combating the sexual abuse and sexual exploitation of children and child pornography, and replacing Council Framework Decision 2004/68/JHA [2011] OJ L335/1.

[97] *Ibid*, Art 2 and Arts 3–6.

[98] *Ibid*, Arts 3–6.

[99] *Ibid*, Art 7.

[100] *Ibid*, Arts 3–6.

[101] *Ibid*, Art 9.

[102] *Ibid*, Art 12. For further analysis, see in the context of content regulation ch 5 and in the context of cyber-terrorism, see ch 7.

[103] Council Framework Decision 2004/757/JHA of 25 October 2004 laying down minimum provisions on the constituent elements of criminal acts and penalties in the field of illicit drug trafficking [2004] OJ L335/8, see, in particular, Recital 3.

[104] *Ibid*, Art 2(1).

Criminal liability is also to be imposed on those who attempt, aid and abet or incite such acts.[105] Provisions in the original proposal which suggested higher sentences in the event that the conduct was carried out by certain categories of person, notably doctors, pharmacists, court officials, police officers and teachers are conspicuously absent in the final draft.[106] Instead Member States must ensure that the conduct referred to is punishable by 'effective, proportionate and dissuasive criminal penalties' and in certain cases by 'criminal penalties of a maximum of at least between one and three years of imprisonment'.[107]

In its implementation report, the Commission criticises the implementation measures undertaken by the Member States as unsatisfactory and states that there has been 'little progress in the alignment of national measures in the fight against drug trafficking'.[108] This is perhaps a reflection of underlying policy differences between the Member States as regards the question how best to tackle the issue with those favouring de facto criminalisation in some cases pitted against those that support strict and draconian punishment in all cases.[109] There continues to be considerable differences in the national drug policies of the Member States and in the 'treatment of drug use and drug users'. This is said to be due to 'the diverse shape of the illicit drug problem in different Member States', but it is 'also to do with social and cultural factors within a country and with the history of the development of drug policy in each Member State'.[110] Although there is a clear legal basis in Article 83(1) TFEU for tackling serious drug trafficking, there might also be scope for action on the basis of Article 168(1) TFEU which instructs the Union to 'complement the Member States' action in reducing drugs-related health damage, including information and prevention'. The Commission has now published a proposal for a directive in this area.[111]

(v) Money Laundering

The Framework Decision on money laundering was created to reinforce the 1990 Council of Europe Convention on Laundering, Search, Seizure and Confiscation

[105] *Ibid*, Art 3.

[106] See proposal for a Council framework decision laying down minimum provisions on the constituent elements of criminal acts and penalties in the field of illicit drug trafficking [2001] OJ C 304 E/172, Art 5(2).

[107] Council Framework Decision 2004/757/JHA of 25 October 2004 laying down minimum provisions on the constituent elements of criminal acts and penalties in the field of illicit drug trafficking [2004] OJ L335/8, Art 4.

[108] Report from the Commission on the implementation of Framework Decision 2004/757/JHA laying down minimum provisions on the constituent elements of criminal acts and penalties in the field of illicit drug trafficking, Brussels, 10 December 2009, COM (2009) 669 final.

[109] See also Peers, *EU Justice and Home Affairs Law* (n 3) 787.

[110] European Union Committee of the House of Lords, *The EU Drugs Strategy*, 26th Report (London, 2012) para 29.

[111] Proposal for a Directive of the European Parliament and of the Council amending Council Framework Decision 2004/757/JHA of 25 October 2004 laying down minimum provisions on the constituent elements of criminal acts and penalties in the field of illicit drug trafficking, as regards the definition of drug, Brussels, 17 September 2013, COM (2013) 618 final.

of the Proceeds from Crime[112] and must be considered within the context of administrative measures designed to control money laundering.[113] It requires Member States to refrain from making or upholding reservations to Article 2 of the 1990 Convention, which concerns the confiscation of instruments and the proceeds of crime, in order to 'expand the applicability of confiscation measures to a wide scope of offences'.[114] Member States are also compelled by Article 1(b) to limit reservations to Article 6 of the 1990 Convention, in so far as serious offences are concerned. Article 6 of the 1990 Convention reads:

> 1. Each Party shall adopt such legislative and other measures as may be necessary to establish as offences under its domestic law, when committed intentionally:
>
> a. the conversion or transfer of property, knowing that such property is proceeds, for the purpose concealing or disguising the illicit origin of the property or of assisting any person who is involved in the commission of the predicate offence to evade the legal consequences of his actions;
> b. the concealment or disguise of the true nature, source, location, disposition, movement, rights with respect to, or ownership of, property, knowing that such property is proceeds;
>
> and, subject to its constitutional principles and the basic concepts of its legal system;
>
> c. the acquisition, possession or use of property, knowing, at the time of receipt, that such property was proceeds;
> d. participation in, association or conspiracy to commit, attempts to commit and aiding, abetting or facilitating and counselling the commission of any of the offences establish in accordance with this article.

Serious offences are defined by the Framework Decision as 'in any event' including 'offences which are punishable by deprivation of liberty or a detention order for a maximum of more than one year or, as regards those States which have a minimum threshold for offences in their legal system, offences punishable by deprivation of liberty or a detention order for a minimum of more than six months'.[115]

[112] Council Framework Decision of 26 June 2001 on money laundering, the identification, tracing, freezing, seizing and confiscation of instrumentalities and the proceeds of crime (2001/500/JHA) [2001] OJ L182/1.

[113] Notably Directive 2005/60/EC of the European Parliament and of the Council of 26 October 2005 on the prevention of the use of the financial system for the purpose of money laundering and terrorist financing [2005] OJ L309/15; Commission Directive 2006/70/EC of 1 August 2006 laying down implementing measures for Directive 2005/60/EC of the European Parliament and of the Council as regards the definition of 'politically exposed person' and the technical criteria for simplified customer due diligence procedures and for exemption on grounds of a financial activity conducted on an occasional or very limited basis [2006] OJ L214/29.

[114] *Ibid*, Art 1(a) referring to Art 2 of the 1990 Council of Europe Convention on Laundering, Search, Seizure and Confiscation of the Proceeds from Crime, Strasbourg, 8.XI.1990 ETS No 141 (1990 Convention). See Editorial, 'Implementation of Money Laundering Framework Decision Still Has Some Way to Go' (2004) 143 *EU Focus* 10, 11.

[115] Council Framework Decision of 26 June 2001 on money laundering, the identification, tracing, freezing, seizing and confiscation of instrumentalities and the proceeds of crime (2001/500/JHA) [2001] OJ L182/1, Art 1(b).

The Framework Decision also gives directions to the Member States with regard to their provisions on sentencing, stating that they should ensure that the offences referred to in Article 6(1)(a) and (b) of the 1990 Convention, in so far as they are to be considered 'serious' offences, are 'punishable by deprivations of liberty for a maximum of not less than four years'.[116] The Commission's second implementation report on the Framework Decision demonstrates both wide variations in the penalties imposed in the various Member States and that several Member States still have some way to go in order to completely transpose the provisions into their domestic laws.[117]

(vi) Corruption

The Framework Decision on corruption in the private sector sets out to prohibit both active and passive forms of corruption. [118] According to Article 1, Member States must ensure that 'the intentional promising, offering or giving, directly or through an intermediary, to a person who in any capacity directs or works for a private-sector entity an undue advantage of any kind for that person or for a third party, in order that that person should perform or refrain from performing any act, in breach of that person's duties' and when 'carried out in the court of business activities' shall constitute a criminal offence. Passive corruption, defined as 'directly or through an intermediary, requesting or receiving an undue advantage of any kind, for oneself or for a third party, while in any capacity directing or working for a private-sector entity, in order to perform or refrain from performing any act, in breach of one's duties' when committed intentionally, and in the context of business activities, must also be criminalised.

Provision is made for liability of legal persons and for the criminalisation of instigation and aiding and abetting.[119] Express regulation of jurisdiction is set out in Article 7. It is of particular interest that Article 1 allows Member States to restrict the scope of the provision to cases where it can be shown that the prohibited acts were committed intentionally. Member States must ensure that the penalties are effective, proportionate and dissuasive and that the conduct referred to in Article 2 is 'punishable by a penalty of a maximum of at least one to three years of imprisonment'.[120]

In its implementation report in 2007, the Commission expressed 'concern' that the transposition of the Framework Decision was still at an 'early stage' in most

[116] *Ibid*, Art 2.

[117] Second Commission report based on Article 6 of the Council Framework Decision of 26 June 2001 on money laundering, the identification, tracing, freezing, seizing and confiscation of instrumentalities and the proceeds of crime, Brussels, 21 February 2006, COM (2006) 72 final, see especially Annexes 1 and 5.

[118] Council Framework Decision of 22 July 2003 on combating corruption in the private sector (2003/568/JHA) [2003] OJ L192/54.

[119] *Ibid*, Art 3.

[120] *Ibid*, Art 4(1) and (2).

Member States.[121] It noted in particular that only two Member States (Belgium and the UK) had correctly transposed the provisions in the 'key' article, Article 2, and that just five had implemented the provisions imposing liability on legal persons. In its conclusions it refers to its lack of authority to initiate infringement proceedings against a Member State and urges the States to act speedily to incorporate the provisions, as 'strong, comprehensive legislation at national level is the foundation for effective protection of the private sector against this economic threat'.[122] According to the Commission, 'several EU States still have to transpose the most detailed provisions on criminalisation of all elements of active and passive bribery and the provisions on the liability of legal persons. Depending on progress, the Commission will consider proposing a directive to replace the Framework Decision'.[123]

(vii) Counterfeiting

(a) Counterfeiting in Connection with the Euro

The first framework decision to be created with the aim of standardising the substantive criminal laws of the Member States concerned counterfeiting of the Euro.[124] The Framework Decision formed part of a hybrid regulatory structure, which also included a first pillar regulation and the International Convention on the Suppression of Counterfeiting Currency.[125] The Framework Decision compels Member States both to accede to this Convention and to punish a variety of acts, including the fraudulent making or altering of currency, by whatever means; the fraudulent uttering of counterfeit currency; the import, export, transport, receiving, or obtaining of counterfeit currency with a view to uttering the same and in the knowledge that it is counterfeit; the fraudulent making, receiving, obtaining or possession of both the means (including instruments, articles and computer programs) for counterfeiting or altering of currency, and holograms or other components of currency which serve to protect against counterfeiting.[126] Member

[121] Report from the Commission to the Council based on Article 9 of the Council Framework Decision 2003/568/JHA of 22 July 2003 on combating corruption in the private sector, Brussels, 18 June 2007, COM (2007) 328 final, 4.

[122] *Ibid.*

[123] *Ibid.*

[124] Council Framework Decision of 29 May 2000 on increasing protection by criminal penalties and other sanctions against counterfeiting in connection with the introduction of the euro (2000/383/JHA) [2000] OJ L140/1, amended by Council Framework Decision 2001/888/JHA of 6 December 2001 amending Framework Decision 2000/383/JHA on increasing protection by criminal penalties and other sanctions against counterfeiting in connection with the introduction of the euro [2001] OJ L329/3.

[125] Council Regulation (EC) No 1338/2001 of 28 June 2001 laying down measures necessary for the protection of the euro against counterfeiting [2001] OJ L181/6 and the International Convention of 20 April 1929 for the Suppression of Counterfeiting Currency.

[126] Council Framework Decision of 29 May 2000 on increasing protection by criminal penalties and other sanctions against counterfeiting in connection with the introduction of the euro (2000/383/JHA)

States must also criminalise the participation in, instigation of, and attempt to commit, any of the acts prohibited in the Article 3(1)(a)–(c).[127]

The Framework Decision further obliges Member States to ensure that the conduct referred to above is also punishable with respect to 'banknotes or coins being manufactured or having been manufactured by use of legal facilities or materials in violation of the rights or conditions under which the competent authorities may issue currency, without these authorities' agreement'.[128] Not only must they ensure that effective, dissuasive and proportionate sanctions are imposed, they must also make sure that the offence of fraudulently making or altering currency is punishable by 'terms of imprisonment' and that the maximum term is 'not less than eight years'.[129] According to the Commission's second report on the implementation of the Framework Decision, only Sweden and Denmark failed to comply with this provision, in that they only permitted the imposition of an eight-year sentence of imprisonment in relation to serious offences.[130] It is instructive that an examination of the various sentencing laws for such offences in the various Member States reveals significant disparities in maximum sentences.[131]

Significantly, the Framework Decision goes further than the Convention by insisting on the introduction of liability for legal persons.[132] This is in line with other similar provisions such as the Second Protocol to the Convention on the protection of the European Communities' financial interests which requires legal persons to be held liable for fraud, corruption and money laundering. Notably, however, Member States are under no obligation to introduce criminal liability for legal persons; the imposition of 'non-criminal fines' will suffice.[133]

(b) Fraud and Counterfeiting of Non-cash Means of Payment

The aim of the Framework Decision on combating fraud and counterfeiting of non-cash means of payment is both to ensure the imposition of repressive penalties for abuse of payment instruments and to encourage operators to provide

[2000] OJ L140/1, Art 3(1)(a), (b), (c) and (d). For comments, see H Weenink, 'The Legal Framework for the Protection of the Euro against Counterfeiting' (2004) 19 *Journal of International Banking Law and Regulations* 276.

[127] *Ibid*, Art 3(2).

[128] *Ibid*, Art 4.

[129] *Ibid*, Art 6(2).

[130] Second Commission Report based on Article 11 of the Council Framework Decision of 29 May 2000 on increasing protection by criminal penalties and other sanctions against counterfeiting in connection with the introduction of the euro, Brussels, 3 September 2003, COM (2003) 532 final, para 3.1.

[131] *Ibid*, Annex to the second report, Table 3.

[132] *Ibid*, Art 9.

[133] The Commission has now issued a proposal for a directive to replace the framework decision: Proposal for a Directive of the European Parliament and of the Council on the protection of the euro and other currencies against counterfeiting by criminal law, and replacing Council Framework Decision 2000/383/JHA, Strasbourg, 5 February 2013, COM (2013) 42 final.

protection to the payment instruments which they issue.[134] Consequently, protection is afforded primarily to payment instruments which are 'protected against imitation of fraudulent use'.[135] Member States are required to criminalise various types of intentional conduct including theft or other unlawful appropriation of a payment instrument; counterfeiting or falsification of a payment instrument in order for it to be used fraudulently; receiving, obtaining, transporting, sale or transfer to another person or possession of a stolen or otherwise unlawfully appropriated, or of a counterfeited or falsified payment instrument in order for it to be used fraudulently; fraudulent use of a stolen or otherwise unlawfully appropriated, or of a counterfeited or falsified payment instrument.[136]

The Framework Decision also contains various provisions which relate specifically to computer-related offences and to offences committed with the assistance of specifically adapted devices.[137] Article 3 requires Member States to criminalise the 'performing or causing a transfer of money or monetary value and thereby causing an unauthorised loss of property for another person, with the intention of procuring an unauthorised economic benefit for the person committing the offence or for a third party' by introducing, altering, deleting or suppressing computer data, in particular identification data, or interfering with the functioning of a computer programme or system when committed intentionally and 'without right'. There are separate provisions on participation, instigation and attempt,[138] on the liability of legal persons,[139] on penalties and sanctions,[140] and on jurisdiction.[141] Article 6 of the Framework Decision requires the Member States to take measures to ensure the conduct to be criminalised is punishable by effective, proportionate and dissuasive penalties, including in serious cases, deprivation of liberty. The implementation reports of the Commission highlight the fact that while the Member States have all made the offences punishable by imprisonment, the penalties 'vary widely'.[142] Whereas, for example, Austria provides for a maximum of five years for counterfeiting, receiving and fraudulent use, Cyprus provides for a maximum of 14 years for counterfeiting payment instruments and seven years for using and acquiring them. The Commission concludes in its

[134] Council Framework Decision 2001/413/JHA of 28 May 2001 on combating fraud and counterfeiting of non-cash means of payment [2001] OJ L149/1. A payment instrument is defined in Art 1(a) as 'a corporeal instrument, other than legal tender (bank notes and coins), enabling, by its specific nature, alone or in conjunction with another (payment) instrument, the holder or user to transfer money or monetary value, as for example credit cards, eurocheque cards, other cards issued by financial institutions, travellers cheques and bills of exchange, which is protected against imitation or fraudulent use, for example through design, coding or signature'.

[135] *Ibid*, Art 1(a). See also Recital 10.

[136] *Ibid*, Art 2.

[137] *Ibid*, Arts 3 and 4.

[138] *Ibid*, Art 5.

[139] *Ibid*, Art 7.

[140] *Ibid*, Arts 6 and 8.

[141] *Ibid*, Art 9.

[142] Report from the Commission based on Article 14 of the Council Framework Decision of 28 May 2001 combating fraud and counterfeiting of non-cash means of payment, Brussels, 30 April 2004, COM (2004) 346 final.

second report that the Member States have complied with the requirement to implement Article 6, but that this is 'far from uniform'.[143]

(viii) Attacks on Information Systems

The Commission's implementation report on the Framework Decision on attacks against information systems[144] concluded that although significant progress had been made, there was still work to be done.[145] In 2010, the Commission published a proposal for a directive on attacks against information systems to replace the Framework Decision.[146] The Directive was adopted in 2013.[147]

According to the Directive on attacks against information systems, Member States must criminalise the 'intentional access, without right, to the whole or part of an information system', at least in relation to those cases which are deemed not to be minor; there is no indication however of how 'minor' is to be defined.[148] It is of interest to note the omission of the requirement set out in earlier drafts of the legislation that the actions be committed 'intentionally'.[149] The Directive also requires that illegal system inference and illegal data interference be punished as criminal offences.[150] The former is defined as the intentional serious hindering or interruption of the functioning of an information system by inputting, transmitting, damaging, deleting, deteriorating, altering, suppressing or rendering inaccessible computer data. The latter meanwhile consists of the intentional deletion, deterioration, alteration, suppression or rendering inaccessible of computer data on an information system where it is committed without right.[151] Both Articles require the punishment 'at least of those cases which are not minor'. In addition, the Member States must introduce criminal liability for illegal interception and concerning tools used to commit any of the offences set out in the Directive.[152] Also included in the Directive are provisions obliging Member States to criminalise the

[143] Second Report from the Commission based on Article 14 of the Council Framework Decision of 28 May 2001 combating fraud and counterfeiting of non-cash means of payment, Brussels, 20 February 2006, COM (2006) 65 final, 3.

[144] Council Framework Decision 2005/222/JHA of 24 February 2005 on attacks against information systems [2005] OJ L69/67. For an overview of the Framework Decision, see S Mercado Kierkegaard, 'Here Comes the Cybernators' (2006) 22 *Computer Law and Security Report* 381.

[145] Report from the Commission to the Council based on Article 12 of the Council Framework Decision of 24 February 2005 on attacks against information systems, Brussels, 14 July 2008, COM (2008) 448.

[146] Proposal for a Directive on attacks against information systems and repealing Council Framework Decision 2005/222/JHA, Brussels 30 September 2010, COM (2010) 517. For further analysis, see ch 7 below.

[147] Directive 2013/40/EU of the European Parliament and of the Council of 12 August 2013 on attacks against information systems and replacing Council Framework Decision [2013] OJ L218/8.

[148] *Ibid*, Art 3.

[149] Arts 3(i)–(iii) of the proposal for a framework decision on attacks against information systems.

[150] Directive 2013/40/EU of the European Parliament and of the Council of 12 August 2013 on attacks against information systems and replacing Council Framework Decision [2013] OJ L218/8, Arts 4 and 5.

[151] *Ibid*, Arts 4 and 5.

[152] *Ibid*, Arts 6 and 6.

instigation or aiding and abetting of any of the acts covered in Articles 3 to 7, as well as any attempt to commit any of these acts.[153]

Member States are directed to impose 'effective, proportional and dissuasive criminal penalties' for the offences referred to in Articles 3 to 8.[154] Moreover they are obliged to ensure that the offences referred to in Article 3 to 7 'are punishable by a maximum term of imprisonment of at least two years'[155] and that the offences in Articles 4 and 5 are punishable by a maximum sentence of imprisonment of at least three years.[156] In the event that the acts referred to in Articles 2(2), 3 and 4 are committed within the framework of a criminal organisation, as defined in the Joint Action 98/733/JHA', cause serious damage or are committed against 'a critical infrastructure system', they are to be 'punishable by a maximum sentence of imprisonment of at least five years'.[157] The Directive is considered in detail in chapter 7.

(ix) Organised Crime

The Framework Decision on the fight against organised crime requires that the Member States take the necessary measures to criminalise conduct by a person who intentionally and with knowledge of the aim and activity of the criminal organisation or its intention to commit the offences in question, actively takes part in the organisation's activities;[158] and/ or the agreement with one or more persons to pursue an activity which if carried out would amount to the commission of an offence punishable by a deprivation of liberty of at least four years, irrespective of whether the person actually carries out the activity.[159] It also requires that the Member States ensure that in relation to the offences set out in Article 2(a) a maximum sentence of between two and five years' imprisonment is available, and in the context of those offences set out in Article 2(b), the maximum sentence is the same as that for the offence at which the agreement was aimed or is between two and five years.[160]

C EU Criminal Legislation Areas falling within Article 83(2)

(i) Spam

The E-Privacy Directive requires Member States to 'take appropriate' measures to ensure that unsolicited emails are 'not allowed either with the consent of the sub-

[153] *Ibid*, Art 8(1) and (2).
[154] *Ibid*, Art 9(1).
[155] *Ibid*, Art 9(2).
[156] *Ibid*, Art 9(3).
[157] *Ibid*, Art 9(4).
[158] Council Framework Decision 2008/841/JHA of 24 October 2008 on the fight against organised crime [2008] OJ L300/42, Art 2(a).
[159] *Ibid*, Art 2 (b).
[160] *Ibid*, Art 3(1)(a) and (b).

scribers concerned or in respect of subscribers who do not wish to receive these communications'.[161] A subsequently amendment to the Directive, meanwhile, required Member States in the regulation of spam to ensure that they 'lay down rules on penalties, including criminal sanctions where appropriate'.[162] As we shall see, the majority of Member States provide for the imposition of criminal sanctions for spam-related offences, although the nature of these penalties varies significantly across the continent.[163]

(ii) Intellectual Property

The Commission has long supported the introduction of EU provisions requiring that the Member States ensure the possibility for intellectual property rights to be enforced by way of the criminal law. In 2005, it introduced a proposal for a directive to this effect which would have required Member States to ensure that all intentional infringements of an intellectual property right on a commercial scale, as well as the aiding and abetting of, inciting of, or attempt to commit such an infringement, were treated as criminal offences.[164] It later withdrew this proposal and altered its focus somewhat by instead pushing for the ratification by the EU and its Member States of ACTA, which contained similar provisions. In view of the fact that the ACTA ratification process has now stalled, it is to be expected that the Commission will issue new proposals in this field in the near future.[165]

(iii) Unauthorised Entry, Transit and Residence

A number of legislative instruments have been created in the field of illegal immigration. The Framework Decision on unauthorised entry, transit and residence was adopted in order to require Member States to impose criminal penalties for infringing conduct set out in a similarly entitled directive.[166] Member States must ensure that any person 'who intentionally assists a person who is not a national of

[161] Directive 2002/58/EC of the European Parliament and of the Council of 12 July 2002 concerning the processing of personal data and the protection of privacy in the electronic communications sector [2002] OJ L201/37.

[162] Directive 2009/136/EC of the European Parliament and the Council of 25 November 2009 amending Directive 2002/22/EC on universal service and users' rights relating to electronic communications networks and services, Directive 2002/58/EC concerning the processing of personal data and the protection of privacy in the electronic communications sector and Regulation (EC) No 2006/2004 on cooperation between national authorities responsible for the enforcement of consumer protection laws [2009] OJ L337/11.

[163] For detailed consideration of these matters, see ch 6.

[164] Proposal for a European Parliament and Council Directive on criminal measures aimed at ensuring the enforcement of intellectual property rights, Brussels, 12 July 2005, COM (2005) 276 final.

[165] For detailed consideration of this issue, see ch 4.

[166] Council Framework Decision of 28 November 2002 on the strengthening of the penal framework to prevent the facilitation of unauthorised entry, transit and residence (2002/946/JHA) [2002] OJ L328/1.

a Member State to enter, or transit across, the territory of a Member State'[167] or 'who, for financial gain, intentionally assists a person who is not a national of a Member State to reside within territory of a Member State' in breach of the laws of the State concerned on the entry or transit of aliens, shall be criminally liable.[168] They are also required to impose criminal sanctions for the instigation, assisting or attempt to commit such conduct.[169] The definition of authorised entry set out in Article 1(1)(a) differs significantly from analogous provisions in other instruments such as the Europol Convention and the Protocol against the smuggling of migrants by land, sea and air, supplementing the United Nations Convention against Transnational Organized Crime,[170] in that it removes the need for prosecutors to prove that the assistance was rendered for financial gain. Although Member States may, if they wish, make a defence available 'in cases where the aim of the behaviour is to provide humanitarian assistance to the person concerned', there is no escaping the fact that this represents an inversion of the burden of proof, principally, it would seem, in order to surmount the problems associated with proving financial gain.[171]

Member States are required to impose 'effective, proportionate and dissuasive criminal penalties', and in the event that infringements are committed or instigated for 'financial gain', to ensure that the conduct is punishable by 'custodial sentences with a maximum of not less than eight years' if the offence was committed within the context of a criminal organisation or was committed while 'endangering the lives of the persons who are the subject of the offence'.[172] The Commission's report on the implementation of the Framework Decision notes that while all of the Member States have ensured that the conduct referred to is punishable under the criminal law, there is still a considerable variety of penalties which range 'from fines as minimum penalties to imprisonment of up to 15 years as maximum penalties in aggravating circumstances'. It notes however that 'this is not contrary to the Framework Decision, since it only provides for minimum approximation'.[173]

[167] Council Directive 2002/90/EC of 28 November 2002 defining the facilitation of unauthorised entry, transit and residence [2002] OJ L328/17, Art 1(1)(a).

[168] *Ibid*, Art 1(1)(b).

[169] *Ibid*, Art 2.

[170] United Nations Convention Against Transnational Organized Crime, GA Res 25, annex I, UN GAOR, 55th Sess, Supp No 49, 44, UN Doc A/45/49 (Vol.I) (2001), not in force.

[171] See also A Weyembergh, 'Approximation of Criminal Laws, the Constitutional Treaty and the Hague Programme' (2005) 42 *CMLR* 1567, 1589.

[172] Council Framework Decision of 28 November 2002 on the strengthening of the penal framework to prevent the facilitation of unauthorised entry, transit and residence (2002/946/JHA) [2002] OJ L328/1, Art 1(1) and (3).

[173] Report from the Commission based on Article 9 of the Council Framework Decision of 28 November 2002 on the strengthening of the penal framework to prevent the facilitation of unauthorised entry, transit and residence, Brussels 6 December 2006, COM (2006) 770 final, 6.

(iv) Employment of Illegal Migrants

A directive regulating the criminal liability of employers of illegal third country migrants was adopted in 2009. It does not apply to the UK, Ireland or Denmark.[174] The Directive prohibits the employment of third-country nationals who are unlawfully residing in a Member State[175] and requires Member States to criminalise employers who 'intentionally' infringe the requirement to undertake sufficient checks to ensure that their employees are lawfully resident in the Member State or to maintain documentation to this effect if: 'the infringement continues or is persistently repeated'; 'the infringement is in respect of the simultaneous employment of a significant number of illegally staying third-country nationals'; 'the infringement is accompanied by particularly exploitative working conditions'; the 'infringement is committed by an employer who, while not having been charged with or convicted of an offence pursuant to [legislation on trafficking in human beings], uses work or services extracted from an illegally staying third-country national with the knowledge that he or she is a victim of trafficking in human beings'; or 'the infringement relates to the illegal employment of a minor'.[176] The Member States are obliged criminalise incitement to or aiding and abetting in such conduct[177] and to ensure that infringements are subject to 'effective, proportionate and dissuasive sanctions'.[178]

(v) Environmental Crime, including Ship-Source Pollution

In 2003, the Council adopted a Framework Decision on the protection of the environment through the criminal law which set out a number of offences which the Member States were required to establish as criminal offences under their domestic laws.[179] The Commission subsequently successful sought the annulment of this legislation on the basis that the correct legal basis for such legislation was the EC Treaty and not the EU Treaty.[180] The Directive on the protection of the environment through the criminal law requires the Member States to criminalise a wide variety of unlawful conduct if committed 'intentionally or with at least serious negligence'[181]

[174] Directive 2009/52/EC of the European Parliament and of the Council of 18 June 2009 providing for minimum standards on sanctions and measures against employers of illegally staying third-country nationals [2009] OJ L168/24.

[175] *Ibid*, Art 3(1).

[176] *Ibid*, Art 4 and Art 9(1).

[177] *Ibid*, Art 9(2).

[178] *Ibid*, Art 10.

[179] Council Framework Decision 2003/80/JHA of 27 January 2003 on the protection of the environment through the criminal law [2003] OJ L29/55.

[180] Case 176/03 *Commission v Council* [2005] ECR I-7879.

[181] Directive 2008/99/EC of the European Parliament and of the Council of 19 Nov 2008 on the protection of the environment through the criminal law [2008] OJ L328/28, Art 3. Aiding and abetting and inciting the commission of the offences must also to be criminalised, Art 4 and the Member States must ensure that legal persons can also be held liable, Art 6.

and to ensure that the offences are 'punishable by effective, proportionate and dissuasive criminal penalties'.[182]

The Council Framework Decision on ship source pollution was annulled under similar circumstances[183] and a Directive on ship-source pollution and the introduction of penalties adopted.[184] This Directive was amended and renamed in 2009 to include criminal penalties to reinforce its substantive provisions.[185] The Member States must ensure that 'ship-source discharges of polluting substances, including minor cases of such discharges', into waters as defined in Article 3, 'if committed with intent, recklessly or with serious negligence', is considered to be a criminal offence[186] and punishable by 'effective, proportionate and dissuasive criminal penalties'.[187] In addition, the Member States must ensure that aiding and abetting and inciting the commission of the offences is also criminalised,[188] and that legal persons can be held criminally liable.[189]

(vi) Racism and Xenophobia

In 2008, after a drafting process lasting several years, the Council finally adopted a Framework Decision on combating certain forms and expressions of racism and xenophobia by means of criminal law.[190] This is one of the only areas regulated by way of a framework decision which is not referred to in Article 83(1) TEFU. The legal basis for further action is likely to be Article 19(1) TFEU in conjunction with Article 83(2) TFEU.[191] The Framework Decision requires that Member States criminalise various types of 'intentional' racist or xenophobic conduct, including: (a) publicly inciting violence or hatred directed against a group of persons or a

[182] *Ibid*, 5.

[183] Case 440/05 *Commission v Council* [2007] ECR I-9097 concerning Council Framework Decision 2005/667/JHA of 12 July 2005 to strengthen the criminal-law framework for the enforcement of the law against ship-source pollution [2005] OJ L255/164 and Directive 2005/35/EC of the European Parliament and of the Council of 7 September 2005 on ship-source pollution and on the introduction of penalties for infringements [2005] OJ L255/11. For comment, see M Hedemann-Robinson, 'The EU and Environmental Crime: The Impact of the ECJ's Judgment on Framework Decision 2005/667 on Ship Source Pollution' (2008) 20 *Journal of Environmental Law* 279.

[184] Directive 2005/35/EC of the European Parliament and of the Council of 7 September 2005 on ship-source pollution and on the introduction of penalties for infringements [2005] OJ L255/11.

[185] Directive 2009/123/EC of 21 October 2009 amending Directive 2005/35/EC on ship-source pollution and on the introduction of penalties for infringements [2009] OJ L280/52.

[186] Directive 2005/35/EC of the European Parliament and of the Council of 7 September 2005 on ship-source pollution and on the introduction of penalties for infringements [2005] OJ L255/11 as amended, Art 4(1) and Art 5a(1).

[187] *Ibid*, Art 8a.

[188] *Ibid*, Art 5b.

[189] *Ibid*, Art 8b and 8c.

[190] Council Framework Decision 2008/913/JHA of 28 November 2008 on combating certain forms and expressions of racism and xenophobia by means of criminal law [2008] OJ L328/55. See also the earlier Proposal for a Council Framework Decision on combating racism and xenophobia, Brussels, 28 November 2001, COM (2001) 664 final.

[191] The importance of combating racism and xenophobia is also referred to in Article 67(3) though it is questionable whether this provision would provide the legal basis for action, see above.

member of such a group defined by reference to race, colour, religion, descent or national or ethnic origin; (b) committing an act referred to in (a) by the public dissemination or distribution of tracts, pictures or other material; (c) publicly condoning, denying or grossly trivialising crimes of genocide, crimes against humanity and war crimes, as defined in Articles 6, 7 and 8 of the Statute of the International Criminal Court, directed against a group defined by reference to race, colour, religion, descent or national or ethnic origin when the conduct is carried out in a manner likely to incite violence or hatred against such a group or a member of such a group; (d) publicly condoning, denying or trivialising the crimes, defined in Article 6 of the Charter of the International Military Tribunal appended to the London Agreement of 8 April 1945, directed against a group defined by reference to race, colour, religion, descent or national or ethnic origin when the conduct is carried out in a manner likely to incite violence or hatred against such a group or a member of such a group.[192] Member States are also required to criminalise the incitement, aiding and abetting or attempting of the prohibited conduct[193] and ensure that the conduct outlined in Article 1 is punishable by a maximum prison sentence of between one and three years.[194] They are also required to ensure that racist and xenophobic motives are considered as aggravating factors or that such motivation is taken into account by the courts in sentencing[195] and that legal persons can be held liable for the conduct outlined in Articles 1 and 2.[196]

(vii) Insider Dealing and Market Manipulation

In 2011, the Commission issued a proposal for a Directive on insider dealing and market manipulation based on Article 83(2) TFEU on the grounds that 'market abuse can occur across border and harms the integrity of financial markets which are increasingly integrated in the Union' and that 'divergent approaches to the imposition of criminal sanctions for market abuse offences by Member States leave a certain scope for perpetrators who can often make use of the most lenient sanction systems'.[197] The UK Government has intimated that the UK will not opt in, although it stresses that its decision 'not to opt in at this point in time is a reflection of the sequencing of the Commission's proposal, rather than particular concerns as to the substance', while noting that 'the UK already covers all of the offences in its criminal law'.[198]

[192] Council Framework Decision 2008/913/JHA of 28 November 2008 on combating certain forms and expressions of racism and xenophobia by means of criminal law [2008] OJ L328/55, Art 1.

[193] *Ibid*, Art 5.

[194] *Ibid*, Art 3.

[195] *Ibid*, Art 4

[196] *Ibid*, Art 5.

[197] Proposal for a Directive on criminal sanctions for insider dealing and market manipulation, Brussels, 20 October 2011, COM (2011) 654 final, at 5.

[198] See the written statement of the Financial Secretary to the Treasury (Mr Mark Hoban), Hansard, Commons Debates, 20 February 2012: Column 58WS.

In the context of insider dealing, the proposal requires Member States to ensure that the following conduct is criminalised if committed intentionally: (a) when in possession of inside information, using that information to acquire or dispose of financial instruments to which that information relates for one's own account or for the account of a third party. This also includes using inside information to cancel or amend an order concerning a financial instrument to which that information relates where that order was placed before entering into possession of that inside information; or (b) disclosing inside information to any other person, unless such disclosure is made in the lawful course of the exercise of duties resulting from employment or profession.[199] In relation to market manipulation, the intentional commission of the following activity must also be criminalised: (a) giving false or misleading signals as to the supply of, demand for, or price of, a financial instrument or a related spot commodity contract; (b) securing the price of one or several financial instruments or a related spot commodity contract at an abnormal or artificial level; (c) entering into a transaction, placing an order to trade, or any other activity in financial markets affecting the price of one or several financial instruments or a related spot commodity contract, which employs a fictitious device or any other form of deception or contrivance; (d) dissemination of information which gives false or misleading signals as to financial instruments or related spot commodity contracts, where those persons derive, for themselves or another person, an advantage or profit from the dissemination of the information in question.[200] The Member States must ensure that inciting or aiding and abetting the offences is also criminalised, that legal persons can be held liable and that the offences are punished by way of 'effective, proportionate and dissuasive sanctions'.[201]

D Criminal Legalisation falling under other Treaty Provisions

(i) Protection of EU's Financial Interests

The protection of the financial interests of the EU has long been considered a matter of considerable importance and the PIF Convention and its protocols were adopted in order to address concerns that differences in the laws of the Member States were hindered attempts to combat fraud against the Union's interests. The PIF Convention defines fraud affecting the Communities' interests as, in respect of expenditure, 'any intentional act or omission' relating to 'the use or presentation of false, incorrect or incomplete statements or documents' or the 'non-disclosure of information in violation of a specific obligation' which has as its effect 'the misappropriation or wrongful retention of funds' from the general

[199] Proposal for a Directive on criminal sanctions for insider dealing and market manipulation, Brussels, 20 October 2011, COM (2011) 654 final, Art 3.

[200] *Ibid*, Art 4.

[201] *Ibid*, Arts 5, 6, and 7.

budget of, or budgets managed by or on behalf of, the Communities, or the 'misapplication of such funds for the purposes other than those for which they were originally intended'.[202] Also included within the definition is, with respect of revenue, 'any intentional act or omission' relating to the 'use of false, incorrect or incomplete statements or documents', the 'non-disclosure of information in violation of a specific obligation', or the 'misapplication of a legally obtained benefit' which has as its effect the illegal diminution of the resources of the general budget of, or budgets managed by or on behalf of, the Communities.[203] Member States are required to ensure that the commission, participation in, instigation of and the attempt to commit such conduct (unless it constituted minor fraud), is punishable by 'effective, proportionate and dissuasive criminal penalties, including, at least in cases of serious fraud, penalties involving deprivation of liberty'.[204]

The Corruption Protocol,[205] which was subsequently added to the Convention, was intended to tackle 'acts of corruption which involve national and Community officials and damage, or are likely to damage, the European Communities' financial interests'.[206] 'Passive corruption' is defined as

> the deliberate action of an official, who, directly or through an intermediary, requests or receives advantages of any kind whatsoever, for himself or her a third party, or accepts a promise of such an advantage, to act or refrain from acting in accordance with his duty or in the exercise of his functions in breach of his official duties in a way which damages or is likely to damage the European Communities' financial interests.[207]

Active corruption meanwhile is defined as

> the deliberate action of whosoever promises or gives, directly or through an intermediary, an advantage of any kind whatsoever to an official for himself or for a third party for him to act or to refrain from acting in accordance with his duty or in the exercise of his functions in breach of his official duties in a way which damages or is likely to damage the European Communities' financial interests.[208]

Member States were required to criminalise both active and passive corruption and to ensure that Community officials and members of the Commission, European Parliament, Court of Justice and Court of Auditors, were treated for the purposes of the criminal law in the same way as, or 'assimilated' to, their national

[202] Convention on the Protection of the European Communities' Financial Interests [1995] OJ C316/49, Art 1(a).

[203] *Ibid*, Art 1(b).

[204] *Ibid*, Art 2.

[205] Protocol drawn up on the basis of Article K.3 of the Treaty on European Union to the Convention on the Protection of the European Communities' Financial Interests [1996] OJ C313/2 (Corruption Protocol).

[206] Explanatory Report on the Second Protocol to the Convention on the Protection of the European Communities' Financial Interests OJ [1999] C 91/8. See also L Ferola, 'Anti-Bribery Measures in the European Union: A Comparison with the Italian Legal Order' (2000) 28 *International Journal of Legal Information* 512, 521–25.

[207] Protocol drawn up on the basis of Article K.3 of the Treaty on European Union to the Convention on the Protection of the European Communities' Financial Interests [1996] OJ C313/2, Art 2.

[208] *Ibid*, Art 3.

equivalents in the Member States.[209] They were also obliged to ensure that the commission, participation in and instigation of the conduct set out in the Protocol be 'punishable by effective, proportionate and dissuasive criminal penalties, including in serious cases, penalties involving deprivation of liberty'.[210] A Second Protocol which requires Member States to establish money laundering related to the proceeds of 'serious' fraud, as defined in Council Directive 91/308/EEC, and to active and passive corruption as a criminal offence was adopted in 1999.[211]

In 2012, the Commission issued a proposal for a Directive on the fight against fraud to the Union's financial interests based on Article 325(4) of the TFEU rather than on Article 83(2) TFEU. According to the proposal 'Article 325 sets out the EU's competence to enact the necessary measures in the fields of prevention of and fight against fraud and any other illegal activities affecting the Union's financial interests which "act as a deterrent"'.[212] It is likely that any attempts to enact legislation on the basis of Article 325 TFEU will be contested,[213] not least because of the procedural law implications.[214]

IV EU Criminal Law and Policy after Lisbon

There are, as we have seen, two express justifications in the Lisbon Treaty for the need for EU criminal law: to ensure the effectiveness of EU policy and to deal with the problem of cross-border crime in order to promote the EU area of freedom, security and justice. The competence to 'establish minimum rules with regard to the definition of criminal offences and sanctions' for the purposes of ensuring the effectiveness of EU policy is a continuation of the approach of the Commission under the old first pillar.[215] The EU competence for tackling serious crime in the context of the AFSJ must be understood meanwhile as a continuation of the EU third pillar policy. Questions remain, however, about the means of establishing these minimum rules. The development of EU criminal law is dependent on the manner in which criminal laws are created and enforced. In this regard there are two main principles which have traditionally governed the creation of EU criminal law: harmonisation of the law and the notion of mutual recognition.

[209] *Ibid*, Art 4.

[210] *Ibid*, Art 5.

[211] Second Protocol, drawn up on the basis of Article K.3 of the Treaty on European Union, to the Convention on the Protection of the European Communities' Financial Interests [1997] OJ C221/12, Art 2.

[212] Proposal for a Directive of the European Parliament and of the Council, on the fight against fraud to the Union's financial interests by means of the criminal law, Brussels, 11 July 2012, COM (2012) 363 final, at 6.

[213] See the analysis of the UK House of Commons European Scrutiny Committee, 12th Report of Session 2012–13 (London, 2012) at 10.27.

[214] *Ibid.*

[215] Case C 176/03 *Commission v Council* (n 180).

The principle of mutual recognition is generally considered to have been introduced by the ECJ in the *Cassis de Dijon* case in which it was held that Member States must allow goods sold legally in another Member State to be sold in their own country.[216] In the criminal law context, the principle generally refers to the notion that judgments and decisions taken in one Member State will be recognised in all other Member States. This notion which was introduced by the British Presidency in 1998 has enjoyed considerable success and is considered to be one of the 'cornerstones' of EU criminal law policy.[217] It is particularly important in relation to criminal procedure law and a number of instruments in the field – notably the European Arrest Warrant (EAW) – which rely heavily on the principle[218] and is referred to directly in Article 82 TFEU: 'Judicial cooperation in criminal matters in the Union shall be based on the principle of mutual recognition of judgments and judicial decisions'. Its relevance is less clear in the substantive criminal law context and it is not mentioned in Article 83 TFEU.

Mutual recognition is said to allow for integration without total harmonisation.[219] It is not surprising, therefore, that it has been considered by some to constitute an alternative to harmonisation.[220] It is questionable, however, whether in the context of the substantive criminal law this can be said to be the case. Sole reliance on mutual recognition would require Member States to recognise foreign judgments, even if their laws were quite different, which in many cases would be likely to be politically unacceptable. Harmonisation of the substantive criminal law might be considered to be a means of securing mutual recognition rather than a goal in itself, for instance as a sign of political unity in the EU.[221] The application

[216] Case 120/78 *Rewe-Zentral AG v Bundesmonopolverwaltung für Branntwein* [1979] ECR 649.

[217] P Asp, 'Mutual Recognition and the Development of Criminal Law Cooperation within Europe' in EJ Husabø and A Strandbakken (eds), *Harmonisation of Criminal Law in Europe* (Antwerpen, Intersentia, 2005) 26.

[218] Council Framework Decision of 13 June 2002 on the European arrest warrant and the surrender procedure between Member States (2002/584/JHA) [2002] OJ L190/1, Recital 7. See too Council Framework Decision 2008/978/JHA of 18 December 2008, on the European evidence warrant for the purposes of obtaining objects, documents and data for use in proceedings in criminal matters [2008] OJ L350/72; Council Framework Decision 2003/577/JHA of 22 July 2003 on the execution of orders freezing property and evidence [2003] OJ L196/45; Council Framework Decision 2005/214/JHA of 22 March 2005 on application of mutual recognition to financial penalties [2005] OJ L76/16 (as amended by Council Framework Decision 2009/299/JHA of 26 February 2009 amending Framework Decisions 2002/584/JHA, 2005/214/JHA, 2006/783/JHA, 2008/909/JHA and 2008/947/JHA, thereby enhancing the procedural rights of persons and fostering the application of the principle of mutual recognition to decisions rendered in the absence of the person concerned at the trial [2009] OJ L81/24).

[219] *Ibid*, 29.

[220] *Ibid*, 31 referring to the British Presidency. See too European Council, EU Presidency Conclusions, 4–5 November 2004, Annex 1: *The Hague Programme: Strengthening Freedom, Security and Justice in the European Union*, Brussels, 13 December 2004, 3.3.1: mutual recognition and not approximation lies at the heart of the EU criminal justice policy.

[221] See eg European Council, EU Presidency Conclusions, 4-5 November 2004, Annex 1: *The Hague Programme: Strengthening Freedom, Security and Justice in the European Union*, Brussels, 13 December 2004, Council Document 16054/04, II, General Orientations, General Principles, 4 and Mutual Recognition, 3.3.2 Approximation of law: 'The European Council recalls that the establishment of the minimum rules concerning aspects of procedural law is envisaged by the existing and future treaties in order to facilitate mutual recognition of judgments and judicial decisions and police and judicial

of the notion of mutual recognition to the criminal sphere might require a degree of standardisation of the criminal law through agreement of 'common definitions, incriminations and sanctions'.[222] This type of argument was frequently made in the context of the EAW. The EAW controversially abolished the 'dual criminality' rule for certain crimes, where the crime could be subject to a sentence of at least three years[223] and doubts were raised about potential for difficulties to arise in cases where the criminal laws of Member States differ significantly.[224] On this basis harmonisation of the criminal laws of the Member States was often portrayed as a means of lessening concerns about the abolition of the dual criminality requirement in certain cases. Nevertheless it is doubtful, particularly in view of the fact that the EAW was agreed before there had been any broad agreement regarding harmonisation of the crimes covered by the EAW, whether the drive towards harmonisation of the law can be seen to rest in any meaningful sense on the abolition of the dual criminality requirement.

Even if the assumption that the aim of harmonisation is to further the goals of mutual recognition is correct, the question then arises as to 'how much' harmonisation is necessary in order to further these interests? Is a list of common criminal offences sufficient (as with the EAW) or is wide ranging harmonisation necessary? If it is simply a question of securing general agreement that certain conduct (terrorism, child pornography, insider dealing) be considered to be criminal across the EU, it could be argued that in many respects there is no real need for harmonisation in the first place. This suggests that the harmonisation of the law, although often linked to mutual recognition or the abolition of the dual criminality rule, is better understood as a goal in its own right. The harmonisation of the criminal law can be seen in the broader context of the evolving role of the EU institutions in matters involving justice and home affairs as facilitating the transfer of competence from the Member States to the EU.[225]

The EU is now actively involved in creating substantive criminal law. Initial reluctance to acknowledge 'harmonisation' as the principal goal driving the creation of criminal laws,[226] has been replaced by express recognition of harmonisation as an

cooperation in criminal matters having a cross border dimension. The approximation of substantive criminal law services the same purposes and concerns areas of particular serious crime with cross border dimensions'.

[222] Presidency Conclusions of the Tampere European Council, 15 and 16 October 1999, Milestone 48. See also the Presidency Conclusions of the Brussels European Council, November 2004, 3.3.2 Approximation of law, in which it is stated that in order to ensure 'more effective implementation within national systems, JHA Ministers should be responsible within the Council for defining criminal offences and determining penalties in general'.

[223] *Ibid*, Art 2(2).

[224] See eg S Peers, 'Mutual Recognition and Criminal Law in the European Union: Has the Council got it Wrong?' (2004) 41 *CMLR* 5, 25. See also Mitsilegas, *EU Criminal Law* (n 19) 101–103.

[225] S Skinner, 'The Third Pillar Treaty Provisions on Police Cooperation: Has the EU Bitten off More than it Can Chew?' (2002) 8 *Columbia Journal of European Law* 203.

[226] See European Council, EU Presidency Conclusions, 4–5 November 2004, Annex 1*: The Hague Programme: Strengthening Freedom, Security and Justice in the European Union*, Brussels, 13 December 2004, 3.3.1: mutual recognition and not approximation lies at the heart of the EU criminal justice policy.

objective of EU law[227] and an explicit legal basis. The 'approximation of the criminal' is expressly referred to in the context of the Article 83(2) TFEU criminal law competence to protect EU policy. There is no direct reference to approximation or harmonisation in Article 83(1) TFEU, which regulates serious crime with a cross-border dimension, but it is telling that the same terminology is used in both provisions: the EU has the competence to 'establish minimum rules concerning the definition of criminal offences and sanctions'.

Two principal questions arise in relation to the EU harmonisation of the criminal law: why is the criminal law necessary in the first place and why is the EU best placed to determine the definition and scope of these criminal laws? These questions are currently of crucial importance in view of the extended competence of the EU and the increased jurisdiction of the CJEU and in light of the UK's decision to opt out of many of the measures. It is crucial that the EU is able to provide clear justification for its role in the context of criminalisation and in relation to the harmonisation of the criminal law.

The EU institutions frequently refer to the 'transnational' nature of crimes and the 'cross-border' dimension of crime as one of the principal justifications for EU involvement in the criminal law.[228] This is now clearly recognised in the TFEU, which gives the EU competence to harmonise the criminal law in the areas of particularly serious crime with a cross-border dimension.[229] It is common to find reference in the legislation to the 'international scale'[230] of the problem of crime and to the international dimension: the 'transnational and borderless character of modern information systems' results in 'trans-border' attacks on information systems and thus gives rise to an 'urgent need for further action to approximate criminal laws in this area'.[231]

References to the international, trans-border nature of crime are often precursors to claims that the Member States are unable to sufficiently combat certain types of crime on their own or that the EU is better placed to enforce a 'comprehensive' approach. It is no coincidence that such language mirrors that of the subsidiarity principle set out in Article 5 TEU.[232] Corruption and environmental

[227] See eg Communication from the Commission to the European Parliament, the Council, the European Economic and Social Committee and the Committee of the Regions, Towards an EU Criminal Policy: Ensuring the effective implementation of EU policies through criminal law, Brussels, 20 September 2011, COM (2011) 573, at 2.

[228] See S Peers, 'The European Union and Substantive Criminal Law: Reinventing the Wheel?' (2002) 33 *Netherlands Yearbook of International Law* 47, 55.

[229] Art 83 TFEU.

[230] Council Framework Decision 2001/413/JHA of 28 May 2001 on combating fraud and counterfeiting of non-cash means of payment [2001] OJ L149/1.

[231] Council Framework Decision 2005/222/JHA of 24 February 2005 on attacks against information systems [2005] OJ L69/67, Recital 5. Similar statements were to be found in the (annulled) Council Framework Decision 2003/80/JHA of 27 January 2003 on the protection of the environment through the criminal law [2003] OJ L29/55, Recital 1; Council Framework Decision of 22 July 2003 on combating corruption in the private sector (2003/568/JHA) [2003] OJ L192/54, Recital 1: 'not just a domestic problem but also a transnational problem'.

[232] This provision was previously set out in Art 5 EC Treaty and allows the EU to take measures if 'the objectives of the proposed action cannot be sufficiently achieved by Member States' action in the

offences are thus referred to as problems 'most effectively tackled by means of a European Union joint action'[233] and as 'jointly faced by Member States, which should therefore take concerted action',[234] while the aim of ensuring that 'fraud and counterfeiting involving all forms of non-cash means of payment are recognised as criminal offences' cannot, 'in view of the international dimension', 'be sufficiently achieved by Member States', but can be 'better achieved at Union level'.[235] Similarly 'the serious criminal offence of trafficking in human beings' must be 'addressed not only through individual action by each Member State but by a comprehensive approach in which the definition of the constituent elements of criminal law common to all Member States, including effective, proportionate and dissuasive sanctions, forms an integral part',[236] while the objectives of the provisions on combating terrorism 'cannot be sufficiently achieved by the Member States unilaterally, and can therefore, because of the need for reciprocity be better achieved at the level of the Union'.[237]

The perceived inability of the Member States to tackle crime unilaterally is in turn frequently linked to the 'effectiveness' of investigating and prosecuting crime: 'Significant gaps and differences in Member States' laws in this area may hamper the fight against organised crime and terrorism, and may complicate effective police and judicial cooperation in the area of attacks against information systems'.[238] Consequently it is necessary for '[c]riminal law in the area of attacks against information systems to be 'approximated in order to ensure the greatest possible police and judicial cooperation in the areas of criminal offences relation to attacks against information systems and to contribute to the fight against organised crime and terrorism'.[239]

framework of their national constitutional system and can therefore be better achieved by action on the part of the Community'.

[233] Council Framework Decision of 22 July 2003 on combating corruption in the private sector (2003/568/JHA) [2003] OJ L192/54, Recital 1.

[234] Council Framework Decision 2003/80/JHA of 27 January 2003 on the protection of the environment through the criminal law [2003] OJ L29/55 (annulled), Recital 1.

[235] Council Framework Decision 2001/413/JHA of 28 May 2001 on combating fraud and counterfeiting of non-cash means of payment [2001] OJ L149/1, Recital 4. See also the Explanatory Memorandum to the Proposal for a Council Framework Decision laying down minimum provisions on the constituent elements of criminal acts and penalties in the field of illicit drug trafficking, Brussels, 23 May 2001, COM (2001) 259 final, 3: 'The aims of this framework decision cannot be achieved by the Member States, given the transnational dimension of the offence, and can therefore best be attained by the European Union'.

[236] Council Framework Decision of 19 July 2002 on combating trafficking in human beings (2002/629/JHA) [2002] OJ L203/1, Recital 7.

[237] Council Framework Decision 2002/475/JHA of 13 June 2002 on combating terrorism [2002] OJ L164/3, Recital 9. See also the Proposal for Council Framework Decision of to strengthen the criminal-law framework for the enforcement of the law against ship-source pollution, Brussels, 2 May 2003, COM (2003) 227 final: 'the objectives of the proposed action cannot be achieved adequately by the Member States separately, but can, owing to the cross-border character of the damage which may be caused by the behaviour concerned, be better achieved by the Union'.

[238] Council Framework Decision 2005/222/JHA of 24 February 2005 on attacks against information systems [2005] OJ L69/67, Recital 5.

[239] *Ibid*, Recital 7. See too the Explanatory Memorandum to the Proposal for a Council Framework Decision laying down minimum provisions on the constituent elements of criminal acts and penalties in the field of illicit drug trafficking, Brussels, 23 May 2001, COM (2001) 259 final, 2.

Differences in the criminal laws of the Member States are often referred to as providing criminals with an advantage, by allowing them to choose the Member State with the most lenient laws or simply by making the prosecution and investigation of crime more complicated.[240] Diversity in the nature of the regulation of crime at the national level and differences in the definition and punishment of crime are referred to as constituting 'barriers to international judicial cooperation'[241] and thus as justifying harmonisation of the law by the EU. The explanatory memorandum to the proposal for a framework decision on combating the sexual exploitation of children and child pornography, for instance, referred to 'the need to address diverging legal approaches in the Member States'.[242] There was no mention, however, of the basis on which this conclusion was reached, no critique of the pre-existing provisions, such as those in the Cybercrime Convention, nor any explanation as to why they were deemed inadequate.[243] Similarly, the Framework Decision on racism and xenophobia refers to the importance of defining 'a common criminal law approach in the European Union to this phenomenon in order to ensure that the same behaviour constitutes an offence in all Member States',[244] but immediately qualifies this by acknowledging that the legislation is 'limited to very serious forms of racism'. In the words of the UK European and Scrutiny Committee report on the earlier proposal: 'the proposal does not in fact achieve the objective of prescribing common rules, and no explanation if offered as to why it is said to be necessary to ensure "that the same behaviour constitutes an offence in all Member States"'.[245]

Diversity between Member States in the criminal law response to an issue suggests that there may not be consensus on the need or desirability of criminalisation. This in turn gives rise to questions about whether the EU is best placed to determine the boundaries of criminalisation. Further, if closer cooperation between the Member States is considered to be an 'obvious response' to the 'phenomenon' of cross-border crime,[246] the empirical basis for this phenomenon is

[240] See eg A Weyembergh, 'Approximation of the Criminal Law, the Constitutional Treaty and the Hague Programme', (2005) 42 *CMLR*1567, 1579; A Bernardi, 'Opportunité de l'harmonisation' in M Delmas-Marty, G Giudicelli-Delage and E Lambert-Abdelgawad (eds), *L'harmonisation des sanctions pénales en Europe* (Paris, Société de legislation compare, 2003) 461.

[241] Joint action/96/443/JHA of 15 July 1996 adopted by the Council on the basis of Article K.3 of the Treaty on European Union, concerning action to combat racism and xenophobia [1996] OJ L185/5.

[242] Communication from the Commission to the Council and the European Parliament, Combating trafficking in human beings and combating the sexual exploitation of children and child pornography, Brussels, 22 January 2001, COM (2000) 854 final, at 21.

[243] Council Framework Decision 2004/68/JHA of 22 December 2003 on combating the sexual exploitation of children and child pornography [2004] OJ L13/44, Recital 7.

[244] Council Framework Decision 2008/913/JHA of 28 November 2008 on combating certain forms and expressions of racism and xenophobia by means of criminal law [2008] OJ L328/55, Recital 4.

[245] European Scrutiny Committee, 11th Report, Session 2006–07 (London, 2007) at 23, para 5.9.

[246] C van den Wyngaert, 'Eurojust and the European Public Prosecutor in the *Corpus Juris* Model: Water and Fire?' in N Walker (ed), *Europe's Area of Freedom, Justice and Security* (Oxford, Oxford University Press, 2004) 201.

considerably less clear.[247] This suggests that the well-rehearsed statements about cross-border crime may mask other grounds for the harmonisation of the criminal law. In short, the reasons provided by the EU for its involvement in the substantive criminal law often appear overly general and, more often than not, fail to establish a scientific or empirical basis for the creation of criminal law. This does not necessary mean, however, that the EU's involvement cannot be justified, only that it has failed to adequately explain the need for its role in the context of creating and harmonising the criminal law.

The introduction of the Treaty of Lisbon is said to have moved 'the debate on EU criminal law harmonisation from the inter-pillar constitutional debate to the questions of "why criminal law" and "what kind of criminal law" for the EU'.[248] In the following chapters we will analyse the EU's criminal law involvement in one particular area – the information and communication technology sector – in an effort to achieve a more detailed understanding of the policies driving the EU's approach. This will allow us to better analyse the justifications for the EU's involvement in the criminal law. The EU has displayed considerable interest in regulating the information society, which in view of the cross-border nature of the Internet, coupled with the rapidly changing nature of the digital environment should come as little surprise. The criminal law response of the EU to ICT (information and communications technology) matters is of particular interest as it allows consideration of issues relating both to cross-border regulation of crime and to the effective implementation of EU policy.

In chapter 3 we will consider how the EU's criminal law provisions fit in to its broader regulatory approach to the information society. This will provide a basis in the following chapters for assessing the process of criminalisation and harmonisation of the substantive criminal law in the field of information technology.

[247] K Nuotio, 'Harmonisation of Criminal Sanctions in the European Union – Criminal Law Science Fiction' in EJ Husab and A Strandbakken (eds), *Harmonization of Criminal Law in Europe* (Antwerp, Intersenia, 2005) 91 et seq. See also RT Naylor, '"Marlboro Men" review of M Naím, Illicit: How Smugglers, Traffickers and Copycats are Hijacking the Global Economy' (2007) 29 *London Review of Books* 37: 'And while it is doubtless true that there is more economic crime across borders today, there is also much more legal business, and no proof that the proportion of illegality is increasing faster. Indeed to the extent that exchanges are becoming liberalised, flows more transparent, taxes cut and regulations relaxed, illicit trafficking across border is more likely to be shrinking relative to total economic transactions. What is increasing is the amount of noise made about it'.

[248] Mitsilegas, *EU Criminal Law* (n 19) 112; see too Herlin-Karnell, 'EU Competence after Lisbon' (n 22) 346.

3

EU Legislation in the Field of Information and Communications Technology

Governments of the Industrial World, you weary giants of flesh and steel . . . You have no sovereignty where we gather. You have no moral right to rule us nor do you possess any methods of enforcement we have true reason to fear. Cyberspace does not lie within your borders.[1]

I Introduction

The information and communication technology (ICT) sector now represents one of the most important industries in the Western world. A combination of the globalisation of communication and the borderless availability and accessibility of information has led to the construction of a new social reality in which the concept of 'global information space' has become increasingly important:

> As distinct from conventional geographical space, this means space connected by information networks. It is space without regional boundaries. . . . Information has no national boundaries. When global information space is formed, world-wide communication activities among citizens that cross all national boundaries will be set in motion . . . When this happens, the spirit of globalism, prevailing against conflicting national interests and differences, will become broadly and deeply rooted in the minds of the people.[2]

The European Commission was quick to recognise the technical, economic and societal developments in the information society and to develop a market-based legal framework, aimed at promoting competition in the context of borderless information services.[3] It has produced a steady stream of action plans and

[1] John Perry Barlow, Declaration of the Independence of Cyberspace.

[2] Y Masuda, *The Information Society as Post-Industrial Society* (Bethesda, World Future Society, 1981); see also MU Porat, 'Global Implications of the Information Society' (1978) 28 *Journal of Communication* 70.

[3] See Communication from the Commission to the Council, the European Parliament, the Economic and Social Committee and the Committee of the Regions, Europe's way to the information society, An action plan, Brussels, 19 July 1994, COM (94) 347 final; Europe and the Global Information Society, Recommendations of the High-level Group on the Information Society to the Corfu European Council

initiatives[4] and in doing so has attempted to develop an integrated master plan for the information society and audio-visual media sectors. Three of the Commission's priorities are of particular interest in this context. First, it has sought to promote the creation of a 'single European information space' in order to foster the creation of an open and competitive internal market for the information society and the media. Second, it has highlighted the importance of strengthening innovation and investment in ICT research, with a view to promoting growth and creating more and 'better' jobs. Third, it has stressed the importance of developing an inclusive European information society, which promotes growth and employment in a manner which is consistent with sustainable development and which is focused on promoting better public services and quality of life.[5] It is important here to note the significance of free market policies in relation to the Commission's approach.

In the context of the implementation of the first priority – the creation of a European Information Space with affordable and fast broadband service, rich and diverse content and digital services – the issue of Internet and network security took on increasing importance. Trust in digital services was deemed to be directly contingent on investors and users being sufficiently protected from the threat of sabotage, destruction of data, fraud, harmful content or breaches of confidentiality. This in turn led to criminal law and policy matters becoming increasingly important in the context of the European ICT regulatory framework.[6] This chapter will provide an overview of legislative developments at the EU level in order to demonstrate that while criminal law matters rarely play a central role in policy making in this sector, the EU developments in the field have nevertheless had a considerable impact on certain aspects of the criminal law. This impact has become more and more evident in recent years.

(Bangemann group), Bulletin of the European Union Supplement 2/94, 16 et seq; European Commission, Living and Working in the Information Society: People First, Green Paper, Brussels, 24 July 1996, COM (96) 389 final. The implications for regulation, see European Commission, Green Paper on the convergence of the telecommunications, media and information technology sectors and the implications for regulation – Towards an approach for the information society, Brussels, 3 December 1997, COM (97) 623 final, 10 et seq.

[4] Communication from the Commission to the Council and the European Parliament, eEurope 2002: Impact and Priorities A communication to the Spring European Council in Stockholm, 23–24 March 2001, Brussels, 13 March 2001, COM (2001) 140 final; Communication from the Commission to the Council, the European Parliament, the Economic and Social Committee and the Committee of the Regions, The eEurope 2005 action plan: an information society for everyone, Brussels, 28 May 2002, COM (2002) 263 final; Communication from the Commission to the Council, the European Parliament, the Economic and Social Committee and the Committee of the Regions, 'i2010 – A European Information Society for growth and employment', Brussels, 1 June 2005, COM (2005) 229 final.

[5] Communication from the Commission to the Council, the European Parliament, the Economic and Social Committee and the Committee of the Regions, 'i2010 – A European Information Society for growth and employment', Brussels, 1 June 2005, COM (2005) 229 final, 4.

[6] Stressed in Communication from the Commission to the European Parliament, the Council, the Economic and Social Committee and the Committee of the Regions, On fighting spam, spyware and malicious software, Brussels, 15 November 2006, COM (2006) 688 final; Communication from the Commission to the European Parliament, the Council and the Committee of the Regions, Towards a general policy on the fight against cyber crime, Brussels, 22 May 2007, COM (2007) 267 final.

II The Development of the EU Legislation concerning ICT

A Improvements in Technology

The EU legislation in the field of information and communications technology was initially influenced by what is best described as a general mood of euphoria stemming from the huge advances in technological capabilities. As communication methods were digitalised, the initial stages of a worldwide information network began to emerge. The Commission, in particular, perceived these developments as representing a significant opportunity: It hoped that the new technology would provide a way of overcoming linguistic barriers and of turning diversity within the EU into an advantage.[7] This largely positive outlook was reflected in the legislation. The aim was to provide as much room as possible for technological advances and to avoid hindering developments. In order to achieve this, the initial undertakings of the EU were orientated towards creating a free market, in which all institutions were to be afforded equal opportunities of access to the market. This was deemed to be the best way of providing the sector with a structure capable of supporting and promoting competition.

B Liberalisation as a Legislative Catalyser

(i) Point of Departure in the Member States

The development of the EU legislation in the ICT field was strongly influenced by the fact that the telecommunications market in the majority of Member States was dominated by monopolies. Individual companies controlled the market and there was virtually no competition. In addition, these firms were often wholly or partially tied to government agencies.[8] The potential for competition was further complicated by the fact that the sector was subject to strict regulation.[9] In 1987, this situation was highlighted by the Commission in its Green Paper on the development of

[7] Green Paper, Strategy options to strengthen the European Programme Industry in the context of the audiovisual policy of the European Union, Brussels, 6 April 1994, COM (94) 96 final, 19–14.

[8] Commission Directive 88/301/EEC of 16 May 1988 on competition in the markets in telecommunications terminal equipment [1988] OJ L131/73, 1; A Heffermann, *Telekommunikationsrecht, Liberalisierung und Wettbewerb* (Vienna, Verlag Österreich, 2002) 64; S Mosteshar, *European Community Telecommunications Regulation* (London, Graham & Trotman, 1993) 71; P Nihoul and P Rodford, *EU Electronic Communications Law, Competition and Regulation in the European Telecommunications Market*, 2nd edn, (Oxford, Oxford University Press, 2011) 1.10; H Ungerer and N Costello, *Telekommunikation in Europa, Freie Wahl für den Benutzer im europäischen Binnenmarkt des Jahres 1992: Eine Herausforderung für die Europäische Gemeinschaft* (Brussels, Kommission der Europäischen Gemeinschaften, 1989) 89.

[9] Ungerer and Costello, *Telekommunikation in Europa* (n 8) 89.

the common market for telecommunications services and equipment[10] and taken as the point of departure for its legislative reforms. Several measures were suggested as providing a means to efficiently utilise the opportunities of the sector. One of the central concerns in this regard was the creation of a competitive market in the telecommunications branch.[11] The EU demanded that steps be taken to liberalise the sector and to loosen the domination of the monopolies.[12]

The reaction of the individual Member States to the efforts of the EU can be characterised as somewhat hostile. This can be explained, at least in part, by the fact that in most countries the market leaders or monopolies in the telecommunications branch were entirely or partially state-owned.[13] Liberalisation would thus inevitably result in the state's loss of influence over the monopolies in the sector. The Commission was determined, however, to realise its goals for the ICT sector and it issued two directives, which were both aimed directly at achieving market liberalisation.[14] The principal goal of these directives was to abolish the practice of granting exclusive rights to single operators.

(a) Commission Directive 88/301/EEC

In the first Directive the Commission established rules concerning terminal equipment.[15] The Member States were required to withdraw any special or exclusive rights, which they had granted to public or private bodies, to import, market, connect, bring into service or to maintain telecommunications terminal equipment.[16] All economic operators were to have the right to import, market, connect, bring into service and maintain terminal equipment.[17] The public network termination points were to be made accessible to all users and in order to achieve this new public termination points were to be made public by a set date.[18] In addition, the Member States were required to publish a list of all of the technical specifications and type-approval procedures which were used for terminal equipment.[19] The Directive was amended in 1994 by a directive containing provisions aimed at

[10] Towards a Dynamic European Economy, Green Paper on the development of the common market for telecommunications services and equipment, Brussels, 30 June 1987, COM (87) 290 final; see too Heffermann, *Telekommunikationsrecht, Liberalisierung und Wettbewerb* (n 8) 67–69

[11] *Ibid*, 4.

[12] Nihoul and Rodford, *EU Electronic Communications Law* (n 8) 1.12; T Nöding, *Das neue europäische Telekommunikationsrecht und die Konvergenz der Übertragungswege* (Berlin, Tenea, 2004) 24.

[13] Nihoul and Rodford, *EU Electronic Communications Law* (n 8)1.13.

[14] Commission Directive 88/301/EEC of 16 May 1988 on competition in the markets in telecommunications terminal equipment [1988] OJ L131/73; Commission Directive 90/388/EEC of 28 June 1990 on competition in the markets for telecommunications services [1990] OJ L192/10.

[15] Commission Directive 88/301/EEC of 16 May 1988 on competition in the markets in telecommunications terminal equipment [1988] OJ L131/73, Art 2.

[16] Terminal equipment includes, for instance, modems, telex terminals, data transmission terminals, mobile telephones, receive-only satellite stations not reconnected to the public network of a Member State etc.

[17] Commission Directive 88/301/EEC (n 14), Art 3.

[18] *Ibid*, Art 4.

[19] *Ibid*, Art 5.

regulating satellite communications;[20] again the main aim of the legislation was to promote market liberalisation in the field of satellite communications.

(b) Commission Directive 90/388/EEC

The second Directive was also based on the premise that the establishment and use of telecommunications networks in the Member States was subject to regulatory barriers. This meant that access to the market was largely at the discretion of the individual Member States.[21] The EU was also troubled by the fact that licences to provide telecommunications services were often granted to organisations, which already occupied a dominant position in creating and operating the networks.[22]

In order to address this situation, the Commission obliged the Member States to withdraw 'all special or exclusive rights for the supply of telecommunications services other than voice telephony'. All operators were to be entitled to supply telecommunications services.[23] If a Member State made the supply of such services subject to licensing procedures, they were required to ensure that the conditions for granting the licences were 'objective, non-discriminatory and transparent', that reasons were provided for the refusal to grant a licence and that procedures were in place to enable an appeal against any such refusal.[24] Voice telephony was expressly excluded in Article 2 from the ambit of the Directive. The express exclusion of the important issue of voice telephony from the Directive was one of the principal reasons provided for its amendment in 1996. The separate regulation of this area was no longer considered to be appropriate.[25] The abolition of the exception was intended to guarantee total competition in the telecommunications market and to allow all telecommunications organisations in one Member State to directly provide their service in the other Member States.[26]

(ii) Reaction of the EU to Technological Advances

The technological advances in the ICT field during the 1980s and 1990s had a significant impact on the activities of the EU. The changing parameters brought about by the technological developments led to further activity by the EU institutions. New regulations were issued in various areas relating to information and communications technology. Again, the pursuit of liberalisation was usually the

[20] Commission Directive 94/46/EC of 13 October 1994 amending Directive 88/301/EEC and Directive 90/388/EEC in particular with regard to satellite communications [1994] OJ L268/15, Art 1.

[21] Commission Directive 90/388/EEC of 28 June 1990 on competition in the markets for telecommunications services [1990] OJ L192/10, Recital 2, 5.

[22] *Ibid*, Recital 15.

[23] *Ibid*, Art 2, para 1.

[24] *Ibid*, Art 2 Abs 2.

[25] Commission Directive 96/19/EC of 13 March 1996 amending Directive 90/388/EEC with regard to the implementation of full competition in telecommunications markets [1996] OJ L74/13, Recital 5.

[26] *Ibid*, Recital 6. Art 1, para 2 of the new Directive amended the old Directive and removed the exception concerning voice telephony.

principal factor driving the reforms. The early efforts continued to be influenced by the initial euphoria. In creating legislation, the EU adopted various approaches. In some cases, it addressed specific issues;[27] in other cases it focused its efforts on technological advances and future developments with the potential to impact on the entire information and communications sector.

At the beginning of the 1990s, for instance, the Commission issued a White Paper on growth, competitiveness and the way forward into the twenty-first century.[28] In this Paper, the Commission examined in particular the likely consequences of developments in information technology. It anticipated changes in consumer behaviour, new opportunities for the industry and significant technical advances.[29] In order to be able to exploit these developments, it stressed that it was necessary to promote the use of information technology, to provide basic services, to create an appropriate regulatory framework, to develop training on new technologies and to improve industrial and technological performance.[30]

On the basis of this Paper, it commissioned a team to write a report for the European Council setting out the measures to be adopted in response to the new information structures. This resulted in the creation of the Bangemann report.[31] The report considered first the revolution in the field and the significant opportunities afforded by the developments in information and communication technology. It referred, in particular, to the opportunities to create jobs, to improve equality and to promote quality of life.[32] The report stated that it was necessary to adopt an 'all-European' approach in order to prevent the creation of a 'two tier society of haves and have-nots'.[33] It recommended that the 'public authorities take measures to establish safeguards to ensure the cohesion of the new society' and to promote public acceptance of the new technology.[34] The report concluded that the ICT branch would constitute a global market of 'winners and losers'[35] and that the successful functioning of the market required 'a regulatory environment allowing full competition'. Consequently the report recommended that the Member States:

> [A]ccelerate the ongoing process of liberalization of the telecom sector by: opening up to competition infrastructures and services still in the monopoly area removing non-commercial political burdens and budgetary constraints imposed on telecommunications operators setting clear timetables and deadlines for the implementation of practical measures to achieve these goals.[36]

[27] See eg the regulations concerning the television industry at section II B(iii), below.

[28] Growth, Competitiveness, Employment: The Challenges and Ways Forward into the 21st Century – White Paper, 5 December 1993, COM (93) 700.

[29] *Ibid*, 22–23.

[30] *Ibid*, 24.

[31] Europe and the Global Information Society, Recommendations of the High-level group on the Information Society to the Corfu European Council (Bangemann group), Bulletin of the European Union Supplement 2/94, 5–39.

[32] *Ibid*, 10–11.

[33] *Ibid*, 11.

[34] *Ibid*, 12.

[35] *Ibid*, 13.

[36] *Ibid*, 16.

The abolition of the monopolies and the strengthening of the market were identified as essential to enabling this goal to be met.[37]

The report made it clear that parallel measures would need to be adopted in order to guard against the dangers associated with the new technology. It referred in particular to the protection of intellectual property, the protection of the private sphere and the electronic and legal protection of data.[38] The Bangemann report was the first European document which did not merely focus on the huge opportunities of the new technology. It also referred to the dangers and recommended that the EU consider these in more detail and work towards addressing them. The general tenor of the report was nevertheless considerably influenced by the general mood of excitement towards developments in the information society: the dangers and the measures to be taken to address them were mentioned as an aside.

On the basis of the Bangemann report, the Commission produced an action plan entitled Europe's Way to the Information Society.[39] The Commission's recommendations principally involved taking measures in order to establish a legal framework for the technical advances. The EU was to become a competitive area in which liberalisation of the branch was to be promoted and common standards and tariffs created.[40] At the same time, however, the Commission made it clear that the technological developments were accompanied by various risks. These would require action at a European level. It was deemed necessary to take measures in relation to protection of intellectual property,[41] protection of the private sphere[42] and the electronic and legal protection of data.[43]

(iii) Excursus: Regulation of the Television Industry

It is interesting to note that in its regulation of the ICT sector, the EU treated the television industry separately. An overview of the regulatory structure in this area is of interest not just because of its central importance, but also because it provides a clear illustration of the EU's approach. The radio and television branch was shaped in the second half of the twentieth century by continual technical advances. The development of satellite technology, in particular, brought about

[37] *Ibid*, 16–18.

[38] *Ibid*, 21–23.

[39] Communication from the Commission to the Council, the European Parliament, the Economic and Social Committee and the Committee of the Regions, Europe's way to the information society, An action plan, Brussels, 19 July 1994, COM (94) 347 final.

[40] *Ibid*, 3-4.

[41] Referring to the Amended proposal for a Council Directive on the legal protection of databases, COM (93) 464 final [1993] OJ C308/1.

[42] Referring to the Amended proposal for a Council Directive on the protection of individuals with regard to the processing of personal data and on the free movement of such data, Brussels, 15 October 1992, COM (92) 422 final.

[43] Communication from the Commission to the Council, the European Parliament, the Economic and Social Committee and the Committee of the Regions, Europe's way to the information society, An action plan, Brussels, 19 July 1994, COM (94) 347 final, 5–7.

entirely new opportunities. The new methods of transmission introduced for the first time the possibility of cross-border television. The abolition of territorial borders in the television industry provided the basis for a European television area.[44] In response to these developments, the Commission issued a Green paper on Television without Frontiers.[45] In this Paper the Commission noted that the broadcasting industry was of considerable significance for European integration and for the preservation of free democratic structures within the EU.[46] It referred to the new opportunities brought about by the technical advances[47] and recommended working towards a free, cross-border broadcasting industry in Europe.[48] In order to achieve this, it recommended that certain aspects of the broadcasting legislation of the Member States, including the prohibition on alcohol and tobacco advertising, be harmonised.[49]

On the basis of this Green Paper, a Directive was issued in 1989 on the coordination of certain provisions laid down by law, regulation or administrative action in Member States concerning the pursuit of television broadcasting activities.[50] As is clear from the title, the Directive was principally concerned with ensuring the basic coordination of the relevant regulations in the various Member States.[51] The aim behind these measures was to secure the freedom to provide broadcasting services within the EU without prejudice to various important public interests (such as cultural diversity, consumer protection and the protection of minors) of significance in the individual Member States. Another goal was to promote European audio-visual 'works'.[52]

The Directive was revised in 1997[53] and various new provisions were introduced relating to events considered by a Member State to be of major importance, ie teleshopping and the protection of minors. The most important amendments, however, were those concerning the matter of jurisdiction: according to the Directive, each Member State was deemed to have jurisdiction for the broad-

[44] B Möwes and AK Meider, *Die Revision der EG-Fernsehrichtlinie* (Berlin, Berliner Wissenschafts-Verlag, 2008) 23; see too Television Without Frontiers: Green Paper on the establishment of the common market for broadcasting, especially by satellite and cable, Brussels, 14 June 1984, COM (84) 300 final, 13–16.

[45] Television Without Frontiers: Green Paper on the establishment of the common market for broadcasting, especially by satellite and cable, Brussels, 14 June 1984, COM (84) 300 final, 1.

[46] *Ibid*, 2.

[47] *Ibid*, 11–22.

[48] *Ibid*, 105--208.

[49] *Ibid*, 209–345.

[50] Council Directive 89/552/EEC of 3 October 1989 on the coordination of certain provisions laid down by law, regulation or administrative action in Member States concerning the pursuit of television broadcasting activities [1989] OJ L298/23.

[51] Möwes and Meider, *Die Revision der EG-Fernsehrichtlinie* (n 44) 23.

[52] Council Directive 89/552/EEC of 3 October 1989 on the coordination of certain provisions laid down by law, regulation or administrative action in Member States concerning the pursuit of television broadcasting activities [1989] OJ L298/23.

[53] Directive 97/36/EC of the European Parliament and of the Council of 30 June 1997 amending Council Directive 89/552/EEC on the coordination of certain provisions laid down by law, regulation or administrative action in Member States concerning the pursuit of television broadcasting activities [1997] OJ L202/60; see too Möwes and Meider, *Die Revision der EG-Fernsehrichtlinie* (n 44) 28–29.

casters established in that Member State.[54] The Directive was revised once again in 2007[55] and in 2010[56] and the provisions were modernised in order to adapt to the technical advances and commercial developments. In particular, non-linear audio-visual services (such as on-demand services) were included within the scope of the Directive.

The central amendment to the Directive – introduced in the context of the 1997 revisions, but still of central importance in the context of the more recent revisions[57] – was the introduction of the country of origin principle[58] in respect of broadcasting providers. According to Article 2, paragraph 1 of the Directive:

> Each Member State shall ensure that all audiovisual media services transmitted by media service providers under its jurisdiction comply with the rules of the system of law applicable to audiovisual media services intended for the public in that Member State.

The aim of the country of origin principle was to guarantee Europe-wide legal certainty by requiring that a provider only had to comply with the laws of the Member State in which it was established (the establishment criterion).

C From Liberalisation to Harmonisation

The EU's regulatory approach was initially dominated, as we have seen, by its focus on liberalisation but this was later supplemented by a different preoccupation: convergence. This concept can be understood as encompassing a period of gradual development: the legal and technical structures of the Member States steadily come closer together until such time as they become increasingly similar and total standardisation is achieved.[59] In the context of information and telecommunications technology, the movement towards convergence encompassed various different elements: Convergence of the means of transmission, convergence in the context of terminal equipment, convergence of content, and convergence of user behaviour. Taken together, it was hoped that these element would lead to convergence of the entire market: Instead of restricting their activities to a

[54] Directive 97/36/EC of the European Parliament and of the Council of 30 June 1997 amending Council Directive 89/552/EEC on the coordination of certain provisions laid down by law, regulation or administrative action in Member States concerning the pursuit of television broadcasting activities [1997] OJ L202/60, Art 2, para 2.

[55] Directive 2007/65/EC of the European Parliament and of the Council of 11 December 2007 amending Council Directive 89/552/EEC on the coordination of certain provisions laid down by law, regulation or administrative action in Member States concerning the pursuit of television broadcasting activities [2007] OJ L332/27.

[56] Directive 2010/13/EU of the European Parliament and of the Council of 10 March 2010 on the coordination of certain provisions laid down by law, regulation or administrative action in Member States concerning the provision of audiovisual media services (Audiovisual Media Services Directive) [2010] OJ L95/1.

[57] *Ibid*, Recital 27.

[58] See further below at section II E(ii)(c). It is of note that various exceptions were introduced by the Audiovisual Media Services Directive.

[59] Nöding, *Das neue europäische Telekommunikationsrecht und die Konvergenz der Übertragungswege* (n 12) 4.

small area, the various providers would be able to be active across the whole EU. Finally, this would lead to convergence of law: a uniform legal framework would be created. The aim here was not to create wholly identical rules, but rather to establish a single legal framework.[60]

In 1997, the Commission published a Green Paper on the convergence of the telecommunication, media and information technology sectors and the regulatory implications.[61] The Green Paper adopted a rather narrow definition of convergence. The term was considered to comprise two main elements: the capability of different platforms to transmit similar content and the amalgamation of terminal equipment (such as telephones, televisions and computers).[62] The Green Paper analysed the convergence phenomenon and its impact on the telecommunication, media and information technology sectors. Convergence was not merely concerned with technical challenges; it also involved new ways of establishing economic and societal interaction. An additional aim of the Commission, underpinning its interest in convergence, was the strengthening of the European economy by improving efficiency and competitiveness. The global opportunities of the Internet were perceived to constitute a considerable opportunity for companies of every size. The aim was to create an environment that supported rather than hindered developments in the ICT sector.

A public consultation exercise was undertaken in the context of the creation of the Green Paper[63] and the results were published in a Communication.[64] On the basis of its findings that further EU provisions were desirable, the Commission drafted various proposals for a Directive[65] designed to lead to harmonisation of

[60] *Ibid*, 5–8; C Pichinot, *Konvergenz der Medien in Europa im Spannungsfeld von E-Commerce- und Fernsehrichtlinie* (Göttingen, Cuvillier Verlag, 2005) 6–8.

[61] Green Paper on the convergence of the telecommunications, media and information technology sectors, and the implications for Regulation – Towards an information society approach, Brussels, 3 December 1997, COM (1997) 623 final, see too Pichinot, *Konvergenz der Medien in Europa im Spannungsfeld von E-Commerce- und Fernsehrichtlinie* (n 59) 26–32; W Sauter, 'EU Regulation for the Convergence of Media, Telecommunications, and Information Technology: Arguments for a Constitutional Approach?' (1998) 1 *ZERP-Diskussionspapier* 12–21.

[62] Green Paper on the convergence of the telecommunications, media and information technology sectors, and the implications for Regulation – Towards an information society approach, Brussels, 3 December 1997, COM (1997) 623 final, 1.

[63] See too W Sauter, 'The Consultation on EU Regulation for Convergence' (1999) 10 *Util Law Rev* 3; Sauter, 'EU Regulation for the Convergence of Media, Telecommunications, and Information Technology' (n 61) 22–25.

[64] Communication from the Commission to the Council, the European Parliament, the Economic and Social Committee and the Committee of the Regions, The Convergence of the Telecommunications, Media and Information Technology Sectors, and the Implications for Regulation – Results of the Public Consultation on the Green Paper, Brussels, 10 March 1999, COM (1999) 108 final.

[65] Proposal for a Directive of the European Parliament and of the Council on access to, and interconnection of, electronic communications networks and associated facilities, COM (2000) 384 final [2000] OJ C365E/215; Proposal for a Directive of the European Parliament and of the Council concerning the processing of personal data and the protection of privacy in the electronic communications sector, COM (2000) 385 final [2000] OJ C365E/223; Proposal for a Directive of the European Parliament and of the Council on the authorisation of electronic communications networks and services, COM (2000)386 final [2000] OJ C365E/230; Proposal for a Directive of the European Parliament and of the Council on universal service and users' rights relating to electronic communications networks and services, COM (2000) 392 final [2000] OJ C365E/238; Proposal for a Directive of the European

infrastructure and network regulation at the European level. These proposals were implemented in 2002 by way of a number of directives,[66] which shared the aim of harmonising communication infrastructure, irrespective of the content of the regulation.[67] The basic idea underpinning the so-called 'telecoms reform package' was that a uniform legal framework for the telecommunication sector would result in improved competitiveness. The efforts at promoting convergence in European ICT regulation led to the harmonisation of the regulatory framework for both networks and infrastructure[68] and constituted the first movement towards harmonisation in the sector.

D Specific Areas of Relevance in the Context of the Criminal Law

The Action Plan on Europe's Way to the Information Society[69] demonstrated clearly that by the mid-1990s the focus of the EU was moving away from simple liberalisation. There was increasing awareness of the risks perceived to accompany the technological advances and of the need to combat these problems. As a result, various pieces of legislation were enacted in order to address these threats. In the process, the EU often issued extensive regulation in relation to a specific area and attempted thereby to set out a comprehensive solution to the relevant problem. In order to provide an overview of the specific legislative initiatives, it is useful to focus by way of illustration on a couple of these areas, which are of particular relevance in the criminal law context.

(i) Data Protection

There was early recognition by the EU of the potential for the new technology to pose a threat to some types of data. The first steps towards regulation in the field

Parliament and of the Council on a common regulatory framework for electronic communications networks and services, COM (2000) 393 final [2000] OJ C365E/198.

[66] Directive 2002/22/EC of the European Parliament and of the Council of 7 March 2002 on universal service and users' rights relating to electronic communications networks and services (Universal Service Directive) [2002] OJ L108/51; Directive 2002/21/EC of the European Parliament and of the Council of 7 March 2002 on a common regulatory framework for electronic communications networks and services (Framework Directive) [2002] OJ L108/33; Directive 2002/20/EC of the European Parliament and of the Council of 7 March 2002 on the authorisation of electronic communications networks and services (Authorisation Directive) [2002] OJ L108/21; Directive 2002/19/EC of the European Parliament and of the Council of 7 March 2002 on access to, and interconnection of, electronic communications networks and associated facilities (Access Directive) [2002] OJ L108/7. See further Pichinot, *Konvergenz der Medien in Europa im Spannungsfeld von E-Commerce- und Fernsehrichtlinie* 31.

[67] Pichinot, *Konvergenz der Medien* (n 60) 31; Sauter, 'EU Regulation for the Convergence of Media, Telecommunications, and Information Technology' (n 60) 21.

[68] Pichinot, *Konvergenz der Medien* (n 60) 31.

[69] Communication from the Commission to the Council, the European Parliament, the Economic and Social Committee and the Committee of the Regions, Europe's way to the information society, An action plan, Brussels, 19 July 1994, COM (94) 347 final.

of data protection date back to the beginning of the 1980s.[70] A Convention on data protection was enacted in 1981, but not properly implemented by all of the Member States. In addition, many of the provisions set out in the Convention were deemed to be unsuitable in the context of the digital era and this led the Commission to issue a proposal for a directive.[71] The objective of the proposed legislation was to introduce comprehensive data protection in both the public and private sectors.[72] The final version of the Data Protection Directive was enacted in 1995.[73]

The Directive set out minimum standards for data protection in the EU. The principle aim of the legislation was to ensure the smooth functioning of the single market and the effective protection of fundamental rights and freedoms.[74] This Directive was soon considered, however, to be insufficient, particularly in the telecommunications context. In the context of E-Commerce, for instance, personal data was processed in various ways. In order to provide adequate protection in this area, the data protection principles were subsequently supplemented by further provisions introduced by the E-Commerce Directive.[75] The potential of the Internet to pose a threat to privacy was expressly mentioned and the Directive set out measures to tackle problems specific to the Internet, such as spam.[76] The Commission is currently working to create a comprehensive new European data protection framework. Pursuant to Article 16 TFEU, the comprehensive legal framework will comprise a regulation and a directive.[77]

(ii) Protection of Minors

The issue of the protection of minors was afforded considerable importance at an early stage in the development of the EU's ICT regulation. The EU's regulatory approach in this area began in 1996 when, at an informal conference, the minister

[70] Convention for the Protection of Individuals with regard to Automatic Processing of Personal Data, Strasbourg, 28 January 1981; see too A Savin, *EU Internet Law* (Cheltenham, Edward Elgar, 2013) 195.

[71] Savin, *EU Internet Law* (n 70) 195.

[72] Amended proposal for a Council Directive on the protection of individuals with regard to the processing of personal data and on the free movement of such data, Brussels, 15 October 1992, COM (92) 422 final, 2.

[73] Directive 95/46/EC of the European Parliament and of the Council of 24 October 1995 on the protection of individuals with regard to the processing of personal data and on the free movement of such data [1995] OJ L281/31.

[74] *Ibid*, Recitals 1–10, 34, 37

[75] Directive 2002/58/EC of the European Parliament and of the Council of 12 July 2002 concerning the processing of personal data and the protection of privacy in the electronic communications sector (Directive on privacy and electronic communications) [2002] OJ L201/37.

[76] This matter is considered in detail in ch 6.

[77] Proposal for a Regulation of the European Parliament and of the Council on the protection of individuals with regard to the processing of personal data and on the free movement of such data (General Data Protection Regulation), Brussels, 25 January 2012, COM (2012) 11 final; Communication from the Commission to the European Parliament, the Council, the European Economic and Social Committee and the Committee of the Regions, Safeguarding Privacy in a Connected World A European Data Protection Framework for the 21st Century, Brussels, 25 January 2012, COM (2012) 9 final, 3–4.

for telecommunication, culture and audio-visual polices requested that the Commission present a summary of the problems, which could arise as a result of the development of the Internet. In addition, the Commission was requested to examine whether EU or international rules should be adopted in this field.[78] In October 1996, the Commission presented a Green Paper on the protection of minors and human dignity in audio-visual and information services.[79] The principle underpinning the Green Paper was the belief that combating content which could endanger minors was of fundamental importance to enabling the development of information services in a climate of confidence.[80] The threats to children and young people were considered to be a direct result of the interactive nature of communication in general and the Internet in particular.[81] In this regard the Green Paper recommended that various measures be adopted.

First, it recommended strengthening administrative cooperation. It was stated that the exchange of information should be considered a priority. There was to be comparative analysis of the national legislation and its implementation. In addition, recommendations and guidelines aimed at strengthening cooperation in the context of justice and home affairs and a common regulatory framework for self-regulation were to be drafted. Second, it advocated cooperation with the relevant industries and the promotion of industry codes of conduct. In addition, it suggested an examination of whether common standards on the labelling of material were necessary particularly in the context of material, which could represent a risk to minors. Third, it recommended that there be more emphasis on informing users and raising their awareness of the problems and advocated promoting the access of minors to the new electronic services. This was presented not just as a risk but also as a significant opportunity.[82]

In response to the Green Paper the Council issued a Resolution in 1997 on illegal and harmful content on the Internet,[83] in which it requested that the Member States take some initial steps towards addressing this issue by endorsing and facilitating self-regulation and promoting the availability of filtering systems. Finally, in January 1999 the Council issued a Decision adopting a multiannual Action Plan on promoting the safer use of the Internet by combating illegal and harmful

[78] Resolution of the Council and of the Representatives of the Governments of the Member States, meeting within the Council of 17 February 1997 on illegal and harmful content on the Internet, 1; see too on the development of EU regulations concerning the protection of minors in the context of the internet, G Ege and S Muggli, 'Safer Internet Programm und andere Massnahmen der EU zum Jugendschutz im Internet und in den neuen Medien', in C Schwarzenegger and R Nägeli (eds), *Viertes Zürcher Präventionsforum: Illegale und schädliche Inhalte im Internet und in den neuen Medien – Prävention und Jugenschutz* (Zurich, Schulthess, 2012) 140–142; D Allhutter: '"Illegale und schädigende Internetinhalte": Pornografie und Grundrechte im *Policy Framing* der Europäischen Union' (2004) 4 *Österreichische Zeitschrift für Politikwissenschaft* 423.

[79] Green Paper on the protection of minors and human dignity in audiovisual and information services, Brussels, 16 October 1996, COM (96) 483 final.

[80] *Ibid.*

[81] *Ibid*, 8–10.

[82] *Ibid*, 29–31.

[83] Resolution of the Council and of the Representatives of the Governments of the Member States, meeting within the Council of 17 February 1997 on illegal and harmful content on the Internet.

content on global networks.[84] This represented the first Action Plan in the context of the Safer Internet Program, which is still in operation.[85]

The EU's action concerning the protection of minors in the context of the media was not restricted to the Safer Internet Program; it also encompassed other aspects. The Green Paper was acknowledged and welcomed by the Council. The majority of the measures proposed in the Paper were accepted and pursued in a Council Recommendation.[86] It is unsurprising that the Green Paper and the Recommendation display considerable similarities, because the Recommendation can be traced back to a follow up report on the Green Paper produced by the Commission, in which the Commission set out a proposal for the Council's Recommendation.[87] The main subject of the Recommendation was the protection of minors, which was to be promoted by way of various initiatives. The identification of illegal and harmful content was to be achieved by encouraging self-regulation and by way of the drawing up of codes of conduct, while the handling of such content was to be regulated in law. In order to protect minors from such content, it was deemed necessary to improve technical filters and to promote the responsible use among young people of on-line audio-visual services by educating them in how to deal with such content. Further, as a reaction to the increasing cross-border availability of such content, it was considered necessary to strengthen European and international cooperation.[88]

The Recommendation invited the Commission to produce an evaluation report for the European Parliament and the Council on the adoption of the Recommendation.[89] In this report the Commission stressed again the importance of the protection of minors and noted that the Member States had implemented a number of the recommendations. The Commission stated, however, that it was necessary, in the context of all media services, for further provisions on the pro-

[84] Decision No 276/1999/EC of the European Parliament and of the Council of 25 January 1999 adopting a multiannual Community action plan on promoting safer use of the Internet by combating illegal and harmful content on global networks. On the issue of criminal law regulation of content, see ch 5.

[85] For detailed consideration of this issue, see Ege and Muggli, 'Safer Internet Programm und andere Massnahmen der EU zum Jugendschutz im Internet und in den neuen Medien' 137–187.

[86] Council recommendation of 24 September 1998 on the development of the competitiveness of the European audiovisual and information services industry by promoting national frameworks aimed at achieving a comparable and effective level of protection of minors and human dignity (98/560/EC) [1998] OJ L270/48.

[87] Communication from the Commission to the Council, the European Parliament, the Economic and Social Committee and the Committee of the Regions on the follow-up to the Green Paper on the protection of minors and human dignity in audiovisual and information services including a Proposal for a Council Recommendation concerning the protection of minors and human dignity in audiovisual and information services, Brussels, 18 November 1997, COM (97) 570 final.

[88] Council recommendation of 24 September 1998 on the development of the competitiveness of the European audiovisual and information services industry by promoting national frameworks aimed at achieving a comparable and effective level of protection of minors and human dignity (98/560/EC) [1998] OJ L270/48, sections I and II.

[89] *Ibid*, section III para 4.

tection of minors to be created.[90] In a second evaluation report the Commission emphasised again the view that the protection of children and young people from the harmful effects of the media could only be undertaken by way of a common approach at the EU level. In addition, it complained of the inconsistent implementation of the Recommendation by the Member States.[91]

The Council Recommendation on the protection of minors was amended again in 2006, and in particular, it was recommended that a right of reply be introduced in relation to all online media.[92] In addition, reference was made once again to the importance of promoting the responsible use of media by minors and combating all illegal activities on the Internet which could be harmful to minors.[93] The Recommendations were evaluated by the Commission in 2011 and in its report it noted that 'all Member States are conscious of the challenges for the protection of minors online and are increasingly making efforts to respond to them'.[94] The Commission referred, however, to the fact that the various Member States had adopted a diverse – and in some cases diverging – range of measures and that in some cases the regulatory measures had not been implemented in practice. Consequently, the Commission concluded that it was necessary for further action at the EU level to be undertaken.[95]

(iii) Network Security

Network security, including the issue of computer crime, has also taken on central importance in the last decade in the context of EU ICT legislation. In 2001, the Commission noted that the creation of a safer information society required that action be taken towards improving the safety of information infrastructure and combating computer crime.[96] The international dimension of cybercrime

[90] Evaluation report from the Commission to the Council and the European Parliament on the application of Council Recommendation of 24 September 1998 concerning the protection of minors and human dignity, Brussels, 27 February 2001, COM (2001)106 final, 14–15.

[91] Second Evaluation Report from the Commission to the Council and the European Parliament on the application of Council Recommendation of 24 September 1998 concerning the protection of minors and human dignity, Brussels, 12 December 2003, COM (2003) 776 final.

[92] Recommendation of the European Parliament and of the Council of 20 December 2006 on the protection of minors and human dignity and on the right of reply in relation to the competitiveness of the European audiovisual and on-line information services industry (2006/952/EC) [2006] OJ L378/72.

[93] *Ibid*, section I.

[94] Report from the Commission to the European Parliament and to the Council, the European Economic and Social Committee and the Committee of the Regions on the application of the Council Recommendation of 24 September 1998 concerning the protection of minors and human dignity and of the Recommendation of the European Parliament and of the Council of 20 December 2006 on the protection of minors and human dignity and on the right of reply in relation to the competitiveness of the European audiovisual and online information services industry – Protecting Children in the Digital World, Brussels, 13 September 2011, COM (2011) 556 final, 9.

[95] *Ibid*, 9–10.

[96] Communication from the Commission to the Council, the European Parliament, the Economic and the Social Committee and the Committee of the Regions, Creating a safer information society by improving the security of information infrastructures and combating computer-related crime, Brussels, 26 January 2001, COM (2000) 890 final.

meant that in order for this to be achieved, it was necessary for action to be undertaken at the European level.[97] According to the Commission, this meant that the approximation of the substantive law of the Member States had to be considered to be a priority. The approximation of law was considered to be the only way of ensuring that the victims of computer crime were provided with a minimum level of protection. In addition, approximation would assist in promoting the dual criminality requirement and provide greater clarity for the industry.[98]

In its conclusions the Commission advocated the approximation 'of the substantive criminal law in the area of high-tech crime'.[99] This led to the introduction of the EU Framework Decision on attacks against information systems.[100] The Commission subsequently stated that the Framework Decision was insufficient and that it was necessary to take further steps to harmonise the laws of the Member States in the field of computer crime;[101] the Directive on attacks against information systems was adopted in 2013.[102]

The Commission has stressed that the effort to combat cybercrime is just one aspect of network security and that are other security risks, including the interception of electronic communication, the unauthorised accessing of computers or computer networks (once again a classical computer crime), attacks on the Internet and telephone networks, malicious software, such as viruses, misrepresentation of people or entities (for instance in order to access confidential information) and other security incidents relating to unforeseen and unintentional events (such as natural disasters, human error etc).[103] It proposed that various measures be taken in order to address such threats and recommended that awareness be raised by way of public information campaigns, that a European warning and information system be created and that support be offered for technological advances and for market-orientated standardisation and certification. In addition, it advocated that the Member States incorporate effective and interoperable security solutions in their e-government and e-procurement activities, that international cooperation be strengthened and that the legal framework be clarified (particularly in the context of cybercrime).[104]

[97] *Ibid*, 11.

[98] *Ibid*, 14.

[99] *Ibid*, 31.

[100] Council Framework Decision 2005/222/JHA of 24 February 2005 on attacks against information systems [2005] OJ L69/67.

[101] Communication from the Commission to the European Parliament, the Council and the Committee of the Regions, Towards a general policy on the fight against cybercrime, Brussels, 22 May 2007, COM (2007) 267 final, 7.

[102] See further ch 7.

[103] Communication from the Commission to the Council, the European Parliament, the European Economic and Social Committee and the Committee of the Regions, Network and Information Security: Proposal for A European Policy Approach, Brussels, 6 June 2001, COM (2001)298 final, 10 ff.

[104] *Ibid*, 22 ff.

E Indirect Impact of EU Regulation on European Criminal Law

(i) General Issues

It is important to note that the EU has only recently been afforded express general criminal law making competence for ICT matters, which traditionally fell within the first pillar.[105] It would be incorrect, however, to assume that the previous lack of criminal law making power in the field of ICT means that EU law was irrelevant in the criminal law context.[106] The EU regulation had the potential to indirectly impact on the criminal law and indeed this led to some unintended problems. In order to illustrate this, it is useful to consider the EU regulation of jurisdiction in the context of criminal law matters. A contentious issue arose in this regard in relation to regulations aimed at market deregulation, which also affected the issue of criminal law jurisdiction.

(ii) Jurisdiction and European Criminal Law

(a) General Rules on Jurisdiction

Consideration of the rules on jurisdiction demonstrates that the EU generally follows the general principles of sovereignty. As is the case in the majority of legal systems, jurisdiction is generally regulated in accordance with the principle of territoriality. This means for the purposes of EU law, that a criminal offence committed within the territory of a Member States falls within the jurisdiction of that state.[107] A criminal offence is deemed to have been committed in the place where the offender carried out the acts in pursuit of the offence in question.[108]

This principle is set out in various EU documents, including in Article 4(1) of the Financial Interests Convention (in the context of fraud offences, the country in which the benefit was obtained also has jurisdiction) and Article 12 of Directive 2013/40/EU on attacks against information systems (the state in which the activities were carried out). A special rule on participation in criminal activities is set out in Article 4(1) of the Financial Interests Convention: each Member State has jurisdiction over a person who knowingly assists or induces the commission of an offence while within the territory of any Member State. This rule implies that the EU assumes that the locus of the principal offender and the accessory could well be different and that this could result in different states having jurisdiction.

[105] Directive 2013/40/EU of the European Parliament and the Council of 12 August 2013 on attacks against information systems and replacing Council Framework Decision 2005/222/JHA [2013] OJ L218/14. For an overview of the impact of the Lisbon reforms on the criminal law, see ch 2.

[106] On the potential for Community law to impact on the criminal law, see ch 6.

[107] A Klip, *European Criminal Law*, 2nd edn (Cambridge, Intersentia, 2012) 192.

[108] *Ibid.*

In addition to this general principle, EU criminal law also refers to various other principles in the regulation of jurisdiction,[109] including the flag principle,[110] the active nationality principle,[111] the domicile principle,[112] the protective principle, which allows a state to assert jurisdiction over a person who acts outside its border, but whose actions threaten the state's security or interests,[113] and the principle of universal jurisdiction.[114] Klip suggests that there are only two principles common to many legal systems which are not referred to in the EU legislation: the passive personality principle and the rule of subsidiary jurisdiction (on the basis of a request from the state which would actually have jurisdiction),[115] although even this seems overly generous in view of the fact that the Framework Decision on terrorism appears to refer to a version of the passive personality principle.[116] The EU legislation is particularly influenced by a desire to avoid a situation in which no state has jurisdiction as this would inevitably lead to impunity. Consequently, in the event of doubt, the regulations tend to provide for overlapping jurisdiction.[117] In general it can be said that the rules on jurisdiction within the EU adhere to the 'first come, first served principle'.[118]

In addition to the rules on jurisdiction, the EU has been increasingly concerned with trying to ensure that the decisions of one Member State are recognised in the other Member States. In this regard it has strengthened the *ne bis in idem* principle in an attempt to prevent contradictory decisions.[119] The most important provisions in this area are set out in the Framework Decision on the prevention and

[109] See too Klip, *European Criminal Law* (n 107) 193 ff.

[110] Council Framework Decision of 13 June 2002 on combating terrorism (2002/475/JHA) [2002] OJ L164/3, Art 9(1).

[111] Council Framework Decision 2004/757/JHA of 25 October 2004 laying down minimum provisions on the constituent elements of criminal acts and penalties in the field of illicit drug trafficking [2004] OJ L335/8, Art 8.

[112] Council Framework Decision 2002/475/JHA of 13 June 2002 on combating terrorism [2002] OJ L164/3, Art 9(1).

[113] Council Framework Decision 2005/667/JHA of 12 July 2005 to strengthen the criminal-law framework for the enforcement of the law against ship-source pollution [2005] OJ L255/164, Art 7(1)(f).

[114] Council Framework Decision of 29 May 2000 on increasing protection by criminal penalties and other sanctions against counterfeiting in connection with the introduction of the euro [2000] OJ L140/1, Art 7(2); Directive 2005/60/EC of the European Parliament and of the Council of 26 October 2005 on the prevention of the use of the financial system for the purpose of money laundering and terrorist financing [2005] OJ L309/15, Art 1(3); Council Framework Decision 2005/667/JHA of 12 July 2005 to strengthen the criminal-law framework for the enforcement of the law against ship-source pollution [2005] OJ L255/164, Art 7(1)(g).

[115] Klip, *European Criminal Law* (n 107) 199.

[116] Council Framework Decision 2002/475/JHA of 13 June 2002 on combating terrorism [2002] OJ L164/3, Art 9(1)(4).

[117] BR Killmann, '§10 Systematisierung' in U Sieber, FH Brüner, H Satzeger and B v Heintschel-Heinegg (eds), *Europäisches Strafrecht* (Baden-Baden, Nomos, 2011) n 32.

[118] Klip, *European Criminal Law* (n 107) 200.

[119] See Council Framework Decision 2009/948/JHA of 30 November 2009 on prevention and settlement of conflicts of exercise of jurisdiction in criminal proceedings [2009] OJ L328/42, Recital 3.

settlement of conflicts of exercise of jurisdiction in criminal proceedings.[120] The Framework Decision was designed to guarantee recognition of the *ne bis in idem* principle and thereby to ensure that proceedings were not conducted against the same person in the same case in various Member States.[121] In order to prevent this, Article 1 states that there should be close cooperation between the relevant authorities of the Member States. In order to ensure efficient cooperation, the Member States are required to designate the authorities which have competence to act in accordance with the Framework Decision.[122] In addition, a key element of the legislation is the efficient exchange of information. To this end, the Framework Decision sets out both obligations to contact,[123] and to reply to,[124] other Member States. The Member States are directed to work together to reach a consensual solution.[125] In the event that this is not possible, the relevant authorities are to cooperate with Eurojust.[126] If Eurojust becomes involved, it is obliged to provide a non-binding written opinion on the matter.[127]

(b) *Specific Rules on Jurisdiction in relation to Criminal Offences involving the Internet*

In the context of criminal offences committed via the Internet, it is common for problems of jurisdiction to arise;[128] it is therefore unsurprising that in ICT legislation the matter of jurisdiction is often expressly regulated. Specific rules on jurisdiction are to be found, for instance in Article 12 of the Directive on attacks again information systems:[129]

> 1. Member States shall establish their jurisdiction with regard to the offences referred to in Articles 3 to 8 where the offence has been committed:

[120] *Ibid*; this legislation was enacted the day before the Lisbon Treaty came into force, see C Calliess and M Ruffert Suhr, *EUV/AEUV, Das Verfassungsrecht der Europäischen Union mit Europäischer Grundrechtecharta. Kommentar*, 4th edn (Munich, Beck, 2011) Art 82 AEUV (ex-Art 31 Abs 1 lit a) bis d) EUV), n 14.

[121] Council Framework Decision 2009/948/JHA of 30 November 2009 on prevention and settlement of conflicts of exercise of jurisdiction in criminal proceedings [2009] OJ L328/42, Recital 3

[122] *Ibid*, Art 4.

[123] *Ibid*, Art 5.

[124] *Ibid*, Art 6.

[125] *Ibid*, Art 10(1).

[126] *Ibid*, Art 12(2).

[127] Council Decision of 28 February 2002 setting up Eurojust with a view to reinforcing the fight against serious crime (2002/187/JHA) [2002] OJ L63/1, Art. 7(2), amended by Council Decision 2009/426/JHA of 16 December 2008 on the strengthening of Eurojust and amending Decision 2002/187/JHA setting up Eurojust with a view to reinforcing the fight against serious crime [2009] OJ L138/14, Art. 1(6).

[128] J Clough, *Principles of Cybercrime* (Cambridge, Cambridge University Press, 2010) 405; Savin, *EU Internet Law* (n 69) 248; H Satzger, *Internationales und europäisches Strafrecht. Strafanwendungsrecht. Europäisches Straf- und Strafverfahrensrecht. Völkerstrafrecht*, 6th edn (Baden-Baden, Nomos, 2013) para 5 n 44.

[129] Directive 2013/40/EU of the European Parliament and the Council of 12 August 2013 on attacks against information systems and replacing Council Framework Decision 2005/222/JHA [2013] OJ L218/14.

(a) in whole or in part within their territory; or
(b) by one of their nationals, at least in cases where the act is an offence where it was committed.

2. When establishing jurisdiction in accordance with point (a) of paragraph 1, a Member State shall ensure that it has jurisdiction where:

(a) the offender commits the offence when physically present on its territory, whether or not the offence is against an information system on its territory; or
(b) the offence is against an information system on its territory, whether or not the offender commits the offence when physically present on its territory.

3. A Member State shall inform the Commission where it decides to establish jurisdiction over an offence referred to in Articles 3 to 8 committed outside its territory, including where:

(a) the offender has his or her habitual residence in its territory; or
(b) the offence is committed for the benefit of a legal person established in its territory.

The rules on jurisdiction are essentially the same as those in the earlier framework decision, despite the emphasis placed by the Commission in its proposal on the importance of harmonising the rules on jurisdiction in order to prevent offenders from escaping criminal responsibility.[130] In order to shut perceived loopholes in the legislation, the EU is continually working towards ensuring better and more intensive cooperation between the various prosecuting authorities. In this regard it is intended that the European institutions (EC3, CEPOL, Eurojust) will assist the national authorities in tackling cybercrime.[131] The cooperation should remain at this level; there are no plans for a centralised approach on the part of the EU and in a recent Communication, the Commission declared itself opposed to 'centralised European supervision'.[132]

(c) The Free Market Paradigm as a Contradictory Approach to Criminal Jurisdiction?

The EU's approach to criminal jurisdiction is defined essentially by its expansiveness. The breadth of the rules on jurisdiction is intended to prevent loopholes arising from over-reliance on the territoriality principle. In spite of this it is not inconceivable that the European rules could actually constrain a state's jurisdiction. Indeed the question whether the rules could result in the limitation of jurisdiction in criminal law was subject to considerable discussion in the context of the

[130] Proposal for a Directive of the European parliament and of the Council on attacks against information systems and repealing Council Framework Decision 2005/222/JHA, Brussels, 30 September 2010, COM (2010) 517 final, 3.

[131] Joint communication to the European Parliament, the Council, the European Economic and Social Committee and the Committee of the regions, Cybersecurity Strategy of the European Union: An Open, Safe and Secure Cyberspace, Brussels, 7 February 2013, JOIN(2013) 1 final, 20.

[132] *Ibid*, 17.

country of origin principle. As discussed above, the principle was adopted principally with a view to market liberalisation. According to the principle, only the laws in the country of origin are applicable.[133] Providing that the commercial providers comply with the laws in their country of origin, then the services deemed legal in that country cannot be restricted by other states.[134] Providers should be able to assume that providing they comply with the law in their country of origin, they are entitled to provide services in another state.[135]

The most important legal source of the country of origin principle is to be found in the E-Commerce Directive.[136] Reliance on the country of origin principle is also evident, however, in other EU documents. According to Recital 27 of the Directive on the pursuit of television broadcasting services for instance, the 'country of origin principle should remain at the core of this Directive, as it is essential for the creation of an internal market'.[137] Similarly, it was proposed that the principle be adopted in the Directive on services in the internal market.[138] It was not, however, as we shall see set out in the final version of the Directive due to controversy surrounding the subject.

The introduction of the country of origin principle led to a question, much discussed in the German language literature and as yet unresolved, which has again been subject to consideration in more recent academic literature:[139] is the country of origin principle applicable in the criminal law context? If this were the case, then each service provider would only have to comply with the criminal laws of its country of origin. The controversy surrounding the application of the principle is principally concerned with the vague nature of the provision. It is not

[133] Member States are entitled to derogate from this principle in the context of retransmissions of audiovisual media services which 'manifestly, seriously and gravely infringes' Art 27(1) of the Directive, concerning the protection of minors or Art 6 of the Directive which involves incitement to hatred, Directive 2010/13/EU of the European Parliament and of the Council of 10 March 2010 on the coordination of certain provisions laid down by law, regulation or administrative action in Member States concerning the provision of audiovisual media services (Audiovisual Media Services Directive), Art 3(2)(a).

[134] H Satzger, 'Strafrechtliche Providerhaftung' in PW Heermann and A Ohly (ed), *Verantwortlichkeit im Netz: Wer haftet wofür?* (Stuttgart, Richard Boorberg Verlag, 2003).

[135] C Schwarzenegger, 'Hyperlinks und Suchmaschinen aus strafrechtlicher Sicht' in O Plöckinger, D Duursma and M Mayrhofer (ed), *Internet-Recht. Beiträge zum Zivil- und Wirtschaftsprivatrecht, Öffentlichen Recht, Strafrecht* (Vienna, NWV, 2004) 422–423.

[136] Directive 2000/31/EC of the European Parliament and of the Council of 8 June 2000 on certain legal aspects of information society services, in particular electronic commerce, in the Internal Market (Directive on Electronic Commerce) [2000] OJ L178/1, Art 3 Abs 1 und 2; see too for the detailed consideration of this issue, S Gassner, 'Das Herkunftslandprinzip nach der E-Commerce-Richtlinie', in O Pläckinger, D Duursma and G Helm (eds), *Aktuelle Entwicklungen im Internet-Recht* (Vienna, NWV, 2002) 27–35; G Spindler, 'Herkunftslandprinzip und Kollisionsrecht – Binnenmarktintegration ohne Harmonisierung: Die Folgen der Richtlinie im elektronischen Geschäftsverkehr für das Kollisionsrecht' (2002) 66 *RabelsZ* 633, 633–709.

[137] Directive 2007/65/EC of the European Parliament and of the Council of 11 December 2007 amending Council Directive 89/552/EEC on the coordination of certain provisions laid down by law, regulation or administrative action in Member States concerning the pursuit of television broadcasting activities [2007] OJ L332/27, Recital 27.

[138] See the Proposal for a Directive of the European Parliament and of the Council on services in the internal market, Brussels, 5 March 2004, COM (2004) 2 final.

[139] Satzger, *Internationales und europäisches Strafrecht. Strafanwendungsrecht. Europäisches Straf- und Strafverfahrensrecht. Völkerstrafrecht* (n 128) para 5 n 5.

immediately obvious from the text of Article 3, paragraphs 1 and 2 of the E-Commerce Directive and the Recitals to the Directive whether the provision is applicable in the criminal law context. One reason for this lack of clarity as to the scope of the country of origin principle in criminal law matters was that it allowed the Commission to adopt a 'wait and see' approach to whether it would be accepted by Member States. This would have enabled the principle to be adopted without controversy.[140] The majority of Member States, however, were unimpressed with this approach.

Some commentators have argued that reasons in support of the application of the principle in the criminal law context can be found in the development of EU law. They refer in particular to the importance of the notion of liberalisation in influencing the development of EU legislation in the ICT field. The application of the country of origin principle to the criminal law would fit in with this approach by leading to increased legal certainty and freedom of movement and thereby leading to greater liberalisation.[141] Further, it has been suggested that the development of the Directive itself could be considered to support this view. References to the criminal law, set out in the final draft of the Directive, which could be understood as suggesting that the country of origin principle did not apply to the criminal law, were not included in the original proposal issued by the Commission.[142] The criminal law was subsequently included in the exception clause (Article 3, para 4 of the Directive) in order to ensure that the Member States were able to investigate allegations of criminal activity. Consequently, they argued that it could not be said that the criminal law was fundamentally excluded from the scope of the country of origin principle.[143] In addition, it was argued that the matter at issue was not essentially the harmonisation of the criminal law, but rather mutual recognition. The consequence of the provision was not to create criminal liability, but in fact to prevent criminal liability arising in the relevant country. In view of this, there was no need for any particular EU criminal law competence.[144] The EU's lack of competence to create criminal law was deemed irrelevant as this was in any event only concerned with the creation of distinct criminal offences.[145] Another reason in support of the argument in favour of the inclusion of the criminal law was said to be found in the text of Recital 8 of the E-Commerce Directive, which states that the criminal law should not be

[140] Schwarzenegger, 'Hyperlinks und Suchmaschinen aus strafrechtlicher Sicht' (n 135) 395–434.

[141] See too Satzger, 'Strafrechtliche Providerhaftung' (n 134) 176–177; and H Kudlich, 'Herkunftslandprinzip und internationales Strafrecht' (2004) *HRRS* 282.

[142] Proposal for a European Parliament and Council Directive on certain legal aspects of electronic commerce in the internal market, Brussels, 18 November 1998, COM (1998) 586 final.

[143] K Altenhain, 'Europäisches Herkunftslandprinzip und nationales Strafanwendungsrecht', in F Zieschang, E Hilgendorf and K Laubenthal (eds), *Strafrecht und Kriminalität in Europa* (Baden-Baden, Nomos, 2003) 111.

[144] Kudlich, 'Herkunftslandprinzip und internationales Strafrecht' (n 141) 282.

[145] Spindler, 'Herkunftslandprinzip und Kollisionsrecht – Binnenmarktintegration ohne Harmonisierung: Die Folgen der Richtlinie im elektronischen Geschäftsverkehr für das Kollisionsrecht' (n 136) 682.

harmonised.[146] The introduction of the country of origin principle would mean that there would be no need for the harmonisation of the criminal law.[147] Further, the aims of the E-Commerce Directive would be endangered if the country of origin principle was not applied in the criminal law context.[148] Finally, the criminal law is not in itself set out in the list of exceptions in Article 3, paragraph 4. This means that the criminal law cannot be entirely excluded from the scope of application of the country of origin principle;[149] if this were the case then the exclusions relating to criminal proceeding in Article 3, paragraph 4 would be rendered meaningless.[150]

Many commentators, however, have taken exception to the argument that the country of origin principle applies to criminal law matters. There are various reasons for this view. The Directive permits derogation from the freedom to provide information services requirement (Article 3, paragraph 4 E-Commerce Directive). Some authors have argued that means that the criminal law is entirely excluded from the scope of the provision.[151] Further, Recital 26 of the Directive expressly states that the Member States are entitled 'in conformity with conditions establish in this Directive', to 'apply their national rules on criminal law and criminal proceedings'.[152] It is impossible to reconcile the sweeping non-application of domestic criminal law on the basis of the country of origin principle with this statement.[153]

Other reasons, which suggest that the application of the country of origin principle should not be applied in the criminal law context, or should at least be restricted, include the fact that reliance on the principle would result in improper distinctions. The Directive only concerns 'commercial' providers. Applied in the context of possible offenders, this would mean that commercial (child) pornography providers, Nazi propaganda dealers or online fraud perpetrators could benefit from preferential treatment.[154] Another argument concerns the treatment of criminal law jurisdiction in the context of Internet offences in other pieces of EU legislation. Article 12 of the Directive on attacks against information systems, for instance, states that the territoriality principle is applicable. This principle is in clear contrast to the country of origin principle, in that it provides that the state in which the activity is conducted has jurisdiction, irrespective of the country of origin of the actor. This means that in the context of online offences, the Member

[146] Directive on Electronic Commerce (n 136), Recital 8.

[147] Altenhain, 'Europäisches Herkunftslandprinzip und nationales Strafanwendungsrecht' (n 142) 112.

[148] *Ibid*, 112–113.

[149] Kudlich, 'Herkunftslandprinzip und internationales Strafrecht' (n 141) 281.

[150] Spindler, 'Herkunftslandprinzip und Kollisionsrecht – Binnenmarktintegration ohne Harmonisierung: Die Folgen der Richtlinie im elektronischen Geschäftsverkehr für das Kollisionsrecht' (n 136) 682; G Spindler, 'Das Gesetz zum elektronischen Geschäftsverkehr – Verantwortlichkeit der Diensteanbieter und Herkunftslandprinzip' (2002) *NJW* 926.

[151] Satzger, *Internationales und europäisches Strafrecht. Strafanwendungsrecht. Europäisches Straf- und Strafverfahrensrecht. Völkerstrafrecht* (n 128) para 5 n 53.

[152] Directive on Electronic Commerce (n 136), Recital 26.

[153] Satzger, 'Strafrechtliche Providerhaftung' (n 134) 178.

[154] Schwarzenegger, 'Hyperlinks und Suchmaschinen aus strafrechtlicher Sicht' (n 135) 423; see too Kudlich, 'Herkunftslandprinzip und internationales Strafrecht' (n 141) 283.

States must reject the country of origin principle.[155] Finally, there are a number of negative consequences which could arise as a result of the application of the country of origin principle to the criminal law.[156] These include the possibility of a downward spiral in criminal law protection, whereby Member States seek to reduce the criminal law requirements in respect of service providers in order to convince providers to remain in, or even relocate to, their country.[157]

III Changes in EU Competence

The development of EU legislation in the ICT field can be seen to have been influenced by various measures. The legislative instruments that have been created have only had, however, an indirect impact on the criminal law. This can be explained by the earlier rules on the competence of the EU. It was assumed, on the basis of the TEU and the EC Treaty, that EU regulation of the criminal law could only take place via third pillar measures. Harmonisation of the criminal law by way of framework decisions was only possible in relation to the areas expressly mentioned in the Treaty.[158] The EU had no further criminal law competence to create criminal law or to influence the criminal legal systems of the Member States. This understanding of EU competency was, as we have seen, revolutionised by the European Court of Justice (ECJ) which held that the EC Treaty could only be effectively implemented if the various areas could also be subject to directives aimed at harmonising the criminal law.[159] The developments have since been cemented by the reforms brought about by the Lisbon Treaty[160] and the criminal law competence is now expressly regulated in Article 83(2) TFEU.[161]

[155] Kudlich, 'Herkunftslandprinzip und internationales Strafrecht' (n 141) 283; Schwarzenegger, 'Hyperlinks und Suchmaschinen aus strafrechtlicher Sicht' (n 135) 423.

[156] Schwarzenegger, 'Hyperlinks und Suchmaschinen aus strafrechtlicher Sicht' (n 135) 423.

[157] Kudlich, 'Herkunftslandprinzip und internationales Strafrecht' (n 141) 283.

[158] Satzger, *Internationales und europäisches Strafrecht. Strafanwendungsrecht. Europäisches Straf- und Strafverfahrensrecht. Völkerstrafrecht* (n 128) para 9 n 39.

[159] See further ch 1. The position was rejected, inter alia, by: R Hefendehl, 'Europäischer Umweltschutz: Demokratiespritze für Europa oder Brüsseler Putsch?' (2006) 1 *ZIS* 161; T Pohl, 'Verfassungsvertrag durch Richterspruch. Die Entscheidung des EuGH zu Kompetenzen der Gemeinschaft im Umweltstrafrecht' (2006) 1 *ZIS* 213; Satzger, *Internationales und europäisches Strafrecht. Strafanwendungsrecht. Europäisches Straf- und Strafverfahrensrecht. Völkerstrafrecht* (n 128) para 9 n 39 further references; supported by: O Suhr, 'Strafrechtsharmonisierung in der Europäischen Union: Neue Grenzziehungen und zusätzliche Kontrollaufträge' (2008) *ZEuS* 57.

[160] Satzger, *Internationales und europäisches Strafrecht. Strafanwendungsrecht. Europäisches Straf- und Strafverfahrensrecht. Völkerstrafrecht* (n 128) para 9 n 40.

[161] See further ch 2.

IV Current State of Affairs

As in relation to other areas, the EU has attempted in the IT context to adapt its activities to its general strategy. In this regard, it has repeatedly produced documents which aim to set out an integrated EU approach to the regulation of the information society. The movement began with the program 'eEurope - An information society for all',[162] and various subsequent initiatives (eEurope 2002[163], eEurope 2005[164], i2010[165]) have called for the opportunities afforded by the Internet to be better utilised and for cheaper, quicker and safer Internet to be guaranteed across Europe. The EU has also called for the development of a single Europe information space. In the context of these programmes a wide variety of further projects and activities have been undertaken.

The most recent program is the 'Digital Agenda for Europa'[166] which is part of the 'Europe 2020' strategy.[167] The program aims to develop a digital single market and thereby fits squarely within the liberalisation movement. It aims to promote the interoperability of devices, applications, services and networks and the standardisation of various technical systems. Another objective is the strengthening of public trust in the information society and thus the pursuit of online security. In addition, it advocates promoting various other technical advances (such as faster Internet).[168]

The EU has already taken measures in several of these areas. The Commission has set out a vision of the ICT sector as being of particular importance in the context of European productivity, growth and employment. The opportunities afforded by the sector are to be seized by the EU to the best possible extent which in turn entails promoting the competitiveness and growth of the sector.[169] This is

[162] Communication of 8 December 1999 on a Commission initiative for the special European Council of Lisbon, 23 and 24 March 2000 - eEurope - An information society for all, COM (1999) 687 final.

[163] Communication from the Commission to the Council and the European Parliament, eEurope 2002: Impact and Priorities A communication to the Spring European Council in Stockholm, 23–24 March 2001, Brussels, 13 March 2001, COM (2001) 140 final.

[164] Communication from the Commission to the Council, the European Parliament, the Economic and Social Committee and the Committee of the Regions, The eEurope 2005 action plan: an information society for everyone, Brussels, 28 May 2002, COM (2002) 263 final.

[165] Communication from the Commission to the Council, the European Parliament, the Economic and Social Committee and the Committee of the Regions, i2010 – A European Information Society for growth and employment, Brussels, 1 June 2005, COM (2005) 229 final.

[166] Communication from the Commission of 19 May 2010 to the European Parliament, the Council, the European Economic and Social Committee and the Committee of the Regions, A Digital Agenda for Europe, Brussels, 26 August 2010, COM (2010) 245 final.

[167] Communication from the Commission of 3 March 2010, Europe 2020 A strategy for smart, sustainable and inclusive growth, Brussels, 3 March 2010, COM (2010) 2020 final.

[168] Communication from the Commission of 19 May 2010 to the European Parliament, the Council, the European Economic and Social Committee and the Committee of the Regions, A Digital Agenda for Europe, Brussels, 26 June 2010, COM (2010) 245 final.

[169] Communication from the Commission to the Council, the European Parliament, the European Economic and Social Committee and the Committee of the Regions of 7 September 2007, E-skills for the 21st century: fostering competitiveness, growth and jobs, Brussels, 7 September 2007, COM (2007) 496 final.

well illustrated by the Directive on competition in the markets in telecommunications terminal equipment, which was created in order to promote competitiveness in the sector.[170] The aim of the Directive was to ensure that Member States did not grant specific or exclusive licences for the right to import, market, connect, bring into service and maintain telecommunications terminal equipment. Other EU documents have followed similar objectives.[171]

As well as attempting to further improve liberalisation in the ICT branch, the initiatives have also been increasingly orientated towards promoting a standardised approach in the EU. Various attempts at harmonisation have already been mentioned. An important initiative was the creation of a common regulatory framework for telecommunications networks and services (part of the so-called telecommunications reform package),[172] which has since been updated.[173] In order to ensure satisfactory implementation of this framework, a body of European regulators for electronic communications (BEREC) was established.[174] The aim of this body was to develop and disseminate among the national regulatory authorities regulatory best practice (such as common approaches, methodologies, methods or guidelines) on the implementation of the EU regulatory framework. The body was also to provide assistance to the Member States and to advise the Commission on matters concerning electronic communications.[175] A number of reports from the Commission have addressed the current state of affairs of the single European electronics market. These reports generally highlight the growth in the telecommunications sector and refer to improvements – either by the branch or as a result of EU efforts – which have led to improved competition and the introduction of new technology. At the same time, the Commission often refers to the lack of coordination between the various regulatory approaches of the Member States and recommends further European efforts in this regard.[176]

[170] Commission Directive 2008/63/EC of 20 June 2008 on competition in the markets in telecommunications terminal equipment (Codified version) (Text with EEA relevance) [2008] OJ L162/20.

[171] Commission Directive 2002/77/EC of 16 September 2002 on competition in the markets for electronic communications networks and services [2002] OJ L249/21; Directive 1999/5/EC of the European Parliament and of the Council of 9 March 1999 on radio equipment and telecommunications terminal equipment and the mutual recognition of their conformity [1999] OJ L91/10.

[172] Framework Directive (n 66).

[173] Directive 2009/136/EC of the European Parliament and of the Council of 25 November 2009 amending Directive 2002/22/EC on universal service and users' rights relating to electronic communications networks and services, Directive 2002/58/EC concerning the processing of personal data and the protection of privacy in the electronic communications sector and Regulation (EC) No 2006/2004 on cooperation between national authorities responsible for the enforcement of consumer protection laws [2009] OJ L337/11.

[174] Regulation (EC) No 1211/2009 of the European Parliament and of the Council of 25 November 2009 establishing the Body of European Regulators for Electronic Communications (BEREC) and the Office [2009] OJ L337/1, Art 1, para. 1.

[175] *Ibid*, Art 2.

[176] See, for instance, the most recent report: Communication from the Commission to the European Parliament, the Council, the European Economic and Social Committee and the Committee of the Regions, Progress report on the single European electronic communications market 2009 (15th report), Brussels, 25 May 2010, COM (2010) 253 final; Communication from the Commission to the European

The fact that the sector is subject to lasting, rapid and complex developments has been used by the Commission to promote the standardisation of certain types of technical equipment and network components and as the basis for its argument that the EU regulatory framework should be adapted and that standardised norms be introduced.[177] Other areas have been subject to similar treatment by the EU. The Directive on attacks against information systems, for instance, represents an important instrument for combating cybercrime. In addition, various EU measures set out to provide EU citizens with a safer Internet.[178] Another issue that has been subject to considerable attention from the EU institutions is data protection.[179] The protection of personal data has taken on particular importance in the context of movement towards digitalisation. The individual should be afforded various rights, such as the right of access, the right to have data corrected, deleted or blocked and the 'right to be forgotten'.[180] There has not yet been any specific harmonisation of criminal laws on data protection law. In the academic literature there have been some calls for the EU to promote the adoption of a harmonised criminal law approach to data protection. Sieber, for instance, has suggested that this would 'in view of the aim of securing effective and deterrent penalties for serious data protection violations and the numerous and significant threats to privacy on the Internet . . . be desirable'.[181]

The EU has not just considered the issue of information and communications technology separately, it has also attempted to utilise this technology in other policy areas and has stressed, for instance, that the technical advances should also be introduced in the context of public health, road safety, electronic commerce or energy.[182]

Parliament, the Council, the European Economic and Social Committee and the Committee of the Regions, Progress Report on the single European electronic communications market 2008 (14th Report), Brussels, 24 March 2009, COM (2009)140 final; Communication from the Commission to the European Parliament, the Council, the European Economic and Social Committee and the Committee of the Regions, Progress Report on the single European electronic communications market 2007 (13th Report), Brussels, 19 March 2008, COM (2008)153 final.

177 White Paper, Modernising ICT Standardisation in the EU: the Way Forward, Brussels, 3 July 2009, COM (2009) 324 final.

178 For detailed consideration, see ch 7.

179 See too section IV D(i), above.

180 Communication from the Commission to the European Parliament, the Council, the Economic and Social Committee and the Committee of the Regions of 4 November 2010, A comprehensive approach on personal data protection in the European Union, Brussels, 4 November 2010, COM (2010) 609 final.

181 U Sieber, '§24 Computerkriminalität' in U Sieber, FH Brüner, H Satzeger and B v Heintschel-Heinegg (eds), *Europäisches Strafrecht* (Baden-Baden, Nomos, 2011) n 31.

182 See eg: Communication from the Commission to the European Parliament, the Council, the European Economic and Social Committee and the Committee of the Regions of 12 March 2009 on mobilising Information and Communication Technologies (ICTs) to facilitate the transition to an energy-efficient, low-carbon economy, Brussels, 12 March 2009, COM (2009) 111 final; Communication from the Commission to the Council and the European Parliament of 15 September 2003, Information and Communications Technologies for Safe and Intelligent Vehicles, Brussels, 15 September 2003, COM (2003) 542 final.

V Conclusions

In general the EU's regulatory approach in the context of the ICT sector is characterised by the piecemeal nature of its creation: the regulatory framework is made up of individual pieces of legislation aimed at addressing specific problems. In those areas in which systemisation has been achieved, this has only occurred after a considerable period of time has elapsed – such as in the context of strategy concerning the digital agenda. The fragmented approach of the EU has inevitably resulted in legal ambiguity, which in turn has complicated the task of implementation on the part of the national legislators.[183] The legal apparatus of the EU seems more reminiscent of a patchwork quilt than of a well thought out legal framework.

The criminal law has been afforded very much a subsidiary role in the EU's regulatory approach to the information society. It is evident that the EU's law-making process in this sector has been driven by the desire to promote market liberalisation and remove obstacles to the proper functioning of the free market. In this regard it is clear that the criminal law has the potential not just to assist, but also to impede such objectives. As we shall see in chapter 4, the aims of liberalisation are not always compatible with those underpinning the criminal law.

[183] See too E Hilgendorf, 'Harmonisierung des Internetstrafrechts auf europäischer Ebene', in C Schwarzenegger, O Arter and F Jörg (eds), *Internet-Recht und Strafrecht* (Bern, Stämpfli Verlag, 2005) 286.

4

Criminal Law and the Protection of Intellectual Property Rights

The book, as a book, belongs to the author, but as thought it belongs – the word is not too big – to the human species. Any intelligent being has a right to it. If one of the two rights, that of the writer and that of the human spirit, must be sacrificed, then certainly it should be the right of the writer, as the public interest is our sole preoccupation, and everyone, I declare, should come before us.*

I Intellectual Property and Copyright in the Information Society

A Introduction

The concept of intellectual property is based on a simple principle, namely that 'anything emanating from the working of the human brain',[1] such as an idea or a concept, can be the subject of rights.[2] Intellectual property encompasses creative ideas from science, industry and the arts, such as literary works, music, pictures, technical innovations and other designs.[3] The *property* part of the term makes it clear that the regulation concerns the ownership of, or control over, intellectual activity. Intellectual property rights (IPRs) regulate the manner in which intellectual property is to be dealt with. IPRs differ from traditional real rights (in particular the ownership of moveable and immoveable property), in that they are often granted or held for a limited period of time. Such restrictions, together with other specific rules, are designed to reconcile the interests of the right holder with those of other potential users.[4]

The development of the information society has been of particular importance in the context of IPRs. Intellectual property has gained in significance, particu-

* Victor Hugo, Opening speech of the International Literature Congress of 1878.

[1] IJ Lloyd, *Information Technology Law*, 6th edn (Oxford, Oxford University Press, 2011) 282.

[2] See too C Hesse, 'The Rise of Intellectual Property, 700 b.c.–a.d. 2000: An Idea in the Balance' (2002) *Daedalus* 26, 26.

[3] A Kur and T Dreier, *European Intellectual Property Law* (Cheltenham, Edward Elgar, 2013) 2.

[4] *Ibid*, 2.

larly in the technological field, but also in other areas such as the music industry, as the potential for value creation has shifted from 'real' to 'intellectual' property. This has resulted in intellectual property attaining considerable economic significance.[5] The advances in technology have, however, created new challenges for the protection of intellectual property, especially as regards determining how best to protect intellectual ideas from unauthorised use in the age of the Internet. In this chapter, the steps taken by the European Union (EU) to address these issues will be examined. The focus will be on the criminal law measures, and in particular, on ascertaining the extent to which the EU has sought to promote the protection of intellectual property through recourse to the threat of criminal sanctions.

Intellectual property encompasses three principal areas: copyright, patents and trademarks. As it would be difficult to provide an overview of the entire EU regulatory structure in the intellectual property context in this chapter, the focus will be on copyright. Copyright law is customarily understood as serving to protect activity in the field of literature and art.[6] The creator of the work should be entitled to determine how the work should be used:

> Copyright forms the basis for intellectual and cultural creativity in the field of literature and art. Its aim is to ensure for an author the economic fruits of his labour and to protect his moral interests in the work.[7]

The focus of copyright protection has traditionally been on literary works, musical compositions, performances and films; in more recent times the protection of computer programs and databanks has become increasingly important.[8] This much-discussed subject provides an ideal basis on which to highlight both the EU's regulatory approach to intellectual property and to consider the extent to which it has supported a criminal law response to the subject.

B The Difficulties of Copyright Protection in the Digital Age

The increased potential for copyright violations lies at the heart of attempts to protect these rights in a more appropriate, more focused way, and where necessary, with the assistance of the criminal law. Such violations are generally referred to under the heading 'piracy'. Advances in technology have given rise to new challenges for right holders, both in the context of digital capabilities and as regards 'traditional' areas. The new technological challenges began with the creation of the compact cassette. The audiocassette, which recently celebrated its 50th birthday,[9]

[5] *Ibid*, 9.

[6] Berne Convention for the Protection of Literary and Artistic Works of 9 September 1886, revised at Paris on 24 July 1971, art 2; P Goldstein and B Hugenholtz, *International Copyright. Principles, Law and Practice* (Oxford, Oxford University Press, 2013) 4.

[7] Television Without Frontiers: Green Paper on the establishment of the common market for broadcasting, especially by satellite and cable, Brussels, 14 June 1984, COM (84) 300 final, 300.

[8] Kur and Dreier, *European Intellectual Property Law* (n 3) 241.

[9] See B Dormon, 'Happy 50th birthday, Compact Cassette: How it Struck a Chord for Millions', The Register, 30 August 2013, available at www.theregister.co.uk/2013/08/30/50_years_of_the_compact_cassette/?page=1.

made it possible for music played on the radio or other media to be recorded. As a result of concerns about copyright violations, the British Phonographic Industry began a campaign aimed at deterring such activities entitled 'Home Taping is Killing Music'.[10] The advent of the VHS system gave rise to similar concerns in the context of the film industry. The creation at the end of the 1990s of low-priced CD and DVD burners, which enabled the copying of CDs and DVDs, represented the next important step in technological development. Sales of burners continued to increase until around 2005/2006, but have since declined.[11]

The most recent developments, precipitated by the widespread introduction of broadband Internet access, involve the dissemination of content via the Internet. Illegal downloading of music and other material from the Internet – particularly via P2P (peer to peer) networks[12] – peaked shortly after the turn of the century and has since been on the decline, following the introduction of various opportunities to download material legally.[13] Various legitimate platforms, such as iTunes, were created by the entertainment industry to enable the legal downloading of content and have been successful in recovering some of the lost revenue brought about by illegal downloads.[14] In spite of this, it is notable that new methods for circumventing copyright have emerged, such as specialised recording software used to record music or film data from Internet radio or to capture data streams.[15]

Studies have shown that particularly in the music and TV industries, user behaviour has been significantly influenced by the opportunity to download material for free. This is particularly relevant in the context of younger consumers; 70 per cent of younger consumers possess music or videos which they have downloaded, burned or received from friends.[16] It is interesting, however, to note that there are indications that those who use P2P networks to acquire material unlawfully also purchase more material legally than people who do not use such networks.[17] Steaming of data – whereby data is transferred over the Internet in a continuous steam – provides another means of accessing material for free and has become increasingly popular, particularly among younger people.[18]

[10] *Ibid.*

[11] Gfk, Brennerstudie 2010, available at www.musikindustrie.de/uploads/media/Brennerstudie_2010_Presseversion_FINAL_02.pdf, 12; J Karaganis and L Renkema, 'Copy Culture in the US and Germany' (2013) *The American Assembly* 30.

[12] See too Ch Schwarzenegger, 'Die Internationalisierung des Wirtschaftsstrafrechts und die schweizerische Kriminalpolitik: Cyberkriminalität und das neue Urheberstrafrecht' (2008) 127 ZSR II 435 ff with further references.

[13] Gfk, Brennerstudie 2010, available at www.musikindustrie.de/uploads/media/Brennerstudie_2010_Presseversion_FINAL_02.pdf, 23.

[14] U Dolata, 'Das Internet und die Transformation der Musikindustrie, Rekonstruktion und Erklärung eines unkontrollierbaren Wandels' (2008)18 *BJS* 354.

[15] Gfk, Brennerstudie 2010, available at www.musikindustrie.de/uploads/media/Brennerstudie_2010_Presseversion_FINAL_02.pdf, 29 ff.

[16] Karaganis and Renkema, 'Copy Culture in the US and Germany' (n 11) 5.

[17] *Ibid*, 20 f.

[18] *Ibid*, 23 ff.

Copyright violations are also said to have contributed to the substantial financial losses incurred by the entertainment industry in recent times.[19] Some estimates place the loss of revenue incurred by the music industry in the region of billions of dollars.[20] It is important to note, however, that these losses cannot be attributed solely to illegal activity. The industry failed to react quickly enough to technological advances and failed to implement necessary structural reforms.[21] Equally, it is important to recognise that the repercussions of these losses extend beyond the sector itself; states are also indirectly affected as a result of the inevitable reduction in tax receipts.[22]

It is difficult to quantify the losses suffered by the industry as a result of copyright violations, not least because there is a dearth of accurate data on the economic impact of such rights infringements. It is difficult to avoid making assumptions about the reasons for the loss in revenue, even though there is a possibility that this could have been caused by other factors. It is particularly noticeable that much of the data is provided by the industry itself. In view of this, there is a danger that the impact of piracy could in fact have been overestimated. One problematic assumption commonly made, for instance, is that each piece of music which was downloaded illegally would otherwise have been purchased legally.[23] Irrespective of whether the impact of piracy is overestimated, however, there can be little doubt that copyright violations have resulted in the rights holders – often collecting societies – suffering significant financial losses. The Organisation for Economic Co-operation and Development (OECD) has suggested that in 2005 the international trade in counterfeit and pirated products was worth around $250 billion.[24]

The situation as regards E-books differs markedly from that involving music and video data, not least because the proportion of legally purchased e-versions outnumbers by far the number of illegal downloads.[25] The availability of E-books is relatively small in comparison and thus it is possible that with time the behaviour of those acquiring the books might change.

It is clear that the issue copyright violations and the perceived or actual consequences of such violations did not first arise with the advent of the information

[19] Bundesverband Musikindustrie e V, 'Musik im digitalen Wandel, Eine Bilanz zu zehn Jahren Brennerstudie', February 2012, available at www.musikindustrie.de/fileadmin/news/publikationen/Kompendium_Musik_im_digitalen_Wandel_FINAL.pdf; OECD, The Economic Impact of Counterfeiting and Piracy, 2008, available at www.oecd.org/sti/ind/theeconomicimpactofcounterfeitingandpiracy.htm.

[20] Dolata, 'Das Internet und die Transformation der Musikindustrie, Rekonstruktion und Erklärung eines unkontrollierbaren Wandels' (n 14) 348.

[21] *Ibid*, 348–49.

[22] GAO, 'Report to Congressional Committees, Intellectual Property, Observations on Efforts to Quantify the Economic Effects of Counterfeit and Pirated Goods', April 2010, available at www.gao.gov/new.items/d10423.pdf, 12–13.

[23] T Klopp, 'Verluste durch Filesharing stark übertrieben, zeit-online', 15 April 2010, available at www.zeit.de/digital/internet/2010-04/us-regierung-verluste-filesharing.

[24] OECD, 'The Economic Impact of Counterfeiting and Piracy', 2007, DSTI/IND(2007)9/PART4/REV1.

[25] Karaganis and Renkema, 'Copy Culture in the US and Germany' (n 11) 27 f.

society. Nevertheless there can be little doubt that the problems that the industry has faced and the potential for infringements increased markedly as a result of technological advances. Further, the number of copyright infringements appears to be increasing and might even be considered to have reached a systemic level. Some studies go so far as to suggest that a culture of copying material has developed: 'Nearly half the population in the US and Germany (46 per cent US; 45 per cent DE) has copied, shared, or "downloaded for free" music, movies, and TV shows'.[26] Consequently, it is understandable, particularly when the financial losses are taken into consideration, that the industry is in favour of more stringent copyright protection and more effective instruments for tackling such infringement. This highlights the fact that the quest for modern copyright protection is inextricably linked to the matter of enforcement: how can copyright infringements be combated effectively?

Before considering the EU's response to this question, it is important first to consider, more generally, the role of the criminal law in the context of the copyright enforcement.

C Criminal Law Enforcement of Copyright

These introductory remarks make it clear that copyright infringements, particularly in the digital environment, are routine. While various laws serve to protect copyright, these provisions are routinely violated. This in turn suggests that amendments to copyright laws might be necessary in order to meet the challenges of copyright protection in the Internet age. There are various possible approaches, which could be adopted in this regard, of which two are of particular interest.

Those in favour of a liberal approach are unfazed by the extent of online copyright infringements. This is unsurprising given that they call into question the basis of copyright protection altogether and advocate the redefinition of the entire concept of copyright in the digital age. This would involve strengthening the flow of information and reducing copyright protection to an absolute minimum. Such demands take different forms. Some proponents argue in favour of the significant expansion of freedom of use for cultural institutes, education and science. Others suggest that private users be removed from the scope of copyright law altogether or that a cultural flat rate be introduced. According to this proposition, every person who has an Internet connection would pay a fee which would go towards reimbursing artists; they would in turn be entitled to access data protected by copyright law. None of these variants have been scientifically assessed in any detail and in view of this it is difficult to say whether they nevertheless will be able to prevail in the foreseeable future.[27] This approach highlights the fact that the criminalisation

[26] *Ibid*, 5.

[27] On this subject, see T Kreutzer, 'Auf dem Weg zu einem Urheberrecht für das 21. Jahrhundert. Ideen für eine zukünftige Regulierung kreativer Güter' (2012) 92 *Wirtschaftsdienst* 701, 701–705.

of intellectual property infringement is not undisputed.[28] Problems include the fact that the harm caused is difficult to assess[29] and that it is often difficult to establish who should be held culpable for the offence, leading one commentator to refer to such offences as 'morally ambiguous'.[30]

Another approach is to reinforce the traditional understanding of copyright protection by focusing on the 'property' aspect of copyright law. This involves strengthening both the rights of the right holder and promoting the enforcement of such rights by all means necessary. One way of enforcing copyright is through the criminal law. Current developments seem to be heading in this direction. The music industry has been trying, since the second half of the 1990s, to push through more effective enforcement provisions, including by exerting pressure on international regulators to establish better enforcement mechanisms. In addition to these efforts on the political front, pressure groups have pursued an intense legal battle against copyright infringement, although these have mainly focused on civil legal claims for damages.[31]

Some have suggested that civil legal instruments for enforcing traditional copyright laws are insufficient to deal with the advances in technology.[32] This has led to calls for the development of criminal legal mechanisms, especially in those areas in which the civil legal protection has proven ineffective. One particular aim in this regard is to thwart attempts to profit from mass copyright infringements.[33] In order to address such cases, one suggestion has involved the criminalisation of preliminary activities which take place prior to the actual infringement activity. This would allow for the criminalisation of the distribution of file-sharing software or even the publication of links to streaming portals.[34] Another important issue in this regard is the protection of technical protective measures. Such instruments serve to enable the rights holder to prevent the unauthorised use of his or her work. Proponents of the criminal law response argue that these technical measures must also be protected by the criminal law, which in essence means that the act of circumventing such measures should also be criminalised. Such an approach demonstrates clearly a change of emphasis away from civil law protection to criminal law protection of copyright.[35]

[28] For a good overview of this issue, see M Bitton, 'Rethinking the Anti-Counterfeiting Trade Agreement's Criminal Copyright Enforcement Measures' (2012) 102 *Journal of Criminal Law and Criminology* 37; see too ID Manta, 'The Puzzle of Criminal Sanctions for Intellectual Property Infringement' (2011) 24 *Harvard Journal of Law and Technology* 469.

[29] SP Green, 'Moral Ambiguity in White Collar Criminal Law' (2004) 18 *Notre Dame Journal of Law, Ethics and Public Policy* 501, 510.

[30] *Ibid*, 502, 510.

[31] Dolata, 'Das Internet und die Transformation der Musikindustrie, Rekonstruktion und Erklärung eines unkontrollierbaren Wandels' (n 14) 350–52.

[32] Schwarzenegger, 'Die Internationalisierung des Wirtschaftsstrafrechts und die schweizerische Kriminalpolitik: Cyberkriminalität und das neue Urheberstrafrecht' (n 12) 438.

[33] *Ibid*, 439.

[34] *Ibid*, 439–40.

[35] *Ibid*, 440.

The nature and extent of the criminal law response to copyright infringement is controversial, not least because difficult questions arise as to the correct balance to be achieved between protecting the rights of the right holder, on the one hand, and protecting other interests such as the internal market or individual rights, such as freedom of information, on the other. The criminal law approach to copyright violations varies widely; some countries, such as the USA, have a long history of criminalisation of copyright infringement, while others are considerably more cautious.[36] In addition, the protection of copyright protection in the digital age cannot be divorced from matters such as 'Internet freedom' not least because there is considerable potential for obligations to be placed on Internet subscribers or Internet service provider (ISPs) to ensure that Internet connections are not used to infringe intellectual property.[37] Concerns have also been raised about the potential for excessive use of criminal penalties, particularly in the context of peer-to-peer networks and about the implications of this for individual rights.[38] In short, as soon as the focus moves away from commercial activities and towards the practices of individuals, the criminalisation of copyright infringement becomes controversial.[39] These issues are particularly visible in the context of the EU's attempts to develop regulation in this area.

II EU Copyright Protection Measures

As a result of the changing technological landscape, copyright law has, in recent years, been subject to continuous attempts at reform. This chapter will demonstrate the approach of the EU in this context and particular attention will be paid to the enforcement of copyright and to the role criminal law measures in this regard. Although the EU has placed considerable emphasis on the fact that the measures are designed to target commercial actors involved in large-scale piracy

[36] See the US Copyright Act, 29 Stat 481 (1897).

[37] On the issue of Internet piracy and constitutional concerns, see D Jancic, 'The European Political Order and Internet Piracy: Accidental or Paradigmatic Constitution-Shaping' (2010) 6 *European Constitutional Law Review* 430, 431 and 452; see too C Eckes, E Fahey and M Kanetake, 'International, European, and US Perspectives on the Negotiation and Adoption of the Anti-Counterfeiting Trade Agreement (ACTA)' (2012) 20 *Currents: International Trade Law Journal* 20.

[38] See eg the decision of the European Court of Human Rights in the Pirate Bay case in which the applicants alleged a violation of Art 10 ECHR, *Niej and Sunde Kolmisoppi v Sweden*, no 40397/12, decision of 19 February 2013 and *Ashby Donald v France*, no 36769/08 of 10 January 2013. In both cases the ECtHR was willing to accept that copyright protection amounted to a legitimate interference with the rights of freedom of expression under Art 10 ECHR.

[39] See C Lim Saw and SHS Leong, 'Defining Criminal Liability for Primary Acts of Copyright Infringement – the Singapore Experience', (2008) 5 *Journal of Business Law* 304, 311; see too the position of the European Parliament which stated in its position on the proposal for a new IPR Enforcement Directive that acts 'carried out by private users for personal and not-for-profit purposes' should not fall within the scope of the new Directive, European Parliament, Position of the European Parliament Adopted at First Reading on 25 April 2007 with a View to the Adoption of Directive 2007/.../EC of the European Parliament and of the Council on Criminal Measures Aimed at Ensuring the Enforcement of Intellectual Property Rights, EUR. PARLIAMENT, 7 (25 April 2007).

or counterfeiting, the breadth of the laws developed has given rise to concerns about the potential liability of individual users or indeed the secondary criminal liability of ISPs.[40] In order to understand the EU's approach to counterfeiting and piracy and to be able to analyse its criminal law response, it is essential first to consider its regulatory approach to intellectual property more broadly. This will allow consideration of the rationales underpinning the regulation.

A EU Competence with regard to the Regulation of Copyright Law

The EU was faced with a number of problems in relation to its initial attempts to implement measures in the field of copyright law. Of particular importance in this regard was the fact that the EC Treaty did not set out any specific provisions granting competence to the EU in the field of copyright law.[41] Consequently, the EU was forced to construe such competence from various other provisions, such as the general rule on property rights (ex Article 295 EC Treaty), the free movement of goods (ex Articles 23– 28EC Treaty), or the provisions on competition (ex Articles 81 and 82 EC Treaty).[42]

These problems regarding competence have now been resolved with the introduction of Article 118 TFEU:

> In the context of the establishment and functioning of the internal market, the European Parliament and the Council, acting in accordance with the ordinary legislative procedure, shall establish measures for the creation of European intellectual property rights to provide uniform protection of intellectual property rights throughout the Union and for the setting up of centralised Union-wide authorisation, coordination and supervision arrangements.

This means that the EU now has express competence in the field of copyright law and that regulatory efforts have a clear legal basis.[43] The competence to create criminal law for the purposes of enforcing copyright law, however, remains controversial,[44] although such competence must now be construed as deriving from Article 83(2) of the TFEU.[45]

[40] See too Ch Geiger, 'Weakening Multilateralism in Intellectual Property Lawmaking: a European Perspective on ACTA' (2012) 3 *The WIPO Journal* 166, 168; N Agarwal, 'Evaluating IRPED2: The Wrong Answer to Counterfeiting and Piracy' (2010) 27 *Wisconsin International Law Journal* 790, 791.

[41] Ch Geiger, 'The Construction of Intellectual Property in the European Union: Searching for Coherence', in Ch Geiger (ed), *Constructing European Intellectual Property: Achievements and New Perspectives* (Cheltenham, Edward Elgar, 2013) 6; N Gronau, *Europäisches Urheberrecht Weiterer Harmonisierungsbedarf oder ein einheitliches Europäisches Urheberrechtsgesetz?* (Hamburg, Diplomica Verlag, 2010) 18; V Mogel, *Europäisches Urheberrecht* (Vienna, Verlag Österreich, 2001) 49.

[42] For detailed consideration of the earlier competency problems, see Geiger, 'The Construction of Intellectual Property in the European Union' (n 41) 6 ff; Gronau, *Europäisches Urheberrecht Weiterer Harmonisierungsbedarf oder ein einheitliches Europäisches Urheberrechtsgesetz?* (n 41) 18 ff; Mogel, *Europäisches Urheberrecht* (n 41) 49 ff.

[43] Geiger, 'The Construction of Intellectual Property in the European Union' (n 41) 14.

[44] See Ch Geiger, 'The Anti-Counterfeiting Trade Agreement and Criminal Enforcement of Intellectual Property: What Consequences for the European Union?' in J Rosen (ed), *Intellectual Property Rights at the Crossroads of Trade* (Cheltenham, Edward Elgar, 2012) 169 ff.

[45] See, on the issue of the criminal law competence of the EU post-Lisbon, ch 2.

B Initial Developments in EU Copyright Law

The first references to copyright law are to be found in the Television without Frontiers Green Paper.[46] The Commission set out its understanding of copyright law and emphasised that copyright law was both of economic and of social significance.[47] In the context of the creation of a single audio-visual space in Europe, the cross-border availability of programs was considered to be of particular importance. According to the Green Paper, this could best be achieved through the introduction of statutory licences, which allowed for programs to be transmitted simultaneously and without abridgment.[48] It is particularly notable that the Commission's first steps in this regard were not focused on copyright protection, but rather served to impose certain restrictions on right holders.[49] The proposal for a directive, created on the basis of these recommendations,[50] was met with considerable resistance from both the European Parliament and the Economic and Social Committee and was therefore not implemented in the proposed form.[51] The directive that was subsequently adopted[52] did not include any provisions concerning copyright law; rather there was a movement towards protecting the internal market in the audio-visual industry through requiring the Member States to guarantee the reception of television broadcasts from other Member States.[53]

The EU's main objective in the field of copyright was similar to its goal in most fields, namely to ensure a certain degree of harmonisation of the laws of the various Member States. In its Green Paper on copyright law and the challenge of technology, published in 1988, the Commission highlighted once again the importance of copyright protection. At the same time, however, it made it clear that it was not aiming to achieve the total harmonisation of the copyright laws of the Member States, rather its objective was to address, as suggested by the title, those parts of copyright law that required immediate action.[54] Piracy was considered to be one of the central issues in this regard.[55] In order to combat this issue, the Commission deemed it necessary to adopt a multi-layered approach:

[46] Television Without Frontiers: Green Paper on the establishment of the common market for broadcasting, especially by satellite and cable, Brussels, 14 June 1984, COM (84) 300 final; see further ch 3.

[47] *Ibid*, 300.

[48] *Ibid*, 328 ff.

[49] Mogel, *Europäisches Urheberrecht* 151.

[50] Proposal for a Council Directive on the coordination of certain provisions laid down by law, regulation or administrative action in Member States concerning the pursuit of broadcasting activities, COM (86) 146 final/2 [1986] OJ C179/4.

[51] Mogel, *Europäisches Urheberrecht* (n 41) 151.

[52] Council Directive 89/552/EEC of 3 October 1989 on the coordination of certain provisions laid down by law, regulation or administrative action in Member States concerning the pursuit of television broadcasting activities [1989] OJ L298/23, see further ch 3.

[53] *Ibid*, art 2(2).

[54] Kur and Dreier, *European Intellectual Property Law* (n 3) 245; cf Mogel, *Europäisches Urheberrecht* (n 41) 153

[55] Green Paper on copyright and the challenge of technology – Copyright issues requiring immediate action, Brussels, 7 June 1988, COM (88) 172, 2.

> A relatively comprehensive State-by-State description of the current situation would involve a considerable degree of detail. It seems preferable to concentrate on a limited number of important issues, namely the availability of damages or other financial relief to those whose rights have been violated; the availability of injunctive relief; the possibility of disposing of discovered pirate products and equipment used to produce them in ways which ensure that they will not continue to circulate to the right holders' disadvantage and, finally, the possibility of imposing sufficiently dissuasive criminal sanctions, including imprisonment for serious offences.[56]

The Commission stated that in order to combat piracy, recourse would also have to be had to criminal law measures. It noted that this was necessary in order to deal with those who sought to avoid the consequences of civil judgments and to give a clear indication to the authorities of the need to act against piracy.[57] The Commission referred to various jurisdictions that had introduced criminal laws aimed at targeting piracy and reprimanded those states, which had not introduced such laws.[58] It concluded that it was necessary that the Member States introduce both civil and criminal measures in order to better address the issue of piracy and that it was necessary in this regard that minimum requirements be defined and introduced.[59]

The Green Paper made it clear, however, that the principal objective of the EU was not the expansion of the fight against piracy, but rather the creation of a single market in this area. In particular, it was argued that significant differences in copyright protection could lead to fragmentation of the internal market. This was said to necessitate action designed to eradicate differences between the national laws in order to prevent harmful divergence.[60] Reference was also made to the growing importance of the information and entertainment industries[61] and to the importance of protecting copyright, particularly in view of technological innovation, which allowed for the works of others to be readily misappropriated and reproduced.[62]

The Green Paper followed, by and large, the policy approach of the industry and was focused on towards protecting the interests of users rather than those of right holders.[63] This approach was the subject of considerable criticism.[64] The Commission assessed the reaction to the Green Paper by holding four hearings and in 1990 it published a follow-up report,[65] in which it referred repeatedly to the fact that technological innovation necessitated a common response to copyright

[56] *Ibid*, 2.6.55.
[57] *Ibid*, 2.6.69.
[58] *Ibid*, 2.6.70 ff.
[59] *Ibid*, 2.11 i).
[60] *Ibid*, 1.3.2.
[61] *Ibid*, 1.2.3.
[62] *Ibid*, 1.2.4.
[63] Mogel, *Europäisches Urheberrecht* (n 41) 154.
[64] *Ibid*, 155 with further references.
[65] Follow-up to the Green Paper – Working programme of the Commission in the field of copyright and neighbouring rights, Brussels, 17 June 1991, COM (90) 584 final.

law and that national borders had become increasingly irrelevant.[66] The basic principles underpinning its proposed activity in the field, were first the strengthening of copyright protection and second the need for a comprehensive approach to the subject.[67] It also referred to the importance of dealing with piracy as one its central aims and stressed again the need for more efficient remedies for rights holders and the importance of criminal sanctions in this regard.[68]

The EU subsequently sought by way of a variety of measures to develop a stronger social and cultural policy approach.[69] It adopted various directives which led to the creation of an '*acquis communautaire*' in the field of copyright law.[70] This *acquis* encompasses the following documents:

- Council Directive on the legal protection of computer programs:[71] This Directive required Member States to ensure that computer programs fell within the scope of copyright protection (Article 1(1)). This was deemed necessary due to the fact that the development of such programs required the investment of considerable resources, but they could be copied at a fraction of the cost needed to develop them independently. In order to ensure the enforcement of the rights, the Member States were required to provide for 'appropriate measures' in response to the commission of various activities, including: putting an unauthorised copy of a computer program into circulation; possessing an unauthorised copy of a computer program for commercial purposes; and putting into circulation any measures designed solely to facilitate the unauthorised removal or circumvention of any technical device which may have been applied to protect a computer program (Article 7(1)). The Directive did not elaborate on the definition of 'appropriate measures' and thus the Member States were left to interpret this concept. Further the Directive required the Member States to ensure that unlawful copies of computer programs were liable to seizure (Article 7(2)). The Directive was revised in 2009 in order to take account of various developments, but there were no substantive revisions to Article 7.[72]

[66] *Ibid*, 1.1.
[67] *Ibid*, 1.4.
[68] *Ibid*, 2.1.2.
[69] Mogel, *Europäisches Urheberrecht* 155.
[70] Gronau, *Europäisches Urheberrecht Weiterer Harmonisierungsbedarf oder ein einheitliches Europäisches Urheberrechtsgesetz?* (n 41) 30; J Reinbothe, 'Die Entwicklung des EU-Richtlinienentwurfs zum Urheberrecht im Kontext mit den internationalen Konventionen' in H Prütting et al (ed), *Die Entwicklung des Urheberrechts im europäischen Rahmen* (Munich, CH Beck'sche Verlagsbuchhandlung, 1999) 2; AL Schloetter, 'The Acquis Communautaire in the Area of Copyright and Related Rights: Economic Rights' in TE Synodinou (ed), *Codification of European Copyright Law Challenges and Perspectives* (Alphen aan den Rijn, Kulwer Law International, 2012) 116.
[71] Council Directive 91/250/EEC of 14 May 1991 on the legal protection of computer programs [1991] OJ L122/42. On this Directive, see W Blocher and MM Walter, 'Computer Program Directive' in MM Walter and S Von Lewinski (ed), *European Copyright Law. A Commentary* (Oxford, Oxford University Press, 2010) 5.1.1 ff; Mogel, *Europäisches Urheberrecht*, 158 ff; G Tritton et al, *Intellectual Property in Europe* (London, Sweet and Maxwell, 2008) 4-044 ff.
[72] Directive 2009/24/EC of the European Parliament and of the Council of 23 April 2009 on the legal protection of computer programs (codified version) (Text with EEA relevance) [2009] OJ L111/16.

- Council Directive on rental right and lending right and on certain rights related to copyright in the field of intellectual property:[73] This Directive was created again with a view to achieving and promoting the 'proper functioning of the internal market'. According to the Directive, differences in the laws of the Member States regulating the rental and lending rights of works protected by copyright could distort competition and interfere with the proper functioning of the internal market. Consequently, the Member States were required to issue regulations on the rental and lending of originals and copies of copyright works (Article 1(1)). The Directive also stated that the exclusive right to authorise or prohibit rental and lending belonged to the author, performer or producer of the work (Article 2(1)). Such persons were deemed to retain the right to obtain an equitable remuneration for the rental, even if they had transferred or assigned the rental right (Article 4(1)). The Member States were also required to ensure that the performers or producers were afforded the exclusive fixation (Article 6), reproduction (Article 7) and distribution (Article 9) rights. For the purposes of the implementation of the Directive, the Member States were required to introduce laws, regulations and administrative provisions (Article 15(1)); no further guidance in this regard is to be found in the Directive.
- Council Directive on the coordination of certain rules concerning copyright and rights related to copyright applicable to satellite broadcasting and cable retransmission:[74] The EU determined that in order to enable the cross-border transmission of broadcasts, regulations on copyright in this area were required. This meant that the TV Directive had to be supplemented with reference to copyright. The Member States were obliged to provide an exclusive right for the author to authorise the communication to the public by satellite of copyright works (Article 2) and to ensure that such authorisation be acquired only by agreement (Article 3(1)). Once again, the Directive did not set out any specific rules relating to dealing with infringements of these rights.
- Council Directive harmonizing the term of protection of copyright and certain related rights:[75] In order to prevent long terms of protection in some Member States impeding the free movement of goods, the EU decided to harmonise

[73] Council Directive 92/100/EEC of 19 November 1992 on rental right and lending right and on certain rights related to copyright in the field of intellectual property [1992] OJ L346/61. See too S von Lewinski, 'Rental and Lending Rights Directive' in MM Walter and S von Lewinski (eds), *European Copyright Law: A Commentary* (Oxford, Oxford University Press, 2010) 6.0.1 ff; Mogel, *Europäisches Urheberrecht* (n 41) 174 ff; Tritton et al, *Intellectual Property in Europe* (n 71) 4-060 ff.

[74] Council Directive 93/83/EEC of 27 September 1993 on the coordination of certain rules concerning copyright and rights related to copyright applicable to satellite broadcasting and cable retransmission [1993] OJ L248/15. On this Directive, see T Dreier, 'Satellite and Cable Directive' in MM Walter and S Von Lewinski (ed), *European Copyright Law. A Commentary* (Oxford, Oxford University Press, 2010) 7.0.1 ff; Kur and Dreier, *European Intellectual Property Law* (n 3) 257 ff; Mogel, *Europäisches Urheberrecht* (n 41) 184 ff; Tritton et al, *Intellectual Property in Europe* (n 71) 4-077 ff.

[75] Council Directive 93/98/EEC of 29 October 1993 harmonizing the term of protection of copyright and certain related rights [1993] OJ L290/9. On this Directive, see Mogel, *Europäisches Urheberrecht* (n 41) 219 ff; Tritton et al, *Intellectual Property in Europe* (n 71) 4-085 ff; MM Walter, 'Term Directive' in MM Walter and S Von Lewinski (ed), *European Copyright Law: A Commentary* (Oxford, Oxford University Press, 2010) 8.0.1 ff.

terms of protection across the Community. As a general rule copyright protection is to subsist during the lifetime of the author or director and for a period of 70 years following his or her death (Articles 1 and 2); related rights meanwhile are to subsist for a period of 50 years (Article 3). This Directive was amended on several occasions and a new directive was issued in 2006.[76] This Directive was revised in 2011 and the term of copyright protection for performers and producers of phonograms was extended to 70 years in order to prevent the rights expiring during the lifetime of the artists and resulting in an income gap at the end of their lifetime.[77]

- Directive on the legal protection of databases:[78] Differences within the EU regarding the copyright protection afforded to databases led the EU to adopt regulation aimed at harmonisation in order to protect the proper functioning of the internal market. The necessity for regulation in this area was explained by reference to the considerable human, technical and financial resources required to make such databases and to the fact that it was relatively easy for them to be copied or accessed at a fraction of the cost needed to design them independently. In addition, databases were considered to be a 'vital tool' in the development of the information market within the Community. The storage of ever-larger volumes of data was considered to require continual innovation and thus it was deemed necessary for databanks to be protected by copyright (Article 3). Article 12 requires the Member States to provide appropriate remedies in respect of infringements of the rights provided for in the Directive. The Directive does not, however, set out any definition of appropriate remedies. The Member States are consequently afforded considerable discretion in implementing the provisions. There is clearly potential for criminal sanction to be introduced on the basis of this provision.[79]

In addition to these directives, a variety of other legal instruments are of relevance in the context of copyright law.[80] In its 1998 Green Paper, the Commission stated expressly that a European approach to copyright would have to focus on strengthening the protection of rights – in particular, in order to deal with the problem of

[76] Directive 2006/116/EC of the European Parliament and of the Council of 12 December 2006 on the term of protection of copyright and certain related rights (codified version) [2006] OJ L372/12.

[77] Directive 2011/77/EU of the European Parliament and of the Council of 27 September 2011 amending Directive 2006/116/EC on the term of protection of copyright and certain related rights [2011] OJ L265/1, Recital 5; See too the Proposal for a European Parliament and Council Directive amending Directive 2006/116/EC of the European Parliament and of the Council on the term of protection of copyright and related rights, Brussels, 16 July 2008, COM (2008) 464 final, 2.

[78] Directive 96/9/EC of the European Parliament and of the Council of 11 March 1996 on the legal protection of databases [1996] OJ L77/20. On this Directive, see T Cook, *EU Intellectual Property Law* (Oxford, Oxford University Press, 2010) 3.40 ff; S von Lewinski, 'Database Directive' in MM Walter and S Von Lewinski (ed), *European Copyright Law. A Commentary* (Oxford, Oxford University Press, 2010) 9.0.1 ff; Kur and Dreier, *European Intellectual Property Law* 266 ff; Mogel, *Europäisches Urheberrecht* (n 41) 242 ff; Tritton et al, *Intellectual Property in Europe* (n 71) 4-098 ff.

[79] Von Lewinski, 'Database Directive' (n 78) 9.12.2.

[80] See eg Gronau, *Europäisches Urheberrecht Weiterer Harmonisierungsbedarf oder ein einheitliches Europäisches Urheberrechtsgesetz?* (n 41) 31 ff.

piracy. In this regard it considered criminal sanctions to be one important factor. As is evident from this brief overview of the copyright law *acquis*, however, the various directives created initially in the field did not pick up on this idea. The Member States were only required on isolated occasions to implement effective sanctions in order to address copyright infringements. Further, they were afforded considerable discretion in determining how best to enforce such measures and were entitled to resort to criminal or other types of sanctions.

C Copyright in the Information Society

(i) The Green Paper on Copyright in the Information Society

The challenge of technological innovation was recognised as of particular relevance in the context of copyright law and the EU authorities undertook various measures to protect copyright in the information society. In 1995, the Commission published a Green Paper on the copyright and related rights in the information society.[81] In the first chapter it highlighted the growing importance of the information society in Europe and referred expressly to the fact that the development of the information society had resulted in new challenges for copyright law. The development of new products gave rise in turn to questions about whether they fell within the scope of copyright protection.[82] In the second chapter various important issues were raised and analysed. The Commission referred to the fact that it was essential to create a uniform legal framework for new works and services in order to protect these intellectual ideas. The unauthorised reproduction of material was defined as a form of piracy and referred to as one of the main problems of technological developments.[83] The Commission also referred to new questions raised such as whether the digitisation of works should be covered by a reproduction right.[84] The EU's approach as set out in the Green Paper was maintained in the follow-up document.[85] In contrast to the 1988 Green Paper, there was no express reference in this document to sanctions. Reference was made simply to the need to ensure protection of rights by way of appropriate means; there was no mention of the ways in which such rights were to be enforced.

The European Parliament commented on both of these documents in a Resolution in which it underlined the importance of the development of a European approach to the creation of harmonised rules regarding copyright. In its comment on the Green Paper, the Parliament drew attention to the risks to users that may arise from new technologies designed to contribute to the 'identification and pro-

[81] Green Paper – Copyright and related rights in the information society, Brussels, 19 July 1995, COM (95) 382 final.

[82] *Ibid*, 10 ff.

[83] Green Paper – Copyright and related rights in the information society, COM (95) 382 final, 51.

[84] *Ibid*, 53.

[85] Communication from the Commission – Follow-Up to the Green Paper on Copyright and related Rights in the information Society, COM (96) 568 final.

tection of protected works' and stated that the Commission should ensure that the application of such technology was compatible with the protection of fundamental rights and freedoms of citizens. The Parliament also asserted that it was necessary to provide for civil and criminal penalties for those who 'produce, market, possess, use, manufacture, sell or install devices or who offer, solicit, advertise or perform services capable of rendering systems of protection ineffective'.[86] The Parliament repeated the remarks on the importance of EU measures towards harmonisation in the field of copyright, but refrained from making specific demands as regards the imposition of criminal sanctions.[87]

(ii) The Copyright in the Information Society Directive

(a) The Development of the Directive

On the basis of the Green Paper and the follow-up documents, the Commission produced a proposal for a directive in 1998 on the harmonisation of certain aspects of copyright and related rights in the information society.[88] The Commission's principal objective was to amend the legal framework in order to take account of developments in the information society with a view to promoting the proper functioning of the internal market. In order to protect intellectual creation, it stated that it was essential to ensure that there was a high level of protection of copyright and related rights.[89] Following various amendments introduced by the Parliament, it presented a revised version of the proposal in June 1998,[90] which subsequently provided the basis for the Directive on the harmonisation of certain aspects of copyright and related rights adopted in 2001.[91]

(b) Content of the Directive

The Directive is significantly shaped by the typical economic bias commonly found in most EU documents. The aim of the copyright revision is to ensure that

[86] European Parliament, Resolution on the Green Paper on copyright and related rights in the information society, (COM(95)0382 – C4-0354/95) [1996] OJ C320/177.

[87] *Ibid.*

[88] Proposal for a European Parliament and Council Directive on the harmonization of certain aspects of copyright and related rights in the Information Society, COM (97) 628 final [1998] OJ C108/6, p 6.

[89] *Ibid*, p 6, Recitals 4–8.

[90] Amended proposal for a European Parliament and Council Directive on the harmonisation of certain aspects of copyright and related rights in the Information Society, COM (99) 250 final [1999] OJ C180/6.

[91] Directive 2001/29/EC of the European Parliament and of the Council of 22 May 2001 on the harmonisation of certain aspects of copyright and related rights in the information society [2001] OJ L167/10. See too on the development of the Directive, S von Lewinski and MM Walter, 'Information Society Directive' in MM Walter and S Von Lewinski (ed), *European Copyright Law. A Commentary* (Oxford, Oxford University Press, 2010) 11.0.1 ff; Mogel, *Europäisches Urheberrecht* (n 41) 272–74; Tritton et al, *Intellectual Property in Europe* (n 71) 4-aaa ff.

competition in the internal market is not distorted.[92] According to the Directive, the importance of creative innovation – particularly in the context of the information society – is such that it is necessary for copyright to be afforded a high level of protection in order to ensure the maintenance and development of creativity.[93] The technological developments are perceived to give rise not just to certain advantages, but also to various challenges. On the one hand, they enable the creation of new methods to enable rights holders to restrict or prevent unauthorised infringement of copyright, but on the other, they also enable the circumvention of technical protection provided by these measures.[94]

Article 1(1) makes it clear that the Directive concerns the protection of copyright in the information society, while in the second paragraph, it is made clear that the Directive does not impact on the pre-existing legislation – ie the legal instruments referred to above. The second chapter of the Directive meanwhile sets out the rights of reproduction (Article 2), communication (Article 3) and distribution (Article 4) and the various exceptions to these rights. The Member States are entitled to make various exceptions to, or restrictions on, these rights (Article 5), such as in the context of teaching or scientific research (Article 5(3)(a)) or for the purposes of public security (Article 5(3)(e)).

The third chapter focuses principally on the problem of the circumvention of technical measures designed to protect copyright. If technical measures are used to prevent rights infringement then these measures must also be protected. The Directive encompasses not just the act of circumvention itself, but also various acts designed to facilitate the circumvention of rights. The Member States are obliged to provide adequate legal protection to deal with the circumvention of technical measures (Article 6). This protection must be designed to combat the manufacture, import, distribution, sale, rental, advertisement for sale or rental, or possession for commercial purposes of devices, products or components or the provision of services which are designed to circumvent such technological measures (Article 6(2)). The Directive does not specify the form that this 'legal protection' is to take. The Member States are entitled to resort to the implementation of civil, administrative or criminal sanctions in order to prevent acts designed to circumvent or facilitate the circumvention of technical measures.[95] According to Article 7 of the Directive, the Member States are obliged to provide adequate legal protection against persons who remove or alter information relating to electronic rights-management or who distribute, import for distribution, broadcast, communicate or makes available to the public works from which the electronic rights-management information has been removed or altered without authority. The Directive refers here to intentional acts and it is notable that it does not indicate

[92] Directive 2001/29/EC of the European Parliament and of the Council of 22 May 2001 on the harmonisation of certain aspects of copyright and related rights in the information society [2001] OJ L167/10, Recitals 1, 8.

[93] *Ibid*, Recitals 9, 10.

[94] *Ibid*, Recital 47 ff.

[95] Von Lewinski and Walter, 'Information Society Directive' (n 91) 11.6.7.

the nature that such protection is to take. Once again the Member States are entitled to choose to implement civil, administrative or criminal sanctions.[96]

The fourth chapter sets out various general provisions: Article 8 regulates sanctions and remedies, while Article 9 refers to the continued applicability of other legal provisions and Article 10 sets out the temporal scope of the Directive. The Directive contains various amendments to some of the other directives (Article 11) and the assigns the Commission the task of producing an impact report on the implementation of the Directive (Article 12(1)).

(c) Sanctions in Respect of Infringement

The Directive makes it clear that illegal activities which allow for copyright protection to be circumvented, are a major problem.[97] For this reason, the Member States are required to provide 'appropriate remedies and sanctions' in respect of infringement of the rights and obligations set out in the Directive. These sanctions are to be 'effective, proportionate and dissuasive'. In addition the Member States are obliged to ensure that the sanctions include 'the possibility of seeking damages and/or injunctive relief and, where appropriate, of applying for seizure of infringing material'.[98] According to Article 8 of the Directive:

1. Member States shall provide appropriate sanctions and remedies in respect of infringements of the rights and obligations set out in this Directive and shall take all the measures necessary to ensure that those sanctions and remedies are applied. The sanctions thus provided for shall be effective, proportionate and dissuasive.
2. Each Member State shall take the measures necessary to ensure that rightholders whose interests are affected by an infringing activity carried out on its territory can bring an action for damages and/or apply for an injunction and, where appropriate, for the seizure of infringing material as well as of devices, products or components referred to in Article 6(2).
3. Member States shall ensure that rightholders are in a position to apply for an injunction against intermediaries whose services are used by a third party to infringe a copyright or related right.[99]

The requirement that appropriate sanctions be made available in event of infringement of the rights set out in the Directive does not extend, however, to a requirement that the Member States take a particular course of action in this regard. The provision is somewhat shadowy,[100] not least because there is no express indication as regards the nature of the sanctions that are to be imposed. The terminology reflects that which is to be found in the vast majority of EU regulations.[101] It is

[96] *Ibid*, 11.7.4.

[97] Directive 2001/29/EC of the European Parliament and of the Council of 22 May 2001 on the harmonisation of certain aspects of copyright and related rights in the information society [2001] OJ L167/10, Recital 56.

[98] *Ibid*, Recital 58.

[99] *Ibid*, art 8.

[100] Tritton et al, *Intellectual Property in Europe* (n 71) 4–125.

[101] See eg the legislation regarding cybercrime, in ch 3.

notable in this regard that the Member States are not under any express obligation to create a criminal law response to copyright infringement, but are entitled to create criminal law sanctions if they deem such sanctions to be appropriate. Consequently, these EU regulations have not resulted directly in the harmonisation of the criminal laws of the Member States, but may nevertheless have had an indirect impact on the criminal legal systems.

(d) Implementation of the Directive

In 2007, the Commission published a study which it had commissioned on the implementation of the Directive. The study concluded that the standards set out in the Directive regarding the rights of reproduction and communication to the public had led to a 'satisfactory level of harmonisation of the laws in the Member States'. It noted, however, that in the context of limitations and exceptions harmonisation had not been achieved, principally because of the wide margin of appreciation which had been left to the Member States. The broad definitions of restricted acts were praised as having increased legal certainty. In addition, the study criticised the failure of the EU to provide guidance on the definition of 'appropriate measures' and noted that the Member States were essentially left with 'complete discretion as to the procedures leading up to such measures'.[102] The Commission also published its own report in 2007 on the implementation of the Directive in the Member States, concentrating in particular on the implementation of Articles 5, 6 and 8.[103] It noted that a certain level of harmonisation had been achieved, but also highlighted by way of various examples that uniform implementation of the Directive had not occurred.

D Recent Developments in EU Copyright Law concerning the Criminal Law

(i) Council Regulation (EC) No 1383/2003

In 2003, the Council issued a regulation concerning customs action against goods suspected of infringing certain IPRs.[104] This measure was designed to target the

[102] L Guibault et al, Study on the Implementation and Effect in Member States' Laws of Directive 2001/29/EC on the harmonisation of certain aspects of copyright and related rights in the information society, Executive Summary of final report, Institute for Information Law University of Amsterdam, The Netherlands, February 2007, available at ec.europa.eu/internal_market/copyright/docs/studies/infosoc-exec-summary.pdf.

[103] Commission Staff Working Document, 'Report to the Council, the European Parliament and the Economic and Social Committee on the application of Directive 2001/29/EC on the harmonisation of certain aspects of copy-right and related rights in the information society', Brussels, 30 November 2007, SEC (2007) 1556.

[104] Council Regulation (EC) No 1383/2003 of 22 July 2003 concerning customs action against goods suspected of infringing certain intellectual property rights and the measures to be taken against goods found to have in-fringed such rights [2003] OJ L196/7.

trade in counterfeit goods. The Regulation provides that customs authorities have the power to suspend the release of goods and to inform the right holder. [105] The right holder is also entitled to make an application for action to the customs authorities.[106] In the event that the goods are found to violate copyright law, the Regulation dictates that they will not be permitted to enter Community customs territory or to be re-exported. [107]

Article 8 obliges the Member States to ensure that 'effective, proportionate and dissuasive' penalties are applicable in the event of a violation of the Regulation. It is clear that the Member States must take action in response to such violations, but the nature of this response remains undefined. This means that once again the Member States have considerable discretion in implementing the provision; criminal law penalties represent one of the possible means of addressing violations of the Regulation.

In 2007, the Commission produced a proposal for a revised version of the Regulation with a view to extending its scope and increasing the competence of the customs authorities.[108] The new legislation came into force in 2013. The rules concerning the activities of the customs authorities were broadened and in particular the authorities were afforded increased powers to order the destruction of counterfeit goods.[109] Once again the Member States were required to ensure the implementation of these requirements by introducing effective, proportionate and dissuasive sanctions. [110]

(ii) Directive on the Enforcement of Intellectual Property

The Directive on the enforcement of intellectual property rights (Enforcement Directive, IPRED) was adopted in 2004.[111] The necessity of a directive in this area was based on the notion that innovation and creativity could only be protected if sufficient attention was paid to the effective enforcement of such rights.[112] In addition, differences in enforcing IPRs across the EU were considered to constitute a barrier to the proper functioning of the internal market.[113]

According to Article 1, the Directive is concerned with the 'measures, procedures and remedies necessary to ensure the enforcement of intellectual property rights', which includes industrial property rights. The Member States are obliged

[105] *Ibid*, art 4.
[106] *Ibid*, arts 5–6.
[107] *Ibid*, art 16.
[108] Proposal for a Regulation of the European Parliament and of the Council concerning customs enforcement of intellectual property rights, Brussels, 24 May 2011, COM (2011) 285 final, 3–4.
[109] Regulation (EU) No 608/2013 of the European Parliament and of the Council of 12 June 2013 concerning customs enforcement of intellectual property rights and repealing Council Regulation (EC) No 1383/2003 [2013] OJ L181/15, Arts 17–26.
[110] *Ibid*, Art 30.
[111] Corrigendum to Directive 2004/48/EC of the European Parliament and of the Council of 29 April 2004 on the enforcement of intellectual property rights (OJ L157, 30 April 2004) [2004] OJ L195/15.
[112] *Ibid*, Recital 3.
[113] *Ibid*, Recital 8.

to provide for 'measures, procedures and remedies' to protect IPRs which are fair, equitable and not 'unnecessarily complicated or costly' (Article 3(1)). In addition, they must be 'effective, proportionate and dissuasive' and are to be applied 'in such a manner as to avoid the creation of barriers to legitimate trade and to provide for safeguards against their abuse' (Article 3(2)). A variety of persons are to be entitled to apply for the application of such measures, including the right holder and licensees (Article 4). The Directive does not require enforcement through the criminal law; indeed the Directive expressly states that it does not impact on the substantive or procedural criminal laws of the Member States (Article 2(3)(c)).[114]

The Directive also sets out rules on the admissibility of evidence and on measures for preserving evidence (Articles 6 and 7). Various categories of people are afforded a right of information (Article 8) and a number of provisional and precautionary provisions are listed (Article 9). A central aspect of the Directive is the fact that it obliges the Member States to ensure that the person who infringed the rights of another is held liable to pay the right holder damages appropriate to the actual prejudice suffered by him or her as a result of the infringement (Article 13). In addition, Member States are required to encourage the development of industry codes of conduct (Article 17).

Article 16 of the Directive sets out the possible sanctions available to the Member States:

> Without prejudice to the civil and administrative measures, procedures and remedies laid down by this Directive, Member States may apply other appropriate sanctions in cases where intellectual property rights have been infringed.

The Member States are thus permitted to set out further measures, in addition to the civil and administrative penalties referred to in the Directive for the purposes of protecting IPRs. Such measures could include criminal penalties. This provision is somewhat superfluous in view of the fact that the Member States are in any event permitted to create criminal laws and because the harmonisation of the criminal law falls outwith the scope of the Directive.[115] Article 16 might be considered as inducing Member States to introduce criminal penalties.[116]

The Directive does not include any binding provisions concerning the imposition of criminal penalties in the event of intellectual property violations. In this regard it differs from the Commission's original proposal for a Directive. In its

[114] On the scope of the Directive, see too the Statement by the Commission concerning Article 2 of Directive 2004/48/EC of the European Parliament and of the Council on the enforcement of intellectual property rights (2005/295/EC) [2005] OJ L94/37.

[115] JB Ackermann, '§ 23 Immaterialgüterstrafrecht' in JB Ackermann and G Heine (ed), *Wirtschaftsstrafrecht der Schweiz. Hand- und Studienbuch* (Bern, Stämpfli Verlag, 2013) 731; SM Kierkegaard, 'Taking a Sledgehammer to Crack the Nut: The EU Enforcement Directive' (2005) 21 *Computer Law & Security Review* 494; MM Walter and D Goebel, 'Enforcement Directive' in MM Walter and S Von Lewinski (ed), *European Copyright Law. A Commentary* (Oxford, Oxford University Press, 2010) 13.16.5.

[116] Walter and Goebel, 'Enforcement Directive' (n 115) 13.16.5.

proposal, the Commission noted that there were considerable differences between the member States as regard the imposition of criminal sanctions. All of the Member States had, in line with the TRIPS Agreement,[117] introduced criminal laws, but the nature of these penalties differed significantly. The maximum fine that could be imposed in the event of an infringement varied between a few thousand and several hundred thousand Euros; the terms of imprisonment ranged from a few days to several years.[118] The proposed directive was not intended to contribute directly to the harmonisation of the criminal law, but the Commission noted that 'the effective application of genuinely deterrent sanctions in all Member States would help greatly in combating counterfeiting and piracy'.[119] In other words, the proposal aimed to contribute to some extent to the harmonisation of the criminal law. The criminal law provisions of the proposal are set out in Article 20:[120]

> 1. Member States shall ensure that all serious infringements of an intellectual property right, as well as attempts at, participation in and instigation of such infringements, are treated as a criminal offence. An infringement is considered serious if it is intentional and committed for commercial purposes.
> 2. Where natural persons are concerned, Member States shall provide for criminal sanctions, including imprisonment.
> 3. As regards natural and legal persons, the Member States shall provide for the following sanctions:
>
> (a) fines,
> (b) confiscation of the goods, instruments and products stemming from the offences referred to in paragraph 1, or of goods whose value corresponds to those products.
>
> In appropriate cases, Member States shall also provide for the following sanctions:
>
> (a) destruction of the goods infringing an intellectual property right;
> (b) total or partial permanent or temporary closure of the establishment used primarily to commit the infringement;
> (c) a permanent or temporary ban on engaging in commercial activities;
> (d) placing under judicial supervision;
> (e) judicial winding-up;
> (f) a ban on access to public assistance or subsidies;
> (g) publication of judicial decisions.
>
> 4. [. . .]

[117] See further section IV D below.

[118] Proposal for a Directive of the European Parliament and of the Council on measures and procedures to ensure the enforcement of intellectual property rights, Brussels, 30 January 2003, COM (2003) 46 final, 15–16

[119] *Ibid*, 16.

[120] The Legal Committee of the European Parliament supported this version, see: European Parliament's Committee on Legal Affairs and the Internal Market, 'Report on the Proposal for a Directive of the European Parliament and of the Council on measures and procedures to ensure the enforcement of intellectual property rights' (COM (2003) 46 – C5-0055/2003 – 2003/0024 (COD)), 5 December 2003, A5-0468/2003, no 43.

As mentioned above, this provision was not included in the final version of the Directive and the criminal law was expressly excluded from its scope. This was due in part to the difficulties of achieving consensus in this regard and to the fact that the legal basis of the EU for creating criminal law was extremely contentious.[121] In particular, it was deemed by many commentators to be too broad in that it applied to 'any infringement of intellectual property rights'.[122] This proved particularly alarming in the context of patents and led one patent agent in the UK Patent Office to suggest that it made 'criminals of all of us'.[123]

In 2010, the Commission published a report on the application of the Directive. It noted that considerable progress had been made in harmonising the legal provisions of the Member States in the context of the civil law enforcement of the various rights. In spite of this progress, the 'sheer volume' and financial implications of the IPRs infringements were described as 'alarming'.[124] Consequently it stated that it was necessary to continue to work towards ensuring more effective protection of IPRs.[125]

(iii) Proposal for a Directive on Criminal Measures

In 2005, the Commission issued a proposal for a directive on criminal measures aimed at ensuring the enforcement of intellectual property rights (IPRED2).[126] This was a clear attempt to react to the failed attempt to introduce criminal law penalties in the Enforcement Directive[127] and it is notable that patents were excluded from the scope of the proposed legislation. The proposal referred in particular to piracy as a current and ever-increasing problem. In addition, it suggested that the issue of piracy was increasingly connected to the problem of organised crime. On this basis, it argued that it was necessary to amend the Enforcement Directive in order to allow for the introduction of criminal penalties.[128]

Article 3 of the proposed directive would have required the Member States to ensure that all intentional infringements of IPRs on a commercial scale were treated as criminal offences. In addition, provision was to be made for the crimi-

[121] Kierkegaard, 'Taking a Sledgehammer to Crack the Nut' (n 115) 489; Walter and Goebel, 'Enforcement Directive' (n 115) 13.0.22, 13.16.5; on the issue of the competence of the EU to create criminal law, see ch 2.

[122] Agarwal, 'Evaluating IRPED2: The Wrong Answer to Counterfeiting and Piracy' (n 40) 791.

[123] See V Lowe, 'The Law of Unintended Consequences – A Perspective on the Draft Directive on Criminal Measures to Enforce Intellectual Property Rights' (2006) 163 *Criminal Lawyer* 3.

[124] Communication from the Commission to the European Parliament, the Council, the European Economic and Social Committee and the Committee of the Regions, Application of Directive 2004/48/EC of the European Parliament and the Council of 29 April 2004 on the enforcement of intellectual property rights, Brussels, 22 December 2010, COM (2010) 779 final, 2.

[125] *Ibid*, 9.

[126] Proposal for a European Parliament and Council Directive on criminal measures aimed at ensuring the enforcement of intellectual property rights, Brussels, 12 July 2005, COM (2005) 276 final.

[127] Walter and Goebel, 'Enforcement Directive' (n 115) 13.0.22, 13.16.9–10.

[128] Proposal for a European Parliament and Council Directive on criminal measures aimed at ensuring the enforcement of intellectual property rights, Brussels, 12 July 2005, COM (2005) 276 final.

nalisation of attempts, aiding and abetting and the incitement of such infringements. The Member States would have been required, in line with Article 4, to provide for the imposition of fines for both natural and legal persons and the confiscation of objects, instruments and products stemming from infringements or of goods whose value corresponds to those products. In addition, it would have obliged the Member States to provide for custodial sentences for natural persons of up to four years. Other sanctions included the destruction of the goods infringing an IPR, the total or partial closure, on a permanent or temporary basis, of the establishment used primarily to commit the offence, a permanent or temporary ban on engaging in commercial activities, placement under judicial supervision, judicial winding-up, a ban on access to public assistance or subsidies and the publication of judicial decisions. These sanctions were to be both dissuasive and to serve as a 'channel of information both for right holders and for the public at large'.[129]

In addition, regulations for coordinating criminal proceedings were proposed. In the event of jurisdictional disputes, the Member States would have been entitled to have recourse to the services of Eurojust (Article 5(2)). Article 6 would have ensured that Member States could have initiated criminal proceedings even in the absence of a report or accusation made by a person within their jurisdiction.

The Commission confirmed its support for legislation in this area in 2006 when it produced a revised version of the proposed directive.[130] The impetus for these revisions was the judgment of the ECJ in which the ECJ ruled that the EU had competence to create criminal law in order to ensure the effective implementation of EU law.[131]

Despite initially being welcomed by the European Parliament,[132] the proposal was never adopted. This was due to the controversy surrounding the criminal law competence of the EU which meant that there was no consensus in the Council in favour of the proposal.[133] In 2010, the Commission withdrew the proposal[134] on the basis that it was unlikely to be able to secure the implementation of the directive in the near future.[135] It did so, as we shall see, not because of uncertainty about whether criminal law measures were necessary, but because it planned to achieve the same result by promoting the ratification of the Anti-Counterfeiting

[129] *Ibid*, 4.

[130] Amended proposal for a Directive of the European Parliament and of the Council on criminal measures aimed at ensuring the enforcement of intellectual property rights, Brussels, 26 April 2006, COM (2006) 168 final.

[131] C 176/03 *Commission v Council* [2005] ECR I-07879. See further ch 2.

[132] European Parliament legislative resolution of 25 April 2007 on the amended proposal for a Directive of the European Parliament and of the Council on criminal measures aimed at ensuring the enforcement of intellectual property rights (COM(2006)0168 – C6-0233/2005 – 2005/0127(COD)), P6_TA(2007)0145.

[133] Ackermann, '§ 23 Immaterialgüterstrafrecht' (n 115) 731.

[134] Withdrawal of obsolete Commission Proposals (2010/C 252/04), List of proposals withdrawn [2010] OJ C252/7.

[135] Walter and Goebel, 'Enforcement Directive' (n 115) 13.0.22, 13.16.20.

Trade Agreement (ACTA).[136] A new version of the Enforcement Directive is currently under discussion, although the road map does not make any mention of the possibility of criminal sanctions.[137]

(iv) Further Activities of the Commission

In spite of the fact that attempts to introduce criminal law measures for the purposes of protecting copyright law have failed on two occasions, there are indications that the Commission is nevertheless convinced of the necessity of such legislation in order to ensure the adequate protection of copyright. It has referred on several occasions in its communications to the fact that the comprehensive protection of copyright can only be achieved through strengthening criminal law measures.[138] This applies not just to copyright, but also to industrial property rights[139] which taken together form, according to the Commission, the two main categories of intellectual property.[140] The Commission frequently refers to the relationship between piracy and organised crime and to the fact that, due to the importance of the Internet, IPR infringements increasingly constitute an important aspect of cybercrime.[141] Despite recognising the fact that the majority of Member States have criminal laws aimed at dealing with copyright infringement, it nevertheless is critical of differences in the definitions of criminal activity and in the nature and extent of the sanctions available which is said to restrict the effective fight against piracy at the EU level.[142]

The fight against piracy is considered by the Commission to constitute a considerable problem. Reference is frequently made to the fact that additional measures are necessary to address this danger and to the need to ensure the enforcement of the legally protected rights, although the Commission has failed to clearly state the manner in which this enforcement is to be achieved.[143]

[136] See too Geiger, 'Weakening Multilateralism in Intellectual Property Lawmaking' (n 40) 167.

[137] Roadmap, 'Proposal for a Revision of the Directive on the enforcement of intellectual property rights (Directive 2004/48/EC)', January 2013, available at www.ec.europa.eu/governance/impact/planned_ia/docs/2011_markt_006_review_enforcement_directive_ipr_en.pdf; Ackermann, '§ 23 Immaterialgüterstrafrecht' 731.

[138] Commission Staff Working Document, 'Analysis of the Application of Directive 2004/48/EC of the European Parliament and the Council of 29 April 2004 on the enforcement of intellectual property rights in the Member States', Brussels, 22 December 2010, SEC (2010) 1589 final, 25; Communication from the Commission to the Council, the European Parliament and the European Economic and Social Committee on a Customs response to latest trends in Counterfeiting and piracy, Brussels, 11 October 2005, COM (2005) 479 final, 5.

[139] Communication from the Commission to the European Parliament, the Council and the European Economic and Social Committee, An Industrial Property Rights Strategy for Europe, Brussels, 16 July 2008, COM (2008) 465 final, 14.

[140] *Ibid*, 2.

[141] Commission Staff Working Document, 'Analysis of the Application of Directive 2004/48/EC of the European Parliament and the Council of 29 April 2004 on the enforcement of intellectual property rights in the Member States', Brussels, 22 December 2010, SEC(2010) 1589 final, 25.

[142] *Ibid.*

[143] Communication from the Commission to the European Parliament, the Council, the European Economic and Social Committee and the Committee of the Regions on creative content online in the Single Market, Brussels, 3 January 2008, COM (2007) 836 final, 7–8.

The various documents produced by the Commission do not refer expressly to criminal or civil measures in this field. They do demonstrate, however, that copyright has been and continues to be of considerable interest to the EU authorities and that there has been a constant drive to strengthen copyright protection and to improve the mechanisms for enforcing these rights. The Commission has argued in favour of taking measures to develop a coherent, uniform Europe-wide patent system[144] and better cooperation between the Member States in this regard,[145] to ensure appropriate copyright protection in the context of scientific activities,[146] to improve the enforcement of IPRs within the internal market – without directly aiming for the introduction of criminal penalties,[147] and to strengthen the European Observatory on Counterfeiting and Piracy.[148] In producing these documents, the Commission has sought to reinvigorate and sustain the European debate on copyright protection.[149]

Copyright is also referred to as one of the principal targets in the strategy paper Europe 2020. In the context of the flagship initiative 'innovation union', the Commission was given the task of creating a standardised EU patent system and a patent court and to modernise the EU's copyright framework.[150] The efforts of the EU are focused principally on economic policy objectives. The uniform enforcement of protection and IPRs more generally is considered to be of central importance to the strengthening of the EU internal market.[151] The Commission's endeavours in the context of the digital internal market are also concerned with copyright. In this regard the focus of the Commission is on ensuring that copyright is able to properly fulfil its role in the new digital environment, not least

[144] Communication from the Commission to the European Parliament and the Council, Enhancing the patent system in Europe, Brussels, 3 April 2007, COM (2007) 165 final.

[145] Council Regulation (EU) No 1260/2012 of 17 December 2012 implementing enhanced cooperation in the area of the creation of unitary patent protection with regard to the applicable translation arrangements [2012] OJ L361/89; Regulation (EU) No 1257/2012 of the European Parliament and of the Council of 17 December 2012 implementing enhanced cooperation in the area of the creation of unitary patent protection [2012] OJ L361/1; Council Decision of 10 March 2011 authorising enhanced cooperation in the area of the creation of unitary patent protection, 2011/167/EU [2011] OJ L76/53; Proposal for a Council Decision authorising enhanced cooperation in the area of the creation of unitary patent protection, Brussels, 14 December 2010, COM (2010) 790 final.

[146] Green Paper, Copyright in the Knowledge Economy, Brussels, 16 July 2008, COM (2008) 466 final.

[147] Communication from the Commission to the Council, the European Parliament and the European Economic and Social Committee, Enhancing the enforcement of intellectual property rights in the internal market, Brussels, 11 September 2009, COM (2009) 467 final.

[148] Communication from the Commission to the European Parliament, the Council, the European Economic and Social Committee and the Committee of the Regions, Single Market Act Twelve levers to boost growth and strengthen confidence 'Working together to create new growth', Brussels, 13 April 2011, COM (2011) 206 final, 9.

[149] Communication from the Commission to the European Parliament and the Council, Enhancing the patent system in Europe, Brussels, 3 April 2007, COM (2007) 165 final, 15.

[150] EUROPE 2020 A strategy for smart, sustainable and inclusive growth, Brussels, 3 March 2010, COM (2010) 2020 final, 12.

[151] Communication from the Commission to the European Parliament, the Council, the European Economic and Social Committee and the Committee of the Regions, An Integrated Industrial Policy for the Globalisation Era Putting Competitiveness and Sustainability at Centre Stage, Brussels, 28 October 2010, COM (2010) 614 final, 9.

because it is considered to be of central importance to the further development of the digital internal market:[152]

> Over the next two years the Commission will continue to work for a modern copyright framework that remains fit for purpose and seeks to foster innovative market practices in order to guarantee effective recognition and remuneration of rights holders.[153]

In order to strengthen the internal market and to enable better enforcement of the rights of licensing agencies, the Commission issued a proposal in 2013 for a directive on collective management of copyright and related rights and multi-territorial licensing of rights in musical works for online uses in the internal market.[154] Express reference is made to the obligation of the Member States to use administrative measures to enforce the provisions of the directive.[155]

Copyright and its enforcement is not just of interest to the Commission, the European Council has also referred to the need to develop a strategy to combat counterfeiting and piracy. In a Resolution in 2008, the Council instructed the Commission and the Member States to take further action in this regard.[156] It is interesting to note that the Council referred expressly to the proposal for a Directive on criminal law measures aimed at ensuring the enforcement of IPRs, but refrained itself from expressing any preference for the resort to criminal sanctions.[157]

The EU considers the issue of increased copyright protection and the fight against piracy as representing matters of central importance. The focus has principally been on civil law measures designed to provide the party whose rights have been infringed with damages for the rights infringement. But other measures such as customs provisions and the European Observatory for Counterfeiting and Piracy have also been created. The Commission's repeated attempts to introduce criminal law measures to contribute to the enforcement of copyright have so far proven unsuccessful. In spite of this it seems likely that the Commission will continue to push for the introduction of such measures, not least because the Commission is planning a wide-ranging revision of European copyright law in 2014.[158]

[152] Communication from the Commission, On content in the Digital Single Market, Brussels, 18 December 2012, COM (2012) 789 final, 2.

[153] *Ibid*, 5.

[154] Proposal for a Directive of the European Parliament and of the Council on collective management of copyright and related rights and multi-territorial licensing of rights in musical works for online uses in the internal market, Brussels, 11 July 2012, COM (2012) 372 final.

[155] *Ibid*, Art 38.

[156] Council resolution of 25 September 2008 on a comprehensive European anti-counterfeiting and anti-piracy plan [2008] OJ C253/1, no 15–16.

[157] *Ibid*, no 6.

[158] Communication from the Commission, On content in the Digital Single Market, Brussels, 18 December 2012, COM (2012) 789 final, 5.

III Extra-European Initiatives

In addition to the various EU measures, there are a number of international agreements which are of relevance in the context of copyright protection and the criminal law. The EU often refers to these conventions and treaties and either introduces regulations on the basis of these agreements or requires that the Member States adhere to their terms. These two areas – EU law and international relations – are closely linked.[159]

Initial international developments in copyright law were undertaken on the basis of bilateral treaties. Copyright laws in Europe traditionally applied only to national publications which meant that foreign works were either not protected or received only very limited protection.[160] From around the second half of the nineteenth century, countries began to create bilateral treaties in order to address this issue and afford the works published in the contracting country a certain degree of protection. Those countries which exported a considerable volume of works, notably France and the UK, found it particularly difficult to form such alliances.[161] The copyright protection stemming from such bilateral treaties was extremely limited. Not only did the level of protection differ significantly from treaty to treaty, but also any amendments to the treaties resulted in a long drawn out process of negotiation.[162] Consequently from around the end of the nineteenth century, there was a movement towards the regulation of copyright by way of multilateral treaties. The following section contains a short overview of the most important and influential treaties on copyright law. Once again the focus here is on the enforcement of copyright.

A The Berne Convention

The Berne Convention for the Protection of Literary and Artistic Works of 9 September 1886 is the oldest international instruments in the field of copyright protection and highlights the fact that this subject was subject to cross-border concern, long before the introduction of the EU measures. The Convention was initially signed by Belgium, France, Germany, Haiti, Liberia, Italy, Spain, Switzerland, Tunisia and the UK and was subject to several revisions in the course of the twentieth century; it was last amended on 24 July 1971. All the EU Member States are signatories to the Convention.[163] The Convention regulates jurisdictional issues and sets out various minimum standards. The country of

[159] Mogel, *Europäisches Urheberrecht* (n 41) 40.

[160] Goldstein and Hugenholtz, *International Copyright. Principles, Law and Practice* (n 6) 31.

[161] *Ibid*, 32.

[162] *Ibid*, 33.

[163] See for a detailed account of the development Goldstein and Hugenholtz, *International Copyright. Principles, Law and Practice* (n 6) 34–38.

origin rule is set out in Article 5(1) as the guiding jurisdictional principle. As a general rule, domestic law regulates the extent of copyright protection in the country of origin; if, however, an author is not a national of the country of origin of the work for which he is protected under the Convention, he or she is entitled to enjoy in that country the same rights as national authors (Article 5(3)). The minimum standards set out in the Convention, which are all framed as the exclusive rights of the author, include: moral rights (Article 6bis), the term of protection (Article 7), translation rights (Article 8), rights of reproduction (Article 9), certain rights in dramatic and musical works (Article 11), broadcasting and related rights (Article 11bis), certain rights in literary works (Article 11ter), rights of adaption, arrangement and alteration (Article 12) and cinematographic rights (Article 14).

In order to ensure enforcement of these rights, the Convention provides that unauthorised copies be subject to seizure (Article 16) and for the creation of an assembly charged with maintaining and development the implementation of the Convention (Articles 22 – 26). The Member States are also obliged, in line with Article 36, to adopt such measures as are necessary to ensure the application of the Convention (para 1) and to ensure that on ratification national law will give effect to the provisions of the Convention (para 2). The Convention does not set out any specific rules on the manner in which the rights are to be implemented.

B The Universal Copyright Convention

The creation of UNESCO led to the introduction of a new instrument designed to protect copyright on the international stage. A central aspect of the Universal Copyright Convention signed in Geneva in 1952 was the obligation on the Member States to provide the same level of protection for foreign works as was afforded to domestic works (Article II). The terms of protection are set out in Article IV, while Article V regulates translation rights. The signatory states are obliged to take the measures necessary to ensure the application of the Convention (Article X), but are once again afforded complete discretion as to determining the best way of achieving compliance.

C The Rome Convention

The International Convention for the Protection of Performers, Producers of Phonograms and Broadcasting Organizations was concluded in Rome in 1961.[164] As with the Berne Convention, this Convention seeks to ensure that performers, producers of phonograms and broadcasting organisations of the other contracting states are afforded the same level of protection as would be provided to a

[164] International Convention for the Protection of Performers, Producers of Phonograms and Broadcasting Organizations, Rome on 26 October 1961, Preamble.

national (Articles 4–6). Specific provisions regulate broadcasting rights (Article 7(1)(a)) and rights of reproduction (Article 7(1)(c) and Article 10).

Article 26 obliges the Member States to take such measures as are necessary to ensure the application of the Convention (para 1) and to ensure that domestic law gives effect to its provisions following ratification (para 2). There is no express reference to the manner in which the Convention is to be implemented; this matter is left to the discretion of the Member States.

D The TRIPS Agreement

The Agreement on Trade-Related Aspects of Intellectual Property Rights (TRIPS) is an international agreement which sets out minimum standards for the national legal systems in the context of copyright law. It forms Annex 1C to the WTO Copyright Treaty and was signed in Marrakesh in April 1994. The focus of the Treaty was necessarily influenced by the connection to the foundation of the World Trade Organisation; according to the preamble the principal aim of the Agreement is to reduce distortions and impediments to international trade.[165]

Of central importance to the Agreement are the principles of national treatment (Article 3) and the most-favoured-nation treatment (Article 4).[166] According to the latter principle, any advantage, favour, privilege or immunity granted by a Member to the nationals of any other country shall be accorded immediately and unconditionally to the nationals of all other Members. The Agreement also regulates various aspects of intellectual property, including copyright. Various minimum standards in the field of copyright and related rights are set out including in relation to computer programs and compilations of data (Article 10) and rental rights (Article 11). According to the Agreement, the terms of protection must subsist for a period of at least 50 years from the end of the calendar year of the authorised publication or, failing such authorised publication, at least 50 years from the making of the work (Article 12). In addition, various rights are afforded to performers, producers of phonograms and broadcasting organisations (Article 14).

Various methods of enforcement are referred to in the Agreement. The Member States are obliged to ensure that enforcement procedures are available under their law so as to permit effective action against any act of infringement of IPRs covered by the Agreement (Article 41(1)). These procedures must be fair and equitable and must not be unnecessarily complicated or costly, or entail unreasonable time limits or unwarranted delays (Article 41(2)). The Member States are obliged to make civil judicial procedures available to right holders (Article 42), including in the context of injunctions (Article 44), damages (Article 45) and other remedies (Article 46). In order to facilitate a fast and effective means of addressing rights infringements, the Agreement also sets out various provisional measures (Article 50).

[165] See on the development of the Agreement, Kur and Dreier, *European Intellectual Property Law* (n 3) 24–25.

[166] Mogel, *Europäisches Urheberrecht* (n 41) 45.

Criminal law sanctions are expressly set out in Article 61:

> Members shall provide for criminal procedures and penalties to be applied at least in cases of wilful trademark counterfeiting or copyright piracy on a commercial scale. Remedies available shall include imprisonment and/or monetary fines sufficient to provide a deterrent, consistently with the level of penalties applied for crimes of a corresponding gravity. In appropriate cases, remedies available shall also include the seizure, forfeiture and destruction of the infringing goods and of any materials and implements the predominant use of which has been in the commission of the offence. Members may provide for criminal procedures and penalties to be applied in other cases of infringement of intellectual property rights, in particular where they are committed wilfully and on a commercial scale.

This provision expressly obliges the signatory states to adapt their criminal justice systems in order to ensure that intentional unauthorised acts of trademark counterfeiting or copyright piracy on a commercial scale are criminalised. In the context of imposing penalties, the Member States are, however, afforded considerable discretion in that they are only required to ensure that the custodial sentences or fines imposed are sufficient to have a deterrent effect. The only specific requirement is that the level of the sentence corresponds to that applied in the context of serious offences. Some commentators have suggested that the sentencing framework in cases of theft or fraud might be applicable in such cases.[167] But even the extent of the criminalisation itself is somewhat unclear, not least because important terms such as 'wilful'[168] or 'commercial scale' are not delineated and are thus left to the Member States to define.[169]

In 2002, the International Association for the Protection of Intellectual Property published a report on the implementation of Article 61of TRIPS. In this report it noted that all of the criminal justice systems examined were in conformity with the TRIPS Agreement. In spite of this it noted that the extent and actual implementation of the criminal law provision in the various Member States differed substantially.[170] These differences in the implementation of Article 61 of TRIPS in the criminal legal systems of the Member States were the subject of criticism from the Commission.[171]

[167] Schwarzenegger, 'Die Internationalisierung des Wirtschaftsstrafrechts und die schweizerische Kriminalpolitik: Cyberkriminalität und das neue Urheberstrafrecht' (n 12) 447; D Vaver, *Some Aspects of the TRIPS Agreement: Copyright Enforcement and Dispute Settlement* (Oxford, Routledge, 2000) 6.

[168] Lim Saw and Leong, 'Defining Criminal Liability for Primary Acts of Copyright Infringement – the Singapore Experience' (n 39) 307.

[169] Geiger, 'The Anti-Counterfeiting Trade Agreement and Criminal Enforcement of Intellectual Property' (n 44) 168; H Grosse Ruse-Khan, 'Criminal Enforcement and International IP law' in Ch Geiger (ed), *Criminal Enforcement of Intellectual Property. A Handbook of Contemporary Research* (Cheltenham, Edward Elgar, 2012) 174–75.

[170] AIPPI, Summary Report, 'Question Q169, Criminal Law Sanctions with regard to the Infringement of Intellectual Property rights', available at www.aippi.org/download/commitees/169/SR169English.pdf.

[171] Proposal for a Directive of the European Parliament and of the Council on measures and procedures to ensure the enforcement of intellectual property rights, Brussels, 30 January 2003, COM (2003) 46 final, 13–16

E The WIPO Copyright Treaty (WCT) and the WIPO Performances and Phonograms Treaty (WPPT)

The World Intellectual Property Organisation (WIPO) was founded in 1967 as a sub organisation of the United Nations.[172] In 1996, two new international treaties were finalised at an international conference on international copyright organised by the WIPO in Geneva: the WIPO Copyright Treaty (WCT) and the WIPO Performances and Phonograms Treaty (WPPT).[173] The aim of the WCT was to revise the Berne Convention in order take account of the developments of the digital age.[174] The scope of the Convention was increased to include computer programs (Article 4) and databanks (Article 5). In addition, authors were granted rights of distribution (Article 6), rental (Article 7) and communication to the public (Article 8). The WPPR was designed to extend the protection afforded to performers and producers of phonograms[175] by granting them rights of national treatment (Article 4), moral rights (Article 5), rights of reproduction (Articles 7 and 11), rental rights (Article 9 and 13) and rights in respect of making their work available (Article 10 and 14). Further, the Treaty grants performers and procedures the right to remuneration for broadcasting and communication to the public (Article 15).

Both Treaties oblige the contracting states to provide adequate and effective legal remedies against the circumvention of any technical protection measures designed to guard against the unlawful or unauthorised infringement of copyright (Article 11 WCT; Article 18 WPPT). They are also obliged to protect against the unauthorised removal or alteration of electronic rights management information (Article 12(1)(i) and (2) WCT; Article 19(1)(i) and (2) WPPT). The Treaties contain various provisions regarding implementation. The contracting states are obliged to take such measures as are necessary to ensure the application of the Treaties and to ensure that measures for enforcing the provisions are available in their legal system in order to guarantee an effective means of tackling the infringement of the rights set out in the Treaties. Such measures are to include expeditious remedies to prevent infringements and remedies which constitute a deterrent to further infringements (Article 14 WCT and Article 23 WPPT). The Treaties also require that appropriate legal protection be guaranteed by way of substantive penalties. There is, however, no express reference to criminal penalties.[176] The EU

[172] Mogel, *Europäisches Urheberrecht* (n 41) 46.

[173] European Commission, Press Release, 'WIPO Diplomatic Conference Concludes its Work: Two New Treaties on Intellectual Property Adopted in Geneva on 20 December 1996', IP/96/1244, Brussels, 20 December 1996.

[174] WIPO Copyright Treaty, Preamble; Mogel, *Europäisches Urheberrecht* (n 41) 47.

[175] WIPO Performances and Phonograms Treaty (WPPT), Preamble; Mogel, *Europäisches Urheberrecht* (n 41) 47.

[176] Schwarzenegger, 'Die Internationalisierung des Wirtschaftsstrafrechts und die schweizerische Kriminalpolitik: Cyberkriminalität und das neue Urheberstrafrecht' (n 12) 448.

approved both Treaties[177] and the Commission was authorised to represent the Community at the meetings of the Assemblies referred to in the WCT and WPPT Treaties.[178]

F The Convention on Cybercrime

The Convention on Cybercrime of the Council of Europe also contains provisions relating to copyright. The inclusion of such provisions is justified by reference to the fact that criminal offences related to copyright infringement constitute one of the most common forms of computer and Internet crime.[179] Consequently, the following provision was included in the Convention:

> Article 10: Offences related to infringements of copyright and related rights
>
> 1 Each Party shall adopt such legislative and other measures as may be necessary to establish as criminal offences under its domestic law the infringement of copyright, as defined under the law of that Party, pursuant to the obligations it has undertaken under the Paris Act of 24 July 1971 revising the Berne Convention for the Protection of Literary and Artistic Works, the Agreement on Trade-Related Aspects of Intellectual Property Rights and the WIPO Copyright Treaty, with the exception of any moral rights conferred by such conventions, where such acts are committed wilfully, on a commercial scale and by means of a computer system.
> 2 Each Party shall adopt such legislative and other measures as may be necessary to establish as criminal offences under its domestic law the infringement of related rights, as defined under the law of that Party, pursuant to the obligations it has undertaken under the International Convention for the Protection of Performers, Producers of Phonograms and Broadcasting Organisations (Rome Convention), the Agreement on Trade-Related Aspects of Intellectual Property Rights and the WIPO Performances and Phonograms Treaty, with the exception of any moral rights conferred by such conventions, where such acts are committed wilfully, on a commercial scale and by means of a computer system.
> 3 A Party may reserve the right not to impose criminal liability under paragraphs 1 and 2 of this article in limited circumstances, provided that other effective remedies are available and that such reservation does not derogate from the Party's international obligations set forth in the international instruments referred to in paragraphs 1 and 2 of this article.

The Convention on Cybercrime requires that the contracting parties criminalise acts committed by 'means of a computer system' and 'on a commercial scale'. This reference to the 'commercial scale' suggests that the offender must generate a certain amount of profit by carrying out these activities in an organised

[177] Council Decision 2000/278/EC of 16 March 2000 on the approval, on behalf of the European Community, of the WIPO Copyright Treaty and the WIPO Performances and Phonograms Treaty [2000] OJ L89/6, art 1.

[178] *Ibid*, art 3(1).

[179] Council of Europe, Explanatory Report, CETS No 185, Convention on Cybercrime, 35 and 107.

manner.[180] The determination of which acts are to be criminalised is to be made by reference to various other documents, notably the Berne Convention, the TRIPS Agreement, the Rome Convention and the WPPT. Article 61 of TRIPS is to be understood as constituting a minimum standard in this regard.[181] Article 11 of the Convention also requires that intentional acts of inciting or aiding and abetting a criminal offence in the sense of Article 10 are also criminalised. There is no obligation to impose liability in respect of the attempted commission of such a criminal offence (Article 11(2)).

The obligation on the contracting states to impose criminal sanctions is mitigated considerably by the provisions in paragraph 3. The contracting states are entitled to refrain from imposition criminal penalties, providing that they ensure that other effective remedies are available. Further a prerequisite to the arising of the obligations in Article 10 of the Convention is that the other contracting state has also ratified the Convention.[182]

The harmonisation of the criminal law is afforded particular relevance (Articles 14–21) and these provisions apply to all criminal offences committed using a computer system and to all measures of securing electronic evidence. Consequently, the coercive measures set out in the Convention on Cybercrime must also be made available in all criminal proceedings concerning copyright, providing that the criminal activities take place in the digital environment.[183]

IV ACTA

The Anti-Counterfeiting Trade Agreement (ACTA) is a multilateral trade agreement which is principally concerned with copyright matters. The EU was directly involved in the development of the agreement as negotiating party. In addition, the process was closely followed in Europe and provoked considerable controversy. In view of this it is useful to consider the scope of ACTA and to consider the implications of this project for the criminal law enforcement of copyright in Europe.

[180] J Beer, *Die Convention on Cybercrime und österreichisches Strafrecht* (Linz, Trauner Verlag, 2005) 207; Schwarzenegger, 'Die Internationalisierung des Wirtschaftsstrafrechts und die schweizerische Kriminalpolitik: Cyberkriminalität und das neue Urheberstrafrecht' (n 12) 450.

[181] Council of Europe, Explanatory Report, CETS No 185, Convention on Cybercrime, 116; Schwarzenegger, 'Die Internationalisierung des Wirtschaftsstrafrechts und die schweizerische Kriminalpolitik: Cyberkriminalität und das neue Urheberstrafrecht' (n 12) 450.

[182] Schwarzenegger, 'Die Internationalisierung des Wirtschaftsstrafrechts und die schweizerische Kriminalpolitik: Cyberkriminalität und das neue Urheberstrafrecht' (n 12) 451.

[183] *Ibid*, 452.

A The Origins of ACTA

The issue of piracy was stated as one of the principal reasons for the need for ACTA. The various documents referred to above were created in order to address these developments, but were considered to be insufficient to deal with the extent of the problem. The USA and the EU, in particular, were not entirely satisfied with the international rules applicable to the protection of intellectual property. At a meeting of the TRIPS council,[184] it was suggested that better enforcement of IPRs protection was necessary. There was resistance to this suggestion, however, because of fears that enforcement issues would end up becoming a permanent subject of discussion at the TRIPS council meetings. Consequently, the decision was made to begin negotiations on a new international agreement.[185] Australia, Canada Japan, Jordan, Korea, Morocco, Mexico, New Zealand, Singapore, Switzerland, the United Arab Emirates, the USA and the EU took part in the first negotiations in 2008.[186] A total of 11 rounds of negotiations took place between June 2008 and October 2010 before agreement was reached on a final version of the Agreement. A final meeting was held in Sydney and the final version of ACTA was presented in December 2010.[187]

One of the main problems of ACTA related to the manner in which it was created. The negotiations took place in secret which resulted in the project being shaped by a complete lack of transparency.[188] In the USA, for example, information concerning the Agreement was classified as constituting a matter of 'national security'.[189] This culture of secrecy led to public interest groups being largely excluded from the whole process.[190]

Various organisations attempted both in the USA and within the EU to obtain information about ACTA, but these attempts proved fruitless. The first document which made reference to the content of the Agreement was a discussion paper which was published on the Wikileaks website.[191] This secretiveness led to considerable speculation about the possible content of the Agreement, which in turn increased the pressure on those states involved as more and more calls were made for increased transparency. In order to comply with these requests – and indeed

[184] Agreement on Trade-Related Aspects of Intellectual Property Rights (TRIPS), art 68.

[185] M Blakeney, *Intellectual Property Enforcement, A Commentary on the Anti-Counterfeiting Trade Agreement (ACTA)* (Cheltenham, Edward Elgar, 2012) 44–46 with further references.

[186] Office of the United States Trade Representative, Trade Facts, Anti-Counterfeiting Trade Agreement (ACTA), 4 August 2008, available at www.ustr.gov/sites/default/files/uploads/factsheets/2008/asset_upload_file760_15084.pdf.

[187] Blakeney, *Intellectual Property Enforcement* 57–62 with further references.

[188] R D'Erme, Ch Geiger, H Grosse Ruse-Khan, C Heinze, T Jaeger, R Matulionyte and A Metzger, 'The Impact of the Anti-Counterfeiting Trade Agreement on the Legal Framework for IP Enforcement in the European Union' in Ch Geiger (ed), *Constructing European Intellectual Property. Achievements and New Perspectives* (Cheltenham, Edward Elgar, 2013) 394.

[189] Blakeney, *Intellectual Property Enforcement* (n 185) 68.

[190] *Ibid.*

[191] http://wikileaks.org/wiki/Proposed_US_ACTA_multilateral_intellectual_property_trade_agreement_%282007%29; Blakeney, *Intellectual Property Enforcement* (n 185) 71.

in an attempt to prevent further damage to the proposed agreement – a consolidated version of ACTA was published after the eighth round of negotiations.[192]

B Content

ACTA is based on the notion that the effective enforcement of IPRs is of crucial importance to the world economy and that piracy, in particular, poses a particular threat with the potential to give rise to considerable losses. In order to combat this, it was considered necessary to promote better international cooperation and to extend the enforcement mechanisms of the TRIPS Agreement. At the same time there was recognition of the danger that such enforcement mechanisms could themselves constitute barriers to trade.[193] This highlights the fact that the Agreement aims to take account of the need to balance various interests.[194]

The first chapter sets out various introductory provisions and definitions and states that nothing in the Agreement shall serve to invalidate the provisions of other treaties (Article 1). The contracting states are obliged to implement the Agreement but are free to determine the most appropriate means of so doing (Article 2(1)). The second chapter sets out the legal framework for the enforcement of IPRs. Every contracting state is obliged to ensure that enforcement mechanisms are available under its law in order to ensure effective action against rights infringements (Article 6(1)). These proceedings must be fair and equitable and must not be unnecessarily complicated or costly or entail unreasonable time limits or unwarranted delays (Article (6(2)). The contracting state must ensure that civil procedures are available (Article 7)[195] which enable a party whose rights have been infringed the opportunity to seek injunctions (Article 8), damages (Article 9), as well as other appropriate remedies (Article 10). The states must also ensure that the party responsible for the rights infringement can be obliged to provide information in respect of the infringement (Article 11) and that provisional measures are available (Article 12).

In order to ensure legal protection at an international level, the contracting states are obliged to implement various border measures for the purposes of ensuring the effective enforcement of IPRs (Article 13ff).[196] The provisions on enforcement by way of the criminal law are set out in Articles 23 and are considered in detail below.

[192] Consolidated Text, Prepared for Public Release, Anti-Counterfeiting Trade Agreement, PUBLIC Predecisional/Deliberative Draft, April 2010, available at http://trade.ec.europa.eu/doclib/docs/2010/april/tradoc_146029.pdf; Blakeney, *Intellectual Property Enforcement* (n 185) 74–75; R Urpmann-Wittzack, 'Das Anti-Counterfeiting Trade Agreement (ACTA) als Prüfstein für die Demokratie in Europa' (2011) *Archiv des Völkerrechts* 105.

[193] Anti-Counterfeiting Trade Agreement, 3 December 2010, Preamble.

[194] Urpmann-Wittzack, 'Das Anti-Counterfeiting Trade Agreement (ACTA) als Prüfstein für die Demokratie in Europa' (n 192) 107.

[195] For detailed discussion of the civil law enforcement mechanisms in ACTA, see Blakeney, *Intellectual Property Enforcement* (n 185) 138–64.

[196] For discussion of the border measures in ACTA, see Blakeney, *Intellectual Property Enforcement* (n 185) 165–94.

ACTA contains a separate section on the enforcement of IPRs in the digital environment. The general provisions on enforcement are also to be implemented in the context of copyright infringement in the digital context.[197] In spite of this there is clear recognition of the need to ensure that that legitimate online activity, such as online trading, is not unduly impeded.[198] The contracting states are required to promote cooperation in the business community, with a view to effectively combating rights violations (Article 27(3)). In this context, a principal concern is strengthening cooperation between providers and right holders.[199] The contracting states are entitled to oblige online service providers to provide information sufficient to identify subscribers whose account was allegedly used for infringement (Article 27(4)). In addition the states are obliged to provide effective legal remedies against the circumvention of technical protective measures.[200] In particular, they are required to take action against the manufacture, importation or distribution of a device or product, including computer software or provision of a service that is primarily designed or produced for the purpose of circumvention a technological measure or has only a limited commercially significant purpose other than circumventing an effective technological measure (Article 27(6). In addition, the states are required to afford adequate protection against the alteration or removal of electronic rights management information (Article 27(7)). The third chapter (Articles 28-32) regulates enforcement practices, while chapter 4 (Articles 33–35) governs international cooperation. In addition, provision is made for the creation of an ACTA committee responsible for overseeing the implementing of and the further development of the Agreement (Article 36).

A comparison of the final version of the Agreement with the earlier drafts (which it must be noted are not easily reconstructed) reveals that the scope of ACTA was significantly reduced.[201] The final version is much less extreme and controversial as several disputed passages were removed.[202] The 'taming' of the Agreement can be seen as a reaction to the international protests. The final version does not contain, for instance, binding rules on provider liability; in this regard it merely states that better cooperation should be promoted.[203] The draft published in 2010 set out more far-reaching rules in this regard.[204]

[197] Anti-Counterfeiting Trade Agreement, 3 December 2010, Art 27(1).

[198] *Ibid*, Art 27(2).

[199] Blakeney, *Intellectual Property Enforcement* (n 185) 287.

[200] Anti-Counterfeiting Trade Agreement, 3 December 2010, Art 27(5).

[201] Urpmann-Wittzack, 'Das Anti-Counterfeiting Trade Agreement (ACTA) als Prüfstein für die Demokratie in Europa' (n 192) 105–106 with further references.

[202] Geiger, 'The Anti-Counterfeiting Trade Agreement and Criminal Enforcement of Intellectual Property' (n 44) 168.

[203] Anti-Counterfeiting Trade Agreement, 3 December 2010, Art 27(3).

[204] Consolidated Text, Prepared for Public Release, Anti-Counterfeiting Trade Agreement, PUBLIC Predecisional/Deliberative Draft, April 2010, available at http://trade.ec.europa.eu/doclib/docs/2010/april/tradoc_146029.pdf, art 2.18(3).

C The Criminal Law Provisions

ACTA sets out various provisions on the use of criminal penalties to enforce IPRs (Articles 23–26):

Article 23: Criminal Offences

1 Each Party shall provide for criminal procedures and penalties to be applied at least in cases of wilful trademark counterfeiting or copyright or related rights piracy on a commercial scale. For the purposes of this Section, acts carried out on a commercial scale include at least those carried out as commercial activities for direct or indirect economic or commercial advantage.
2. [. . .]
3. A Party may provide criminal procedures and penalties in appropriate cases for the unauthorized copying of cinematographic works from a performance in a motion picture exhibition facility generally open to the public.
4. With respect to the offences specified in this Article for which a Party provides criminal procedures and penalties, that Party shall ensure that criminal liability for aiding and abetting is available under its law.
5. Each Party shall adopt such measures as may be necessary, consistent with its legal principles, to establish the liability, which may be criminal, of legal persons for the offences specified in this Article for which the Party provides criminal procedures and penalties. Such liability shall be without prejudice to the criminal liability of the natural persons who have committed the criminal offences.

Article 24: Penalties

For offences specified in paragraphs 1, 2, and 4 of Article 23 (Criminal Offences), each Party shall provide penalties that include imprisonment as well as monetary fines sufficiently high to provide a deterrent to future acts of infringement, consistently with the level of penalties applied for crimes of a corresponding gravity.

Article 25: Seizure, forfeiture, and destruction

1. With respect to the offences specified in paragraphs 1, 2, 3, and 4 of Article 23 (Criminal Offences) for which a Party provides criminal procedures and penalties, that Party shall provide that its competent authorities have the authority to order the seizure of suspected counterfeit trademark goods or pirated copyright goods, any related materials and implements used in the commission of the alleged offence, documentary evidence relevant to the alleged offence, and the assets derived from, or obtained directly or indirectly through, the alleged infringing activity.
2. [. . .]
3. With respect to the offences specified in paragraphs 1, 2, 3, and 4 of Article 23 (Criminal Offences) for which a Party provides criminal procedures and penalties, that Party shall provide that its competent authorities have the authority to order the forfeiture or destruction of all counterfeit trademark goods or pirated copyright goods. [. . .]
4. With respect to the offences specified in paragraphs 1, 2, 3, and 4 of Article 23 (Criminal Offences) for which a Party provides criminal procedures and penalties,

that Party shall provide that its competent authorities have the authority to order the forfeiture or destruction of materials [. . .]

5. With respect to the offences specified in paragraphs 1, 2, 3, and 4 of Article 23 (Criminal Offences) for which a Party provides criminal procedures and penalties, that Party may provide that its judicial authorities have the authority to order:

   (a) the seizure of assets the value of which corresponds to that of the assets derived from, or obtained directly or indirectly through, the allegedly infringing activity; and
   (b) the forfeiture of assets the value of which corresponds to that of the assets derived from, or obtained directly or indirectly through, the infringing activity.

Article 26: Ex officio criminal enforcement

Each Party shall provide that, in appropriate cases, its competent authorities may act upon their own initiative to initiate investigation or legal action with respect to the criminal offences specified in paragraphs 1, 2, 3, and 4 of Article 23 (Criminal Offences) for which that Party provides criminal procedures and penalties.

These provisions make it clear that ACTA provides for extensive criminal law penalties. Although some commentators have suggested that level of criminalisation set out in ACTA does not exceed that set out in TRIPS,[205] this is by no means clear. In particular, the definition in Article 23(1) of 'commercial' activities, as those which are undertaken 'for direct or indirect commercial advantage', is extremely broad, and underlines the fact that the scope of ACTA extends beyond that of Article 61 of the TRIPS Agreement.[206] The commercial use clause is conspicuously absent in Article 23(3).[207] Of particular concern in the context of Article 23 is the potential for acts which are commonly deemed to come within the 'private use' exception in national law, such as private downloading of material, to fall within the definition of 'commercial scale' under ACTA.[208] Article 23(1) defines 'wilful copyright piracy' as a criminal offence. In this context it closely mirrors the definition in TRIPS of 'pirated copyright goods':[209]

> 'pirated copyright goods' shall mean any goods which are copies made without the consent of the right holder or person duly authorized by the right holder in the country of production and which are made directly or indirectly from an article where the making of that copy would have constituted an infringement of a copyright or a related right under the law of the country of importation.[210]

[205] Ackermann, '§ 23 Immaterialgüterstrafrecht' (n 115) 730.

[206] Blakeney, *Intellectual Property Enforcement* (n 185) 201; Ch Geiger, 'Of ACTA, "Pirates" and Organized Criminality – How "Criminal" Should the Enforcement of Intellectual Property Be?'(2010) 41 *ILC* 631; Grosse Ruse-Khan, 'Criminal Enforcement and International IP law' (n 169) 187; P Sugden, 'How Long is a Piece of String? The Meaning of "Commercial Scale" in Copyright Piracy' (2009) 31 *European Intellectual Property Review* 202.

[207] See too Geiger, 'Weakening Multilateralism in Intellectual Property Lawmaking' (n 40) 174.

[208] Eckes, Fahey and Kanetake, 'International, European, and US Perspectives on the Negotiation and Adoption of the Anti-Counterfeiting Trade Agreement (ACTA)' (n 37) 20.

[209] Blakeney, *Intellectual Property Enforcement* (n 185) 206–207.

[210] Agreement on Trade Related Aspects of Intellectual Property Rights (TRIPS), art 51 n 14.

Article 23(4) requires the criminalisation of the aiding and abetting of such an offence. Some have suggested that this provision, read in conjunction with Articles 27(1) and 23(5), could give rise to criminal liability of ISPs and social networks for aiding and abetting wilful copyright piracy by their members.[211] This in turn could have considerable implications for internet freedom as ISPs are forced to monitor user behaviour and potentially report violations of IPRs. The reference to incitement, which was evident in earlier drafts, is conspicuous by its absence;[212] any reference to the criminalisation of attempts is similarly absent.

ACTA, like TRIPS, does not set out any minimum penalties, but leaves it to the Member States to ensure that appropriate dissuasive custodial sentence or fines are available. The level of the sentence must reflect that imposed in the context of similarly serious criminal offences (Article 24); it is likely that this would lead to considerable differences in the implementation of ACTA as a consequence of divergence in the legal systems of the contracting states.[213] ACTA also differs from TRIPS in that its provisions on seizure, forfeiture and destruction, while similar to those set out in the TRIPS Agreement, are more extensive.[214] Objects subject to seizure, for instance, need only be described in such detail as is necessary to allow them to be identified for the purposes of seizure.[215] In addition, the authorities are entitled to order the forfeiture or destruction of any counterfeit trademark goods or pirated copyright goods[216] or any materials or implements used in the creation of such goods and, in the context of serious offences, any assets obtained directly or indirectly through the unlawful copyright or trademark infringement.[217]

D The Ratification Process: Protest and Collapse in the EU

ACTA was signed by Australia, Canada, Japan, Morocco, New Zealand Singapore, South Korea and the USA in October 2011, by the EU and its Member States in January 2012[218] and by Mexico in July 2012.[219] Japan is the only country to date to have ratified the Agreement.[220] In order for ACTA to enter into force, it must be ratified by a further five states.[221] The long drawn out nature of the process of

[211] Eckes, Fahey and Kanetake, 'International, European, and US Perspectives on the Negotiation and Adoption of the Anti-Counterfeiting Trade Agreement (ACTA)' (n 37) 20.

[212] Consolidated Text, Prepared for Public Release, Anti-Counterfeiting Trade Agreement, PUBLIC Predecisional/Deliberative Draft, April 2010, available at http://trade.ec.europa.eu/doclib/docs/2010/april/tradoc_146029.pdf, art 2.15(2).

[213] J Gibson, 'The Directive Proposal on Criminal Sanctions' in Ch Geiger (ed), *Criminal Enforcement of Intellectual Property. A Handbook of Contemporary Research* (Cheltenham, Edward Elgar, 2012) 264; Blakeney, *Intellectual Property Enforcement* (n 185) 216.

[214] Gibson, 'The Directive Proposal on Criminal Sanctions' (n 213) 264; see further Blakeney, *Intellectual Property Enforcement* (n 185) 206.

[215] Anti-Counterfeiting Trade Agreement, 3 December 2010, Art 25(2).

[216] *Ibid*, Art 25(3).

[217] *Ibid*, Art 25(4) and 25(5).

[218] www.mofa.go.jp/policy/economy/i_property/acta1201.html.

[219] www.mofa.go.jp/policy/economy/i_property/acta1207.html.

[220] www.mofa.go.jp/policy/economy/i_property/acta_conclusion_1210.html.

[221] Anti-Counterfeiting Trade Agreement, 3 December 2010, Art 40(1).

ratification can be explained by the large international protests against the Agreement. The secretive and non-transparent nature of the development of ACTA led to considerable speculation and to misgivings about the substance of the Agreement.[222] It is notable, however, that the anti-ACTA movement continued even after the publication of the final version of the Agreement. A number of street protests were held, Government websites were subject to denial of service attacks and various petitions were submitted. One of these addressed to the European Parliament demanded that its Members 'stand for a free and open Internet' and was signed by over 2.8 million people. As a result of this, various Member States decided not to ratify the Agreement.[223]

In mid-2011, the Commission recommended that the EU ratify ACTA,[224] but the European Parliament, concerned by the continuing protests and reservations about the Agreement, refused to do so. A vote on the ratification of ACTA was soundly rejected: 478 Members of Parliament voted against the Agreement, while only 39 MEPs were in favour and 165 MEPs abstained.[225] Consequently, the EU and its Member States will not, or at least not in the near future, ratify the Agreement. The collapse of the ratification process in the EU has resulted in the movement towards implementation of the Agreement stalling. Switzerland, for instance, has intimated that it will not, for the time being, ratify the Agreement.[226] Other contracting states, notably the USA and Japan, have however announced their intention to push for progress.[227]

E The Importance of ACTA in the EU

In 2009, the Commission referred to ACTA as a possible means of improving the enforcement of IPRs in Europe.[228] In 2010, the European Parliament even adopted

[222] Geiger, 'The Anti-Counterfeiting Trade Agreement and Criminal Enforcement of Intellectual Property' (n 44) 167.

[223] I Baraliuc, S Depreeuw and S Gutwirth, 'Copyright Enforcement in the Digital Age: A post-ACTA View on the Balancing of Fundamental Rights' (2013) 21 *Int J Law Info Tech* 93.

[224] Proposal for a Council Decision on the conclusion of the Anti-Counterfeiting Trade Agreement between the European Union and its Member States, Australia, Canada, Japan, the Republic of Korea, the United Mexican States, the Kingdom of Morocco, New Zealand, the Republic of Singapore, the Swiss Confederation and the United States of America, Brussels, 24 June 2011, COM (2011) 380 final.

[225] Plenary Session Press Release, 'European Parliament Rejects ACTA', 4 July 2012, available at www.europarl.europa.eu/news/en/news-room/content/20120703IPR48247/html/European-Parliament-rejects-ACTA.

[226] Der Bundesrat, Medienmitteilung, Schweiz wartet mit der Unterzeichnung des ACTA-Abkommens zu, 9 May 2012, available at www.ige.ch/fileadmin/user_upload/Juristische_Infos/d/medienmitteilungen/ACTA_d_09052012.pdf; see too Eckes, Fahey and Kanetake, 'International, European, and US Perspectives on the Negotiation and Adoption of the Anti-Counterfeiting Trade Agreement (ACTA)' (n 37) 20 who note that many Member States have halted the ratification process.

[227] Office of the United States Trade Representative, 2013 Special 301 Report, available at www.ustr.gov/sites/default/files/05012013%202013%20Special%20301%20Report.pdf, 12: 'The United States is working with Japan and other negotiating parties to bring ACTA into force'.

[228] Communication from the Commission to the Council, the European Parliament and the European Economic and Social Committee, Enhancing the enforcement of intellectual property rights in the internal market, Brussels, 11 September 2009, COM (2009) 467 final, 4.

a Resolution in which it stated that ACTA was wholly compatible with the EU's *acquis communautaire*.[229] This led a group of European academics to produce an opinion on ACTA[230] in which they noted that there was no European *acquis* on matters relating to the enforcement of IPRs by way of the criminal law.[231] The Commission in turn issued a response to this opinion in which it stated that the Agreement was in fact compatible with EU law.[232] It expressed its agreement with the position that there was no specific European *acquis*, but argued that this was irrelevant as in this context ACTA did not go beyond Article 61 of the TRIPS Agreement and therefore did not require the creation of further EU legislation. As we have seen, however, there are important differences between TRIPS and ACTA, not least because ACTA sets out more extensive criminal enforcement provisions, leading some commentators to suggest that ACTA 'altered the balance in favor of the right holders'.[233]

The defensive stance of the Commission highlights once again its aim to ensure the implementation of criminal law mechanisms of enforcement at the EU level. In particular, it is safe to assume that the decision to withdraw the proposed directive in September 2009 was connected to the belief that the finalisation of ACTA was imminent. As mentioned above, it is to be expected that the Commission will take further measures in order to ensure the introduction of criminal law enforcement measures in the intellectual property context; the problems which it has encountered in the context of ACTA makes this all the more likely. Even though implementation failed within the EU as a result of considerable pressure from the general public, it is likely that the Commission will introduce a new proposal for criminal law enforcement of IPRs which contains the same or similar provisions as those set out in ACTA.[234] This means that despite its failure, ACTA is nevertheless likely to have a considerable impact on EU intellectual property law.[235]

The collapse of ACTA, however, also clearly demonstrates that this is not likely to be an easy task. The nature of the process underlines a central problem with the EU legislative process, namely its lack of democratic legitimacy and its top down approach to law making. The new rules on the enforcement of intellectual property law were created first in an international agreement, and then transferred into EU law and subsequently into national legislation. In the context of these controversial provisions, this approach was doomed to failure.

[229] European Parliament resolution of 24 November 2010 on the Anti-Counterfeiting Trade Agreement (ACTA), P7_TA(2010)0432.

[230] Opinion of European Academics on Anti-Counterfeiting Trade Agreement, JIPITEC 2011, Vol 2, 65–72; see further D'Erme et al, 'The Impact of the Anti-Counterfeiting Trade Agreement on the Legal Framework for IP Enforcement in the European Union' (n 188) 394–408.

[231] Opinion of European Academics on Anti-Counterfeiting Trade Agreement, JIPITEC 2011, Vol 2, 67.

[232] Commission Services Working Paper, Comments on the 'Opinion of European Academics on Anti-Counterfeiting Trade Agreement', 27 April 2011, available at http://trade.ec.europa.eu/doclib/docs/2011/april/tradoc_147853.pdf.

[233] Eckes, Fahey and Kanetake, 'International, European, and US Perspectives on the Negotiation and Adoption of the Anti-Counterfeiting Trade Agreement (ACTA)' (n 37).

[234] Geiger, 'The Anti-Counterfeiting Trade Agreement and Criminal Enforcement of Intellectual Property' 176; Gibson, 'The Directive Proposal on Criminal Sanctions' (n 44) 265–66.

[235] Gibson, 'The Directive Proposal on Criminal Sanctions' (n 213) 263.

V Conclusions

There can be little doubt that the opportunities afforded by the Internet have had a considerable impact on everyday life. Certain industries, such as the entertainment industry, have been particularly affected by these developments. User and consumer behaviour has been fundamentally altered by the online opportunities, as advances in technology have provided new ways to access content without the authority of right holders. The considerable financial impact of the copying, downloading and streaming of such material has meant that the entertainment industry has been particularly active in pushing for changes to IPRs enforcement, appropriate to the digital environment. There are clear indications from within the EU of its desire to improve copyright protection. Questions arise, however, about the nature and extent of the EU's response to this matter.

The approach of the EU demonstrates quite clearly that the principal aim is not the harmonisation of the criminal law in this area, but the harmonisation of some aspects of intellectual property law with a view to the protection of the proper functioning of the internal market. The criminal law, while potentially of relevance in the context of the enforcement of IPRs, also has the potential to give rise to impediments to the internal market.

The Commission's repeated attempts to implement criminal legal enforcement mechanisms have, for the moment and for a variety of reasons, failed. One reason for this is uncertainty about whether there is in fact any need for EU legislation on the enforcement of IPRs by way of the criminal law. Although the majority of European countries have criminal law provisions dealing with copyright infringement, the approaches differ considerably. The existence of such difference is referred to by the EU as justifying the need for EU legislation to harmonise the criminal laws of the Member States, principally in order to enable the prosecution of cross-border nature of copyright infringement on a commercial scale.[236] But it is precisely the existence of differences in the approaches of the Member States in this regard which calls into question the EU's involvement; there is limited consensus as to what exactly is to be criminalised. There is little agreement between the Member States as to the nature and extent of criminalisation in the context of copyright violations.[237]

The potential breadth of the proposed criminal law provisions, particularly as a result of provisions such as those on aiding and abetting and uncertainty about the definition of 'commercial use', has given rise to concern, as has the potential

[236] Indeed, as was recognised by the Commission in its attempt to secure agreement for an international Agreement, it is questionable whether unilateral action at the European level is insufficient to deal with the cross-border nature of the problem.

[237] Geiger, 'The Anti-Counterfeiting Trade Agreement and Criminal Enforcement of Intellectual Property' (n 44) 169.

for the provisions to impact on the individual consumers or users and to negatively affect internet freedom.[238]

This in turn highlights the fact that it is essential that the EU explains not just why harmonisation is necessary, but also why criminalisation is required. Although it frequently stresses that the criminal law provisions on copyright are designed principally to tackle the problems of piracy and counterfeiting at an international level, it is unclear whether the proposed response is well suited to achieving this goal: 'the EU fails to provide evidence as to how requiring Member States to implement uniform criminal measures will deter commercial infringement or mitigate its economic and social consequences'.[239] Harmonisation of the criminal might be accepted by Member States in the context of criminal offences which have a common basis across the EU (such as offences concerning the sexual exploitation of children or denial of service attacks). In the absence, however, of consensus as to whether the matter at issue is one which should fall within the scope of the criminal law, evidence for, and indeed justification of, the creation of criminal law takes on crucial importance. This is a matter which is likely to become more important in the future in view of the EU's competence in the context of Article 83(2) TFEU to create criminal law for the purposes of ensuring the effectiveness of EU policy.

[238] Opinion of the Economic and Social Committee on the 'Communication from the Commission to the European Parliament, the Council, the European Economic and Social Committee and the Committee of the Regions, A Single Market for Intellectual Property Rights: Boosting Creativity and Innovation to Provide Economic Growth, High Quality Jobs and First Class Products and Services in Europe', 18 January 2012, CEDE 143/2012 – int/591: The focus of legislation such as ACTA on 'increasing protection for right holders by means of customs, police and administrative cooperation measures continues to favour a certain view of rights ownership. Other doubtless more fundamental human rights, such as the right to information, health, sufficient food, the right of farmers to select seeds and the right to culture, are not taken sufficiently into consideration, and this will impact on future European legislation geared towards the harmonisation of Member States'; see too D Korff and I Brown, 'Opinion on the Compatibility of ACTA with the European Convention on Human Rights and EU Charter of Fundamental Rights', October 2011, study prepared for the Greens/ European Free Alliance in the European Parliament, available at: http://rfc.act-on-acta.eu/fundamental-rights.

[239] Agarwal, 'Evaluating IRPED2: The Wrong Answer to Counterfeiting and Piracy' (n 40) 813.

5

Content Regulation and the Criminal Law

If you don't like my lyrics, you can press fast forward/ Got beef with radio if I don't play they show/ They don't play my hits, well I don't give a sh*t, so.*

I Introduction

One of the principal targets of the European Union's policy makers in the context of the information society is content considered to be so unacceptable as to merit criminal law regulation. Various types of content, including material relating to child sexual abuse, incitement to terrorism, illegal glorification of violence, and racism and xenophobia, have been subject to the attention of the EU institutions.[1] While not directed solely at content disseminated by means of the Internet or audio-visual media, the various pieces of legislation are linked, as we shall see, by the fact that their existence is commonly justified by the reference to potential for new communication networks to enable the easy and widespread distribution of such material.

Content regulation, particularly when it involves the use of criminal sanctions, is a controversial subject. The determination of what constitutes 'criminal' as opposed to 'lawful' content depends to a large extent on the political and cultural context in which issues such as censorship, freedom of expression and more broadly the relationship between the individual and the government are determined. In the EU this is further complicated, in spite of acceptance of the EU Charter,[2] by differences in the interpretation of fundamental rights such as the freedom of expression. If the differentiation between criminal and lawful content is dependent on the interpretation of constitutional constraints and the relationship between the individual and the state, then this will necessarily prove difficult

* Jay-Z, '99 Problems' (Roc-A-Fella, Def Jam, 2004)

[1] See eg Communication from the Commission to the European Parliament, the Council and the Committee of the Regions, Towards a General Policy on the Fight Against Cyber Crime, Brussels, 22 May 2007, COM (2007) 267 final.

[2] Charter of Fundamental Rights of the European Union of 7 December 2000, as adapted at Strasbourg on 12 December 2007 (2010/C 83/02) [2010] OJ C83/389.

in the absence of agreement on constitutional principles.[3] The contested nature of a common European constitutional framework is best illustrated by the failure of the 'Constitutional Treaty' in 2005; but deep-seated disagreement between the Member States with regard to the interpretation of principles such as freedom of expression has also significantly obstructed attempts to push through various specific pieces of legislation.[4]

The existence of such disagreement is interesting not just because it highlights problems with the current institutional set up of the EU, but also because it seems to cast some doubt on whether the goals strived for in the legislation are best achieved, or indeed achievable at all, through recourse to the criminal law. The provisions criminalising various types of content are especially interesting precisely because of the uncertainty about the proper role of the criminal law in this context. The imposition of criminal liability, despite the existence of other less invasive means of control, is undesirable and has the potential to negatively impact on the legitimacy of the law.[5] In addition, divergence between the Member States is likely to complicate efforts to achieve harmonisation in this area. The provisions considered in this chapter were developed in the context of the third pillar. The majority now fall within the scope of Article 83(1) TFEU which provides a basis for the creation of common standards in the context of the criminalisation of serious offences with a cross-border dimension.

This chapter will begin with an examination of the EU regulatory approach to content regulation and will then go on to consider the basis on which unlawful content is to be distinguished from lawful content in the context of European constitutional provisions on freedom of expression. This will provide the basis for more detailed analyses of those provisions which have been identified by the institutions of the EU as requiring express regulation, namely terrorism, racism and child pornography. In examining the various pieces of legislation, particular consideration will be given to the reasons provided in support of the need for EU involvement and the nature of implementation of the provisions in the Member States. In view of the fact that these areas now fall within Article 83 TFEU, analysis of implementation takes on considerable importance. Inconsistent

[3] On the various conceptions of the rule of law within Europe, see D Mineshima, 'The Rule of Law and EU Expansion' (2002) 24 *Liverpool Law Review* 73. See also E Herlin-Karnell, *The Constitutional Dimension of European Criminal Law* (Oxford, Hart, 2012) ch 4.

[4] It took almost a decade, for instance, for consensus to be reached on the Framework Decision on Racism and Xenophobia. See also V Mitsilegas, 'The Third Wave Third Pillar Law: Which Direction for EU Criminal Justice' (2009) 34 *EL Rev* 523, 527 referring to negotiation and adoption of the legislation as lengthy and 'cumbersome'.

[5] See M Kaifa-Gbandi, 'The Importance of Core Principles of Substantive Criminal Law for a European Criminal Policy Respecting Fundamental Rights and the Rule of Law' (2011) 1 *European Criminal Law Review* 7, and for an interesting examination of the ultima ratio principle N Jareborg, 'Criminalization as Last Resort (*Ultima Ratio*)' (2004) 2 *Ohio State Journal of Criminal Law* 521. The ultima ratio principle is recognised by the Commission as of importance, see Communication from the Commission, Towards an EU Criminal Policy: Ensuring the effective implementation of EU policies through criminal law, Brussels, 20 September 2011, COM (2011) 573 final, at 7: 'criminal law must always remain a measure of law resort'.

application of the provisions calls into question both the possibility of approximation and the main justification for the EU's involvement in the criminal law.

II The Development of Content Regulation and the Role of ICT

While the remit of the provisions discussed in this chapter is not confined to the regulation of content in the context of information and communications technology (ICT), the spectre of the Internet in particular looms large in the reasons provided for the justification of the existence of such provisions.[6] EU policy on content regulation, which stretches back more than a decade, can be seen as having developed principally as a result of the perception that it was necessary to regulate the Internet, which is referred to as having 'established itself as one of the main building blocks of the Global Information Infrastructure and as an essential enabler of the Information Society in Europe' and held up as the 'symbol of convergence between telecommunications, computer and content industries'.[7] In 1996, the European Commission published a Green Paper on the Protection of Minors and Human Dignity in Audiovisual and Information Services, which referred to the 'radically evolving world of audiovisual and information services' and to the transition 'from a broadcast world to an environment where conventional television will exist alongside on-line services and indeed hybrid products'.[8] The Green Paper and the Commission's Communication on 'Illegal and Harmful Content on the Internet' were published simultaneously[9] and the two documents were described at the time as being 'fully complementary as regards timing and scope'.[10]

The unique characteristics of the Internet – wide usage, resistance to tampering, its global nature and so on – were seen to pose certain specific problems in relation both to the combating of crime and to the prosecution of those responsible. The Commission frequently alludes to the problems which could arise if

[6] See eg the opening line of the Commission Staff Working Document attached to the Communication from the Commission to the Parliament, the Council and the Committee of Regions, 'Towards a General Policy on the Fight against Cyber Crime', Brussels 22 May 2007, SEC (2007) 641, 2: 'The use of the Internet has exploded in recent years, and the appearance of new phenomena and new techniques have created a situation of increased insecurity'.

[7] Communication of the Commission to the European Parliament, the Council, the Economic and Social Committee and the Committee of the Regions, Illegal and Harmful Content on the Internet, Brussels, 16 October 1996, COM (1996) 487.

[8] Commission, Green Paper on the Protection of Minors and Human Dignity in Audiovisual and Information Services, Brussels, 16 October 1996, COM (1996) 483 final.

[9] Communication of the Commission to the European Parliament, the Council, the Economic and Social Committee and the Committee of the Regions, Illegal and Harmful Content on the Internet, Brussels, 16 October 1996, COM (1996) 487.

[10] Commission, Green Paper on the Protection of Minors and Human Dignity in Audiovisual and Information Services, Brussels, 16 October 1996, COM (1996) 483 final.

certain acts were categorised or penalised differently in the various Member States.[11] The need for regulation at the EU level is explained by reference to the international reach of the Internet and the difficulties facing the Member States in enforcing their standards in the absence of common provisions:

> Due to the international nature of the Internet, even if the legislation of the concerned country forbids such contents and require criminal prosecution, it may also occur the author, content provider, and the host service provider, may all be beyond the reach of national law enforcers. Criminal law only operates within national frontiers. In order to avoid loopholes for criminal activities, it would be therefore important, that Member States would define certain minimum common standards in their penal legislation'.[12]

The 'highly decentralised and transnational nature' of the Internet is described as making international cooperation essential.[13] The Green Paper on the protection of minors identifies, 'irrespective of differences in national legislation', certain types of content, notably 'child pornography, extreme gratuitous violence and incitement to racial or other hatred, discrimination, and violence', and suggests that access to it 'be banned for everyone, regardless of the age of the potential audience or the medium used'. Although the Commission's Communication on illegal and harmful content referred to a much broader range of conduct which could 'be misused as a vehicle for criminal activities',[14] there can be little doubt that the principal focus of the EU organs has been on the 'dissemination, especially via the Internet, of pornography, in particular child pornography, racist statements and information inciting violence'.[15] The importance of regulating these types of content in the information and communications context has been highlighted in general policy documents on the regulation of the Internet, such as in the various Community programmes on promoting safer use of the internet as well as in the specific policy documents promoting EU action in relation to illegal content.

In April 2000, the European Parliament adopted a resolution specifically addressing the problem of child pornography on the Internet,[16] and this was followed up in May 2000 in a Council decision[17] and in December 2003 in a Council framework decision aimed at addressing the sexual exploitation of children more

[11] See eg Communication of the Commission to the European Parliament, the Council, the Economic and Social Committee and the Committee of the Regions, Illegal and Harmful Content on the Internet, Brussels, 16 October 1996, COM (1996) 487, at 5.

[12] *Ibid*, 17 (the linguistic errors are all in the original Communication).

[13] *Ibid*, 11.

[14] *Ibid*, 3; see too written question No 2874/98 by Jean-Yves Le Gallou to the Commission, Action on illegal and harmful content on the Internet [1999] *OJ C142/52*.

[15] Communication from the Commission, Creating a Safer Information Society by Improving the Security of Information Infrastructures and Combating Computer-related Crime, Brussels, 26 January 2001, COM (2000) 890 final, at 12.

[16] European Parliament legislative resolution of 11 April 2000 on the initiative of the Republic of Austria with a view to adopting a Council decision to combat child pornography on the Internet (10317/1999 (C5-0318/1999 (1999/0822(CNS)) [2001] OJ C40/41.

[17] Council Decision 2000/375/JHA of 29 May 2000 to combat child pornography on the Internet [2000] OJ L138/1.

broadly.[18] The measures undertaken by the EU institutions have primary involved attempts to approximate the criminal laws of the Member States in this field,[19] to delineate the boundaries of criminal responsibility for the various types of Internet providers,[20] and to promote effective cooperation between Member States in prosecuting such criminal activity.[21]

The decision to promote the safe use of the Internet and new online technologies through combating illegal and harmful content was based both on the desire to create a safe environment for Internet users and on the realisation that the proliferation of harmful content had the potential to 'adversely affect the establishment of the necessary favourable environment for initiative and undertakings to flourish'.[22] The focus on Internet regulation was a natural progression from earlier undertakings in the context of audio-visual and information services.[23] In addition the EU institutions have sought to encourage industry self-regulation, to promote the development of filtering systems, and to establish a system of hotlines to enable people to report illegal content,[24] while simultaneously introducing provisions requiring Member States to criminalise certain activities associated with illegal content.[25]

The role of the Internet as an expedient in the Commission's proposals for common EU criminal laws is clearly evident in its various legislative proposals. The proposal for a framework decision on combating racism and xenophobia referred to the 'dissemination of racist and xenophobic contents on the Internet' as a 'worrying issue' and noted that the Internet is a 'relatively cheap and highly effective tool for racist individuals or groups to spread hateful ideas to an audience of thousands if not millions' while providing a great deal of impunity to authors. In view of this it claimed that the EU's 'determination to implement

[18] Council Framework Decision 2004/68/JHA of 22 December 2003 on combating the sexual exploitation of children and child pornography [2004] OJ L13/44.

[19] Notably the Council Framework Decision 2004/68/JHA of 22 December 2003 on combating the sexual exploitation of children and child pornography [2004] OJ L13/44.

[20] European Parliament Resolution on the Commission communication on illegal and harmful content on the internet, 24 July 1997.

[21] Council Decision 2000/375/JHA of 29 May 2000 to combat child pornography on the Internet [2000] OJ L138/1.

[22] Decision No 276/1999/EC of the European Parliament and of the Council of 25 January 1999 adopting a multi-annual Community action plan on promoting safer use of the Internet by combating illegal and harmful content on global networks [1999] OJ L33/1, para 2, as amended by Decision No 1151/2003/EC of the European Parliament and of the Council of 16 June 2003 amending Decision No 276/1999/EC adopting a multi-annual Community action plan on promoting safer use of the Internet by combating illegal and harmful content on global networks [2003] OJ L162/1; and Decision 854/2005/EC of the European Parliament and of the Council of 11 May 2005 establishing a multi-annual Community Programme on promoting safer use of the Internet and new online technologies [2005] OJ L149/1.

[23] See especially Commission, Green Paper on the Protection of Minors and Human Dignity in Audiovisual and Information Services, Brussels, 16 October 1996, COM (1996) 483 final.

[24] See Safer Internet Programme (1999–2004) and Safer Internet Plus (2005–2008); Communication from the Commission to the European Parliament, the Council, the European Economic and Social Committee and the Committee of the Regions, European Strategy for a Better Internet for Children, Brussels, 2 May 2012, COM (2012) 196 final.

[25] See further ch 3.

common penal provisions also in this field would contribute to provide Internet-users with a safe and crimeless environment'.[26] The Commission implies that the Internet is the driving force in the need for legislation and states that its 'basic idea' is to ensure that 'what is illegal off-line is illegal on line'. But here it is faced with the problem that while most, if not all, Member States have legislation outlawing racist conduct or incitement to racial hatred their 'scope, content and enforcement still differ considerably'. In order to overcome this problem it determined that 'it is time to achieve further progress in this area'.[27]

The various pieces of legislation also emphasise the preoccupation with the Internet and other audio-visual media as providing a forum for the commission of criminal offences and as justifying the need for legislation. The 2008 Framework Decision on combating terrorism refers to the fact that: 'The terrorist threat has grown and rapidly evolved in recent years, with changes in the modus operandi of terrorist activists and supporters including the replacement of structured and hierarchical groups by semiautonomous cells loosely tied to each other. Such cells inter-link international networks and increasingly rely on the use of new technologies, in particular the Internet'.[28] It goes on to note that the: 'The Internet is used to inspire and mobilise local terrorist networks and individuals in Europe and also serves as a source of information on terrorist means and methods, thus functioning as a "virtual training camp". Activities of public provocation to commit terrorist offences, recruitment for terrorism and training for terrorism have multiplied at very low cost and risk'.[29] Similarly the Directive on the sexual abuse and exploitation of children and child pornography refers to the fact that: 'Child pornography . . . and other particularly serious forms of sexual abuse and sexual exploitation of children are increasing and spreading through the use of new technologies and the Internet'.[30]

Although the scope of the various provisions regulating terrorism, racism and the sexual abuse and exploitation of children are not confined to the ICT context,[31] there can be little doubt that the desire to regulate the online environment was a driving force in the EU's treatment of content regulation. It is notable that this legislation has primarily been targeted at users and content providers, rather than access and service providers.[32]

[26] Proposal for a Council Framework Decision on combating racism and xenophobia, Brussels 28 November 2011, COM (2001) 664 final, Explanatory Memorandum, at 5–6.

[27] *Ibid*, at 6.

[28] Council Framework Decision 2008/919/JHA of 28 November 2008 amending Framework Decision 2002/475/JHA on combating terrorism [2008] OJ L330/21, Recital [3] of the preamble.

[29] *Ibid*, Recital [4] of the preamble.

[30] Directive 2011/92/EU of the European Parliament and of the Council of 13 December 2011 on combating the sexual abuse and sexual exploitation of children and child pornography, and replacing Council Framework Decision 2004/68/JHA [2011] OJ L335/1, Recital [3] of the preamble.

[31] See Appendix 1 for a list of all offences.

[32] J Henn, 'Targeting Transnational Content Regulation' (2003) 21 *Boston University International Law Journal* 157, at 166.

III Distinguishing Criminal from Lawful Content

A Criminal Content in the EU Policy Documents and Legislation

The EU provisions seek to prohibit unlawful content, but this inevitably gives rise to the question, what is unlawful or criminal content? The various policy documents, as a general rule, separate such content into two categories: harmful content and illegal content. Illegal content is considered obviously and universally unlawful, whereas the decision about whether content is 'harmful' or not is considered to depend on 'cultural differences' and requires 'that international initiatives take into account different ethical standards in different countries in order to explore appropriate rules to protect people against offensive material whilst ensuring freedom of expression'.[33] Harmful content has been defined by the Commission, for instance, as 'content which is defined as such by law and so made subject to measures intended to restrict access by minors, or quite simply content which individual parents do not wish their child to see'.[34]

The Commission has referred to illegal content as including 'child pornography and racist material'[35] and in a response to a written question stated that illegal content 'relates to a wide variety of issues including national security (instructions on bomb-making, illegal drug production, terrorist activities); protection of minors (abusive forms of marketing, violence, pornography); protection of human dignity (incitement to racial hatred or racial discrimination); economic security (fraud, instructions on pirating credit cards); information security (malicious hacking); protection of privacy (unauthorised communication of personal data, electronic harassment); protection of reputation (libel, unlawful comparative advertising); and intellectual property (unauthorised distribution of copyrighted works, e.g. software or music)'.[36] In distinguishing illegal and harmful content, the Commission's representative referred to the fact that the publication of harmful content could not be restricted 'because of the principle of freedom of expression'.[37] The assumption underpinning the EU legislation in this field seems to be that content involving terrorism, child pornography and racism is obviously criminal and thereby falls outside the scope of protection offered by fundamental rights and freedoms such as Article 10 ECHR.

[33] Communication of the Commission to the European Parliament, the Council, the Economic and Social Committee and the Committee of the Regions, Illegal and Harmful Content on the Internet, Brussels, 16 October 1996, COM (1996) 487, at 11.

[34] Communication from the Commission, Follow-up to the multiannual Community action plan on promoting safer use of the Internet by combating illegal and harmful content on global networks, Brussels, 22 March 2002, COM (2002) 152 final, at 8.

[35] *Ibid*, 7.

[36] Written question No 2874/98 by Jean-Yves Le Gallou to the Commission, Action on illegal and harmful content on the Internet [1999] *OJ C142/52*.

[37] *Ibid.*

B Constitutional Constraints

(i) Freedom of Expression

Constitutional standards have the potential to impact on the determination of whether content is criminal. This makes it necessary in establishing the definition of criminal content, to consider the role of constitutional restraints and in particular the principle of the freedom of expression on EU legislation. The right to freedom of expression and information is set out in the Charter of Fundamental Rights of the European Union and includes both the 'freedom to hold opinions and to receive and impart information and ideas without interference by public authority and regardless of frontiers' and the guarantee that 'the freedom and pluralism of the media' be 'respected'.[38] The Charter attained binding legal force equal to that of the treaties with the introduction of the Lisbon Treaty in December 2009.[39] Freedom of expression is also guaranteed in a number of human rights instruments, notably in the European Convention on Human Rights (ECHR).[40] The ECHR is especially important in this regard, not just because the case law of the ECHR is the principal European source of interpretation of constitutional rights and freedoms, but also because the Lisbon Treaty provides the basis for the accession of the EU to the ECHR.[41]

Freedom of expression has been held by the European Court of Human Rights (ECtHR) to be essential to enabling 'pluralism, tolerance and broadmindedness without which there is no democratic society'.[42] In *Handyside* the ECtHR confirmed that this meant that ideas or information which 'offend, shock or disturb the State or any sector of the population' had to be regarded as being of the same importance as those which were 'favourably received or regarded as inoffensive or a matter of indifference'.[43] Fundamental to the essence of freedom of expression is thus acceptance of the fact that it protects sentiments, speech or content which may be not only controversial, but also objectionable and even deeply disconcerting. Examples of speech, which has been upheld as being worthy of protection

[38] Art 11 of the Charter of Fundamental Rights of the European Union of 7 December 2000, as adapted at Strasbourg on 12 December 2007 (2010/C 83/02) [2010] OJ C83/389.

[39] See Art 6(1) TEU. The UK and Poland both secured an 'opt out' from the Charter, see Protocol 7 to the Charter of Fundamental Rights of the European Union, although the significance of this 'opt out' is contested, see S Peers, 'The Opt-Out that Fell to Earth: The British and Polish Protocol Concerning the EU Charter of Fundamental Rights' (2012) 12 *Human Rights Law Review* 375.

[40] Art 10 ECHR. The principle of freedom of expression is also set out in the Universal Declaration of Human Rights (UDHR), the International Covenant on Civil and Political Rights (ICCPR).

[41] Art 6(2) TEU. The corresponding Council of Europe provision is set out in Protocol 14 to the ECHR.

[42] For a good overview of Art 10 ECHR, see R Reed and J Murdoch, *Human Rights Law in Scotland*, 3rd edn (London, Bloomsbury, 2011) at 898, paras 7.48–7.113.

[43] *Handyside v United Kingdom* Series A no 24 (7 December 1976), para 49. See also *The Observer and the Guardian* Series A no 216 (26 November 1991); *Thorgeir Thorgeirson v Iceland* Series A no 239 (26 April 1995); *Prager and Oberschlick v Austria* Series A no 313 (26 April 1995).

under Article 10 ECHR include: pornographic material,[44] the giving of information to women about the possibility of obtaining an abortion,[45] blasphemous works of art[46] and a television program in which the racist views of young people on immigrant groups were aired.[47]

According to the ECtHR's case law, particular protection is afforded to upholding freedom of 'the press' and expression which is deemed to be 'political'. It is incumbent on the press to 'impart information and ideas on political issues just as on those in other areas of public interest'.[48] States are permitted to interfere with freedom of expression if this is deemed to be 'necessary in a democratic society' in order to protect various interests, including national security, territorial integrity or public safety, the prevention of disorder or crime, the protection of health or morals, the protection of the reputation or rights of others, the confidentiality of information received in confidence and the preservation of the authority and impartiality of the judiciary.[49] These exceptions must, however, 'be construed strictly, and the need for any restrictions must be established convincingly'.[50] The determination of whether the interference with the notion of freedom of expression is sufficient to warrant a finding of a violation of Article 10 ECHR rests on the determination of the proportionality of this interference.

In a number of cases the ECtHR has had to consider the compatibility of convictions for glorification of, or incitement to, terrorism or violence with the right to freedom of expression.[51] As a general rule the ECtHR will consider the nature of the words used, the context in which they were made and the consequences or possible consequences of the speech in assessing the proportionality of the interference.[52] The ECtHR has proven slow to intervene to strike down convictions for hate crimes[53] and the case law suggests a readiness on the part of the ECtHR to allow the national courts a considerable margin of appreciation and to restrict its assessment to determining whether the national court was 'entitled' to reach its conclusion.[54] It is notable here that the lack of consensus among the contracting states results has resulted in a cautious approach by the Strasbourg authorities.

[44] *Handyside v United Kingdom* (n 43) (The Little Red Schoolbook).

[45] *Open Door and Dublin Well Woman v Ireland* Series A no 246-A (29 October 1992).

[46] *Müller and Others v Switzerland* Series A no 133 (24 May 1998).

[47] *Jersild v Denmark* Series A no 298 (23 September 1994).

[48] *Lingens v Austria* Series A no 103 (8 July 1986).

[49] Art 10(2) ECHR.

[50] See eg *Sürek v Turkey (No 1)* Reports 1999-IV (8 July 1999), para 58.

[51] For comment, see S Sottiaux, 'Leroy v France: Apology of Terrorism and the Malaise of the European Court of Human Rights' Free Speech Jurisprudence' (2009) *European Human Rights Law Review* 415; U Belavusau, 'A Dernier Cri from Strasbourg: An Ever Formidable Challenge of Hate Speech' (2010) 16 *European Public Law* 373.

[52] See eg *Sürek v Turkey (No 1)* (n 50), para 62.

[53] See eg *Leroy v France* no 36109/03 (2 October 2008); *Soulas and Others v France* no 15948/03 (10 July 2008); *Balsyté-Lideikiené v Lithuania* no 72596/01 (4 November 2008).

[54] See eg *Leroy v France* (n 53), para 48. See too G Millar, 'The European Protection of Freedom of Expression; Reflections on Some Recent Restrictive Trends', available at www-ircm.u-strasbg.fr/seminaire_oct2008/docs/Millar_Trends_in_the_Recent_Case-Law.pdf, at 1.

This means that the freedom of expression guarantee in the ECHR is considerably weaker than that applied in many Member States. This is potentially problematic in that the EU need only abide by guarantees the standard set out in the Charter and the ECHR. This gives rise to the possibility that the Member States may be obliged to enact criminal laws which impinge on their constitutional standards in this area.[55]

Article 10 ECHR only protects 'democratic' speech. Speech that infringes Article 17 ECHR will not fall within the ambit of Article 10.[56] The general purpose of Article 17 ECHR is 'to prevent individuals or groups with totalitarian aims from exploiting in their own interests the principles enunciated by the Convention'.[57] This principle is, however, to be applied cautiously: 'it applies only to persons who threaten the democratic system of the [parties to the Convention] and then to an extent strictly proportionate to the seriousness and duration of the threat'.[58] This has been held to be the case, for example, in the context of a prohibition on standing for election as a member of a pro-Nazi party and in relation to the conviction for possessing leaflets inciting racial discrimination. In such cases the applicants could not claim a right to freedom of expression, as the speech was such as to violate Article 17 ECHR.[59] The ECtHR has held that there is 'no doubt that, like any other remark directed against the Convention's underlying values, the justification of a pro-Nazi policy could not be allowed to enjoy the protections afforded by Article 10'.[60] Almost all of the cases in which Article 17 has been applied involve holocaust denial.[61] The ECtHR refused, for instance, to apply Article 17 ECHR in *Leroy v France* which concerned the conviction of a French cartoonist following the publication of a cartoon said to represent an 'apology for terrorism'.[62]

While it is permissible for states or communities to introduce constraints – whether of a civil or criminal in nature – on speech or content, these must be compatible with the right to freedom of expression. The absence of a clear understanding of the boundaries of a European conception of freedom of expression, however, clearly has the potential to interfere with harmonisation in this area. One way to improve this situation would be for the EU to ensure that its legislative proposals are in conformity with the standards set out in the Charter and in the ECHR. Indeed the Commission has published several documents in which it expresses its commitment to ensuring the compatibility of its legislative proposals

[55] See eg the CJEU's ruling in Case C-399/11 *Stefano Melloni v Ministerio Fiscal* [2013] ECR I.

[56] Art 17: 'Nothing in this Convention may be interpreted as implying for any State, group or person any right to engage in any activity or perform any act aimed at the destruction of any of the rights and freedoms set forth herein or at their limitation to a greater extent than is provided for in the Convention'.

[57] *Norwood v United Kingdom* no 23131/03 (16 November 2004) (inadmissible).

[58] *De Becker v Belgium* no 214/56 (1960) Series B no 2, para 279.

[59] *Glimmerveen and Hagenbeek v Netherlands* nos 8348 and 8406/78 (1980) 18 DR 187.

[60] *Lehideux and Isorni v France GC* Reports 1998-VII (23 September 1998), para 53.

[61] One exception is *Norwood v United Kingdom* no 23131/03 (16 November 2004).

[62] It did not however find a violation of Art 10 and the judgment has been criticised as essentially marking out 'apology as a separate category of unprotected speech under Art. 10', Sottiaux, 'Leroy v France' (n 51) 425.

with the Charter.[63] The impact of these commitments is nevertheless questionable.[64] If Member States have a higher standard of protection than that set out in Article 10 ECHR or the Charter, then differences in the implementation of the provisions are likely to arise.[65]

The various EU provisions that have been created with a view to regulating illegal and harmful content are of little help in assessing the importance attributed to fundamental rights during the drafting process. They tend to refer vaguely to the value of freedom of expression without providing any insight as to what this implies or to the balancing exercise which is to be undertaken in order to determine the proportionality or necessity of interferences with the freedom of expression. Typically the instruments set out the legitimacy of the aim and an express commitment to the fundamental freedoms set out in the Charter and the ECHR. According to the Framework Decision on combating racism and xenophobia, for instance, 'racism and xenophobia violate the principles of liberty and democracy' and 'constitute a threat against groups of persons which are target of such behaviour'.[66] The Framework Decision expressly states that the measures which it is imposing are 'in accordance with the principle of proportionality'[67] and that it 'respects the fundamental rights and observes the principles recognised by Article 6 of the Treaty on European Union and by the European Convention for the Protection of Human Rights and Fundamental Freedoms, in particular Articles 10 and 11 thereof, and reflected in the Charter of Fundamental Rights of the European Union'.[68] There is however no detailed consideration of the proportionality of the provisions or any indication of the criteria according to which the proportionality of the measures was determined. A similar approach is to be found in the Directive on combating child pornography[69] and the Framework Decision on terrorism.[70]

[63] Commission, 'Compliance with the Charter of Fundamental Rights in Commission Legislative Proposals: Methodology for Systematic and Rigorous Monitoring', Brussels, 27 April 2005, COM (2005) 172 final; Commission, Strategy for the effective Implementation of the Charter of Fundamental Rights by the European Union, Brussels, 19 October 2010, COM (2010) 573 final; Commission, 'Operational Guidance on Taking Account of Fundamental Rights in Commission Impact Assessments', Brussels, 6 May 2011, SEC (2011) 567 final.

[64] For an interesting examination of these issues, see I De Jesus Butler, 'Ensuring Compliance with the Charter of Fundamental Rights in Legislative Drafting: The Practice of the European Commission' (2012) 37 *EL Rev* 397.

[65] But see the judgment of the CJEU in Case C-399/11 *Stefano Melloni v Ministerio Fiscal* [2013] ECR I for consideration of the difference between the Charter and national constitutions. In *Melloni* the CJEU ruled that the application of Spanish constitutional standards in the context of trials in absentia, which were stricter than those set out in the ECHR, constituted an unlawful interference with the European Arrest Warrant.

[66] Council Framework Decision 2008/913/JHA of 28 November 2008 on combating certain forms and expressions of racism and xenophobia by means of the criminal law [2008] OJ L328/55, Recitals 1 and 5.

[67] *Ibid*, Recital 13.

[68] *Ibid*, Recital 14.

[69] Directive 2011/92/EU of the European Parliament and of the Council of 13 December 2011 on combating the sexual abuse and sexual exploitation of children and child pornography, and replacing Council Framework Decision 2004/68/JHA [2011] OJ L335/1, at 50.

[70] Council Framework Decision 2008/919/JHA of 28 November 2008 amending Framework Decision 2002/475/JHA on combating terrorism [2008] OJ L330/21, at 13.

It is fair to say that while the principle of freedom of expression is recognised as a fundamental freedom, the EU instruments do little to explain the nature of the proportionality requirement or the balancing test used in determining the need for legislation. Although the case law of the ECtHR could be used to assist in this regard, its case law in areas in which there is no European consensus is unclear and inconsistent and it is doubtful therefore whether it could be considered to do much to constrain the creation of laws in this area.

(ii) Internet Freedom, Network Neutrality and Censorship

The regulation of the Internet takes on particular significance when viewed from the perspective of the freedom of expression and fundamental rights more broadly. Some have argued that access to the Internet must be considered to constitute a fundamental right.[71] Indeed, a BBC World Service poll found that almost 80 per cent of adults considered access to the Internet to be a fundamental right.[72] The Internet's 'design and raison d'être' are said to be 'open architecture, freedom of expression, and neutral network of networks'.[73] Although it is difficult to regulate online behaviour, it is less difficult to *regulate the architecture of the Net.*[74] In view of this, it is no surprise that censorship of the Internet is widespread. A study of Internet filtering conducted by the Open Net Initiative found that 25 of the 41 countries analysed showed evidence of filtering or blocking.[75] Governments frequently exert pressure on big technology firms such as Yahoo, Google or Microsoft in order to enable monitoring of individuals and censorship of information.[76]

Within the EU the main issues concerning regulation of the Internet are not concerned with political censorship, but rather with obligations placed on technological companies and ISPs to monitor and, where necessary, bar certain types of content. In this context, legal standards and internet service provider (ISP) driven standards are closely linked. ISPs keen to avoid liability may adopt stricter standards than those set out in law; this in turn has the potential to have a chilling effect on freedom of expression. A good example of this is provided by the Irish Internet provider Eircom. Eircom's terms of use for its broadband service state that: 'Customers may not use the Facility to create, host or transmit offensive or obscene material, or engage in activities, which are likely to cause offence to

[71] For consideration of this matter, see P De Hert and D Kloza, 'Internet (access) as a New Fundamental Right: Inflating the Current Rights Framework? (2012) 3 *European Journal of Law and Technology* 3; N Coulson and AEJ Hutchinson, 'Should Access to the Internet be a Fundamental Right?' (2010) 12 *E-Commerce Law and Policy* 12.

[72] http://news.bbc.co.uk/2/shared/bsp/hi/pdfs/08_03_10_BBC_internet_poll.pdf.

[73] See R Cohen-Almagor, 'Freedom of Expression, Internet Responsibility, and Business Ethics: The Yahoo! Saga and Its Implications' (2012) 106 *Journal of Business Ethics* 353, 363.

[74] On this distinction, see L Lessig, *Code and Other Laws of Cyberspace* (New York, NY, Basic Books, 1999) 43 f.

[75] See C Stromdale, 'Regulating Online Content: A Global View' (2007) 13 *Computer and Telecommunications Law Review* 173, 173.

[76] See eg the report by Amnesty International, 'Undermining Freedom of Expression in China', July 2006.

others on any grounds including, but not limited to race, creed, or sex'. This obligation exceeds, by far, the requirements set out in law.[77] In regulating the liability of ISPs for content, it is thus of crucial importance that regard is had to the importance of network neutrality and the freedom of expression.

C Identifying Illegal Content

Illegal content, for EU purposes, can only be identified by the fact that it is defined as such in EU legislation. While it is clear that the EU legislature considers constitutional principles such as freedom of expression as constraints on its power of criminalisation, the extent to which these principles act as constraints and the manner in which this occurs is unclear. The EU has determined broad categories of 'content' deemed to be unlawful, but it is important to bear in mind that even in this context, the freedom of expression might be of relevance. A number of provisions in various framework decisions and directives require Member States to criminalise a variety of content. Some offences, notably those relating to child pornography, are widely accepted as necessary even though questions remain as to their scope, while others, such as some of the provisions on terrorist offences are the subject of considerable controversy both as regards their desirability in the first place and their extent.

IV EU Provisions Criminalising Content

A Terrorist Content

(i) Terrorist Offences and Offences Linked to Terrorist Activities

The EU has produced two framework decisions on 'combating terrorism': the first in 2002 and the second amending the earlier legislation in 2008. The potential for the Internet to be used for terrorist purposes was one of the main reasons provided by the EU for the need to amend its terrorism legislation.[78] The Internet is referred to as having the potential to 'inspire and mobilise local terrorist networks and individuals' and as a source of 'information on terrorist means and methods' such as to amount to a 'virtual training camp'.[79] The criminal law

[77] www.eircom.net/policy, para 4.8; for comment, see D Mac Sithigh, 'Regulating the Medium: Reactions to Network Neutrality in the European Union and Canada' (2011) 14 *Journal of Internet Law* 3.

[78] Council Framework Decision 2008/919/JHA of 28 November 2008 amending Framework Decision 2002/475/JHA on combating terrorism [2008] OJ L330/21, Recital 4. See also the UNODC communication, 'The Use of the Internet for Terrorist Purposes' (New York, UN, 2012).

[79] The Internet is said to be the ideal forum for terrorists to conduct their activities, see T Stevens, 'New Media and Counter-Narrative Strategies' in: EJAM Kessels (ed), *Countering Violent Extremist Narratives* (The Hague, National Coordinator for Counterterrorism, July 2010), at 114.

provisions are therefore intended to 'contribute to the more general policy objective of preventing terrorism through reducing the dissemination of those materials which might incite persons to commit terrorist attacks'.[80] The Framework Decision on combating terrorism does not contain specific provisions focused solely on the criminalisation of speech or content.[81] A number of the provisions are nevertheless of relevance in that they criminalise various types of content.

(a) *Terrorist Offences*

The most important provisions of the 2002 Framework Decision for the purposes of this chapter are those which define 'terrorist groups' and 'terrorist offences'. According to the 2002 Framework Decision, a 'terrorist group' is 'a structured group of more than two persons, established over a period of time and acting in concert to commit terrorist offences'.[82] The Framework Decision requires the criminalisation of the intentional participation in the activities of a terrorist group, 'including by supplying information or material resources or by funding its activities in any way with the knowledge that such participation will contribute to the criminal activities of the terrorist group'.[83] It also sets out a common definition of a 'terrorist offence' which the Member States are obliged to adopt. It lists various offences which are to be considered terrorist offences if, 'given their nature or context', they could 'seriously damage a country or an international organisation' and if they are committed intentionally with the aim of:

- 'seriously intimidating a population';
- 'unduly compelling a Government or international organisation to perform or abstain from performing any act'; or
- 'seriously destabilising or destroying the fundamental political, constitutional, economic or social structures of a country or an international organisation'.[84]

The following offences are to be classed as terrorist offences: (a) attacks upon a person's life which may cause death; (b) attacks upon the physical integrity of a person; (c) kidnapping or hostage taking; (d) causing extensive destruction to a Government or public facility, a transport system, an infrastructure facility, including an information system, a fixed platform located on the continental shelf, a public place or private property likely to endanger human life or result in major economic loss; (e) seizure of aircraft, ships or other means of public or

[80] Council Framework Decision 2008/919/JHA of 28 November 2008 amending Framework Decision 2002/475/JHA on combating terrorism [2008] OJ L330/21, Recital 7.

[81] Council Framework Decision of 13 June 2002 on combating terrorism (2002/475/JHA) [2002] OJ L164/3, as amended by Council Framework Decision 2008/919/JHA of 28 November 2008 amending Framework Decision 2002/475/JHA on combating terrorism [2008] OJ L330/21, Art 2(2)(b).

[82] Council Framework Decision of 13 June 2002 on combating terrorism (2002/475/JHA) [2002] OJ L164/3, Art 2(1).

[83] *Ibid*, Art 2(2)(b). The offences shall be punished by maximum custodial sentence of 'not less than eight years': *Ibid*, Art 5(3).

[84] *Ibid*, Art 1(1).

goods transport; (f) manufacture, possession, acquisition, transport, supply or use of weapons, explosives or of nuclear, biological or chemical weapons, as well as research into, and development of, biological and chemical weapons; (g) release of dangerous substances, or causing fires, floods or explosions – the effect of which is to endanger human life; (h) interfering with or disrupting the supply of water, power or any other fundamental natural resource – the effect of which is to endanger human life; (i) threatening to commit any of the acts listed in (a) to (h).[85] The Member States must ensure that these offences 'are punishable by custodial sentences heavier than those imposable under national law' for such offences in the absence of the special intent, unless the sentence to be imposed already represents the maximum possible sentence under national law.[86]

Each Member State must ensure that it is a criminal offence to attempt to commit any of the terrorist offences, apart from the possession of weapons, explosives or of nuclear, biological or chemical weapons and the threat to commit a terrorist offence.[87] In addition, the Member States are required to ensure that it is an offence to aid and abet[88] or to incite[89] the commission of a terrorist offence and that the punishment for doing so is a custodial sentence.[90]

The criminalisation of 'incitement' to commit terrorist offences is of particular importance in the ICT context, not least because the Internet 'provides an abundance of material and opportunities to download, edit, and distribute content that may be considered unlawful glorification of, or provocation to, acts of terrorism'.[91] It is important here, however, to note that even in those Member States which provide for incitement as an inchoate offence, it is unlikely that a vague connection between terrorist content on an internet site and a terrorist offence will be sufficient to allow for a criminal prosecution. In order for a conviction to be successful it will, as a general rule, be necessary to prove a causal link between the content and the terrorist act or plot. In a Staff Working Document accompanying the proposal for a new framework decision, the Commission noted that it was 'doubtful that the Framework Decision on combating terrorism requires Member States to ensure that a significant part of the dissemination of

[85] *Ibid.*

[86] *Ibid*, Art 5(1). Member States may allow for a reduction in the maximum sentence if the offender 'renounces terrorist activity; and provides the administrative or judicial authorities with information which they would not otherwise have been able to obtain, helping them to: (i) prevent or mitigate the effects of the offence; (ii) identify or bring to justice the other offenders; (iii) find evidence; or (iv) prevent further offences referred to in Articles i to 4', Art 6.

[87] *Ibid*, Art 4(3); these offences must be 'punishable by custodial sentences heavier than those imposable under national law for such offences in the absence of the special intent required pursuant to Article 1(1), save where the sentences imposable are already the maximum possible sentences under national law', see Art 5(1).

[88] *Ibid*, Art 4(1).

[89] *Ibid*, Art 4(2).

[90] *Ibid*, Art 5(1): The sentences to be imposed for such offences must be 'heavier than those imposable under national law for such offences in the absence of the special intent required pursuant to Article 1(1), save where the sentences imposable are already the maximum possible sentences under national law'.

[91] UNDOC, 'The Use of the Internet for Terrorist Purposes' chs 1, 10.

messages through the Internet encouraging the commission of terrorist offences or providing for terrorist expertise, either accessible to anyone (i.e. website), restricted (i.e. chat forum) or addressed to pre-selected candidates for recruitment, is made punishable'.[92] Difficulties in this regard explain why the EU authorities deemed it necessary to introduce new offences in the amending legislation in 2008.

(b) Publicly Provoking the Commission of a Terrorist Offence

The amendments to the terrorism legislation introduced by the 2008 Framework Decision[93] required the Member States to ensure that public provocation to commit a terrorist offence was classified as an 'offence linked to terrorist activities'.[94] The Member States were also obliged to ensure that the aiding and abetting of such an offence was also to be considered criminal.[95] Public provocation is defined as:

> the distribution, or otherwise making available, of a message to the public, with the intent to incite the commission of one of the offences listed in Article (1)(1)(a) to (h), where such conduct, whether or not directly advocating terrorist offences, causes a danger that one or more such offences may be committed.[96]

The first thing to note about this provision is its extreme breadth. Not only is there no requirement that a terrorist offence actually be committed,[97] there is no need for the prosecution to prove a causal link between the incitement and a subsequent terrorist act. This mirrors a similar provision of the Council of Europe's Convention on the Prevention of Terrorism[98] and means that the reach of the criminal law is extended to cover speech which indirectly incites or risks inciting terrorist acts. There is thus considerable potential for the criminalisation of 'legitimate political debate'.[99] The provision can be seen in the context of, and indeed as supporting, broad offences of glorifying or encouraging of terrorism which have been enacted in many jurisdictions in the last decade.[100]

[92] Commission Staff Working Document, Accompanying document to the Proposal for a Council Framework Decision amending Framework Decision 2002/475/JHA on combating terrorism, Brussels, 6 November 2007 COM (2007) 650 final.

[93] Council Framework Decision 2008/919/JHA of 28 November 2008 amending Framework Decision 2002/475/JHA on combating terrorism [2008] OJ L330/21.

[94] Council Framework Decision of 13 June 2002 on combating terrorism (2002/475/JHA) [2002] OJ L164/3, as amended by Council Framework Decision 2008/919/JHA of 28 November 2008 amending Framework Decision 2002/475/JHA on combating terrorism [2008] OJ L330/21, Art 3(1)(a).

[95] *Ibid*, Art 4(1).

[96] *Ibid*, Art 3(1)(a).

[97] *Ibid*, Art 3(3).

[98] *Ibid*, Art 8.

[99] See too the concerns of the International Commission of Jurists, Briefing Paper: Amendment to the Framework Decision on Combating Terrorism – Provocation to Commit a Terrorist Offence, at 2.

[100] See notably the UK's Terrorism Act 2006 which criminalises statements including those which glorify terrorist acts. For comment: A Hunt, 'Criminal Prohibitions on Direct and Indirect Encouragement of Terrorism' (2007) *CLR* 441; DG Barnum, 'Indirect Incitement and Freedom of

Notable convictions in this context include the case of Bilal Ahmad in the UK.[101] Ahmad was found to have placed an entry on Revolutionmuslim.com calling on others to attack Members of the UK Parliament. He also provided a list of every MP who had voted for the war in Iraq, with a link to a website listing their personal details, advised that the best place to find them in order to kill them would be at their constituency surgery and posted a link to a Tesco online shopping service which could be used to purchase knives. In addition, he praised the actions of a woman who had been convicted a few days earlier of attempting to murder her MP in his surgery with a knife.[102] There was no indication that anybody acted 'on the exhortations in the article and he took it down in a very short space of time'.[103] He was sentenced to an extended sentence of 17 years, comprising a custodial sentence of 12 years and an extension period of five years following his conviction for soliciting to murder. In a French case involving the dissemination of terrorist-related material, the multiple accused received prison sentences ranging from 18 months to six years.[104] They were arrested for posting messages calling for jihad against France on a propaganda website and for planning attacks.

The offence as defined in the 2008 Framework Decision has been subject to considerable criticism both because of its wide scope and because of uncertainty about the commitment to fundamental human rights guarantees, notably freedom of expression. The definition of 'terrorist offence' is undeniably broad and this breadth is expanded further by the definition of provocation which does not require that the speech actually results in a terrorist act, only that the speech 'causes a danger' that an offence may be committed. In the words of the International Commission of Jurists: 'This test leaves some doubt as to the level and the imminence of the risk necessary for the offence of provocation to be committed'.[105] The focus is moved away from the commission of actual acts to the control of those who are perceived to represent a threat, even though no unlawful act has actually been committed or perhaps even contemplated by a third party.[106] Many commentators have compared the breadth of the provocation offence with

Speech in Anglo-American Law' (2006) *European Human Rights Law Review* 258; S Chehani Ekaratne, 'Redundant Restriction: The UK's Offence of Glorifying Terrorism' (2010) 23 *Harvard Human Rights Journal* 205. See too E Barendt, 'Incitement to, and Glorification of, Terrorism' in I Hare and J Weinstein (eds), *Extreme Speech and Democracy* (Oxford, Oxford University Press, 2009) 445 ff.

101 *R v Ahmad* [2012] EWCA Crim 959. It is notable that the under s 58 of the Terrorism Act 2000 it is an offence to collect or have in one's possession any record of information likely to be useful to a person committing or preparing an act of terrorism – there is no need for evidence that the person is engaged in activity connected to terrorism. See *R v K* [2008] 3 All ER 526; *R v G and J* [2009] UKHL 13.

102 *Ibid*, at 13.

103 *Ibid*, at 16.

104 *Public Prosecutor v Arnaud, Bedache, Guihal and others* (Tribunal Correctionnel de Paris, 26 January 2012).

105 International Commission of Jurists, Briefing Paper (n 99), at 5.

106 See Mitsilegas, 'The Third Wave of Third Pillar Law. Which Direction for EU Criminal Justice?' (2009) 34 *EL Rev* 526 citing in support M Kaiafa-Gbandi, 'The Prevention of Terrorism and the Criminal Law of Pre-Preventive Enforcement: New Criminal Acts for the Fight against Terrorism in the European Union' (in Greek) (2009) *Poinika Chronika* 385.

the US incitement standard set out in *Brandenburg v Ohio*[107] which requires that the provocation 'is directed to inciting or producing imminent lawless action' and 'is likely to incite or produce such action'.[108]

It is questionable whether a speech which might be said to 'cause a danger' that an offence may be committed, even though the likelihood of such an offence being committed is remote, can be said to comply with the right to freedom of expression.[109] In this regard the lack of any express balancing of the necessity of such provisions and the nature of the interference with constitutional guarantees such as freedom of expression is problematic.

(c) *Recruiting and Training Terrorists*

Other amendments brought about by the 2008 Framework Decision concern the recruitment and training of terrorists. The enactment of these provisions reflected concerns that terrorist organisations 'increasingly use propaganda distributed via platforms such as password-protected websites and restricted-access Internet chat groups as a means of clandestine recruitment'.[110] According to the Framework Decision, the Member States must ensure that the 'recruitment for terrorism', defined as 'soliciting another person to commit one of the offences listed in Article 1(1)(a) to (h) or Article 2(2)',[111] is classified as an 'offence linked to terrorist activities'.[112] As is the case with regard to the offence of public provocation, there is no requirement that a terrorist offence actually be committed'.[113] The Member States may, but are not obliged to, punish the attempt to commit the offence.[114]

The potential for the Internet to be used as a potential 'alternative' training ground for terrorists and for the various media that provide platforms for dissemination of materials to constitute to 'virtual training camps' is expressly referred to in the 2008 Framework Decision.[115] It requires that the 'training' of terrorists be criminalised and the Member States are required to ensure that this is classified as an 'offence linked to terrorist activities'.[116] Training is defined as 'providing instruction in the making or use of explosives, firearms or other weapons or noxious or hazardous substances, or in other specific methods or techniques,

[107] *Brandenburg v Ohio* 395 US 444, 447 (1969).

[108] See eg SM Boyne, 'Free Speech, Terrorism, and European Security: Defining and Defending the Political Community' (2010) 30 *Pace Law Review* 417, 451.

[109] For a critical look at the ECtHRs approach to glorification of terrorism, see Sottiaux, 'Leroy v France' (n 51).

[110] UNDOC, ch 1 at [5] citing S Gerwehr and S Daly, 'Al-Qaida: terrorist selection and recruitment' in D Kamien (ed) *The McGraw-Hill Homeland Security Handbood* (New York, McGraw-Hill, 2006) 83.

[111] Council Framework Decision 2008/919/JHA of 28 November 2008 amending Framework Decision 2002/475/JHA on combating terrorism [2008] OJ L330/21, Art 3(1)(b).

[112] *Ibid*, Art 3(2)(b). The aiding and abetting of such an offence is also to be considered criminal, Art 4(1).

[113] *Ibid*, Art 3(3).

[114] *Ibid*, Art 4(4).

[115] *Ibid*, Recital [4].

[116] *Ibid*, Art 3(2)(c).

for the purposes of committing one of the offences listed in Article 1(1)(a) to (h), knowing that the skills provided are intended to be used for this purpose'.[117] Again the Member States must ensure that the law is framed in such a ways as to make it clear that there is no requirement that a terrorist offence must actually be committed for liability to be imposed.[118] The Member States may, but are not obliged to, punish the attempt to commit the offence.[119]

(ii) Liability of ISPs

Internet providers store and disseminate vast amounts of data (both legal and illegal) and as a general rule will not know of the content of that data or be able to assess whether it is lawful in accordance with the laws of the countries in which the data is transmitted.[120] The 2002 Framework Decision makes express provision for the liability of legal persons and requires that the Member States take necessary measures to ensure that legal persons can be held liable for any of the offences referred to in the Framework Decision if the offences were

> committed for their benefit by any person, acting either individually or as part of an organ of the legal person, who has a leading position within the legal person, based on one of the following:
>
> (a) a power of representation of the legal person;
> (b) an authority to take decisions on behalf of the legal person;
> (c) an authority to exercise control within the legal person.[121]

In addition Member States must ensure that legal persons can be 'held liable where the lack of supervision or control by a person referred to in paragraph 1' has 'made possible' the commission of any of the offences referred to in the Framework Decision 'for the benefit of that legal person by a person under its authority'.[122] The wide scope of these provisions is clear and thus questions arise as to the liability of host providers, responsible for storing third party content and of access providers, responsible for transmitting third party content.

The provision has to be read, however, in conjunction with the E-commerce Directive which regulates the liability of intermediary service providers. According to Article 15 of the Directive, service providers cannot be obliged to 'monitor the information which they transmit or store, nor a general obligation actively to seek

[117] *Ibid*, Art 3(1)(c). The aiding and abetting of such an offence is also to be considered criminal, Art 4(1).

[118] *Ibid*, Art 3(3).

[119] *Ibid*, Art 4(4).

[120] See too U Sieber 'Instruments of International Law: Against Terrorist Use of the Internet' in M Wade and A Maljevic (eds), *A War on Terror?: The European Stance on a New Threat* (New York, Springer, 2010) 192.

[121] Council Framework Decision of 13 June 2002 on combating terrorism (2002/475/JHA) [2002] OJ L164/3, as amended by Council Framework Decision 2008/919/JHA of 28 November 2008 amending Framework Decision 2002/475/JHA on combating terrorism [2008] OJ L330/21, Art 7(1).

[122] *Ibid*, Art 7(2).

facts or information indicating illegal activity'. Service providers will only be liable if they have 'actual knowledge of illegal activity or information' and fail to take prompt action when informed.[123] The fact that access providers are exempt from liability unless they had knowledge of illegal information of activity demonstrates that the focus of the EU has been very much on holding individual users liable rather than on imposing liability on service or host providers. This is partly a consequence of worries about allowing governments to censor the Internet and partly due to the practical and financial burdens that would accompany demands that providers monitor all content before it is posted. Many websites and other platforms have voluntarily put in place systems for dealing with such terrorist. YouTube, for instance, has introduced a system which allows users to flag potential terrorism-related content on the website. Twitter, meanwhile, sets out prohibited conduct in its rules and reserves the right to remove or refuse to distribute content which violates these rules.[124]

(iii) Jurisdiction

The provisions on jurisdiction are defined by their broad scope. Each Member State is obliged to take 'the necessary measures' to establish jurisdiction for terrorist offences if: (a) the offence is committed in whole or in part in its territory. Each Member State may extend its jurisdiction if the offence is committed in the territory of a Member State; (b) the offence is committed on board a vessel flying its flag or an aircraft registered there; (c) the offender is one of its nationals or residents; (d) the offence is committed for the benefit of a legal person established in its territory; or (e) the offence is committed against the institutions or people of the Member State in question or against an institution of the EU or a body set up in accordance with the Treaty establishing the European Community or the Treaty on European Union and based in that Member State.[125] In the event that an offence falls within the jurisdiction of more than one Member State, the Member States are to cooperate to determine which state is to prosecute the offences.[126]

(iv) Implementation in the Member States

The Commission's first implementation report on the Framework Decision emphasised the failure of many of the Member States to comply with their obligation to provide information by the stated deadline on the implementation of the

[123] Directive 2000/31/EC of the European Parliament and of the Council of 8 June 2000 on certain legal aspects of information society services, in particular electronic commerce, in the Internal Market (Directive on Electronic Commerce) [2000] OJ L178/1, Art 14.

[124] UNDOC, 'The Use of the Internet for Terrorist Purposes', at 128.

[125] Council Framework Decision of 13 June 2002 on combating terrorism (2002/475/JHA) [2002] OJ L164/3, Art 9(1).

[126] *Ibid*, Art 9(2).

provisions in national law.[127] It noted that several Member States, including the UK, Germany and Italy had not transposed the obligation in Article 1 to create a special category of terrorist offences as required,[128] while only four Member States had created legislation which fully complied with the obligation in Article 3 in the context of offences linked to terrorist activities.[129] In addition, the UK, Germany and Italy had not provided as required by Article 3 for enhanced penalties for all relevant offences.[130] Problems were also evident in the context of liability of legal persons.[131]

In its second report on implementation, published in 2007, the Commission noted that its concerns regarding Articles 1 and 5 had not been addressed by the UK, Germany and Italy.[132] In addition, Spain and the UK had failed to properly introduce legislation on the liability of legal persons.[133] The rules on jurisdiction had only been partially implemented and only two Member States had correctly implemented the rules on jurisdiction in Article 9(2).[134] In conclusion, the Commission noted that while most of the Member States evaluated for the first time (the Member States which joined the EU on 1 May 2004 and Greece, Luxembourg and the Netherlands) had achieved satisfactory implementation of the main provisions, with regard to the other Member States, evaluated for the second time, 'the main deficiencies identified in the first evaluation report remain unchanged'.[135]

The UK Government responded to the report by stating that it believed the UK complied with Article 1 as the UK regarded 'terrorism as a crime and the perpetrators of terrorism are prosecuted using the ordinary criminal law' and that individuals could be 'prosecuted for the offences listed in the Framework Decision without the need for each of those offences to be reclassified in UK law as "terrorist offences"'.[136] It rejected criticism of its compliance with the sentencing provisions in Article 5 noting that 'the courts do in practice impose heavier penalties on those convicted of offences related to terrorism' and that in the UK 'judicial discretion does not amount to a free hand when a judge is imposing a sentence'.[137] Finally, on the issue of liability of legal persons the Minister noted that the requirements of the Framework Decision were 'met by the UK through the general law on the commission of criminal offences by legal persons and the possibility of a

[127] Report from the Commission based on Article 11 of the Council Framework Decision of 13 June 2002 on combating terrorism, Brussels 8 June 2004, COM (2004) 409 final, 6.

[128] *Ibid.*

[129] *Ibid.*

[130] *Ibid.*

[131] *Ibid*, 7.

[132] Report from the Commission based on Article 11 of the Council Framework Decision on 13 June 2002 on combating terrorism, Brussels, 6 November 2007, COM (2007) 681 final, 7.

[133] *Ibid*, 9.

[134] *Ibid*, 7 and 9 (Lithuania and Ireland).

[135] *Ibid*, 10.

[136] See UK Parliament, Select Committee on European Scrutiny, Fifth Report, 6 November 2007 (citing the Explanatory Memorandum of 29 November 2007 of the Minister of State for Security, Counter-terrorism, Crime and Policing), para 17.11.

[137] *Ibid*, para 17.12.

civil claim for damages and the administrative assets recovery procedure under the Proceeds of Crime Act 2002'.[138]

The UK Government's response underlines the problems of assessing implementation. According to the Commission, the UK's offences were not tailored to terrorist offences and because the sentencing guidelines applied to all serious offences, it concluded that the UK had not ensured heavier custodial sentences in the specific case of terrorist intent. The UK countered that there was no need for specific legislation and those convicted of terrorist offences inevitably received a higher sentence in practice; a suggestion which seems to be borne out in practice by cases such as that of Bilal Ahmad.[139] This demonstrates unwillingness on the part of the Government to make unnecessary and potentially far-reaching changes to its criminal and sentencing laws. It also highlights the formalistic approach of the Commission in assessing implementation which appears unwilling to take into account the manner in which the law is applied.

B Child Pornography

(i) Introduction and Definitions

The Directive on combating the sexual abuse and sexual exploitation of children and child pornography,[140] which replaced the similarly titled Framework Decision,[141] includes a number of provisions designed to establish a common European criminal legal framework for regulating child pornography offences, including those committed through the use of new technologies and the Internet.[142] The Directive is not identical to the earlier legislation, but has instead been modified to address its perceived shortcomings. These include the fact that it only 'approximates legislation' in relation to a limited number of offences, that it 'does not address new forms of abuse and exploitation using information technology' and 'does not contain adequate measures to prevent offences'.[143]

According to the Commission, developments in information technology have exacerbated the problems in investigating, prosecuting and preventing child pornography by 'making it easier to produce and distribute child sexual abuse images

[138] *Ibid*, para 17.13.

[139] *R v Ahmad* (n 101).

[140] Directive 2011/92/EU of the European Parliament and of the Council of 13 December 2011 on combating the sexual abuse and sexual exploitation of children and child pornography, and replacing Council Framework Decision 2004/68/JHA [2011] OJ L335/1.

[141] Council Framework Decision 2004/68/JHA of 22 December 2003 on combating the sexual exploitation of children and child pornography [2004] OJ L13/44.

[142] The UK, Denmark and Poland were entitled in the context of their opt-out to refrain from implementing this Directive; on opt-outs, see ch 2. The UK has opted in, see JR Spencer, 'Opting Out of EU Criminal Justice?' (2012) 7 *Archbold Review* 6.

[143] See the Commission's Proposal for a Directive of the European Parliament and of the Council on combating the sexual abuse, sexual exploitation of children and child pornography, repealing Framework Decision 2004/68/JHA, Brussels, 29 March 2010, COM (2010) 94 final, 3.

while offering offenders anonymity and spreading responsibility across jurisdictions'.[144] The main developments brought about by the Directive are changes to the definition of child pornography, increased criminal penalties, the criminalisation of the possession or acquisition of such materials, the introduction of a new offence of 'grooming' and legal provision allowing for the blocking of websites containing child pornography.[145]

A 'child' is classed for the purposes of the Directive as 'any person below the age of 18 years'.[146] This is in line with the United Nations Optional Protocol to the Convention on the Rights of the Child on the sale of children, child prostitution and child pornography.[147] Although the Optional Protocol does not expressly mention the age of a 'child', there is reference to the UN Convention on the Rights of the Child which states that a child is a human being 'below the age of 18 years unless, under the law applicable to the child, majority is attained earlier'.[148] By contrast, the Council of Europe Convention on Cybercrime defines a minor as a person under the age of 18 but allows contracting states to define a child as a person under the age of 16.[149] The decision to define a child as a person under the age of 18 was not entirely uncontroversial. Prior to the coming into force of the Framework Decision many European jurisdictions had defined a child, for the purposes of child pornography, as a person under the age of 16[150] or even 14.[151]

The discussions during the drafting of the Cybercrime Convention reflected the fact that there were considerable differences between the jurisdictions as to the age of consent to sexual activity and the age of majority. There is considerable disparity in the age of consent to sexual activity, which varies widely across the continent from 13 in Spain to 18 in Greece and Malta. The harmonisation of the age of consent was 'not identified as an objective for the time being'.[152] The definition of a child as a person under the age of 18 in the child pornography provisions was considered as problematic by some in that it led to incoherence in national sexual offences legislation.[153] It meant that in England and Wales, for instance, a

[144] *Ibid*, 2.

[145] For an overview of these developments and for criticism, see S Kierkegaard, 'To Block or not to Block – European Child Porno Law in Question' (2011) 27 *Computer Law & Security Review* 573.

[146] Directive 2011/92/EU of the European Parliament and of the Council of 13 December 2011 on combating the sexual abuse and sexual exploitation of children and child pornography, and replacing Council Framework Decision 2004/68/JHA [2011] OJ L335/1, Art 2(a).

[147] New York, 25 May 2000, 2171 UN Treaty Series 227.

[148] Art 1 UN Convention on the Rights of the Child, New York, 20 November 1989, 1577 UN Treaty Series 3.

[149] Council of Europe Convention on Cybercrime, Budapest, 23 November 2001, 3.2.2: '3. For the purposes of paragraph 2 above, the term "minor" shall include all persons under 18 years of age. A party, may, however, require a lower age-limit, which shall be not less than 16 years'.

[150] Eg England: s 1 of the Protection of Children Act 1978 and s. 160 of the Criminal Justice Act 1988; Scotland: s 52(2) of the Civic Government (Scotland) Act 1982.

[151] Eg Austria – see Materialen zu 294 DB (XX II GP) *Strafrechtsänderungsgesetz* 2003.

[152] Report from the Commission, Based on Article 12 of the Council Framework Decision of 22 December 2003 on combating the sexual exploitation of children and child pornography, Brussels, 16 November 2007 COM (2007) 716 final, at 5.

[153] AA Gillespie, 'The Sexual Offences Act 2003: Tinkering with "Child Pornography"' (2004) *Criminal Law Review* 361, at 362.

17 year old was entitled to consent to sexual activities, but was prohibited from making or distributing a pornographic image of him or herself. The Commission seemed to recognise these issues, but nevertheless argued that adequate protection of minors from exploitation required that the age of the child be fixed at 18 on the basis that 'even though children under the age of eighteen have reached the maturity to take an informed decision about involving themselves in sexual activities, this should therefore not include depictions of such activities'.[154] The Directive addresses this issue in part by permitting states to refrain from criminalising the possession or production of pornographic material involving children who have reached the age of consent, as defined in national law,[155] where that material is produced and possessed with the consent of those children and only for the private use of the persons involved.[156] Following the introduction of the EU legislation, the vast majority of jurisdictions have ensured that a child is defined for these purposes as a person under the age of 18.

Child pornography is defined in the Directive as including not only pornographic material involving actual children,[157] but also pornographic material involving adults who look like children (youthful adult pornography)[158] and computer-generated pornographic material involving children, although not created using any actual children (virtual-child pornography).[159] Offences relating to virtual pornographic images of children (so called pseudo-photographs) were also included in the Framework Decision and although very similar to the offences set out in Article 9 of Title 3 of the Cybercrime Convention, only a minority of European jurisdictions had enacted criminal law provisions prohibiting such pseudo photographic images prior to the introduction of the Framework Decision. One of the reasons for this was the difficulty in identifying the 'harm' associated with images which do not 'involve, let alone harm, any children in the production process'.[160] This also seems to be accepted in the explanatory report

[154] Communication from the Commission to the Council and the European Parliament, Combating trafficking in human beings and combating the sexual exploitation of children and child pornography, Proposal for a Council Framework Decision on combating trafficking in human beings, Proposal for a Council Framework Decision on combating the sexual exploitation of children and child pornography, Brussels, 22 January 2001, COM (2000) 854 final/2, 22.

[155] Directive 2011/92/EU of the European Parliament and of the Council of 13 December 2011 on combating the sexual abuse and sexual exploitation of children and child pornography, and replacing Council Framework Decision 2004/68/JHA [2011] OJ L335/1, Art 2(b).

[156] *Ibid*, Art 8.

[157] Directive 2011/92/EU of the European Parliament and of the Council of 13 December 2011 on combating the sexual abuse and sexual exploitation of children and child pornography, and replacing Council Framework Decision 2004/68/JHA [2011] OJ L335/1, Art 2 (c)(i): 'any material that visually depicts a child engaged in real or simulated sexually explicit conduct'; Art 2 (c)(ii): 'any depiction of the sexual organs of a child for primarily sexual purposes'.

[158] *Ibid*, Art 2 (c)(iii): 'any material that visually depicts any person appearing to be a child engaged in real or simulated sexually explicit conduct or any depiction of the sexual organs of any person appearing to be a child, for primarily sexual purposes'.

[159] *Ibid*, Art 2 (c)(iv): 'realistic images of a child engaged in sexually explicit conduct or realistic images of the sexual organs of a child, for primarily sexual purposes'.

[160] Justice Kennedy joined by Justices Stevens, Souter, Ginsberg and Breyer in *Ashcroft v Free Speech Coalition* 122 S Ct 1389 (2002), at 1397.

accompanying the Cybercrime Convention in which it is written that the corresponding provisions 'aim at providing protection against behaviour that, while not necessarily creating harm to the "child" depicted in the material, as there might not be a real child, might be used to encourage or seduce children into

Table 1: Age of a 'Child' Prior to and Following Implementation of EU Legislation

Country	Age: Before	Age: After	Criminal law provisions	Express reference to EU provisions?
Austria	14	18	s 207a of the Criminal Code	Yes: the changes were deemed necessary to bring Austrian criminal law into line with EU law.[161]
France	18	18	Art 227-23 Code Pénal	No: age was already fixed at 18.[162]
Germany	14	18	§ 182ff StGB	Yes[163]
Italy	18	18	600ter and 600quarter of the Penal Code, as amended by Act no 269 of 3 August 1998 on Child Pornography.	No: Already fixed at 18.
Switzerland	16	N/A	Art 197(1) StGB	N/A
England/ Wales/ NI	16	18	s 7(6) of the Protection of Children Act 1978 and s 160 of the Criminal Justice Act 1988, both as amended by s 45 of the Sexual Offences Act 2003.	No: No mention of the Framework Decision in the explanatory notes to either the Bill or the Act.
Scotland	16	18	s 52(2) of the Civic Government (Scotland) Act 1982, as amended by s 16 of the Protection of Children and Sexual Offences (Scotland) Act 2005.	Yes: Specific mention in the Headnote to the 2005 Act. See also Justice 1 Committee Official Report of 4 May 2005, col 1772.

[161] See Materialien zu 294 dB (XXII GP) Strafrechtsänderungsgesetz – Regierungsvorlage, at 2 and 19–20, available at www.parlament.gv.at/PAKT/VHG/XXII/I/I_00294/fname_010159.pdf.

[162] See eg Law of 98-468 of 17 June 1998, art 17, OJ 18 June 1998.

[163] See the explanatory notes to the German Government's legislative draft, available at http://dipbt.bundestag.de/dip21/brd/2006/0625-06.pdf.

participating in such acts, and hence form part of a subculture favouring child abuse'.[164]

Similarly in the explanatory note to the Framework Decision, there seems to be acknowledgement of the fact that as the second paragraph covers pornographic material where there is no actual sexual exploitation of children behind the depiction, the interest that is to be protected differs from that referred to in paragraph 1 which seeks to protect actual children from abuse:

> [W]hile paragraph 1 seeks to protect children from sexual abuse, paragraph 2 seeks to protect children from being used as sexual objects and to prevent pseudo child pornographic depictions to become more widespread with a potential to underpin sexual exploitation of children.[165]

It is possible that these broad provisions, which seem to test the boundaries of the criminal law,[166] will nevertheless prove difficult to reconcile with constitutionally protected notions of free speech and the presumption of innocence. This reflects too the difficulties with the justifications provided for some of the provisions. Williams has shown how, in the UK, the legislative emphasis has gradually shifted from the protection of the children depicted in the photographs towards attacking possession: 'The emphasis shifted from protecting children from harm to attacking possession itself. The measure was largely unopposed; everyone was revolted by child pornography, no-one defended it and if the Act helped to find and punish those who should be caught under s. 1 of the 1978 Act it was seen as an acceptable measure'.[167] She sees in the criminalisation of pseudo-images an even clearer 'move away from the direct protection of children', citing numerous studies that cast doubt on the prime justification for such provisions, namely the harm thesis, which postulates that 'photographs (pseudo or real) cause individuals to sexually abuse children'.[168] She concludes that 'a large part of the intent of the law is protection of moral standards and sensibilities' and suggests that 'politicians, lawyers and society . . . think long and hard about why they want to stamp out this material' and about 'what it is that needs controlling' and about 'whether the present legal construction [is] the most effective way forward'.[169] This is certainly lacking in the EU legislative process.

[164] Explanatory report to the Convention on Cybercrime, para 102.

[165] Explanatory memorandum to the Proposal for a Council Framework Decision on combating exploitation of children and child pornography, COM (2000) 854 final, at para 3.

[166] L Böllinger, 'Die EU-Kommission und die Sexualmoral' (2006) 2 *Hanse Law Review* 5, 6.

[167] KS Williams, 'Child Pornography Law: Does it Protect Children?' (2004) 26 *Journal of Social Welfare and Family Law* 245, at 251–52.

[168] Citing inter alia M Taylor and E Quayle, *Child Pornography: An Internet Crime* (Hove, Brunner-Routledge, 2003) 80–83, 86–87; D Howit, 'Pornography and the Paedophile: Is it Criminogenic?' (1995) 68 *British Journal of Medical Psychology* 15; J Proulx, C Perrault and M Ouimet, 'Pathways in the Offending Process of Extrafamilial Sexual Child Molesters' (1999) *11 Journal of Research and Treatment* 117; KL Williams, T Howell, BS Cooper, JC Yuille and DL Paulhus, 'Deviant Sexual Thoughts and Behaviours: the Roles of Personality and Pornography Use' (May 2004) Department of Psychology, University of British Columbia. Part of Presentation at the Annual Conference of the American Psychological Society, Chicago, IL.

[169] Williams, 'Child Pornography Law' (n 167) 258.

A similar provision in the United States' Child Pornography Prevention Act 1996 (CPPA), which extended the prohibition on child pornography to 'any visual depiction, including any photograph, film, video, picture, or computer, or computer-generated image or picture' that 'is, or appears to be, of a minor engaging in sexually explicit conduct',[170] was held by the US Supreme Court to be unconstitutional on the basis that it was overly broad and thus violated the First Amendment right to free speech.[171] The Government in the *Free Speech Coalition* case had relied on four principal arguments. First, that 'virtual child pornography' indirectly harmed children and led to child abuse; second, that such virtual images could persuade those viewing them to commit crimes; third, that the elimination of child pornography was a valid aim in its own right; and fourth, that criminalising virtual child pornography would make it easier to prosecute offenders by freeing the prosecution from the burden of proving that the images were in fact real.

The US Supreme Court rejected all of these arguments. It did not accept that 'virtual child pornography' was '"intrinsically related" to the sexual abuse of children'. Moreover it rejected the contention that the possibility that virtual pornography might encourage unlawful acts was sufficient to justifying banning it. Instead it held that 'the prospect of crime . . . by itself does not justify laws suppressing protected speech'.[172] Neither was it convinced that the elimination of the market for child pornography could be achieved through the prohibition also of virtual images. Instead it mooted the possibility that the market for virtual child pornography if legal would provide a legal alternative thereby eliminating the market for actual child pornography. Finally, the US Supreme Court rejected the Government's contention that the criminalisation of virtual child pornography would assist in the prosecution of actual child pornography offences noting that 'the Government may not suppress lawful speech as the means to suppress unlawful speech'. Protected speech does not become unprotected speech merely because it resembles the latter.[173] It remains to be seen whether the European provisions will be subject to the same constitutional-type challenges as in the United States,[174] although in view of the less strict approach adopted by the Strasbourg court in the context of freedom of expression, this seems unlikely.

(ii) Child Pornography Offences

The Directive sets out a number of offences concerning child pornography.[175] Member States are entitled to refrain from criminalising youthful adult pornogra-

[170] 18 USC §2256(8)(A).

[171] *Ashcroft v The Free Speech Coalition* (n 160).

[172] *Ibid*, at 1399.

[173] *Ibid*, at 1404.

[174] See the concerns of Böllinger, 'Die EU-Kommission und die Sexualmoral' (n 166).

[175] Directive 2011/92/EU of the European Parliament and of the Council of 13 December 2011 on combating the sexual abuse and sexual exploitation of children and child pornography, and replacing Council Framework Decision 2004/68/JHA [2011] OJ L335/1, Art 5.

phy in cases in which the person appearing to be a child was 18 years of age or older at the time of the depiction.[176] These offences are not limited to the online environment; the increasing availability of such material has nevertheless been an important factor in driving the EU approach to legislation in the area.

(a) The Acquisition or Possession of Child Pornography

Member States are required to criminalise the acquisition or possession of child pornography and to ensure that it is punishable with a maximum term of imprisonment of at least one year.[177] They are afforded the discretion to determine whether or not to criminalise the acquisition or possession of material involving children who have reached the age of sexual consent, as defined in national law, in cases in which the material is only possessed with the consent of those children and only for the private use of the persons involved, in so far as the acts did not involve any abuse.[178] In addition, Member States are permitted to refrain from criminalising virtual child pornography[179] providing that it is produced and possessed by the producer for his or her private use and providing no pornographic material[180] has been used for the purposes of its production and there is no risk of dissemination of the material.[181]

Notably absent is any definition of conduct such as 'acquisition' or 'possession'. This is surprising in view of difficulties in definition, which have arisen particularly in the IT context in jurisdictions that have already enacted provisions criminalising child pornography offences undertaken by means of a computer system. In England and Wales, following *R v Bowden*,[182] for instance, printing or downloading images from the Internet were deemed to fall into the category 'making a photograph' rather than possessing such an image, while the English lower courts have held that sending an indecent image of a child via the internet to another person, constituted the act of distributing an image in the sense of s 1(1)(c) of the Protection of Children Act 1978.[183] This type of distinction has, following the incorporation of the Directive, significant consequences in view of the different sentencing ranges.[184]

[176] *Ibid*, Art 7.

[177] *Ibid*, Art 5(2).

[178] *Ibid*, Art 8(3).

[179] In the sense of Art 2(c)(iv).

[180] As defined by Art 2(c)(i), (ii), or (iii).

[181] *Ibid*, Art 8(1).

[182] *R v Bowden (Jonathan)* [2000] 2 WLR 1083. *See also R v Smith and Jayson* The Times, 23 April 2002 (CA, 7 March 2002) where the English Court of Appeal held that downloading such an image constituted 'making' for the purposes of s 1(1) of the Protection of Children Act 1978 (1978 Act). See too *Atkins v Director of Public Prosecutions* [2000] All ER 425.

[183] *R v Fellows and Arnold* (first instance), unreported, but see C Manchester, 'More About Computer Pornography' (1996) *Criminal Law Review* 645.

[184] See Annex 1. In England the maximum sentence is up to 10 years' imprisonment for those offences committed on or after the 11 of January 2001, and three years' imprisonment for those committed before that date, when tried on indictment, or up to six months' imprisonment and/ or a fine if tried summarily.

Member States are only required to ensure that intentional conduct is prohibited.[185] The Directive does not define the concept of intent. The conduct is only to be punished if it is committed 'without right',[186] which means that the Member States are entitled to offer a defence in cases in which the accused can show that the material was access for medical, scientific or other legitimate purposes, including for the purposes of preventing, detecting or investigating crime.[187] Additionally, Member States must ensure that inciting or aiding and abetting the commission of the offence are criminalised.[188] The Directive is silent as to what is to be considered to constitute 'aiding and abetting' or 'incitement'. This lack of clarification in the terminology of the Framework Decision could be expected to lead to differences in interpretation, difficulties in application and to have an adverse effect on the stated aim of harmonisation.[189]

(b) Knowingly Obtaining Access, by Means of Information and Communication Technology, to Child Pornography

Member States must ensure that the offence of knowingly obtained access to child pornography by means of information and communication technology is punishable by way of a maximum sentence of imprisonment of at least one year. This offence was introduced in order to ensure that the criminalisation of those cases where viewing child pornography from websites without downloading or storing the images did not amount to 'possession of' or 'acquiring' child pornography.[190] Only intentional conduct must be prohibited.[191] The person must intentionally access the site where the child pornography is available and must also know that such images can be found there.[192] The Member States must also ensure that inciting or aiding and abetting the commission of the offence are criminalised.[193] The conduct is only to be punished if it is committed 'without right'.[194]

[185] Directive 2011/92/EU of the European Parliament and of the Council of 13 December 2011 on combating the sexual abuse and sexual exploitation of children and child pornography, and replacing Council Framework Decision 2004/68/JHA [2011] OJ L335/1, Art 5(1).

[186] *Ibid*, Art 5(1).

[187] *Ibid*, Art 5(1).

[188] *Ibid*, Art 7(1).

[189] On this point, see ch 7.

[190] Proposal for a Council Framework Decision on combating the sexual abuse, sexual exploitation of children and child pornography, repealing Framework Decision 2004/68/JHA, Brussels 25 March 2009, COM (2009) 135 final, 7.

[191] Directive 2011/92/EU of the European Parliament and of the Council of 13 December 2011 on combating the sexual abuse and sexual exploitation of children and child pornography, and replacing Council Framework Decision 2004/68/JHA [2011] OJ L335/1, Art 5(1).

[192] Kierkegaard, 'To Block or not to Block' 579.

[193] Directive 2011/92/EU of the European Parliament and of the Council of 13 December 2011 on combating the sexual abuse and sexual exploitation of children and child pornography, and replacing Council Framework Decision 2004/68/JHA [2011] OJ L335/1, Art 7(1).

[194] *Ibid*, Art 5(1).

(c) The Distribution, Dissemination or Transmission of Child Pornography

The distribution, dissemination or transmission of child pornography is to be punished by a maximum term of imprisonment of at least two years.[195] Again, Member States are only required to ensure that intentional conduct is prohibited.[196] The Directive does not define the concept of intent. The conduct is only to be punished if it is committed 'without right'.[197] The Member States must also criminalise the attempt to distribute, disseminate or transmit child pornography[198] and must provide for the criminalisation of the inciting or aiding and abetting of the commission of the offence.[199]

(d) Offering, Supplying or Making available Child Pornography

The offence of offering, supplying or making available child pornography must be criminalised and punished by way of a maximum sentence of imprisonment of at least two years.[200] Member States are only required to ensure that intentional conduct is prohibited.[201] The conduct is only to be punished if it is committed 'without right'.[202] The Member States must ensure that the attempt to offer or supply child pornography or to make it available is a criminal offence and must provide that inciting or aiding and abetting the commission of the offence also constitutes a criminal offence.[203]

(e) The Production of Child Pornography

The Member States must criminalise the production of child pornography and must make the offence punishable by a maximum sentence of imprisonment of at least three years.[204] As is the case in the content of the possession of child pornography, Member States may decide whether or not to criminalise the production of material involving children who have reached the age of sexual consent, if the material is only produced with the consent of those children and only for the private use of the persons involved, in so far as the acts did not involve any abuse.[205] They may also decide not to criminalise virtual child pornography providing that it is produced and possessed by the producer for his or her private use and providing

195 *Ibid*, Art 5(4).
196 *Ibid*, Art 5(1).
197 *Ibid*, Art 5(1).
198 *Ibid*, Art 7(2).
199 *Ibid*, Art 7(1).
200 *Ibid*, Art 5(5).
201 *Ibid*, Art 5(1).
202 *Ibid*, Art 5(1).
203 *Ibid*, Art 7.
204 *Ibid*, Art 5(6).
205 *Ibid*, Art 8(3).

no pornographic material has been used for the purposes of its production and there is no risk of dissemination of the material.[206] Member States are only required to ensure that intentional conduct is prohibited.[207] The conduct is only to be punished if it is committed 'without right'.[208] The Member States are under an obligation to ensure that the attempt to produce child pornography and the inciting of or aiding and abetting in the commission of the offence are criminalised.[209]

(iii) Grooming and other Criminal Offences in the IT Environment

(a) Pornographic Performances

The Directive instructs the Member States to ensure that the coercing or forcing a child to participate in pornographic performances or threatening a child for such purposes is punishable by a maximum term of imprisonment of at least eight years if the child has not reached the age of sexual consent and of at least five years' imprisonment if the child is over that age.[210] Pornographic performance is defined as a 'live exhibition aimed at an audience, including by means of information and communication technology, of a child engaged in real or simulated sexually explicit conduct or of the sexual organs of a child for primarily sexual purposes'.[211] This definition is intended to include online pornographic performances on public and private peer-to-peer (P2P) networks. Member States are only required to ensure that intentional conduct is prohibited.[212] Member States must also provide for the criminalisation of the inciting or aiding and abetting of the commission of the offence[213] and they must ensure that the attempt to coerce or force a child to participate in pornographic performances or threatening a child for such purposes is a criminal offence.[214]

(b) Causing or Recruiting a Child to Participate in Pornographic Performances

Causing or recruiting a child to participate in pornographic performances or profiting from or otherwise exploiting a child for such purposes shall be punishable by a maximum term of imprisonment of at least five years if the child has not reached the age of sexual consent and of at least two years' imprisonment if the child is over age.[215] Only intentional conduct must be prohibited.[216] Member

[206] *Ibid*, Art 8(1).
[207] *Ibid*, Art 5(1).
[208] *Ibid*, Art 5(1).
[209] *Ibid*, Art 7.
[210] *Ibid*, Art 4(3).
[211] *Ibid*, Art 2(e).
[212] *Ibid*, Art 4(1).
[213] *Ibid*, Art 7(1).
[214] *Ibid*, Art 7(2).
[215] *Ibid*, Art 4(2).
[216] *Ibid*, Art 4(1).

States must also provide for the criminalisation of the inciting or aiding and abetting of the commission of the offence.[217] The Member States must ensure that the attempt to commit the offence is also criminalised.[218]

(c) Knowingly Attending Pornographic Performances

Knowingly attending pornographic performances involving the participation of a child is to be punished by a maximum sentence of imprisonment of at least two years if the child has not reached the age of sexual consent and of at least one year if the child is over that age.[219] Member States are only required to ensure that intentional conduct is prohibited[220] and must also provide for the criminalisation of the inciting or aiding and abetting of the commission of the offence.[221] The Member States may decide whether this offence applies to a pornographic performance that takes place in the context of a consensual relationship where the child has reached the age of sexual consent or between peers who are close in age and degree of psychological and physical development or maturity, in so far as the acts did not involve any abuse or exploitation and no money or other form of remuneration or consideration is given as payment in exchange for the pornographic performance.[222]

(d) Grooming

The new offence of 'grooming' is outlined in the Directive and follows closely the wording of the equivalent provision in the Council of Europe Convention on Cybercrime. It is defined as:

> The proposal, by means of information and communication technology, by an adult to meet a child who has not reached the age of sexual consent, for the purpose of committing any of the offences referred to in Article 3(4) and Article 5(6), where the proposal was followed by material acts leading to such a meeting shall be punishable by a maximum term of imprisonment of at least 1 year.[223]

Member States are only required to ensure that intentional conduct is prohibited.[224] They are also required to ensure that the attempt by means of information and communication technology to commit the offences of acquiring or possessing child pornography or knowingly obtaining access to child pornography by an adult soliciting a child who has not reached the age of sexual consent to provide

[217] *Ibid*, Art 7(1).
[218] *Ibid*, Art 7(2).
[219] *Ibid*, Art 4(4).
[220] *Ibid*, Art 4(1).
[221] *Ibid*, Art 7(1).
[222] *Ibid*, Art 8(2).
[223] *Ibid*, Art 6(1).
[224] *Ibid*, Art 6(1).

child pornography depicting that child is punishable.[225] In addition, they must also provide for the criminalisation of the incitement of or aiding and abetting in the commission of the offence.[226]

(iv) Liability of ISPs

Member States are obliged to take the measures necessary 'to ensure that legal persons may be held liable for any of the offences referred to in Articles 3 to 7 committed for their benefit by any person, acting either individually or as part of an organ of the legal person, and having a leading position within the legal person, based on: (a) a power of representation of the legal person; (b) an authority to take decisions on behalf of the legal person; or (c) an authority to exercise control within the legal person'.[227]

Member States must ensure that a legal person held liable is punishable 'by effective, proportionate and dissuasive sanctions, which shall include criminal or non-criminal fines and may include other sanctions, such as: (a) exclusion from entitlement to public benefits or aid; (b) temporary or permanent disqualification from the practice of commercial activities; (c) placing under judicial supervision; (d) judicial winding-up; or (e) temporary or permanent closure of establishments which have been used for committing the offence'.[228] They are also required to take the necessary measures to ensure that 'legal persons may be held liable where the lack of supervision or control by a person referred to in paragraph 1' has made the commission, by a person under its authority, of any of the offences referred to in Articles 3 to 7 for the benefit of that legal person.[229] In such a case the legal person must be punishable 'by sanctions or measures which are effective, proportionate and dissuasive'.[230]

Notwithstanding reference to the liability of legal persons, there is no express reference to provider liability. Although ISPs are generally able to rely on the country of origin principle in this regard,[231] it is notable that Member States are entitled to provisionally derogate from this principle in the context of audiovisual services if a television broadcast coming from another Member State 'manifestly, seriously and gravely infringes' the obligation in Article 27 to protect minors in television broadcasting.[232]

225 *Ibid*, Art 6(2).
226 *Ibid*, Art 7(1).
227 *Ibid*, Art 12(1).
228 *Ibid*, Art 13(1).
229 *Ibid*, Art 12(2).
230 *Ibid*, Art 13(2).
231 Directive 2000/31/EC of the European Parliament and of the Council of 8 June 2000 on certain legal aspects of information society services, in particular electronic commerce, in the Internal Market (Directive on Electronic Commerce) [2000] OJ L178/1. See further ch 3.
232 Directive 2010/13/EU of the European Parliament and of the Council of 10 March 2010 on the coordination of certain provisions laid down by law, regulation or administrative action in Member States concerning the provision of audiovisual media services (Audiovisual Media Services Directive) [2010] OJ L95/1, Art 3(2)(a) in conjunction with Art 27.

(v) Blocking Websites

The Directive also requires Member States to 'take the necessary measures to ensure the prompt removal of web pages containing or disseminating child pornography hosted in their territory and to endeavour to obtain the removal of such pages hosted outside of their territory'.[233] They may also, but are not required to,[234] 'take measures to block access to web pages containing or disseminating child pornography towards the Internet users within their territory. These measures must be set by transparent procedures and provide adequate safeguards, in particular to ensure that the restriction is limited to what is necessary and proportionate, and that the users are informed of the reason for the restriction. Those safeguards shall also include the possibility of judicial redress'.[235] There is no need for judicial authorisation of the requirement that an ISP block an Internet address. It was recently announced that Google and Microsoft have expanded their systems to block child abuse material from their search engines.[236] Google employs around 200 engineers, who are responsible for improving this technology. It 'strictly controls search results for 100,000 terms related to underage sex abuse', has 'edited its auto-complete feature, and will point searches for the most explicit search terms towards warnings and links to expert help'. It has also developed a video ID tool 'which uses digital fingerprinting technology to identify and block child abuse videos, even if they have been edited and repurposed'. Microsoft is considering using a comparable video ID on its own video services, and has a similar tool for photos called Photo DNA.[237] Google and Microsoft are also developing tools to identify and prevent distribution of material on P2P networks by removing direct links to content. Blocking seems to be the ideal solution for regulating illegal content on the Internet, yet it is important to note both that such technology might result in the inadvertent blocking of legal sites and that such technology does not delete unlawful content, but merely hides it, giving rise to the possibility that those with the ability to bypass the filter can still access the content.[238]

[233] Directive 2011/92/EU of the European Parliament and of the Council of 13 December 2011 on combating the sexual abuse and sexual exploitation of children and child pornography, and replacing Council Framework Decision 2004/68/JHA [2011] OJ L335/1, Art 25(1).

[234] In favour of mandatory blocking: Kierkegaard, 'To Block or not to Block' (n 145) 581.

[235] Directive 2011/92/EU of the European Parliament and of the Council of 13 December 2011 on combating the sexual abuse and sexual exploitation of children and child pornography, and replacing Council Framework Decision 2004/68/JHA [2011] OJ L335/1, Art 25(2).

[236] J Kiss, 'How Microsoft, Google and ISPs aim to halt child abuse images', *The Guardian*, 18 November 2013.

[237] *Ibid.*

[238] For detailed consideration of these issues, see J Kortlander, 'Is Filtering the New Silver Bullet in the Fight against Child Pornography on the Internet? A Legal Study into the Experiences of Australia and Germany' (2011) 17 *Computer and Telecommunications Law Review* 199, 207.

(vi) Jurisdiction

The Member States are obliged to take the necessary measures to establish jurisdiction if the offence is committed in whole or in part within their territory or if the offender is one of their nationals.[239] Member States are also required to ensure that they have jurisdiction if an offence referred to in Articles 5 and 6, and in so far as is relevant, in Articles 3 and 7, is committed by means of information and communication technology accessed from their territory, whether or not it is based on their territory.[240] Jurisdiction in the context of commercial activity is also regulated in the E-Commerce Directive, which generally limits liability of ISPs on the basis of the country of origin principle,[241] although it is notable that the Audiovisual Media Services Directive provides for derogation from this principle in respect of television broadcasts which 'manifestly, seriously and gravely' infringe the physical, mental or moral development of minors.[242]

(vii) Implementation in the Member States

In its implementation report, the Commission referred to a high level of compliance concerning the application of the provisions[243] and stressed that the legislation in the Member States ensured a 'high level of protection of children from sexual exploitation and abuse'.[244] It is notable that many Member States complied despite the fact that they were required to make important amendments to their criminal laws in order to increase the scope of criminal liability by raising the age of the definition of a child. Indeed this high level of compliance led the Commission to stress the need for more legislation to deal with offences committed in the context of electronic communications technologies. The successful implementation of these provisions might be attributable to the fact that this is an area of criminal law which is already tightly regulated in most Member States and which enjoys broad public acceptance.

[239] Directive 2011/92/EU of the European Parliament and of the Council of 13 December 2011 on combating the sexual abuse and sexual exploitation of children and child pornography, and replacing Council Framework Decision 2004/68/JHA [2011] OJ L335/1, Art 17(1)(a) and (b).

[240] *Ibid*, Art 17(3).

[241] For discussion, see ch 3 above.

[242] See Directive 2010/13/EU of the European Parliament and of the Council of 10 March on the coordination of certain provisions laid down by law, regulation or administrative action in Member States concerning the provision of audiovisual services (Audiovisual Media Services Directive) [2010] OJ L95/1, Art 3(2)(a).

[243] See Report from the Commission based on Article 12 of the Council Framework Decision of 22 December 2003 on combating the sexual exploitation of children and child pornography, Brussels 16 November 2007, COM (2007) 716 final, 6

[244] *Ibid*, 8.

C Racist and Xenophobic Content

(i) Introduction and Definitions

The most important criminal law provisions on racist content are set out in the Framework Decision on combating certain forms of racism and xenophobia, which came into force in December 2008 after a protracted drafting process that had lasted almost a decade.[245] Racist content has also been targeted inter alia in a joint action[246] and in a European Parliament legislative resolution.[247] The difficulties in reaching consensus on the Framework Decision were largely attributed to significant differences within Europe in relation to the criminalisation of speech[248] rather than scepticism about the ability of the criminal law to interfere with a pattern of inherent racism in society.[249] In the UK, where the freedom of speech is often assumed to be taken more seriously than in other European jurisdictions, one of the concerns was that the provisions of the proposed framework decision were 'excessively subjective and did not seem to require that the relevant conduct be carried out in a manner which was likely to incite others to violence or hatred or to be likely to disturb the peace'.[250] The UK has a long tradition of criminalising incitement to violence, but does not have a tradition of pure speech offences, such as defamation. This led to a compromise whereby the UK was willing to agree to provisions where there was only an obligation to criminalise conduct which constituted incitement to violence. Whereas denial of the holocaust is not in itself an offence, it would be considered an offence if it was 'done in a manner that was likely to incite race hatred or violence'.[251] The Member States may choose only to

[245] A proposal for a framework decision was published by the Commission in 2001: Proposal for a Council Framework Decision on combating racism and xenophobia, Brussels 28 November 2001, COM (2001) 664. See also the subsequent proposal: Proposal for a Council Framework Decision on combating racism and xenophobia, Brussels, 17 April 2007, 8544/07 DROIPEN 34. For comment, see JJ Garman, 'The European Union Combats Racism and Xenophobia by Forbidding Expression: An Analysis of the Framework Decision' (2008) 39 *University of Toledo Law Review* 843.

[246] Joint Action of 15 July 1996 adopted by the Council on the basis of Article K.3 of the Treaty on European Union, concerning action to combat racism and xenophobia (96/443/JHA) [1996] OJ L185/5.

[247] European Parliament legislative resolution on the proposal for a Council framework decision on combating racism and xenophobia (COM (2001) 664 - C5-0689/2001 - 2001/0270(CNS)).

[248] See eg the comments of Luxembourg's then justice minister: 'we have to take into account that Europe has different attitudes towards freedom of speech. Because of internal political discussions in some Member States, and in the absence of provisions regarding mutual legal assistance in the proposed framework decision, we could not find unanimous agreement . . .', Press Release of the Luxembourg Presidency of the Council of the European Union 2005, 'No agreement on the framework decision on combating racism and xenophobia at the Justice and Home Affairs Council', 2 June 2005.

[249] V Jenness, 'The Hate Crime Canon and Beyond: A Critical Assessment' (2001) 12 *Law and Critique* 279–308; L Ray and D Smith, 'Racist Offenders and the Politics of 'Hate Crime' (2001) 12 *Law and Critique* 203–21; LJ Moran, 'Affairs of the Heart: Hate Crime and the Politics of Crime Control' (2001) 12 *Law and Critique* 331–44.

[250] UK Select Committee on European Scrutiny Eleventh Report, 2003, 'Racism and Xenophobia', para 6.2.

[251] See the comments of the then UK Justice Minister, Oral evidence of 15 January 2003, Q. 3: 'Clearly the position, for example, in Germany on Holocaust denial is substantially different from the position

punish conduct which is either carried out in a manner 'likely to disturb public order or which is threatening, abusive or insulting'.[252]

It is questionable whether these provisions represent a departure from traditional reluctance to criminalise speech in the UK or whether they merely represent an expansion of existing incitement rules. The UK incitement provisions are undeniably broad in that there is no requirement that a third party is in fact influenced by the alleged incitement and the prosecution is not required to prove that accused actually intended to incite racial hatred. Even if the prosecution cannot prove that the accused 'intended to stir up racial hatred' they may still secure a prosecution if they can show that 'hatred was likely to be stirred up, not simply liable or possible'.[253]

Racism and xenophobia are not defined in the Framework Decision, which refers instead to hatred which 'should be understood as referring to hatred based on race, colour, religion, descent or national or ethnic origin'.[254] 'Descent' meanwhile is understood as relating 'mainly to persons or groups of persons who could be identified by certain characteristics (such as race or colour)'.[255]

(ii) Racist and Xenophobic Offences

(a) Publicly Inciting Violence or Hatred

Member States are required to ensure that publicly inciting violence or hatred directed against a group of persons or a member of such a group defined by reference to race, colour, religion, descent or national or ethnic origin is criminalised.[256] The offence must be punishable by a sentence of imprisonment of at least between one and three years.[257] The reference to religion 'is intended to cover, at least, conduct which is a pretext for directing acts against a group of persons or a member of such a group defined by reference to race, colour, descent, or national or ethnic origin'.[258] The Framework Decision also requires Member States to criminalise the 'aiding and abetting' in the commission of such conduct.[259] They must ensure that these offences are punishable by unspecified 'effective, proportionate and dissuasive criminal penalties'.[260]

as we are used to it. We may think that people are unwise or even mad to deny that there was a Holocaust but it is not a criminal offence by itself in Britain'.

[252] *Ibid*, Art 1(2); for a comparison of the Hate speech rules of the ECtHR and the US Supreme Court, see R Kiska, 'Hate Speech: A Comparison between the European Court of Human Rights and the United States Supreme Court Jurisprudence' (2012) 25 *Regent University Law Review* 107.

[253] See the CPS Guidance, 'Violent Extremism and Related Criminal Offences', available at www.cps.gov.uk/publications/prosecution/violent_extremism.html.

[254] Council Framework Decision 2008/913/JHA of 28 November 2008 on combating certain forms and expressions of racism and xenophobia by means of the criminal law [2008] OJ L328/55, Recital 9.

[255] *Ibid*, Recital 7.

[256] *Ibid*, Art 1(1)(a)

[257] *Ibid*, Art 3(2).

[258] *Ibid*, Art 1(3).

[259] *Ibid*, Art 2(2).

[260] *Ibid*, Art 3(1).

In 2006, Neil Martin was sentenced to two years and eight months' imprisonment following his conviction for posting highly offensive racists messages on a website set up to commemorate a teenager who had been murdered.[261]

(b) Publicly Inciting Violence or Hatred by Publicly Disseminating Materials

Publicly inciting violence or hatred directed against a group of persons or a member of such a group defined by reference to race, colour, religion, descent or national or ethnic origin by the public dissemination or distribution of tracts, pictures or other material is to be classed as a criminal offence.[262] The offence must be punishable by a sentence of imprisonment of at least between one and three years.[263] The Framework Decision also requires Member States to criminalise the 'aiding and abetting' in the commission of such conduct.[264]

(c) Publicly Condoning, Denying or Grossly Trivialising Crimes of Genocide, Crimes against Humanity and War Crimes

Publicly condoning, denying or grossly trivialising crimes of genocide, crimes against humanity and war crimes as defined in Articles 6, 7 and 8 of the Statute of the International Criminal Court, directed against a group of persons or a member of such a group defined by reference to race, colour, religion, descent or national or ethnic origin when the conduct is carried out in a manner likely to incite to violence or hatred against such a group or a member of such a group is to be classed as a criminal offence.[265] The offence must be punishable by a sentence of imprisonment of at least between one and three years.[266] The Member States must ensure that the 'instigating'[267] and the 'aiding and abetting' in the commission of such conduct is criminalised.[268] They must ensure that these offences are punishable by unspecified 'effective, proportionate and dissuasive criminal penalties'.[269] The Member States are entitled to restrict the punishment of denying or grossly trivialising these crimes if they have been 'established by a final decision of the national court of this Member State and/or an international court, or by a final decision of an international court only'.[270]

[261] CPS Guidance, 'Violent Extremism and Related Criminal Offences', at 7.

[262] Council Framework Decision 2008/913/JHA of 28 November 2008 on combating certain forms and expressions of racism and xenophobia by means of the criminal law [2008] OJ L328/55, Art 1(1)(b).

[263] *Ibid*, Art 3(2).

[264] *Ibid*, Art 2(2). They must ensure that these offences are punishable by unspecified 'effective, proportionate and dissuasive criminal penalties', *ibid*, Art 3(1).

[265] *Ibid*, Art 1(1)(c).

[266] *Ibid*, Art 3(2).

[267] *Ibid*, Art 2(1).

[268] *Ibid*, Art 2(2).

[269] *Ibid*, Art 3(1).

[270] *Ibid*, Art 1(4).

(d) Publicly Condoning, Denying or Grossly Trivialising the Crimes Defined in Article 6 of the Charter of the International Military Tribunal

Publicly condoning, denying or grossly trivialising the crimes defined in Article 6 of the Charter of the International Military Tribunal appended to the London Agreement of 8 August 1945, directed against a group of persons or a member of such a group defined by reference to race, colour, religion, descent or national or ethnic origin when the conduct is carried out in a manner likely to incite to violence or hatred against such a group or a member of such a group'.[271] The offence must be punishable by a sentence of imprisonment of at least between one and three years.[272] The Member States must ensure that the 'instigating'[273] of and the 'aiding and abetting' in the commission of such conduct is criminalised.[274] The Member States are entitled to restrict the punishment of denying or grossly trivialising these crimes to those offences which have been 'established by a final decision of the national court of the Member State and/or an international court, or by a final decision of an international court only'.[275]

(iii) Liability of ISPs

Each Member State must take 'the necessary measures' to ensure that legal persons can be held liable for the conduct referred to in Articles 1 and 2, 'committed for its benefit by any person, acting individually or as part of an organ of the legal person, who has a leading position within the legal person, based on: (a) a power of representation of the legal person; (b) an authority to take decisions on behalf of the legal person; or (c) an authority to exercise control within the legal person'.[276] A legal person is defined as: 'any entity having such status under the applicable national law, with the exception of States or other public bodies in the exercise of State authority and public international organisation'.[277] The Member States are required to ensure that a legal person in such as case is 'punishable by effective, proportionate and dissuasive penalties, which shall include criminal or non-criminal fines and many include other penalties, such as: (a) exclusion from entitlement to public benefits or aid; (b) temporary or permanent disqualification from the practice of commercial activities; (c) placing under judicial supervision; (d) a judicial winding-up order'.[278] In addition, Member States must ensure that in cases other than those provided for in paragraph 1 'a legal person can be held

[271] *Ibid*, Art 1(1)(d).
[272] *Ibid*, Art 3(2).
[273] *Ibid*, Art 2(1).
[274] *Ibid*, Art 2(2). They must ensure that these offences are punishable by unspecified 'effective, proportionate and dissuasive criminal penalties', *ibid*, Art 3(1).
[275] *Ibid*, Art 1(4).
[276] *Ibid*, Art 5(1).
[277] *Ibid*, Art 5(3).
[278] *Ibid*, Art 6(1).

liable where the lack of supervision or control by a person referred to in paragraph 1 . . . has made possible the commission of the conduct referred to in Articles 1 and 2 for the benefit of that legal person by a person under its authority'.[279]

ISPs are as a general rule not liable for transmission or short storage of a third-party's illegal content. In Germany, for instance, liability will only arise if they 'initiate, select or modify the information'.[280] Host providers, who store content for longer, will only be subject to liability if they are aware of the illegal content and fail to take appropriate and prompt action.[281] In most cases they will deal with such content by blocking access to, or by removing, the information, despite the lack of specific provisions requiring this. In October 2012, for instance Twitter blocked access to a neo-Nazi account after the request of the German government, thereby activating for the first time its local censorship policy, which allows it to block content in specific countries if tweets violate local laws. The tweets, while no longer visible to users in Germany, could be viewed by users in the rest of the world.[282]

(iv) Jurisdiction

Each Member State is obliged to take action against offences committed wholly or partly within its territory.[283] A Member State may, but is not obliged to, take action if the offence is committed by one of its nationals or for the benefit of a legal person that has its head office in that territory.[284] In the context of offences committed 'through an information system', each Member State must ensure that its jurisdiction extends to cases in which the offender commits the conduct when physically present in its territory, even though the content is hosted in another country, or where the content is hosted on an information system in its country, irrespective of whether or not the offender is physically present in the country at the time.[285] The law of England and Wales, for instance, applies to content published online, even if it is hosted in another country as long as a substantial measure of activities take place in England and Wales.[286]

[279] *Ibid*, Art 5(2). Such offences must be punishable by unspecified 'effective, proportionate or dissuasive penalties' *ibid*, Art 6(2).

[280] MDTtV, § 7 Abs 1 and § 8; see further YA Timofeeva, 'Hate Speech Online: Restricted or Protected? Comparisons of Regulations in the United States and Germany' (2003) 12 *Journal of Transnational Law and Policy* 262.

[281] Directive on Electronic Commerce [2000] OJ L178/1.

[282] BBC online, 'Twitter Blocks Neo-Nazi Account to Users in Germany', 18 October 2012, available at www.bbc.co.uk/news/technology-19988662.

[283] Council Framework Decision 2008/913/JHA of 28 November 2008 on combating certain forms and expressions of racism and xenophobia by means of the criminal law [2008] OJ L328/55, Art 9(1).

[284] *Ibid*, Art 9(1) in conjunction with Art 9(3).

[285] *Ibid*, Art 9(2) in conjunction with Art 9(1)(a).

[286] See eg the case of *R v Sheppard and Whittle* [2010] EWCA Crim 65 (material prepared and uploaded in England and Wales), M Taylor, 'British Extremists who Fled to US jailed for Inciting Racial Hatred Online', *The Guardian*, 10 July 2009.

Jurisdiction in respect of commercial activity is restricted by the country of origin principle in the E-Commerce Directive. The Member States are entitled, in accordance with the Audiovisual Media Services Directive, to provisionally derogate from the country of origin principle if a 'television broadcast coming from another Member State manifestly, seriously and gravely infringes' Article 6 of the Directive.[287] According to Article 6, the Member States 'shall ensure by appropriate means that audiovisual media services provided by media service providers under their jurisdiction do not contain any incitement to hatred based on race, sex, religion or nationality'.[288]

(v) Implementation in the Member States

The Commission has not yet published its implementation report on the application of the Framework Decision, but it referred to some unofficial, preliminary findings at the Fundamental Rights Conference in Vilnius.[289] It noted that while almost all Member States had criminal laws which prohibited the conduct in Article 1(a), the terminology used and the criteria applied differed significantly. In addition, it noted that several Member States did not have provisions which criminalised condoning, denying or grossly trivialising the crimes set out in Articles 6, 7 and 8 of the Statute of the International Criminal Court. Further, a large number of Member States did not have criminal laws prohibiting the condoning, denial or gross trivialisation of 'Nazi crimes'. Compliance with the provisions on jurisdiction in the context of information society systems was also poor and only one Member State had fully transposed the jurisdictional rules into its legislation. These provisional findings demonstrate that the Member States have not shown much enthusiasm towards implementing these provisions. In view of the protracted drafting process and considerable differences in the Member States,[290] this is perhaps unsurprising. There can be little doubt that harmonisation of the criminal law in this area is a long way off.

V Conclusions

This overview of the EU's criminal law regulation of content highlights various issues which are common to all three instruments. First, although freedom of speech is repeatedly referred to as an important constitutional principle, it appears

[287] Audiovisual Media Services Directive [2010] OJ L95/1, Art 3(2)(a).

[288] *Ibid*, Art 6.

[289] European Commission, Justice, EU Framework Decision on racism and xenophobia, Articles 3 and 6 of the Audiovisual Media Services Directive, Fundamental Rights Conference, Vilnius, 12–13 November 2013.

[290] See the reports of the European Commission against Racism and Intolerance of the Council of Europe, available at www.coe.int/t/dghl/monitoring/ecri/library/publications.asp.

to have little impact as a restraint on the legislative provisions as the speech subject to regulation is essentially seen as not worthy of protection. This is unfortunate, not least because the potential for criminalisation under the provisions is considerable. Second, censorship of the Internet through the imposition of restrictive obligations on ISPs to monitor content has largely been avoided, although restrictive industry self-regulation has the potential to have a chilling effect. The requirement that ISPs monitor content was rejected by providers themselves as unduly restrictive and by the Commission on the basis that it constituted an obstacle to the proper functioning of the free market. Third, the rules established on jurisdiction give Member States broad scope to initiate prosecutions in the context of Internet crime. Fourth, although only one of the instruments makes express provision for the blocking of content, such procedures are used by ISPs in all spheres of illegal content. This is potentially problematic in that ISPs may be inclined to go further than would be required by law in labelling content illegal.[291] Finally, although the EU has relied on the Internet to justify its role in developing these provisions, these provisions are broad in scope and it is important that there is proper examination of the need for EU criminal law regulation.

The Commission has outlined in detail its desire to regulate content and has made much of the importance of doing so in the digital age. In spite of this it is clear that considerable differences between the Member States remain, particularly in the context of the interpretation of fundamental rights. In view of this it is unsurprising that the implementation of the provisions that require the Member States to regulate content has not been successfully achieved in all of the areas regulated. While the Member States have faithfully implemented some of the provisions, notably those concerning the sexual abuse and exploitation of children, they have failed to implement many of the others. A true assessment of the implementation of the provisions is difficult to establish, however, from the Commission's reports. The Commission appears to adopt a relatively formalistic approach to the evaluation of implementation which is not inclined to look beyond the text of the provisions implemented to consider the true nature of implementation in practice.

Divergence in implementation obviously has the potential to significantly derail attempts to harmonise the criminal law. In the context of the third pillar legislation, the Commission's activities were hampered by its limited options for dealing with Member State's failure to implement or correctly implement the provisions. It is possible that the broader role afforded to the Court of Justice of the European Union (CJEU) to interpret legislation falling within Article 83(1) TEFU could improve compliance with the legislation adopted for the purposes of setting out minimum standards in the context of the criminal law. At the same time, however, the fact that some Member States are entitled to opt out of the

[291] See on this point DE Bambauer, 'Orwell's Armchair' (2012) 79 *University of Chicago Law Review* 863 who suggests that America has begun to censor the Internet through 'soft blocking' of online material.

legislation stemming from the third pillar and that some, such as the UK, have already intimated their intention not to opt back in to legislation on matters such as terrorism and racism, means that questions remain as to the potential for harmonisation of the criminal law in the context of serious cross-border criminality.

6

Criminal Law and the Safeguarding of Privacy

Privacy is something you can sell but you can't buy it back.*

I Introduction

A Information Technology and Privacy

The Internet is simultaneously the largest repository of information, the largest market place, and the most potent means of communication that has ever existed. Users can benefit from almost limitless possibilities to instantaneously interact with other users, and transact with merchants across the globe. However, the size of the market creates intense competition between suppliers, each with the imperative of identifying and informing potential consumers in the online environment. In this atmosphere, personal information of Internet users becomes a hugely valuable commodity for companies and corporations seeking to inform and maximise the effectiveness of their marketing approaches.

The online social networking site 'Facebook' exemplifies these challenges. Founded in 2004, Facebook is one of the most frequently visited websites on earth, allowing users to develop profiles and connect with each other across the globe. Yet Facebook's success as a business lies in the fact that it now holds the personal information of over one billion users.[1] Facebook makes money by selling advertisements targeted through the information users share.[2] While there is no subscription or membership fee levied to gain access to this social system, dues

* Bob Dylan, *Chronicles, Volume One* (New York, Simon & Shuster, 2004) 118.

[1] www.businessweek.com/articles/2012-10-04/facebook-the-making-of-1-billion-users.

[2] 'The vast majority (of facebook revenue) comes from advertising – responsible for 82 percent of revenue in the first quarter of 2012. The company appeals to advertisers with its reach, but even more important, the fact that it can target ads with "relevance," based on all the personal information users decide to share. Perhaps more interesting, Facebook can target ads with "social context" – which means highlighting users' friends connections with a brand or business. And people are much more likely to respond favorably to a message if they know a friend has endorsed the brand or just "checked in" at a store', see www.cnbc.com/id/47450450/Inside_Facebookrsquos_Money_Machine.

are paid in the valuable currency of personal information. As one journalist put it: 'The dirty secret of the Web is that the "free" content and services that consumers enjoy come with a hidden price: their own private data'.[3]

The combination of these vast interlinked potentialities of the Internet – communication, markets and information – offers profound and often insidious challenges to the right to privacy. Effective participation in this digital world demands the sacrifice of personal information, whether engaging in online social networks such as Facebook, making online purchases, or conducting online banking. Increasingly, such sacrifice goes unnoticed: 'This is an age which happily invades its own privacy'.[4] What is at stake is the right of the user, the individual, to 'selective disclosure'.[5] The key question becomes under what conditions the disclosure of information is made. What happens to the information once disclosed? With whom is it shared? In each case, the individual's privacy becomes a currency of exchange that he or she consents to give away in exchange for certain gains, whether social, economic or in terms of efficiency. However, at some point, the privacy cost of participation comes to outweigh the value of the gain.[6]

In normal life, these elements – the market, communications and personal privacy – are regulated tightly. In the online world, a form of anarchy is the modus operandi. This is the constant paradox of the Internet. While its key virtue is essentially anarchic (unregulated communication and free, often anonymous expression), it simultaneously depends for its usefulness upon the protection of some element of user privacy. Privacy is finely balanced with free expression. If the balance tips too far in either direction, whether due to intervention or lack thereof, this can disincentivise participation in the digital world. This in turn can affect the diversity of speech and behaviour, as well as the functioning of the e-commerce market. These are the balances along which regulatory regimes, whether domestic or supra-national, must function.

B The EU and Privacy

In the EU the broad right of an individual to privacy is included in Article 7 of the Charter of Fundamental Rights of the European Union, which states that '[e]veryone has the right to respect for his or her private and family life, home and communications'. More specifically, the right to protection of personal data is found in Article 8 of the Charter, which states:

1. Everyone has the right to the protection of personal data concerning him or her.
2. Such data must be processed fairly for specified purposes and on the basis of the consent of the person concerned or some other legitimate basis laid down by law.

[3] http://online.wsj.com/article/SB10001424052970204190704577024262567105738.html.

[4] C Nevin, 'Surveillance Over Europe' (Summer 2009) *Economist Intelligent Life Magazine*.

[5] J Van Dijk, *The Network Society*, 2nd edn (London, Sage, 2006) 114.

[6] A McStay, 'I Consent: An Analysis of the Cookie Directive and its Implications for UK Behavioural Advertising' (2012) 15 *New Media and Society* 596, 599.

> Everyone has the right of access to data which has been collected concerning him or her, and the right to have it rectified.

Article 16 TFEU reasserts the right to protection of personal data, and further specifies that the European Parliament and the Council of Europe shall be responsible for developing rules to ensure the protection of this right in relation to the processing of personal data by Union institutions.[7] The Court of Justice is clear that this right to protection of data is not absolute. Limitations may be imposed as long as provided by law, respecting the essence of the right, proportional, necessary, and in pursuit of an interest recognised by the EU or to protect the rights of others.[8]

It is important to note that within the context of the EU, the traditional focus, particularly in the context of the former first pillar, is upon safeguarding the functioning of the market.[9] Privacy, and its linked element security, are important elements in ensuring consumer confidence and protection, which in turn are important for this efficient functioning of the market. The effect of privacy problems from a market perspective is to affect the optimal flow of information, thereby increasing economic costs and hindering the system's capability to ensure maximum benefits.[10] As such, the development of privacy regulation in the EU can be said to have as its core logic the promotion of market interests which are the foundation of the EU, such as effective competition, encouraging technological innovation, market development and ensuring consumer protection.[11] In this context the criminal law can be viewed not as primarily concerned with the public interest (as is conventional for domestic legal systems), but instead as a safeguard for treaty objectives through the prescribing of acts harmful to these market-based objectives.

II Key Issues for Privacy in the Information Age

This chapter will look at three different privacy issues of the information age that the EU has, to varying extents, sought to address: cookies, cyberstalking, and

[7] Art 16(2) TFEU states: 'The European Parliament and the Council, acting in accordance with the ordinary legislative procedure, shall lay down the rules relating to the protection of individuals with regard to the processing of personal data by Union institutions, bodies, offices and agencies, and by the Member States when carrying out activities which fall within the scope of Union law, and the rules relating to the free movement of such data. Compliance with these rules shall be subject to the control of independent authorities'.

[8] Joined Cases C-92/09 and C-93/09 Volker und Markus Schecke and Eifert [2010] ECR I-11063.

[9] See further ch 3.

[10] PA Norberg, DA Horne and D Horne, 'Standing in the Footprint: Including the Self in the Privacy Debate and Policy Development' (2009) 43 *Journal of Consumer Affairs* 495, 495–515.

[11] Communication from the Commission to the Council, the European Parliament, the Economic and Social Committee and the Committee of the Regions, Towards a new framework for Electronic Communications infrastructure and associated services – The 1999 Communications Review, Brussels, 10 November 1999, COM (1999) 539 final.

spam. For each, we will outline the issue, and then assess how the EU has responded. Spam, a phenomenon the EU has been particularly active in combating, will be used as a case study, allowing examination of Member State implementation of EU measures in that area, and assessment of the extent and effectiveness of the EU's criminal law approach in pursuit of this policy objective.

A Cookies

(i) Introduction

The collection and processing of personal information on the Internet takes place in a wide variety of ways. Some are clearly nefarious and criminal in intention – bugs, spyware, and hidden identifiers, for example, are utilised without the consent of the user and have potentially deleterious effects on personal privacy. However, there are some methods and means of collecting information that are more ambiguous in both intention and effect. An everyday aspect of online life, 'cookies', in some way exemplify the challenges presented by the Internet overall. Their usefulness to the user is laced with a threat to privacy.

Cookies are small pieces of computer code left by a website on the visitor's computer. These small pieces of code are sent from a web server, stored on the computer, and allow the server to later recognise the computer. Unlike the aforementioned bugs or spyware, they can serve as extremely useful tools for both users and website operators. They are used for session management, personalisation and tracking. They allow the website to remember the user and orient the webpage to his needs. They increase efficiency by removing the need for constant and repetitive reauthentication, and also orient the website according to a user's preferences.[12] In essence, cookies provide the Internet with a memory.[13]

However, this 'memory' also presents a risk. The information cookies collect – user names, email addresses, passwords, personal information and preferences, search records[14] – can be used to create a market profile of the user, which can then be sold for commercial purposes without the user's knowledge or consent. They are part of a greater tendency towards behavioural advertising, which tracks users activities online for the purposes of serving advertising tailored to what appears to be the user's interests.[15]

While this is not malicious in the same way as malware, it nonetheless represents a violation of the user's privacy, which they were not aware of and did not consent to. The extent of a cookie's threat is dependent on the sensitivity of the information it holds, and whether this information is distributed to third

[12] A Savin, *EU Internet Law* (Cheltenham, Edward Elgar Publishing, 2013) 214.

[13] Article 29 Data Protection Working Party, Opinion 04/2012 on Cookie Consent Exemption, Adopted on 7 June 2012, 4.

[14] D Garrie, M Armstrong and A Blakley, 'Voice over Internet Protocol: Reality v. Legal Fiction' (2005) 52 *Fed Law* 34, 38.

[15] McStay, 'I Consent' (n 6) 597.

parties.[16] The decision as to what information the cookie gathers, and whether it is distributed, lies in the hands of the cookie issuer, not the user. In fact, the user is not able to influence the content at all,[17] but can normally only choose, via his or her Internet browser, which cookies to block. This is a more complex task than it seems, because it is sometimes hard to tell exactly what information is being stored. Often a lack of information about cookies and how to reject them, results in inaction on the part of the user, and the collection of personal information as a result. This inaction cannot be said to be genuine consent to the loss of privacy, but is rather akin to enforced agreement. Consent can't merely be passive, but must be actively 'given'.[18]

(ii) Different Types of Cookies

There are four basic categories of cookies.[19] 'Session cookies' are those which store information only for the duration of the user's session. Once the web browser is closed, they are erased. In contrast, a 'persistent cookie' remains stored in the user's hard drive even after the session is finished. They endure until a final expiry date is reached, which could be as little as a few minutes, or as far as years, away. 'Persistent cookies' are normally used to collect user identifying information, such as website preferences. A further differentiation is made between 'first-party cookies', which belong to the site where the user chose to visit, and 'third party cookies', which emanate from sources external to the site, and show content that is retrieved indirectly. In general, the lifespan of persistent cookies, and the external nature of third party cookie, make them greater threats to privacy than first person session cookies.

(iii) EU Regulation of Cookies

As we have seen, cookies can serve an important function in e-commerce. However, early drafts of the Directive on Privacy and Electronic Communications proposed a ban on cookies without consent. There was a fear that customer data was being collected without knowledge, and that this threat to consumer privacy 'would ultimately undermine consumers' confidence in electronic commerce and

[16] Savin, *EU Internet Law* (n 12) 214.

[17] J Merati-Kashani, *Der Datenschutz im E-Commerce – Die rechtliche Bewertung der Erstellung von Nutzerprofilen durch Cookies* (Munich, Beck, 2005) 154.

[18] Article 29 Data Protection Working Party, Opinion 04/2012 on Cookie Consent Exemption, Adopted on 7 June 2012, 8.

[19] Examples within these four categories include: (1) user input cookies (eg session-id, used for the duration of a session or persistent cookies limited to a few hours in some cases; (2) authentication cookies, used for authenticated services, for the duration of a session; (3) user centric security cookies, used to detect authentication abuses, for a limited persistent duration; (4) multimedia content player session cookies, such as flash player cookies, for the duration of a session; (5) load balancing session cookies, for the duration of session; (6) third party social plug-in content sharing cookies, for logged in members of a social network.

seriously damage the prospect of it being at the forefront of development in the EU'.[20] A Parliamentary amendment proposed that the use of devices to store information or to gain access to information stored in the terminal equipment of a subscriber (such as cookies) 'may seriously intrude the privacy of these users. The use of such devices should therefore be prohibited unless the explicit, well-informed and freely given consent of the user concerned has been obtained'.[21] If successful, this would have signalled the adoption of a strong so-called 'opt-in' system, despite the fact that most sites depend on cookies for basic functionality.

However, this approach was subject to considerable lobbying from the Interactive Advertising Bureau Europe,[22] and a less stringent approach was eventually adopted. The final version introduced a more flexible 'opt-out' regime.[23]

According to Article 5(3) of the Directive on Privacy and Electronic Communications:

> Member States shall ensure that the use of electronic communications networks to store information or to gain access to information stored in the terminal equipment of a subscriber or user is only allowed on condition that the subscriber or user concerned is provided with clear and comprehensive information in accordance with Directive 95/46/EC, inter alia about the purposes of the processing, and is offered the right to refuse such processing by the data controller.[24]

It goes on to specify two exemptions. First, that this provision shall not 'prevent any technical storage or access for the sole purpose of carrying out or facilitating the transmission of a communication over an electronic communications network'. Second, it shall not affect the situation where the cookie is 'strictly necessary in order to provide an information society service explicitly requested by the subscriber or user'.

The 2009 revision of the Directive adjusts Article 5(3), affecting information collected from users' computers, including cookies:

> Member states shall ensure that the storing of information, or the gaining of access to information already stored, in the terminal equipment of a subscriber or user is only allowed on condition that the subscriber or user concerned has given his or her consent, having been provided with clear and comprehensive information, in according with Directive 95/46/EC, inter alia, about the purposes of the processing.

[20] Savin, *EU Internet Law* (n 12) 214.

[21] European Parliament, Report on the proposal for a European Parliament and Council Directive concerning the processing of personal data and the protection of privacy in the electronic communications sector, Brussels, 13 June 2001, COM (2000) 385, A5-0270/2001.

[22] For an informative overview of the influence of the lobbyists on the creation of the Directive, see S Mercado-Kierkegaard, 'Taking a Sledgehammer to Crack the Nut: The EU Enforcement Directive' (2005) 21 *Computer Law & Security Review* 488.

[23] L Edwards, 'Articles 6–7, ECD. Privacy and Communications Directive 2002' in L Edwards (ed), *The New Legal Framework for E-Commerce in Europe* (London, Hart, 2005) 31.

[24] Directive 2002/58/EC of the European Parliament and of the Council of 12 July 2002 concerning the processing of personal data and the protection of privacy in the electronic communications sector [2002] OJ L 201/37, Art 5(3).

This adjustment changes the EU approach to cookies, from an opt-out system in the original 2002 Directive, to a more stringent opt-in system. Basically, the user must give consent to the use of cookies,[25] and must be furnished with full information.

(iv) Uncertainties in EU Regulation

The EU's approach, while clearly stricter and more cognisant of the privacy threat represented by cookies, presents some problems in application.[26] Most users deal with cookies through the use of web browser settings. Cookies allowed through user browser settings will constitute consent. Recital 66 states that 'where it is technically possible and effective . . . the user's consent to processing may be expressed by using the appropriate settings of a browser or other application'. Another question left ambiguous under Article 5(3) concerns the frequency of consent. Often cookies are most useful to users on sites often frequented. Must the user 'opt-in' on each individual site visit? Recital 25 acknowledges the importance of cookies for legitimate users, and provides clarification on this issue, stating that 'information and the right to refuse may be offered once', but may cover 'any future use that may be made of those devices during subsequent connections'. In real terms, this means that the opportunity to opt-in should be presented on the first occasion a user visits a web page. Once consent has been given (the user has 'opted in') permission may not be sought for future visits. In addition, a website using several cookies for different purposes will only require consent once as long as information presented on the cookies is clear and comprehensive.

There are two exceptions to this though. First, if the cookie is used 'for the sole purpose of carrying out the transmission of a communication over an electronic communications network'. Second, if the cookie is 'strictly necessary in order for the provider of an information society service explicitly requested by the subscriber or user to provide the service'. It is the purpose and the specific implementation or processing being achieved that is relevant for determining whether or not a cookie can be exempted from consent according to Article 5(3).

We can see from the second criterion that the scope of cookies exempt from requiring consent is intended to be highly limited. Two tests must be met: First, the information society service or functionality has been explicitly requested by the user (requires a positive action by the user), and second, the cookie is strictly needed to enable the information society service or functionality (without the

[25] A Thürauf, 'Cookie Opt-in in Grossbritannien – Zukunft der Cookies?' (2012) 1 *Zeitschrift für Datenschutz* 24.

[26] A further 2012 directive on the protection of individuals with regard to the processing of person data was proposed on 25th January 2012: Proposal for a Directive of the European Paliament and of the Council on the protection of individuals with regard to the processing of personal data by competent authorities for the purposes of prevention, investigation, detection or prosecution of criminal offences or the execution of criminal penalties, and the free movement of such data, Brussels, 25 January 2012, COM (2012) 10 final.

cookie, the service will not work). This judgement of what is strictly necessary is made from the perspective of the user, not the service provider. This link between the necessity of the cookie and the delivery of a service requested by the user is backed up by Recital 66 of Directive 2009/136/EC.[27]

What general conclusions can be drawn about the repercussions of these exemptions for common forms of cookies? It is hard to envisage a situation where a third party cookie would ever be considered strictly necessary, as they normally offer services entirely devolved from that requested by the user. Also, session cookies are more likely to be exempt than persistent cookies, as it is less likely a user's request will extend beyond the end of a session. 'User-input' cookies, for example, for shopping across a number of pages within one site, will generally be exempt. As will authentication cookies, like those used in banking websites across multiple pages after logging in. However, this will only apply to session cookies, and not those that persist across multiple browser sessions. Security cookies, for example, those that detect repeated failed login attempts, will be exempt. User interface customisation cookies, like those that store a language preference for a website, will also be exempt. However, third party cookies for the purpose of behavioural advertising will require consent.

(v) Implementation and Effectiveness

Member States were obliged to implement the 2009 revision to the 2002 Directive by 25 May 2011.[28] As of September 2012, 14 of 16 countries surveyed had fully implemented the updated Directive.[29] Germany and Poland had not fully implemented, though laws had been drafted and were awaiting ratification. Examples of full implementation include France, where the Directive was transposed into law by an ordinance of 24 August 2011. Article 32 II of the French Data Protection Act now creates an 'opt-in' system for cookies. In the UK, Article 6 of the Privacy and Electronic Communications Regulations 2003 was updated in 2011.[30] The new provision allows the Information Commissioner to hand out civil monetary penalties of up to 500,000 GBP[31] – a significant amount. In reality, however, the

[27] 'Exceptions to the obligation to provide information and offer the right to refuse should be limited to those situations where the technical storage or access is strictly necessary for the legitimate purpose of enabling the use of a specific service explicitly requested by the subscriber or user'.

[28] Directive 2009/136/EC of the European Parliament and of the Council of 25 November 2009 amending Directive 2002/22/EC on universal service and users' rights relating to electronic communications networks and services, Directive 2002/58/EC concerning the processing of personal data and the protection of privacy in the electronic communications sector and Regulation (EC) No 2006/2004 on cooperation between national authorities responsible for the enforcement of consumer protection laws [2009] OJ L337/11, Art 4(1).

[29] Briefing Note by Bird & Bird Law Firm, 'Implementation of the E-Privacy Directive Across Europe (as of March 2013)', Navailable at www.twobirds.com/~/media/PDFs/BB%20Cookie%20Table%20 21-03-13_FINAL.pdf.

[30] See Art 6 of the Privacy and Electronic Communications (EC Directive) (Amendment) Regulations 2011.

[31] *Ibid*, Art 11.

risk of actual penalty or prosecution is considered low.[32] This reality perhaps reflects the general norm across the EU.

This probably shows that regulation is not the most potent method of addressing privacy concerns with cookies. While a regulation such as Directive 2009/136/EC can be left open to future technological advances through non-use of technology specific terms, laws are frequently left behind, obsolete in view of technological developments. The best means for maintaining online privacy still comes from the inherently reflexive nature of technology itself. As new threats develop, technology emerges to combat it. In reality, the issue of cookies is currently addressed through the approaches of browser privacy settings. This allows a user to maintain control over privacy while not being burdened with reading security certificates site-by site. This approach balances privacy with efficiency, and while not optimal, it seems a compromise between the interests of the user and the webpage operator.

B Cyberstalking

(i) Introduction

While cookies and spam are generally produced for economic gain of the issuer, cyberstalking is an example of how rapidly technological advancement, and the gathering of information it facilitates, can be co-opted for the wholly nefarious purposes of harassment.

Conventional stalking has been described as 'a course of conduct in which one individual inflicts on another repeated unwanted intrusions and communication, to such an extent that the victim fears for his or her safety'.[33] The possible reasons for this behaviour are many, including jealousy, obsession and the desire to control. 'Cyberstalking' is essentially stalking that utilises new technologies, including email, internet and other communications services. It has been defined as 'the repetitive harassment or threat of an individual through the Internet or other electronic means of communication'.[34] Like conventional stalking, it is normally characterised by a lack of physical violence, but substantial psychological impact. There are generally four categories of cyberstalking: (1) communicating with the victim; (2) publishing information about the victim; (3) targeting the victim's computer; and (4) placing the victim under surveillance. As such, a wide scope of acts can be considered cyberstalking. It could be as simple as gathering information from someone's publicly available Facebook page, or as extreme as the employment of complex spyware or malware to collect information on an individual from a digital

[32] J Hayes, 'Cookie Law: A Hostage to Fortune?' (September 2012) *Engineering & Technology* 67.

[33] R Purcell, M Pathe and PE Mullen, 'Stalking: Defining and Prosecuting a New Category of Offending' (2004) 27 *International Journal of law and Psychiatry* 157, 157.

[34] P Bocij, 'Victims of Cyberstalking: An Exploratory Study of Harassment Perpetrated via the Internet' (2003) *First Monday* 8, 10, available at: www.firstmonday.org.

device. It is linked with the issues of cyberbullying or cyber-smearing, which can be particularly serious, as the posting or distribution of false information online has a huge potential audience, and can remain accessible for a long time.

Conventional stalking can have serious effect on the victim. This has been the subject of a number of studies, which indicate that victims can suffer effects including changes in personality, insomnia, and even symptoms of post-traumatic stress disorder.[35] An estimated 30 per cent of female victims and 20 per cent of males sought counselling, while 7 per cent never return to work as a result of stalking.[36] However, these figures apply to stalking, not cyberstalking, for which no figure are available. Similarly, and in common with many cybercrimes, cyberstalking suffers from a difficulty in assessing the extent and impact of the problem.[37] Estimates on the prevalence of cyberstalking vary so much as to be useless.[38] What is certain is that the online environment is well suited for stalking behaviour. It offers anonymity to the stalker, which is conducive to a loss of normal restraint amid a lack of personal accountability. The Internet offers a direct line of impersonal communication, that the stalker can use to contact and harass the victim. This harassment is possible without personal contact and with substantially reduced risk of detection and punishment. Finally, the Internet offers access to a wealth of personal information and the technology to gather it. As in all aspects of the Internet, knowledge is power. The more personal information the stalker gathers, the more power over the victim he or she has.

(ii) Regulation of Cyberstalking

Cyberstalking is challenging from a regulatory perspective, as it can encompass a variety of diverse behaviours, some of which, are not criminal. As such, in general, in most jurisdictions, cyberstalking is prosecuted as a subset of stalking more generally. This is reflected in how stalking is dealt with in widely divergent manners across Europe.[39] Differences in terminology are rife, while only 8 of 25 European

[35] For example: E Blaauw, L Sheridan and FW Winkel, 'Designing Anti-stalking Legislation on the Basis of Victims' Experiences and Psychopathology' (2002) 9 *Psychiatry, Psychology and Law* 136–145.

[36] P Tjaden and N Thoennes, 'Stalking in America: Findings from the National Violence Against Women Survey', *National Institute of Justice and Centers for Disease Control and Prevention Research in Brief* (1998).

[37] The committee that drafted the Council of Europe Convention on Cybercrime contends that one of the major challenges in combating cybercrime is assessing the extent and impact of the criminal act (Council of Europe, Explanatory Report, CETS No 185, Convention on Cybercrime, Consideration 133).

[38] They range from 474,000 to 18.75 million annual cyberstalking victims across the world. P Bocij, 'Victims of Cyberstalking'(n 34) 47.

[39] Modena Group on Stalking, 'Protecting Women from the New Crime of Stalking: A Comparison of Legislative Approaches Within the European Union. Final report' (2007) *University of Modena and Reggio Emilia for the European Commission* 79.

countries surveyed specifically legislate against stalking.[40] Even where legislation exists, the scope of criminalisation differs between countries, particularly in relation to the required mental state for the crime, the relevance of the reaction of the victim, prescribed penalties, and whether a single act can constitute stalking. These seem to stem from differences in beliefs in why stalking should be punishable; anglo-saxon countries focus on the fear caused, whereas continental countries emphasise the importance of privacy.[41]

(iii) The Approach of the EU

The EU does not regulate cyberstalking specifically, but partial aspects can fall within certain regulations of the EU. Directive 2002/58/EC is focused on e-privacy more generally, but encompasses certain acts which can be a feature of cyberstalking. Recital 24 highlights that the equipment of users of electronic communications networks forms part of their private sphere that requires protection under the European Convention on Human Rights (ECHR). As such, the use of spyware, web-bugs, hidden identifiers, which can access, gain information and trace activities of the user, can only be used 'for legitimate purposes, with the knowledge of the users concerned'.[42]

Article 5 specifies that Member States must prohibit unauthorised 'listening, tapping, storage or other kinds of interception or surveillance of communications'.[43] The use of electronic communications networks to store information or gain access to information stored on equipment of a subscriber is only allowed 'on condition that the subscriber or user concerned is provided with clear and comprehensive information in accordance with Directive 95/46/EC, inter alia about the purposes of the processing, and is offered the right to refuse such processing by the data controller'.[44] Directive 95/46/EC is concerned with data protection. Article 7(a) of this Directive ensures that Member States shall 'provide that personal data may be processed only if the data subject has unambiguously given his consent'.[45] Article 24 obligates Member States to adopt suitable

[40] Actually, with the more recent Italian, Czech, Hungarian and Luxembourg criminalisation there are now 12 countries that have enacted specific anti-stalking legislation.

[41] S 107a Austrian Penal Code ('Beharrliche Verfolgung'); Art 460ter Belgian Penal Code ('belaging'); S 264 Danish Penal Code ('forfølgelse'); Para 238 German Penal Code ('beharrlicher Nachstellungen'); S 10(1) Non-Fatal Offences against the Person Act 1997 (Ireland); Art 251a and 251b Maltese Penal Code ('fastidju'); Art 285b Dutch Penal Code ('belaging'); and the Protection from Harassment Act 1997 (UK).

[42] Directive 2002/58/EC of the European Parliament and of the Council of 12 July 2002 concerning the processing of personal data and the protection of privacy in the electronic communications sector [2002] OJ L201/37, Recital 24.

[43] *Ibid*, Art 5(1).

[44] *Ibid*, Art 5(3).

[45] Directive 95/46/EC of the European Parliament and of the Council of 24 October 1995 on the protection of individuals with regard to the processing of personal data and on the free movement of such data [1995] OJ L281/31, Art 7(a).

measures to ensure full implementation, and 'shall in particular lay down the sanctions to be imposed in case of infringement'.[46]

Notwithstanding the above, there seems little prospect of specific legislation on cyberstalking at the EU level. Attempts have been made to encourage the EU in this direction. In response to a letter in from a member of the European Parliament on the issue, the Commission acknowledged the importance of the crime, but referred to current, non-specific aspects of existing legislation as a suitable response.[47] This seems likely to be the approach for the foreseeable future, and perhaps reflect the fact that cyber stalking has very little nexus to economic interests the EU prioritises.

C Spam

(i) Introduction

Spam is a ubiquitous feature of the modern online environment, described as 'the scourge of email inboxes, plying cheap drugs, septic tanks, new mortgages and bigger manhoods'.[48] The term is one commonly applied and understood, yet without precise definition or legal meaning.[49] Generally, it is used to describe unsolicited, unwanted, bulk emails.[50] 'Unsolicited Commercial Email' (UCE) is sometimes used for more precision, while 'Unsolicited Bulk Material' also encompasses spam not distributed via email, such as posts in website comment feeds. Overall, spam messages are normally commercial but of 'the lowest social utility,'[51] advertising goods and services such as pornography, get rich quick pyramid schemes, and dating websites. However, unsolicited email messages may also carry malicious software and spyware,[52] dubbed by some as 'aggravated spam'.[53] In truth, for most users, the actual content of the irritant mail will be of little relevance; as one website put it: 'If it's sent unsolicited and in bulk, it is spam plain and simple'.[54]

In 2003, a Silicon Valley tech worker Charles Booher threatened to shoot, torture, and send anthrax spores to a company who had spammed his computer.[55]

[46] *Ibid*, Art 24.

[47] European Parliament, Parliamentary Questions, 19 November 2012, available at www.europarl.europa.eu/sides/getAllAnswers.do?reference=E-2012-008581&language=EN.

[48] 'Winning the War on Spam', *The Economist*, 20 August 2005, 46.

[49] The term itself is actually a colloquialism with obscure roots in a British television comedy sketch of the 1970s: 'Spamalot' by Monty Python.

[50] Communication from the Commission on unsolicited commercial communications or 'spam', Brussels, 22 January 2004, COM (2004) 28 final, 4.

[51] PJ Kozyris, 'General Report' in PJ Kozyris (ed), *Regulating Internet Abuses: Invasion of Privacy* (Alphen aan den Rijn, Kluwer Law International, 2007) 3.

[52] Communication from the Commission on Fighting spam, spyware and malicious software, Brussels, 15 November 2006, COM (2006) 688 final, 3 n 4.

[53] Kozyris, 'General Report' (n 51) 4.

[54] www.spamhaus.org/news/article/9/.

[55] The survivor of testicular cancer was particularly enraged at spam touting penis enlargements. See www.usatoday30.usatoday.com/tech/news/2004-02-11-spam-cover_x.htm.

While his reaction was extreme, most Internet users could perhaps sympathise slightly with what newspapers dubbed 'spam-rage'. At the individual level, spam is one of the most frustrating by-products of the Internet, an annoying inconvenience to Internet users. A 2005 UK survey showed 46 per cent of users said they received too much spam.[56] Spam emails oblige monitoring and take time for the user to deal with. As such, it undermines the efficiency of email communication. In the act of filtering, desired emails can be lost. Yet spam is complex from a regulatory perspective. The issue is an example of 'small impact bulk victimisation'.[57] This means that while the individual harm caused is relatively minor, the problem lies in the collective harm, which is highly dispersed.

It is estimated that 80 to 90 per cent of all emails sent worldwide are spam.[58] It is this, the sheer dimensions of the spam issue that make it a predominantly economic issue. Internet service providers (ISPs) suffer loss from bandwidth used in sending mails, and costs for filtering. This cost is passed on to the consumer. Corporations commit resources to filtering technology. As the EU began legislating on spam, it estimated that spam was costing EU businesses more than 2.25 bn Euros a year.[59]

The social impact of spam upon the global internet commons has also been a concern. If public trust, the fuel upon which the Internet market thrives, diminishes, then e-commerce will suffer.[60] The constant stream of emails containing content which is offensive, fraudulent, or constitutes 'phishing,' undermines public trust. It is estimated that only 10 per cent of spam is actually attempting to advertise genuine products.[61] A proportion of the remaining 90 per cent functions as a vehicle for other more individually harmful impositions, such as malware. 'Botnets' – computers coopted to send even more spam – can be created using malware sent with spam.[62] It also creates an incentive to undertake further data breaches, as spammers rely on huge lists of email addresses. Gathering these lists requires what is known as 'harvesting', where spammers, or those who sell data to spammers, harvest addresses from newsgroups, websites or ISP directories.

Over time, press, TV, telephone, and door-to-door salesmen have all burdened people with unwanted commercial intentions. Yet all have been regulated, limited in terms of time manner and place. In the online world, the regulation of spam has proved a difficult objective. This is the focus of the second part of the chapter.

[56] J Clough, *Principles of Cybercrime* (Cambridge, Cambridge University Press, 2010) 233.

[57] D Wall, 'Digital Realism and the Governance of Spam as a Cybercrime' (2005) 10 *European Journal of Criminal Law Policy and Research* 309, 319–20.

[58] Kozyris, 'General Report' (n 51) 2.

[59] http://news.bbc.co.uk/2/hi/business/3068627.stm.

[60] This is market rather than a welfarist approach. L Edwards, 'United Kingdom' in PJ Kozyris (ed), *Regulating Internet Abuses: Invasion of Privacy* (Alphen aan den Rijn, Kluwer Law International, 2007) 184.

[61] D Wall, 'Digital Realism and the Governance of Spam as a Cybercrime' (n 57) 312.

[62] In the spring of 2011, approximately 80 per cent of spam was sent from botnets (compared to 88.2 per cent during 2010), see Symantec Intelligence Report: June 2011, 2, available at www.symantec.com/content/en/us/enterprise/other_resources/b-symc_intelligence_2011_OR.en-us.pdf.

(ii) The Two Regulatory Approaches to Spam

There are two basic possible regulatory approaches to the issue of spam. First, the law can require that users give their consent to receiving spam. This is known as an 'opt-in' system. Frequently, this consent will be needed unless a prior business relationship exists between the sender and the recipient. This is known as a 'soft opt-in' system. Opt-in systems take as their starting point the assumption that users do not want to receive spam, and should therefore be given a chance to object ex ante.

The second basic regulatory approach is requiring that users express their preference to be excluded from receiving spam mail. This so-called 'opt-out' system could require options for 'specific opt-out', such as spam emails including an option to opt-out. Another option is creating 'general opt-out' options, such as a universal exclusion list, whereby those who wish can be added and, in theory, be excluded from spamming lists and therefore from receiving spam.

An opt-out system, to be effective, requires that the sender of spam be clearly identified and contactable, and that the spammer wishes to comply with the rules.[63] It relies upon email users being aware of their option to opt-out, that it is simple and free to do so, and that spammers update their lists and limit their distribution to only those who have not opted out. A further complexity, from an enforcement perspective, is that, due to its presumption in favour of the spam, it requires the examination of individual emails to determine whether a breach has taken place. The overall administrative burden of an opt-out system renders them difficult to implement. By comparison, an opt-in system is simpler to enforce. A violation has clearly taken place whenever an email arrives in the inbox of anyone who had not explicitly 'opted in'.

The weaker opt-out approach, where used, is sometimes justified as a compromise between the ends of protecting privacy and protecting free enterprise. This justification holds little sway. In reality, an opt-out approach only allows the recipient to express his preference after the inconvenience has been suffered. Further, it places the onus on the recipient to take action to prevent the inconvenience of spam. In this way, it seems to assume the existence of spam as a starting point.

Both opt-in and opt-out approaches suffer equally from the basic reality of spam. That is, that a relatively small percentage of spam emails are from legitimate users, seeking to sell a real product, and using the internet as a marketing device. Concealed spammers, who are not identifiable and contactable, are very difficult to locate and prosecute regardless of regulatory system. They operate illegitimately, using the internet's cloak of immunity, and account for the majority of spam. These spammers will not adhere to the rules of an 'opt-out system', requiring the inconvenience of checking 'do not email' lists. Indeed, he or she is more likely to view such a list as a boon to business, revealing a list of confirmed active email addresses, ripe for spamming.

[63] T Verbiest, 'France' in PJ Kozyris (ed), *Regulating Internet Abuses: Invasion of Privacy* (Alphen aan den Rijn, Kluwer Law International, 2007) 50.

(iii) European Legal Framework on Spam

As we have seen above, the regulation of spam is complex. The mode of regulation used will often reflect a legal system's wider approach to the privacy/ freedom of expression dichotomy. For instance, in the USA,[64] the existence of strong freedom of expression principles, which have been held to apply to commercial communications and advertising, means that it has not been possible to directly proscribe unsolicited communications.[65] Instead a less severe 'opt-out' system has been adopted.[66] The EU has, over time, adopted a tougher regulatory approach, prioritising more the importance of individual privacy over expression. The genesis of EU regulation of 'unsolicited communications for purposes of direct marketing'[67] is charted below.[68]

(a) First Steps

Tha Data Protection Directive of 1995[69] was the first EU action in the realm of what is known as 'e-privacy'. It remains an important source of privacy law in the EU, setting a precedent for the prioritisation of privacy, and high benchmarks for the processing of private data. However, it did not mention spam, and indeed was drafted in the very early years of the internet when the full extent of the issue was not yet known. Its focus is the general right of individuals to privacy in relation to personal data. However, if we consider email addresses falling under the category of personal data, and the sending of spam using these email addresses as the processing of personal data, then the Data Protection Directive's terms can be applied to the issue of spam, albeit indirectly.

Article 1 provides that 'Member States shall protect the fundamental rights and freedoms of natural persons, and in particular their right to privacy with respect to the processing of personal data'. Article 7, with a few exceptions,[70] allows the processing of personal data only when 'the data subject has unambiguously given consent'. Article 2(h) defines consent as 'any freely given specific and informed

[64] See shortly for the American approach: Clough, *Principles of Cybercrime* (n 56) 242–44.

[65] W Fritzemeyer and A Law, 'The CAN-SPAM Act-Analysed from a European Perspective' (2005) 11 *Computer and Telecommunication Law Review* 81, 88.

[66] Other countries which employ the opt-out model include South Korea and Columbia.

[67] This is defined as encompassing not only email but also fax communications and other 'automated calling systems' used for the purposes of direct marketing.

[68] Art 13(1) of Directive 2002/58/EC of the European Parliament and of the Council of 12 July 2002 concerning the processing of personal data and the protection of privacy in the electronic communications sector [2002] OJ L201/37 states: 'The use of automated calling systems without human intervention (automatic calling machines), facsimile machines (fax) or electronic mail for the purposes of direct marketing may only be allowed in respect of subscribers who have given their prior consent'.

[69] Directive 95/46/EC on the protection of individuals with regard to processing of personal data and on the free movement of such data [1995] OJ L281/31.

[70] Exceptions: performance of contract, legal obligation, necessary for a official authority in carrying out a task in the public interest, necessary for the controller or third party for the purpose of a legitimate interest.

indication of his wishes'. Article 22 entitles the individual to a judicial remedy for breaches of data processing rights. Article 24 ensures that states lay down 'suitable sanctions' to be imposed in case of infringement.

In relation to spam, the Data Protection Directive is significant in two mains ways. First, it ensures that disclosure of an email address in a certain context does not authorise the use of the address in another context or for another purpose. Second, it should allow the individual the right to object to spam before spam takes place.[71]

The Telecommunications Privacy Directive[72] was the first directive to deal specifically with personal data in the realms of communication. It focused on telephones, and issues such as itemised billing, and unsolicited calls. It introduced an opt-in regime for direct marketing by automatic systems using telecommunications networks.[73] It was left to Member States to decide whether to use opt-in or opt-out systems for other means of communication such as the Internet.

The Distance Selling Directive[74] once more focuses on telephone communication, but specifically linked with marketing. In Article 10(1) it limits the use of automated calling systems through an opt-in system. Prior consent is necessary before someone acting in a commercial or professional capacity initiates contacts through automatic calling or fax. Article 10(2) introduces an opt-out regime for other means of distance communication. Forms of communication other than phone or fax 'may be used only where there is no clear objection from the consumer'. Electronic mail is specifically mentioned in Annex I, the first time it features in a directive. While Article 14 allows for the possibility of more stringent provisions to be employed by Member States, the Directive itself specifies less protection for email and other methods than the opt-in system that it applied to telephone or fax communications.

(b) Addressing Spam Specifically

As we have seen, the EU's initial regulation in this area through the Data Protection Directive and the Distance Selling Directive was not focused on spam, indeed, spam was only implicitly addressed. The first regulation to consider spam as a primary concern came into force in 2000, and is known as the E-Commerce Directive.[75] Recital 30 of the Directive acknowledges that 'the sending of unsolicited commercial communications by electronic mail may be undesirable for consumers and

[71] Verbiest, 'France' (n 63) 51.

[72] Directive 97/66/EC of the European Parliament and of the Council of 15 December 1997 concerning the processing of personal data and the protection of privacy in the telecommunications sector [1998] OJ L24/1.

[73] *Ibid*, Art 12.

[74] Directive 97/7/EC of the European Parliament and of the Council of 20 May 1997 on the protection of consumers in respect of distance contracts [1997] OJ L144/19.

[75] Directive 2000/31/EC of the European Parliament and of the Council of 8 June 2000 on certain legal aspects of information society services, in particular electronic commerce, in the internal market [2000] OJ L178/1.

information society service providers and may disrupt the smooth functioning of interactive networks'. It was focused on commercial communications, which it defined in Article 2(h) as communication 'designed to promote, directly or indirectly, the goods, services or image of a company, organisation or person pursuing a commercial, industrial or craft activity or exercising a regulated profession'.

There were fears that an opt-in system would have a detrimental effect on electronic commerce, which was gaining increasing importance within the EU. As such, the less consumer-oriented opt-out approach was preferred. This approach placed the burden upon those sending the unsolicited commercial emails to regulate their conduct in favour of the consumer. The key provision is Article 7, which states, in the second paragraph, that 'Member States shall take measures to ensure that service providers undertaking unsolicited commercial communications by electronic mail consult regularly and respect the opt-out registers in which natural persons not wishing to receive such commercial communications can register themselves'. This constitutes a specific 'opt-out' system for commercial email communications. The E-Commerce Directive also required, in Article 7(1), that spam be made 'identifiable clearly and unambiguously as such as soon as it is received by the recipient'. Article 15 is clear that providers shall have no obligation to 'monitor the information which they transmit or store, nor a general obligation actively to seek facts or circumstances indicating illegal activity'. Article 20 provided that Member States must ensure enforcement, and apply 'effective, proportionate and dissuasive sanctions'.

This approach proved fraught with difficulty. First, the duty to regularly check registers was not specific enough. How often should one check the registers? Second, it seemed to assume that the problem of spam stemmed from legitimate commercial companies who would self-regulate in this way, and could be held accountable if they didn't. As mentioned earlier, this misjudged the nature of the spam issue. Third, and most importantly, these lists proved to be a valuable commodity for senders of unsolicited commercial email and spam, as they were verified as genuine active accounts. As such, the Directive is widely acknowledged as a limp instrument in relation to spam, too weak to have any effect.

The failure of the Directive led to revisied legislation within two years. The E-Privacy Directive of 2002[76] created, finally, an opt-in system. This represented a sea-change in the EU approach to the regulation of spam, prohibiting (with few exceptions) the use of email for direct marketing purposes unless with prior consent. Recital 40 provides a description of the EU's feelings about spam. It acknowledges the cheap nature of sending such communications, but also that they 'may impose a burden and/ or cost on the recipient'. In relation to the question of volume, it states that this 'may also cause difficulties for electronic communications networks and terminal equipment'. These issues are offered as justification for the requirement of prior explicit consent of the recipients.

[76] Directive 2002/58/EC of the European Parliament and of the Council of 12 July 2002 concerning the processing of personal data and the protection of privacy in the electronic communications sector [2002] OJ L201/37.

Article 13 provides for this new approach to the regulation of spam in the EU. Article 13(1) allows email to natural persons for direct marketing purposes only where prior agreement or consent has been given.[77] Article 13(3) provides that Member States must 'take appropriate measures' to ensure that such unsolicited emails 'are not allowed either without the consent of the subscribers concerned or in respect of subscribers who do not wish to receive these communications, the choice between these options to be determined by national legislation'. Article 13(2) provides an exception, where natural and legal persons have obtained the data in the course of previous business. In this case, they are permitted to use it to advertise similar products. However, there must be an opportunity for the recipient to object, and this must be afforded the recipient with each communication. Article 13(4) specifically prohibits messages that conceal the identity of the sender.[78] Article 13(5) prohibits communications to which the subscriber cannot respond or that conceals information necessary for such. Article 13(6) provides that ISPs have a 'legitimate interest' in preventing such infringements, and can therefore bring legal proceedings against those who infringe.[79] The protection for legal persons in respect of receiving spam is less clear. Article 13(5) provides that Member States must ensure 'that the legitimate interests of subscribers other than natural persons with regard to unsolicited communications are sufficiently protected'.

In terms of acts ancillary to the actual sending of the spam, Article 4 is relevant. Its terms oblige service providers to safeguard the security of its servce through appropriate measures, which must include informing customers of security breaches.[80] In the context of spam, this makes the ISP take technical measures to prevent the spread of spam or viruses. While this is not clear, measures probably can be interpreted as including state-of-the-art technological measures.[81] This imposes upon the ISP an obligation to prevent the harvesting of email addresses.

Directive 2009/136/EC[82] amended the E-Privacy Directive and requires Member States to regulate spam with the option of civil and criminal sanctions.[83] Article 15(a)(1) provides that: 'Member States shall lay down the rules on penalties, including criminal sanctions where appropriate, applicable to infringements of the national provisions adopted pursuant to this Directive and shall take all measures necessary to ensure that they are implemented'. This is the first time

[77] *Ibid*, Art 13(1).

[78] *Ibid*, Art 13(4).

[79] The focus here was on empowering those with the financial clout and interest to pursue cases where the individual may not have sufficient incentive to do so.

[80] Directive 2002/58/EC of the European Parliament and of the Council of 12 July 2002 concerning the processing of personal data and the protection of privacy in the electronic communications sector [2002] OJ L201/37, Art 4(2).

[81] Savin, *EU Internet Law* (n 12) 254.

[82] Directive 2009/136/EC of the European Parliament and of the Council of 25 November 2009 amending Directive 2002/22/EC on universal service and users' rights relating to electronic communications networks and services, Directive 2002/58/EC concerning the processing of personal data and the protection of privacy in the electronic communications sector and Regulation (EC) No 2006/2004 on cooperation between national authorities responsible for the enforcement of consumer protection laws [2009] OJ L337/11.

[83] *Ibid*, Art 15(1)(a).

that criminal sanctions are specifically mentioned in the sphere of data protection. Article 13(6) provides that 'any natural or legal person adversely affected by infringements of national provisions adopted pursuant to this Article . . . may bring legal proceedings in respect of such infringements'. It also extended the protection from spam to messages sent by SMS (short messaging service) or MMS (multi-media messaging service).

(c) Other Relevant Regulations

Other relevant regulations include the Marketing of Consumer Financial Services Directive and the Unfair Commercial Practices Directive. Directive 2002/65/EC[84] focuses on distance marketing of consumer and financial services. While Article 10(1) provides for an opt-in system for distance selling via fax and automated calling systems, in relation to such marketing by email, Article 10(2) leaves discretion to states as to whether to implement an opt-out or opt-in system. This seems contra to the provisions of the E-Privacy Directive, Article 13, which specify an opt-in system for spam except under the two aforementioned exceptions. Directive 2005/29/EC[85] addresses and approximates rules on unfair commercial practices. Article 5(1) prohibits unfair commercial practices. Article 5(4)(b) provides that commercial practices which are 'aggressive' shall be deemed unfair. Spam is considered an 'aggressive practice' under Annex 1 number 2, which states specifically that: 'Making persistent and unwanted solicitations by telephone, fax, email or other remote media except in circumstances and to the extent justified under national law to enforce a contractual obligation'. It is important to note that this only includes 'persistent' acts, and as such, cannot include a single spam message. Its scope of protection is therefore narrower than the previous directives.

(iv) Analysis of the EU's Approach

In essence, the EU legislation outlined above lays out three basic rules:[86]

1) E-mail marketing is subject to prior consent of subscribers. There is a limited exception for emails (or SMS) sent to existing customers by the same person on its similar services or products. This regime applies to subscribers who are natural persons, but Member States can choose to extend it to legal persons.

[84] Directive 2002/65/EC of the European Parliament and of the Council of 23 September 2002 concerning the distance marketing of consumer financial services and amending Council Directive 90/619/EEC and Directives 97/7/EC and 98/27/EC [2002] OJ L271/16.

[85] Directive 2005/29/EC of the European Parliament and of the Council of 11 May 2005 concerning unfair business-to-consumer commercial practices in the internal market and amending Council Directive 84/450/EEC, Directives 97/7/EC, 98/27/EC and 2002/65/EC of the European Parliament and of the Council and Regulation (EC) No 2006/2004 of the European Parliament and of the Council (Unfair Commercial Practices Directive) [2005] OJ L149/22.

[86] Communication from the Commission on Unsolicited Commercial Communications or 'Spam', Brussels, 22 January 2004, COM (2004) 28 final, 9.

2) Disguising or concealing the identity of the sender on whose behalf the communication is made shall be illegal.
3) All e-mails must include a valid return address where to opt-out.

While it represented a substantial step forward for the EU, there are some issues with Directive 2002/58/EC and its subsequent amendment in 2009. In this section we will consider, in brief, four key elements of the E-Privacy Directive: the issue of consent; the existing relationship exception; the legal persons' exception; and the concealing of identity.

(a) The Issue of Consent

The opt-in model primarily turns on the notion of prior consent. An important consequence of this is that the burden of proving that consent has in fact been obtained in advance lies with the sender. Consent, in this context, is to be determined according to Directive 95/45/EC[87] which defines it as: 'any freely given specific and informed indication of his wishes by which the data subject signifies his agreement to personal data related to him being processed'.[88] This definition only hints at the methods which may be acceptable in obtaining this prior consent. Further assistance is provided by Recital 17, which states that there is no one way in which consent is to be obtained; rather, it 'may be given by any appropriate method enabling a freely given specific and informed indication of the user's wishes, including by ticking a box when visiting an Internet website'.

This emphasis on 'specific' and 'informed' consent suggests that general consent to receive marketing mails would not be sufficient to meet the demands of Article 13 of the Directive.[89] Similarly notions of implied or tacit consent would not be compatible with the definition of consent and consequently methods such as pre-ticked boxes on websites would not be acceptable. Moreover, it is likely that consent obtained by fraud or misrepresentation would fail on the 'informed' requirement and would be vitiated.

(b) The Existing Relationship Exception

The importance of balancing the economic interests of businesses with the privacy interests of the consumer is most evident in the second paragraph of Article 13. This contains an exemption from the need for consent for businesses which have pre-existing or on-going dealings with customers and which use the electronic contact

[87] Directive 2002/58/EC of the European Parliament and of the Council of 12 July 2002 concerning the processing of personal data and the protection of privacy in the electronic communications sector [2002] OJ L201/37, Art 2(f) and Recital 17.

[88] Directive 95/46/EC on the protection of individuals with regard to processing of personal data and on the free movement of such data [1995] OJ L281/31, Art 2(h).

[89] See on this point Data Protection Working Party, Opinion 5/2004 on unsolicited communications for marketing purposes under Article 13 of the Directive 2002/58/EC, adopted on 27 February 2004, 5.

details to offer the customer similar products or services. This approach by the EU has been coined a 'soft opt-in' approach.[90]

This exception only applies to those companies which actually obtained the contact details (thus these companies would not be permitted to pass on these details to other companies) and is justified on the basis that the customer had already expressed an interest in the goods or services provided and thus that consent to further communications is implied.

This exception is also subject to further requirements, namely that the recipient must be 'given the opportunity to object, free of charge and in an easy manner, to such use of electronic contact details when they are collected and on the occasion of each message in case the customer has not initially refused such use'.[91]

(c) The Legal Persons' Exception

The distinction made between natural and legal persons is problematic for the EU. The Directive focuses on the protection of individuals. Spam can be a high cost issue for businesses, yet they are not guaranteed to receive the same protection as natural persons under the E-Privacy Directive. Article 13's prior consent exception allows spam where the sender obtains the address through sale of goods or services. However, this is limited to only the natural or legal persons who actually obtained the address, who must only market similar products or services. The question, of course, is which natural or legal persons qualify, and the sufficiency of link to the products and services offered. According to Article 13(5), paragraphs (1) and (3) of the Article apply only to natural persons, while Member States are to ensure 'that the legitimate interests of subscribers other than natural persons with regard to unsolicited communications are sufficient'.

Most Member States enacted an opt-in policy for both natural and legal persons. Italy is an example, imposing an opt-in regime for both natural and legal persons with significant fines and even in some cases jail sentences. However, others chose to differentiate.[92] Some Member States, including France and UK, have chosen to employ an 'opt-out' model in respect of legal persons. Some Member States do not differentiate between legal and natural persons in their legal systems. Overall, the differentiation in the EU regulation complicates the regulation of spam, and results in less protection for legal persons in some jurisdictions of the EU.

[90] See J Palfrey, D Abrams and D Bambauer, 'A Comparative Analysis of Spam Laws: The Quest for a Model Law' (2005) *Background Paper for the ITU WSIS thematic Meeting on Cybersecurity*, available at www.itu.int/osg/spu/cybersecurity/docs/Background_Paper_Comparative_Analysis_of_Spam_Laws.pdf, 17.

[91] Directive 2002/58/EC of the European Parliament and of the Council of 12 July 2002 concerning the processing of personal data and the protection of privacy in the electronic communications sector [2002] OJ L201/37, Art 13(2).

[92] ITU survey showed Portugese legislation applied an opt-in system for natural persons only. To an extent, the UK also made this differentiation. The Netherlands did so, later acknowledging this as an error.

(d) Concealing Identity and Unsubscribing

Article 13(4) 'prohibits' both the sending of electronic mail for the purposes of direct marketing disguising or concealing the identity of the sender on whose behalf the communication is made, and the sending of electronic mail which does not refer to a valid address to which the recipient may send a request that such communications cease. Although these requirements are primarily associated with the 'opt-out' method, it is also important in relation to opt-in systems as it guarantees personal choice by enabling recipients to cancel or alter their communications preferences. This provision is essentially orientated, as is noted in Recital 43, towards ensuring that the Community rules can be effectively enforced. However, this seems somewhat moot in reality, as those companies or individuals who obtain consent or to whom exceptions apply are unlikely to be those using deceptive practices.

(v) Implementation of EU Policy on Spam through the Criminal Law?

(a) Post-Lisbon EU Criminal Law

As outlined in chapter 1, prior to the Lisbon Treaty, the EU only had the explicit competency to regulate particularly serious offences with a cross-border dimension, such as terrorism, trafficking in human beings, drug trafficking, and fraud affecting the EU financial interests.[93] There was no clear legal basis for criminal regulation in other areas, so few measures were taken intended to strengthen implementation of other EU policies.[94] However, Article 83 of the Lisbon Treaty now provides the legal basis for EU criminal law. The list of serious offences remain as so-called 'Euro-Crimes' under Article 83(1), but Article 83(2) of the Lisbon Treaty now sets out a further competency of the EU in relation to criminal law in pursuit of EU policy. It states:

[93] Council Framework Decision of 13 June 2002 on Combating Terrorism (2002/475/JHA) [2002] OJ L164/3; Council Framework Decision 2004/757/JHA of 25 October 2004 laying down minimum provisions on the constituent elements of criminal acts and penalties in the field of illicit drug trafficking [2004] OJ L335/8; Directive on preventing and combating trafficking in human beings and protecting its victims and replacing Council Framework Decision of 19 July 2002 on combating trafficking in human beings (2002/629/JHA) [2002] OJ L101/1; Convention drawn up on the basis of Article K.3 of the Treaty on European Union, on the protection of the European Communities' financial interests [1995] OJ L316/49.

[94] Directive 2008/99/EC of the European Parliament and of the Council of 19 November 2008 on the protection of the environment through criminal law [2008] OJ L328/28; Directive 2009/123/EC of the European Parliament and of the Council of 21 October 2009 amending Directive 2005/35/EC on ship-source pollution and on the introduction of penalties for infringements [2009] OJ L280/52; Directive 2009/52/EC of the European Parliament and of the Council of 18 June 2009 providing for minimum standards on sanctions and measures against employers of illegally staying third-country nationals [2009] OJ L168/24; and Council Framework Decision of 29 May 2000 on increasing protection by criminal penalties and other sanctions against counterfeiting in connection with the introduction of the euro (2000/383/JHA) [2000] OJ L140/1.

> If the approximation of criminal laws and regulations of the Member States proves essential to ensure the effective implementation of a Union policy in an area which has been subject to harmonisation measures, directives may establish minimum rules with regard to the definition of criminal offences and sanctions in the area concerned.

No list of crimes is outlined under Article 83(2), leaving it to the EU institutions to decide whether and how criminal law should be utilised as an enforcement tool. Any action must satisfy the broad criteria that are included within the Article: criminal law measures must be essential to ensure implementation of an EU policy in an area that has been subject to harmonisation measures.[95]

The recent nature of the Lisbon Treaty means that the full significance of Article 83(2) for EU criminal law is not yet known. In a 2011 communication, Towards an EU Criminal Policy, the Commission sought to address some of the uncertainties concerning post-Lisbon Treaty criminal law competencies, setting out how the EU should use criminal law to ensure the effective implementation of EU policies.[96] A two-step approach is outlined on EU criminal law legislation under Article 83(2). A decision must be made whether to adopt a criminal law measure. In this regard, the Treaty requires that criminal law measures must be 'essential' to effective policy implementation. As criminal law always constitutes the 'ultima ratio' measure, legislators must analyse what other measures could achieve the policy goals advanced. Then, a decision must be made on what specific criminal law measures to adopt. The communication mentions a number of key principles.

The communication notes a number of important elements in this two-step approach. First, Article 83 limits the EU to the approximation of 'minimum rules'. Notwithstanding this, the principle of 'legal certainty' requires clear definition of the end pursued in order to inform national law makers implementing EU legislation. In justifying the use of criminal law measures, there must be 'clear factual evidence' from Member States on why, absent EU criminal law, the policy cannot be effectively enforced. This requires careful consideration of what form of sanction will best achieve the policy and 'ensure a maximum level of effectiveness, proportionality and dissuasiveness'. This is important, as the EU can require certain sanction types are made available to judges in national criminal law courts.

Effectiveness requires that the sanction is suitable for the achievement of the intended goal, to ensure adherence to the rules. Proportionality requires that any sanction does not exceed that necessary to achieve the end pursued. Dissuasiveness requires that the sanctions deter those considering perpetration. The Commission highlights that administrative sanctions can in certain circumstances be preferable, 'for example the offence is not particularly severe or occurs in large numbers'.

In relation to the issue of privacy that is the focus of this chapter, the Commission highlighted data protection as one of the main sectors where a criminal law

[95] Communication from the Commission, Towards an EU Criminal Policy: Ensuring the effective implementation of EU policies through criminal law, Brussels, 20 September 2011, COM (2011) 573 final, 6.

[96] *Ibid.*

approach is needed.[97] It cited the dangers towards personal data posed by the internet, since 'rapid technological developments and globalisation have profoundly changed the world around us, and brought new challenges for the protection of personal data'.[98] Article 83(2) can therefore be seen as extending the criminal law competency of the EU into the realm of privacy matters in the online world, which previously fell under the first pillar.

(b) *What Constitutes a Criminal Measure?*

With Article 83(2) representing a somewhat controversial extension of the EU's criminal law competence, it is important to understand when a measure of the EU will be considered as 'criminal'. The jurisprudence of the European Court of Human Rights provides the EU with a definition of what actions constitute criminal measure.[99] The EU to respect the ECHR is now a legal obligation under the Lisbon Treaty, Article 6(2), which provides that 'The Union shall accede to the European Convention for the Protection of Human Rights and Fundamental Freedoms'.[100] For our purposes, the European Court of Human Rights' test for what should be considered 'criminal' can be employed to assess the Member State obligations created by EU directives which define offences and minimum sanctions.

The definition of whether an offence is criminal is sometimes contentious where such an offence is defined as 'disciplinary' or 'regulatory' in nature. The Strasbourg Court's approach to whether an offence shall be 'criminal' under Article 6 (which provides for the right to a fair trial) was defined in the 1976 case of *Engel v Netherlands.*[101] Here, three criteria were laid out as determinants: the domestic classification; the nature of the offence; and the severity of the potential penalty. The first factor is most important, but where an offence is not classified as 'criminal', the latter two are relevant, and may be considered cumulatively where neither is of itself conclusive.[102] It is important to note is that it is the 'potential' penalty under the law, rather than the actual penalty applied which must be assessed. Further, the 'nature of the offence must be deterrent and punitive, not compensatory', and extend to the population at large. [103] The fact that the offence may be minor does not affect whether it is criminal in character.

[97] *Ibid*, 10.

[98] Communication from the Commission, A comprehensive approach on personal data protection in the European Union, Brussels, 4 November 2010, COM (2010) 609 final, 2.

[99] H Satzger, *Internationales und Europäisches Strafrecht, Strafanwendungsrecht – Europäisches Straf- und Strafverfahrensrecht – Völkerstrafrecht*, 4th edn (Baden-Baden, Nomos, 2010) § 8 N 5.

[100] The legal basis for this accession within the ECHR is found in Art 59(2) ECHR, as amended by protocol 14.

[101] *Engel and Others v NL* Series A no 22 (1976) 1 EHRR 647, para 80-85.

[102] *Ezeh and Connors v UK* 2003-X (2003) 39 EHRR 1, para 86.

[103] D Harris, M O'Boyle, C Warbrick, E Bates and C Buckley, *Harris, O'Boyle & Warbrick Law of the European Convention on Human Rights*, 2nd edn (Cambridge, Oxford University Press, 2009) 206.

(c) The Use of EU Criminal Law in Relation to Spam

The E-Privacy Directive came into effect four years before the Lisbon Treaty. As such, in common with the vast majority of former first pillar legislation, the criminal law maintained something of a shadowy role in Directive 2002/58/EC. While there was no direct reference in Article 13 to the imposition of criminal sanctions, the use of the word 'prohibit' certainly seemed to imply that the criminal law could have a role to play in overseeing the application of the provisions of the Article. Further, Member States were not obliged to turn to the criminal law in implementing the Directive, Article 13 could be interpreted as at least some encouragement to Member States to allow recourse to the criminal law. Overall, however, the EU insisted a statute be enacted in each Member State, but 'did not seem particularly concerned with variations in the specifics of the legislation'.[104]

The 2009 amendment made the possibility and encouragement of criminal sanctions explicit, with Article 15(a)(1) specifying that: 'Member States shall lay down the rules on penalties, *including criminal sanctions* where appropriate' (emphasis added). It further provides that: 'The penalties provided for must be effective, proportionate and dissuasive'. Whether criminal in nature, 'the penalties provided for must be effective, proportionate and dissuasive'. A 2004 communication had already stated that 'Member States and competent authorities should in particular [. . .] create adequate possibilities for victims to claim damages and provide for real sanctions, including financial and criminal penalties where appropriate'.[105]

While not obligatory, this represents a gradual shift in the post-Lisbon era of Article 83(2) TFEU competency, ie criminal law measures now openly encouraged in a former first pillar matter. However, in terms of obligations in implementing, it is still ultimately left to Member States to determine what form of sanctions to use in relation to spam offences. Criminal law measures are only obligatory where conduct in the sending of spam falls within the ambit of Council Framework Decision 2005/222/JHA or the Convention on Cybercrime.

(d) Ensuring Implementation of the E-Privacy Directive

The E-Privacy Directive required states to enact transponding laws by 31 October 31 2003. However, by this deadline, nine states still had not complied. These states were France, Germany, Belgium, Finland, Greece, Luxembourg, Netherlands, Portugal and Sweden. By December 2004, the EU, in its annual report on the implementation of the EU electronic communications regulatory package, noted that still

[104] A Mutchler, 'CAN-SPAM Versus the European Union E-Privacy Directive: Does Either Provide a Solution to the Problem of Spam' (2010) 43 *Suffolk UL Rev* 957, 976.

[105] Communication from the Commission on unsolicited commercial communications or 'spam', Brussels, 22 January 2004, COM (2004) 28 final, 29.

only 20 of the EU's present 25 Member States had notified the Commission that they had adopted primary legislation implementing the E-Privacy Directive.[106]

This led the EU to begin proceedings against the non-implementing states in December 2004. These states were Belgium, Greece, Luxembourg, Estonia and the Czech Republic, and cases against Belgium, Greece and Luxembourg reached the European Court of Justice level in 2005 and 2006.[107] By 2007 all states had passed legislation implementing the provisions of the E-Privacy Directive into domestic law. However, even with this level of de jure compliance secured, the Member States still attracted criticism from the Commission, with states being told to improve their enforcement of spam laws.[108] The EU contracted a study to assess enforcement, which again backed up the idea of disparate enforcement.[109] In general, the EU has been critical of the lack of severity of penalties imposed at Member State level, as well as the few cases prosecuted.

(e) Implementation without Harmonisation

While basic implementation of the E-Privacy Directive has been successful across the EU, the Member States have chosen a variety of ways to discharge their obligations. The E-Privacy Directive differs from third pillar legislation in that it could not make explicit a desire to 'harmonise' at the level of the criminal law, at least prior to the Lisbon Treaty. There is clear evidence in the Directive of the belief in the importance of harmonisation:

> For such forms of unsolicited communications for direct marketing, it is justified to require that prior consent of the recipients is obtained before such communications are addressed to them. The single market requires a harmonised approach to ensure simple, Community-wide rules for businesses and users.[110]

Regardless, the lack of clear instruction as to the type and extent of the measures to be taken to prohibit spam, obviously undermined any implicit harmonisation aims. Some countries have used criminal measures to enforce the most serious crimes falling under the provisions of the E-Privacy Directive. Others have used what could be classified as serious administrative measures in the form of fines.[111]

[106] www.edri.org/edrigram/number2.24/report.

[107] Case C-475/04 *Commission v Hellenic Republic* [2006] ECR I-00069; Case C-376/04 *Commission v Belgium* [2005] OJ C143/14; Case C-375/04 *Commission v Luxembourg* [2005] OJ C143/14.

[108] Communication from the Commission on fighting spam, spyware and malicious software, Brussels, 15 November 2006, COM (2006) 688 final.

[109] time.lex, 'Study on activities undertaken to address threats that undermine confidence in the Information Society, such as spam, spyware and malicious software', SMART 2008/0013 (Brussels, 2009).

[110] Directive 2002/58/EC of the European Parliament and of the Council of 12 July 2002 concerning the processing of personal data and the protection of privacy in the electronic communications sector [2002] OJ L201/37, Recital 40.

[111] It is important to note is that under the definition of a 'criminal measure' outlined above, some of the serious administrative measures, particularly fines, could be construed as severe enough penalties to perhaps be considered criminal measures under the third prong of the *Engel* criteria.

It can be said that most jurisdictions within the EU, regardless of the possibility of criminal sanctions, use a primarily civil enforcement model, with an emphasis on administrative penalties. Criminal penalties are associated more with content issues. Much content associated with spam can be prosecuted under existing criminal law.

Overall, an overview of Member State implementation of the spam provisions of the E-Privacy Directive clearly highlights considerable differences in the interpretation and application of the provisions in the various Member States. These differences occur predominantly in relation to three areas: the classification of the nature of the provisions, the sentence imposed, and the applicability of the provisions to communications to legal persons.

In the UK, the E-Privacy Directive is transposed through the Privacy and Electronic Communications (EC Directive) Regulations 2003.[112] Regulation 22 states that a person '[s]hall neither transmit, nor instigate the transmission of, unsolicited communications for the purposes of direct marketing by means of electronic mail unless the recipient of the electronic mail has previously notified the sender that he consents for the time being to such communications being sent by, or at the instigation of, the sender'. Of particular note is that the UK regime does not make provision for the imposition of sanctions where the recipients of the unsolicited communications are legal persons.

The Information Commissioner shall serve an enforcement notice on anyone who he or she believes has contravened the Regulations. Failure to comply with such an enforcement notice constitutes a criminal offence[113] and is punishable, in England and Wales, by a fine of up to £5,000 in the magistrates' court or an unlimited fine in the crown court. However, 'in practice, prosecutions of any kind are rare to non-existent and fines low'.[114] Jail sentences are not available for spam, and while compensation is possible, there is no recorded instance of an individual succeeding in gaining spam damages.

In France Article L34-5(1) of the *Code des Postes et des Communications électroniques* lays out an opt-in system for natural persons, and an opt-out system for legal persons.[115] Paragraph 4 makes it a soft opt-in system. Where a business has already transacted with the recipient, has obtained details in the process of making a sale or negotiating such, and where the recipient has a simple method of refusing his details be used in future for marketing and at each point thereafter, then an exception to the consent exists.[116] Even if a different entity under the law, a company from the same group as the one who previously transacted, will also be exempt if the products or services offered falls into the same category (though this is not defined). This system of regulation was introduced in 2004 as implementation of the 2002

[112] Privacy and Electronic Communications (EC Directive) Regulations 2003, SI 2003/2426.
[113] Data Protection Act 1998, s 47(1).
[114] Edwards, 'United Kingdom' (n 60) 184.
[115] See Verbiest, 'France' (n 63) 45–56.
[116] *Ibid*, 52.

E-Privacy Directive.[117] Violation of the opt-in system is punishable with a fine of only up to 750 Euros for each spam email.[118] Falling somewhere between the UK and Germany's approaches, France's approach applies the opt-in system only to natural persons, and specifies a weaker opt-in protection for legal persons.

In Germany, the relevant law is § 7(2)(3) of the Act Against unfair Competition (UWG), which prevents 'unconscionably pestering [. . . in cases of] advertising using an automated calling machine, a fax machine or electronic mail without the addressees prior express consent'.[119] This is an opt-in system. Provision § 7(3) provides for a soft opt-in in cases where customer relationship exists. Notably, the UWG does not provide for criminal sanctions, though under § 16(1) TMG (Telemediengesetz), administrative offences are applicable, with a fine up to 50,000 Euros. This fine is only applicable when § 6(2) has been violated. This rule states, that it's forbidden to veil or hide the identity of the sender or the commercial nature of a commercial email.[120] In contrast to the UK legislation, the German approach does criminalise spam directed at legal persons, as well as natural persons.

For a more punitive version of this approach, in Italy, those who send spam, irrespective of whether the recipient is a natural or a legal person, are caught by the provisions of the criminal law,[121] with the possibility of custodial sentences.[122] At the opposite end of the spectrum lies Austria, where all spam offences fall within administrative law. According to the Presidency of the Council of the European Union, the variety in penalties varies from between 145 Euros per spam message, to an administrative fine of 450,000 Euros and from warnings to jail sentences.[123]

(vi) The Effectiveness of EU Regulation in Combating Spam

The EU employed all measures within its competency to address the problem of spam. As we have seen, there have been a number of directives drafted, implemented and amended where this was deemed necessary. These regulations can be read as encouraging states to impose criminal sanctions. Proceedings were initiated before the European Court of Justice following the failure of various Member States to comply with the regulations on spam. Even once all of the Member States

[117] T Verbiest, 'Loi pour la confiance dans l'économie numérique: examen du nouveau régime du commerce électronique' (2005) *Acta Universitatis Lucian Blaga* 160.

[118] Contraventions de la quatrième classe, see Art 131-13(4) Code pénal for each spam email («chaque communication»).

[119] See T Hoeren, 'Germany' in PJ Kozyris (ed), *Regulating Internet Abuses: Invasion of Privacy* (Alphen aan den Rijn, Kluwer Law International, 2007) 57–71.

[120] See T Frank, '"You've got (Spam-)Mail" – Zur Strafbarkeit von E-Mail-Werbung' (2004) 20 *Computer und Recht* 123, 123–28.

[121] Italy, Title X s130 Personal Data Protection Code Legislative Decree no 196/2003.

[122] A Funk, G Zeifang, D Johnson and R Spessard, 'Unsolicited Commercial Emails in the Jurisdictions of Germany and the USA: Some Thoughts on the New Anti-spam Laws in Consideration of the Interests of the Parties Involved in Email Traffic' (2004) 5 *Computer Law Review International* 138, 143.

[123] Presidency of the Council of the European Union, Brussels, 24 November 2004, 15148/04.

had transposed the E-Privacy Directive into domestic law, an external report was commissioned that was highly critical of the implementation of these spam laws within Member States.

As outlined in the foregoing section, modes of implementation have differed greatly across the EU, in terms of severity of sanctions, administrative or criminal approach and applicability to legal persons. If the intention of the E-Privacy Directive was to harmonise EU laws on the issue of spam, then clearly the Directive was deficient, allowing the states too wide a scope of possible approaches in implementation. The disparate implementation could be said to be a logical result of European attempts to regulate under the influence and limitations of the former first pillar approach in the context of the criminal law. However, even in the event of perfect harmonisation, it is not clear that the effectiveness of EU regulation on the matter would be greatly enhanced. As one scholar has noted, 'attempts to regulate spam worldwide have been unsuccessful'.[124] The minority explanation for this lack of success is that the effectiveness of spam regulation would require more punitive measures. This mode of thinking is as follows: 'In order for anti-spam Legislation to be effective, it must define penalties that are sufficient to act as a real deterrent'.[125] This concept of deterrence is one that the EU seems to ascribe to, with its apparent encouragement of criminal sanctions and the requirement that measures be 'dissuasive'. Following this logic, the problem of spam within the EU would decrease were states to increase the severity of anti-spam laws implementing the E-Privacy Directive, with increasingly criminal as opposed to administrative sanctions. While tempting, there is little evidence to support this assertion that higher penalties or criminal law sanctions actually have a dissuasive effect upon spammers. Within the EU, Italy's sanctions regime on spam is known as the most severe in the EU,[126] yet it is not noted to be any more successful than that of other Member States with less severe penalties. While America has traditionally been the biggest source of spam, China has recently emerged as a significant source.[127] This is despite the fact that it is said the death penalty is a possible punishment for spamming in China!

The majority view is increasingly that the apparent lack of impact from spam legislation stems more from the nature of the problem the legislation seeks to address, than from deficits in the legislation itself. First, while there are thought to be a very limited number of spammers responsible for most of the world's spam,[128]

[124] Savin, *EU Internet Law* (n 12) 252.

[125] E Moustakas, C Ranganathan and P Duquenoy, 'Combating Spam Through Legislation: A Comparative Analysis of US and European Approaches' (2005) Second conference on email and anti-spam CEAS, available at: www.ceas.cc/2005/papers/146.pdf, 7.

[126] http://news.bbc.co.uk/2/hi/europe/3080396.stm.

[127] In 2012, China became the top source of spam, having not figured in the top 20 sources of spam in 2011. It accounted for 19.5 per cent of all unsolicited mail. Spam originating in the US came second increasing from 13.5 per cent to 15.6 per cent. See Kaspersky Security Bulletin 2012, available at www.securelist.com/en/analysis/204792276/Kaspersky_Security_Bulletin_Spam_Evolution_2012.

[128] As an example, 80 per cent of spam targeting America is thought to originate form as few as 10 known spammers. See Clough, *Principles of Cybercrime* (n 56) 237.

the majority of spam in EU countries, approximately 90 per cent, is sent from outside the EU.[129] The internet allows spammers to operate from any country where an internet connection can be found, transfer to different hosts, and hijack computers in different locations for spamming with relative ease. Frequently the businesses 'advertised' through spam are very difficult to trace, existing only in the online realm or nominally based in jurisdictions with lax regulatory regimes. As such, the EU regime is only applicable to a very small proportion of offenders.[130]

Even where offenders fall within the EU jurisdiction, they are still remarkably hard to trace and prosecute. The experience of the US with its CAN-SPAM legislation, which finds most spammers within its jurisdiction yet is considered a failure,[131] perhaps indicates that jurisdiction is not the key factor either. Rather, some have expressed considerable scepticism toward the notion that legal interventions can prove beneficial in stemming the flow of spam at all.[132] That said, there are now signs that globally the problem of spam appears to be receding somewhat. In 2012, worldwide spam levels decreased to a five-year low. On average, 72.1 per cent of emails sent were spam in 2012. This is 8.2 per cent less than the average for 2011.[133] This is an unprecedented drop. While it is too soon to report the demise of spam, signs are certainly favourable that the problem has passed its zenith. If not regulation, to what can we attribute this improvement?

Most accept that the recent decrease in spam is borne of the increasing success of technical, rather than legal, protection measures.[134] Technical solutions have proved most effective in providing protection against spam. These technical measures include filters, which are ubiquitous, integrated, free, and increasingly successful at ensuring the vast majority of spam email does not reach its intended recipient. Their main benefits are that they move apace with technological advancement (unlike laws which even if drafted to encompass new technology quickly become obsolete), and that they function at a global level. Rather than disparate states across continents, they rely upon the self-regulation of a few

[129] Savin, *EU Internet Law* (n 12) 179. Although UK, Italy and France were also in the top 10. See www.spamhaus.org/statistics/countries/.

[130] The EU has tried to mitigate this problem through entering into a number of agreements with so-called third countries, of which the most important are with the USA and with Asian countries: Commission Decision 2000/520/EC of 26 July 2000 pursuant to Directive 95/46/EC of the European Parliament and the Council on the adequacy of the protection provided by the safe harbour privacy principles and related frequently asked questions provided by the US Department of Commerce (notified under document number C (2000) 2441) [2000] OJ L215/7 and the joint statement on international anti-spam cooperation, signed on 24 February 2005 in London at the 4th ASEM conference on e-commerce (see http://europa.eu/rapid/press-release_IP-05-210_en.htm).

[131] Edwards, 'United Kingdom' (n 60) 196.

[132] See M Butler, 'Spam - the Meat of the Problem' (2003) 19 *Computer Law & Security Review* 388.

[133] Kaspersky Security Bulletin 2012, available at www.securelist.com/en/analysis/204792276/Kaspersky_Security_Bulletin_Spam_Evolution_2012.

[134] Technical strategies include: ISPs, network managers and users utilising filtering software to filter messages sent from known spammers; the use of so-called 'white lists' from which emails can only be received; configuring email servers, or email standard format to make it possible to spot attempts to falsify orgin or content of email; and filtering out email with false reply addresses; industry codes of conduct and appropriate use policies.

major IT players and ISPs who mostly[135] share the interest in combating spam.[136] Overall, ISPs can now make it very difficult for subscribers to bulk-send messages to the extent necessary to gain profit from spam. These technical measures also benefit from the fact that there are now many other cheap, legal avenues for advertising, which detract from spam's appeal to would-be direct marketers.[137]

Regulatory measures to address spam, such as those by the EU, remain necessary, but are not as potent as the technical measures outlined. It is perhaps accurate to state that, whether at the EU or national level, 'passing laws is really only first and rather unsatisfactory step in the process of catching spammers or blocking spam activity'.[138]

III Conclusions

The precise contours of the post-Lisbon EU criminal law landscape have not yet been established, but it is clear that there is greater scope for criminal law regulation in pursuit of policy objectives under Article 83(2) TFEU. However, in relation to data protection and online privacy issues, the EU has not yet sought to utilise this explicit competency. As yet, the EU has largely continued with its former first pillar approach in this area, with criminal law measures suggested in broad terms, but not compulsory for Member States. Under this approach, even successful transposing of EU directives by all Member States will not result in harmonisation between them. However, in the area addressed by this chapter, this lack of full harmonisation does not appear to have had a dire impact on the effectiveness of EU policies.

Criminal legislation often appears a tempting solution to the problems of the day, for policy makers at the domestic and EU level. However, a statement of Cornelis de Jong, the Rapporteur of the European Parliament's Committee on Civil Liberties, Justice and Home Affairs, 'On an EU Approach to Criminal Law', is perhaps prescient. He cautioned that:

> [A]ll too easily criminal law provisions are proposed for their supposedly symbolic and dissuasive effects: they are then aimed at reassuring the European citizens that the EU

[135] It is important to note that according to one respected source, 'Spam continues to plague the Internet because a small number of large Internet Service Providers sell service knowingly to professional spammers for profit, or do nothing to prevent spammers operating from their networks'. See www.spamhaus.org/statistics/networks/.

[136] Edwards, 'United Kingdom' (n 60) 197.

[137] With the emergence of Web 2.0, advertising opportunities on the internet have greatly increased thanks to banners, context-based advertising, and ads on social networks and blogs. Darya Gudkova, Head of Content Analysis & Research Kaspersky Lab, comments: 'This drop is the result of a gradual departure of advertisers from spam to other, more convenient and legal means of promoting goods and services'. See www.kaspersky.com/about/news/spam/2013/Spam_in_2012_Continued_Decline_Sees_Spam_Levels_Hit_5_year_Low.

[138] Edwards, 'United Kingdom' (n 60) 197.

> takes their security seriously and at making it clear to potential criminals that they will be severely punished.[139]

As EU criminal law develops over the coming years, the determination of what is considered 'essential' to the fulfilling of EU policy objectives under Article 83(2) TFEU will be contentious. Data protection online has already been specifically identified by the Commission as an area ripe for an explicit criminal law-based approach under Article 83(2) TFEU, however, the foregoing analysis of the regulation of both cookies and spam suggests regulation (and criminal law) has at best proved of secondary importance to technical approaches in improving protection. If experience in this area portrays any wider lesson, it is perhaps that the number of areas where criminal measures are truly 'essential' will be fewer than the EU institutions will, in time, suggest.

[139] European Parliament, 'Report on an EU Approach on Criminal Law', Committee on Civil Liberties, Justice and Home Affairs Rapporteur: Cornelis de Jong, 24 April 2012, A7-0144/2012, 10.

7

Cybercrime

Cyberspace is now a battlespace. But it's a battlespace you cannot see.*

I Introduction

The first part of this chapter outlines and analyses the criminal law response of the European Union (EU) institutions to the phenomenon of what has broadly become known as 'cybercrime'. It begins by considering the situation where information systems are the target of criminal activity – widely known as 'hacking'. It then goes on to focus on how information systems are used to perpetrate new and potent forms of the traditional crimes of fraud and theft – in particular, identity theft. In the third section we look at the role of computers in modern terrorist activity – so-called cyber-terrorism is considered. The fourth section addresses a linked concept, 'cyber-laundering' – the use of computers to facilitate the process of money laundering.

The EU's criminal law response to 'cybercrime' is based upon the goal and concept of 'harmonisation' of criminal law between its Member States. In the second part of the chapter the significance of this concept is analysed in more detail, and in light of the on-going development of EU criminal law since the Lisbon Treaty, considers one question in particular: what is the significance of the differing 'general part principles' of Member States in relation to the overall goal of harmonisation?

II EU Criminal Law and Cybercrime

A Illegal Interference and Accessing of Computer Systems

(i) Introduction

In May 2013 at the High Court in London, four young men were given lengthy prison sentences for crimes they committed as part of a collective called 'LulzSec'.

* MJ Gross, 'The Silent War', *Vanity Fair*, July 2013.

Over a two-year period they were responsible for accessing some of the most powerful institutions in the world, including media companies like Sony, News International and Fox. They also infiltrated security institutions including the CIA and the UK's Serious Organized Crime Agency (SOCA). They planned and carried out these acts having never met in person, and did so without having to leave their own houses. More complex still, despite all their access to these institutions, there is no evidence that any of them personally profited or had any interest in financial gain.[1] Their case exemplifies the complex task facing legal systems and law enforcement, domestic and supranational, in dealing with the wide variety of individuals, with diverse motives and incentives, who seek to gain access to computer systems without permission.

Through the various treatments of news media and Hollywood films, the term 'hacking' has become part of the modern vernacular.[2] Hacking is a colloquial term for the unauthorised accessing of – and perhaps interference with – computer systems. It is the corollary phenomenon of modern ubiquity of computers, taking root as soon as these information systems began to develop.[3] Such actions can have a broad range of motivations and effects. At one end of the spectrum, there are those individuals and groups whose incentive is only the demonstration and recognition of their skill and expertise.[4] At the other extreme, there are the malign intents of foreign governments, organised crime groups and even terrorists.

The extent to which modern societies depend upon electronic networks and information systems increases year on year. Elements as diverse as economic and banking systems, government service delivery, corporations, military intelligence and personal communication, rely on the effective functioning of ever more complex computer systems. In this 'information society'[5] attacks on these critical elements of infrastructure are potentially highly damaging. As such, these information systems are prime targets for individuals, organised crime groups, international terrorists and even the espionage attempts of governments. Rather than just traditional crimes using computers, this section focuses on where we see computers and networks as the target of criminal activity, with attendant new criminal law offences.

[1] C Arthur, 'LulzSec Hackers Jailed for String of Sophisticated Cyber-attacks' *The Guardian*, 16 May 2013.

[2] The 1983 science fiction film 'Wargames', starring Matthew Broderick was probably the first to focus on hacking. Since then, upwards of 20 Hollywood films have used the phenomenon as a central plot device.

[3] http://news.bbc.co.uk/1/hi/sci/tech/994700.stm.

[4] These individuals are known as 'white–hat' hackers.

[5] In contrast to the former industrial society, members of the information society are not connected by their participation in industrialisation, but through their access to and the use of information and communication technologies (ICT). See M Gercke, 'Europe's Legal Approaches to Cybercrime' (2009) 10 *ERA Forum* 409.

(ii) The EU and 'Hacking'

Safeguarding information systems and the prosecution of those who commit such offences has become a significant issue for the Member States of the EU. Yet, effectively responding to the threat has proven difficult. Information systems frequently function across borders, utilise the internet, and are transnational in character. Correspondingly, so too are the crime groups and terrorists posited as posing the most significant threat to these systems. Any significant gaps or lack of uniformity in the criminal law approach of EU Member States can therefore undermine the police and judicial cooperation necessary to effectively prevent and respond to attacks on information systems.

For these reasons the EU has recognised the need to act to combat computer crime and strengthen the collective security of information infrastructures.[6] Under Article 83(1) TFEU the EU has the explicit competence to harmonise national criminal law in limited areas,[7] with 'computer crime' one area where the EU has the competency to act and identify common standards between Member States. A 2001 communication from the Commission was the first to articulate the increasing risks from cybercrime, and make proposals for action.[8] In particular, the Commission noted the potential implications of not addressing hacking for the EU area of freedom, justice and security.[9] Discrepancies between Member States' rules on the issue necessitated the approximation of rules, meaning that national 'substantive criminal laws should be sufficiently comprehensive and effective in criminalising serious computer-related abuses and provide for dissuasive sanctions'.[10] Those who attack target information systems should be identified and brought to justice, in order that other potential offenders are deterred from committing such acts. Particular emphasis has also been placed upon the risk of attack against essential communication infrastructure.[11] However, while

[6] Communication from the Commission on Creating a Safer Information Society by Improving the Security of Information Infrastructures and Combating Computer-related Crime, Brussels, 26 January 2001, COM (2000) 890 final, 2.

[7] Regarding harmonisation of the criminal law, see A Klip and H Van der Wilt (eds), *Harmonisation and Harmonising Measures in Criminal Law*, vol 186 (The Royal Academy of Arts and Science, Amsterdam, 2002).

[8] Communication from the Commission on Network and Information Security: Proposal for A European Policy Approach, Brussels, 6 June 2001, COM (2001) 298 final, 11 f.

[9] 'The Commission having participated in both the Council of Europe and the G8 discussions, recognises the complexity and difficulties associated with procedural law issues. But effective co-operation within the EU to combat Cybercrime is an essential element of a safer Information Society and the establishment of an Area of Freedom, Security and Justice': Communication from the Commission on Creating a Safer Information Society by Improving the Security of Information Infrastructures and Combating Computer-related Crime, Brussels, 26 January 2001, COM (2000) 890, 23.

[10] *Ibid*, 30.

[11] 'Information and communication infrastructures have become a critical part of our economies. Unfortunately, these infrastructures have their own vulnerabilities and offer new opportunities for criminal conduct. These criminal activities may take a large variety of forms and may cross many borders. Although, for a number of reasons, there are no reliable statistics, there is little doubt that these offences constitute a threat to industry investment and assets, and to safety and confidence in the

the communication highlighted the importance of effective criminalisation,[12] it did not make specific legislative recommendations.

(iii) The 2005 Framework Decision on Attacks against Information Systems

In 2002, the Commission proposed a Framework Decision on attacks against information systems.[13] Modified in part, this proposal was adopted in 2005, with Council Framework Decision on attacks against information systems. The focus of this framework decision was the approximation and harmonisation of criminal laws of Member States in relation to attacks on information systems, 'ensuring that attacks against information systems be sanctioned in all Member States by effective, proportionate and dissuasive criminal penalties and improving and encouraging judicial cooperation by removing potential complications'.[14] This emphasises infrastructure as the targets of attacks.

(a) Definitions

The Framework Decision first defines key terminology. Article 1(a) defines an 'information system' as 'any device or group of inter-connected or related devices [that] . . . performs automatic processing of computer data, as well as computer data stored, processed, retrieved or transmitted by them for the purposes of their operation, use, protection and maintenance'.[15] Article 1(b) further gives 'computer data' a wide interpretation, as 'any representation of facts, information or concepts in a form suitable for processing in an information system, including a program suitable for causing an information system to perform a function'.[16]

(b) Offences

The offences outlined in the Framework Decision constitute a minimum standard for EU states as they develop national laws to counter 'hacking'. Three offences are outlined: illegal access to information systems, illegal system interference, and illegal data interference. Article 2(1) provides that 'intentional access without

information society. Some recent examples of denial of service and virus attacks have been reported to have caused extensive financial damage'. *Ibid*, 2.

[12] '[. . .] to further approximate substantive criminal law in the area of high-tech crime. This will include offences related to hacking and denial of service attacks'. *Ibid*, 31.

[13] Proposal of the Commission for a Council Framework Decision on attacks against information systems, Brussels, 19 April 2002, COM (2002) 173, [2002] OJ C203 E/109. The legal basis for the Framework Decision, indicated in the preamble of the proposal for the Framework Decision is Arts 29, 30(a), 31 and 34(2)(b) TEU.

[14] Council Framework Decision 2005/222/JHA of 24 February 2005 on attacks against information systems [2005] OJ L69/67, Recital 17.

[15] *Ibid*, Art 1(a).

[16] *Ibid*, Art 1(b).

right to the whole or any part of an information system is punishable as a criminal offence'.[17] Article 3 outlines Member State obligations in relation to illegal system interference, stating that 'intentional serious hindering or interruption of the functioning of an information system by inputting, transmitting, damaging, deleting, deteriorating, altering, suppressing or rendering inaccessible computer data is punishable as a criminal offence when committed without right'.[18] Article 4 is concerned with illegal data interference, obligating states to criminalise 'intentional deletion, damaging, deterioration, alteration, suppression or rendering inaccessible of computer data on an information system'.[19] The difference between Article 3 and 4 is very unclear, with the only dissimilarity being the object of protection (Article 3 protects the information system while Article 4 focuses on existing data). Some flexibility is afforded states in implementing these rules in the national context, as each provision mentions they must only do so 'at least in cases which are not minor'.

The Framework Decision also encompasses participation and inchoate offences (also known as art-and-part offences) for the three acts outlined above. Article 5 specifies that the instigation, or aiding and abetting of any of the offences contained in Articles 2, 3 and 4 shall also be an offence. Attempts to commit the crimes shall also be an offence, though Article 5(3) makes this element optional for states. The inclusion of these offences significantly widens the range of acts that states should criminalise in relation to hacking.[20] These terms – instigation, aiding and abetting and attempt – are not defined in the Framework Decision.

(c) Penalties

One of the stated intentions of the Framework Decision, and indeed the general criminalisation of hacking in general, is to act as a deterrent to others. Article 6(1) specifies that penalties for crimes in this area must be 'effective, proportional and dissuasive'.[21] A more precise definition is given to these terms in relation to system interference and data interference offenses under Articles 3 and 4. These crimes must be punishable by between one and three years' imprisonment. Further, if the offender undertook the acts as part of a criminal organisation as defined in the Joint Action on criminal organisations,[22] then this should be considered an aggravating circumstance with a penalty of between two and five years'

[17] *Ibid*, Art 2(1).

[18] *Ibid*, Art 3.

[19] *Ibid*, Art 4.

[20] In particular, many German scholars think that this represents a problem concerning the ultima ratio principle of criminal law. See E Hilgendorf, 'Tendenzen und Probleme einer Harmonisierung des Internetstrafrechts auf Europäischer Ebene' in C Schwarzenegger, O Arter and F Jörg (eds), *Internet-Recht und Strafrecht* (Berne, Stämpfli, 2005) 277.

[21] Council Framework Decision 2005/222/JHA of 24 February 2005 on attacks against information systems [2005] OJ L69/67, Art 6(1).

[22] Council Joint Action 98/733/JHA of 21 December 1998 on making it a criminal offence to participate in a criminal organisation in the Member States of the European Union [1998] OJ L351/1.

imprisonment.[23] In truth, with the Framework Decision being only a baseline standard for states, it is only the minimum penalty specifications that are of real relevance. The mention of maximum penalties of between one and three years really only requires states to enact laws with a maximum penalty of at least one year.[24]

(d) Liability of Legal Persons

Articles 8 and 9 specify the liability of legal persons under the 2005 Framework Decision. Article 8 envisages the extension of criminal liability to legal persons on behalf of whom an impugned individual was acting. Article 8(1) mentions that in order to prosecute the legal person, the individual must either have power of representation of that legal person, decision-making power, or 'the authority to exercise control within the legal person'.[25] Article 8(2) also highlights that a legal person will be liable where the negligence of such an individual has made possible the commission of offences that benefit the legal person.[26] The Framework Decision is careful not to exclude the criminal liability of individuals (natural persons) involved in the crimes.[27] Article 9 specifies penalties for legal persons, highlighting again that they must be 'effective, proportionate and dissuasive'. This includes criminal and non-criminal fines, as well as other punishments such as exclusions from entitlements, disqualifications from commercial practice, judicial supervision or winding-up proceedings.[28]

As mentioned, the nature of cybercrime generally, but particularly hacking, is that it generally operates across borders. As such, jurisdictional issues present potential challenges for the EU's Member States. The Framework Decision specifies in Article 10(1) that a Member State shall have jurisdiction where the offence takes place in whole or in part within its territory, where the offence is promulgated by a national, or, where the crime is committed for the benefit of a legal person with a head office within the Member State's territory.[29] If an act is perpetrated within the jurisdiction of several states (as will often be the case), they must collaborate in order that proceedings may be concentrated in one Member State.[30] It is important to note that criminal procedural law, such as instruments required for the investigation and prosecution of attacks on information systems, were not a part of the Framework Decision.

[23] Council Framework Decision 2005/222/JHA of 24 February 2005 on attacks against information systems [2005] OJ L69/67, Art 7(1).

[24] On this, see M Gercke, 'Der Rahmenbeschluss über Angriffe auf Informationssysteme' (2005) 21 *Computer und Recht* 468, 471.

[25] Council Framework Decision 2005/222/JHA of 24 February 2005 on attacks against information systems [2005] OJ L69/67, Art 8(2) (iii).

[26] *Ibid.*

[27] *Ibid,* Art 8(3).

[28] *Ibid,* Art 9(1).

[29] *Ibid,* Art 10(1).

[30] *Ibid,* Art 10(4).

(e) Link with the Convention on Cybercrime

The Council of Europe plays an important role with regard to the harmonisation of criminal law between European States.[31] Of relevance here is the 2001 Convention on Cybercrime, which entered into force in June of 2004. The EU bodies are cognisant of the importance of complementarity with the Convention. In the proposal for a Council Framework Decision on combating serious attacks against information systems, number 1.6 of the explanations highlighted the importance of complementarity with the Convention on Cybercrime, stating:

> Legislative action at the level of the European Union also needs to take into account development in other international fora. In the context of approximation of substantive criminal law on attacks against information systems, the Council of Europe (C.o.E.) is currently the most far-advanced.

Of course, the EU Framework Decision is applicable to far fewer states; the membership of the EU being 20 compared to the Council of Europe's 47 Member States. In addition, implementation of the Framework Decision is compulsory for EU Member States, which are obliged by Article 12 to ensure implementation by March 2007. This is perhaps the most significant advantage of the Framework Decision as compared to the Convention.[32] However, there remains much in common between the 2005 Framework Decision and the slightly more ambitious Convention on Cybercrime. The Framework Decision's definition of 'computer data' is identical to that in the Cybercrime Convention, whereas the term 'information system' is used rather than 'computer system' in the Convention. The main difference here is that computer systems treat data of any type, whereas information systems (as described in the Framework Decision) are limited to handling computer data as defined in Article 1(b). Further, the provision in the Framework Decision on illegal access to information systems (Article 2), is almost identical to Article 2 of the Convention. Articles 3 and 4, dealing with illegal interference with systems, are also very similar to Articles 5 and 14 of the Convention. In relation to 'art and part' crimes, the Convention differs from the Framework Decision insofar as it doesn't include provisions on instigation.

[31] The Council of Europe, based in Strasbourg and founded in 1949, is an international organisation representing 47 Member States in the European region. The Council of Europe also plays an important role in the harmonisation of Criminal law between its 47 Member States (which count within their number all EU Member States).

[32] M Gercke, 'Die Entwicklung des Internetstrafrechts im Jahr 2005' (2006) 50 *Zeitschrift für Urheber- und Medienrecht* 284, 285; Gercke, 'Der Rahmenbeschluss über Angriffe auf Informationssysteme' (n 24) 469 f; F Sanchez-Hermosilla, 'Neues Strafrecht für den Kampf gegen Computerkriminalität' (2003) 19 *Computer und Recht* 774, 778; S Reindl-Krauskopf, *Computerstrafrecht im Überblick*, 2nd edn (Vienna, Facultas, 2009) 6; D Schuh, *Computerstrafrecht im Rechtsvergleich – Deutschland, Österreich, Schweiz* (Berlin, Duncker & Humblot, 2011) 48.

(f) Implementation of the 2005 Framework Decision

The ever-evolving nature of cybercrime is such that the importance of continuously monitoring the effectiveness of existing legal approaches is paramount.[33] Article 12(2) of the 2005 Framework Decision placed an obligation on Member States to transmit to the Commission the text of any provisions transposing the obligations imposed into their national law. By the specified date of 16 March 2007, only one state, Sweden, had complied. It was found that 7 of the 27 Member States had not fulfilled their obligations at all. It is important to note that, in line with the EU's general approach, the report focused on the formal level implementation of the Framework Decision – whether and how the crimes had been included in the domestic legal framework. The actual application of the rules – frequency of prosecutions, actual length of sentencing, and success in combatting hacking – was not the focus of the report.[34]

Generally, the Commission noted that the implementation has been undertaken in quite divergent manners by the Member States. Many states closely followed the wording of the Framework Decision, while others used more indirect means in pursuit of its goals. Generally, definitions of the Framework Decision were followed quite closely. A number of states (Austria, Czech, Finland, Latvia) took the option of prosecuting only 'cases which are not minor'.[35] The Commission expressed reservations about the approach of these states, stating that 'the concept of 'minor case' must refer to cases where instances of illegal access are of minor importance or where an infringement of information system confidentiality is of a minor degree'.[36]

For Article 3 on illegal system interference, the Commission again found difficulties in the interpretation of 'cases of minor importance', and called for more definition on this point. Among six states that explicitly followed this proviso, the German and Latvian rules, which generally had requirements of 'importance', 'damage' or loss, were not considered stringent enough to meet the requirements of the Framework Decision. The approach of dealing with the new offences using existing, non-cybercrime legislation was also not endorsed. In particular, the Commission expressed reservations about the Danish approach in relation to Articles 3 and 4 of the Framework Decision, which sought to use existing legislation. With the emphasis on 'dissuasive' measures, the Commission reported that

[33] Gercke, 'Europe's Legal Approaches to Cybercrime' (n 5) 410.

[34] Report from the Commission to the Council based on Article 12 of the Council Framework Decision of 24 February 2005 on attacks against information systems, Brussels, 14 July 2008, COM (2008) 448 final.

[35] In Austria, the legal criterion for criminal responsibility is that there must be intent to perpetrate data espionage and to use the data obtained in order to make a profit or to cause damage. The Czech Republic has criminalised illegal access only in cases where the data are subsequently misused or damaged. In Finland, the requirement for criminal responsibility is that the data accessed must be 'endangered'. In Latvia, illegal access is only criminalised 'if substantial injury is caused thereby'.

[36] Report from the Commission to the Council based on Article 12 of the Council Framework Decision of 24 February 2005 on attacks against information systems, Brussels, 14 July 2008, COM (2008) 448 final, 4.

all Member States assessed had implemented appropriate penalties in line with Article 6, while Article 7, with its specifications on aggravated offences has been complied with by 16 out of 20 states.

(iv) Directive on Attacks against Information Systems

The Commission's implementation report also highlighted the appearance of new threats since the adoption of the Framework Decision of 2005, in particular the threat of 'massive simultaneous attacks against information systems' and the emergence of 'botnets', defined as a 'collection of compromised machines running programs under a common command'. In light of the new threats, in 2010 the Commission presented a proposal for a Directive of the European Parliament and of the Council on attacks against information systems that would replace Council Framework Decision of 2005.[37] The purpose was to incorporate and supplement the provisions of the 2005 Framework Decision. Of particular concern was the phenomenon of 'botnets'. The Proposal defines a botnet as:

> A network of computers that have been infected by malicious software (computer virus). Such a network of compromised computers ('zombies') may be activated to perform specific actions, such as attacking information systems (cyber attacks). These 'zombies' can be controlled – often without the knowledge of the users of the compromised computers – by another computer. This 'controlling' computer is also known as the 'command-and-control centre'. The persons who control this centre are among the offenders, as they use the compromised computers to launch attacks against information systems.[38]

The potential damage caused by these botnets is extremely large[39]. The proposal for a directive seems, retrospectively, quite critical of the Framework Decision of 2005, stating 'it approximates legislation only on a limited number of offences, but does not fully address the potential threat posed to society by large scale attacks. Nor does it take sufficient account of the gravity of the crimes and sanctions against them'.[40]

The Directive adopted in 2013 essentially reproduces the offences set out in the former Framework Decision (illegal access to information systems, Article 3; illegal system interference, Article 4; Illegal data interference, Article 5) and seeks in addition to remedy these apparent shortcomings through including a number of additional offences. First, illegal interception is included in Article 6, which requires Member States to criminalise the intentional interception 'by technical

[37] Proposal for a Directive of the European Parliament and of the Council on attacks against information systems and repealing Council Framework Decision 2005/222/JHA, Brussels, 30 September 2010, COM (2010) 517 final.

[38] *Ibid*, 3.

[39] A total of 40,000 and 100,000 connections (ie infected computers) per period of 24 hours.

[40] Proposal for a Directive of the European Parliament and of the Council on attacks against information systems and repealing Council Framework Decision 2005/222/JHA, Brussels, 30 September 2010, COM (2010) 517 final, 4.

means', of 'non-public transmissions of computer data to, from or within an information system'.[41] Article 7 focuses on the tools used for committing offences and requires Member States to criminalise the 'intention production, sale, procurement for use, import, distribution or otherwise making available, of' certain tools for committing the offences.[42] These tools are defined any computers programme 'designed or adapted primarily for the purposes of committing any of the offences referred to in Articles 3 to 6' or any 'computer password, access code, or similar data by which the whole or any part of an information system is capable of being accessed'.[43] The rules on incitement, aiding and abetting and attempt are largely reproduced. The Member States must ensure that the incitement or aiding and abetting of an offence referred to in Articles 3 to 7 is criminalised[44] and must provide for criminal liability for the attempt to commit a crime set out in Articles 4 and 5.[45]

Importantly, the proposal also includes a broader range of penalties. In addition to the 'effective, proportionate and dissuasive penalties' to be imposed in the context of the offences referred to in Articles 3 to 7, then Member States must also provide for a maximum sentence of imprisonment of at least two years in such cases 'at least for cases which are not minor'.[46] In the context of the offences set out in Articles 4 and 5, the Member States must ensure that the offences are punishable by 'a maximum term of imprisonment of at least three years where a significant number of information systems have been affected through the use of a tool, referred to in Article 7, designed or adapted primarily for that purpose'[47] and by a maximum sentence of at least five years if they are committed within the framework of a criminal organisation, if they cause serious damage or if they are committed against a critical infrastructure information system.[48]

The Directive brings the EU regulations marginally closer to the Cybercrime Convention.[49] However, it seems that more detailed analysis of actual implementation effectiveness on a country-by-country basis is required before it can be said for certain that the EU's regulation of attacks on information systems, however stringent, have had any impact on the global phenomenon of hacking.

[41] Directive 2013/40/EU of the European Parliament and of the Council of 12 August 2013 on attacks against information systems and replacing Council Framework Decision 2005/222/JHA [2013] OJ L218/8, Art 6.

[42] *Ibid*, Art 7.

[43] *Ibid*, Art 7(a) and (b).

[44] *Ibid*, Art 8(1).

[45] *Ibid*, Art 8(2).

[46] *Ibid*, Art 9(1) and (2).

[47] Ibid, Art 9(3).

[48] *Ibid*, Art 9(4).

[49] D Brodowski, 'Strafrechtsrelevante Entwicklungen in der Europäischen Union – ein Überblick' (2011) *Zeitschrift für Internationale Strafrechtsdogmatik* 940, 945; Council of the European Union, Outcome of Proceedings, Brussels, 15 June 2011 (11566/11).

B Fraud and Cybercrime

(i) Introduction

With the advent of the Internet and the continuing development of the online world, traditional criminal behaviour has evolved in light of new possibilities presented. Legal systems have struggled to respond to the new forms of criminal behaviour.[50] In particular, for those seeking to steal or defraud, the Internet has proved an exquisitely fertile playing field. It has become the global market place, with banking and purchases increasingly taking place in the online environment. With this method of 'cashless' transacting increasingly the norm, individuals are increasingly familiar and comfortable providing personal, financial information over the Internet. Online, many of the cues and checks through which we would ascertain veracity in person, are absent, which, coupled with the instantaneous nature of online communication, makes it conducive to fraud.[51] Anonymity exacerbates these issues – it is easy to convincingly assume alternate identities. In short, there has never before been such ready, simple, free access to compliant potential victims worldwide. For fraudsters worldwide, the more potential victims within reach, the greater the spread of 'bets' that can be placed, and the more chance there is that one will pay off. This section will consider in brief the EU's response to fraud in general before looking at one particularly important offence, identity theft, in detail.

(ii) The EU Approach to Online Fraud

The EU has focused on addressing fraud directed against the financial interests of the EU, for example, tax evasion and fraud in relation to subsidies. Article 325 TFEU carves out an obligation on the part of the EU and its Member States to cooperate in combating fraud that affects the financial interests of the Union. On this basis, it is perceived that the Commission has additional powers in this area.[52] A distinct organisation was created to combat fraud, the European Anti-Fraud Office (OLAF). This office has the responsibility for investigating and prosecuting such offences.[53] However, there is no specific EU legislation

[50] The new 'online version' of the crimes also leads to legal problems. For instance, the majority of the regulations of fraud require that a person is fooled; the manipulation of a computer or data is not sufficient in itself; see U Sieber, '§ 24 Computerkriminalität' in U Sieber, FH Brüner, H Satzeger and B v Heintschel-Heinegg (eds), *Europäisches Strafrecht* (Baden-Baden, Nomos, 2011) para 24 n 21; M Gercke and PW Brunst, *Praxishandbuch Internetstrafrecht* (Stuttgart, Kohlhammer, 2009) n 159 ff.

[51] J Clough, *Principles of Cybercrime* (Cambridge, Cambridge University Press, 2010) 184.

[52] A Klip, *European Criminal Law: an Integrative Approach* (Cambridge, Intersentia, 2009) 388

[53] G Corstens and J Pradel, *European Criminal Law* (The Hague, Kluwer Law International, 2002) n 473a; S Gless, *Internationales Strafrecht* (Basel, Helbing Lichtenhahn, 2011) n 480; B Hecker, *Europäisches Strafrecht,* 4th edn (Berlin, Springer, 2012) para 4 n 18 ff; C Stefanou, S White and H Xanthaki, *OLAF at the Crossroads – Action against EU fraud* (Oxford, Hart, 2011) 9 ff; S Weitendorf, *Die interne Betrugsbekämpfung in den Europäischen Gemeinschaften durch das Europäische Amt für Betrugsbekämpfung (OLAF)* (Hamburg, Lit, 2007) 53 ff.

focusing on online-based fraud. Rather, it is dealt with within more general documents.[54]

(a) Framework Decision on Combating Fraud

The danger of fraud has been recognised by the EU through the Council Framework Decision of 28 May 2001 combating fraud and counterfeiting of non-cash means of payment. Recital 4 sets out the goals of the Framework Decision, which are 'to ensure that fraud and counterfeiting involving all forms of non-cash means of payment are recognised as criminal offences and are subject to effective, proportionate and dissuasive sanctions in all Member States'. Article 1(a) defines a 'payment instrument' as a 'corporeal instrument, other than legal tender (bank notes and coins), enabling, by its specific nature, alone or in conjunction with another (payment) instrument, the holder or user to transfer money or monetary value'. The most obvious example of such an instrument is a credit card, but could also include traveller's checks, as well as other cheques or bills of exchange.

Articles 2 to 5 set out the relevant offences, which Member States must include within their domestic systems. First, offences related to payment instruments include the intentional theft or unlawful appropriation of a payment instrument[55], the falsification or counterfeiting of such for fraudulent purposes[56], 'receiving, obtaining, transporting, sale or transfer' of a stolen or fraudulent payment instrument,[57] and fraudulent use of such an instrument.[58]

Article 3 addresses the potential of computers and information system in schemes to defraud. Offences include the intentional 'performing or causing a transfer of money or monetary value causing an unauthorised loss of property for another with the intention of procuring an unauthorised economic benefit'. This could be either through 'introducing, altering, deleting or supressing computer data, in particular identification data' or 'interfering with the functioning of a computer programme or system'. Article 4 provides for offences related to specifically adapted devices for the purposes of the commission of fraud as outlined in Articles 2 and 3, meaning that actions prior to the actual fraud are considered punishable.[59] Article 5 provides that each of these crimes contained in Articles 2–4 shall also be criminalised in the modalities of participation, instigation and attempt. Overall, the most common types of computer fraud are covered by this Framework Decision.[60]

[54] Art 8 of the Cybercrime Convention regulates online fraud.

[55] Council Framework Decision 2001/413/JHA of 28 May 2001 on combating fraud and counterfeiting of non-cash means of payment [2001] OJ L149/1, Art 2(a).

[56] *Ibid*, Art 2(b).

[57] *Ibid*, Art 2(c).

[58] *Ibid*, Art 2(d).

[59] Reindl-Krauskopf, *Computerstrafrecht im Überblick* (n 32) 5.

[60] Gercke, 'Europe's Legal Approaches to Cybercrime' (n 5) 412.

Article 6 provides that Member States shall take 'necessary measures' to ensure that the crimes laid out in Articles 2–5 are punished by 'effective, proportionate and dissuasive criminal penalties'. Custodial sentences should be included 'at least in serious cases'. Article 7 extends the scope of the Framework Decision to include liability for legal persons when someone committing fraud has power of representation for the legal person, authority to act on the legal person's behalf, or the authority to exercise control within the legal person. Article 7(2) also highlights the situation where lack of supervision or control by an individual acting for the legal person has made the commission of such a fraud for the benefit of the legal person possible.

(b) *Implementation*

The Member States were required to implement the Framework Decision by June 2003. By that date, not one Member State had informed the Commission of implementation measures. By the time of writing of a 2004 report,[61] five Member States were fully compliant.[62] Belgium felt its existing legislation covered the crimes, but submitted no documentation. Four states were in the process of implementing new legislation.[63] The Commissions stated that: 'several Member States considered that for the most part, their current legislation already corresponds to the obligations of the FD'. In 2006, the Commission produced another report on implementation of the Framework Decision. This report focused on the states that had acceded to the EU in the interim period. By this point, most states were compliant, although particularly in relation to penalties, were 'far from uniform'.[64]

(c) *Preventive Measures*

Intended to complement the Framework Decision, in 2001 the EU also devised a Fraud Prevention Action Plan. This action plan addresses preventive objectives in technological developments (for example, confidence-building standardised security measures such as chip and pin), exchange of information (in order to promote an earlier detection and notification of fraud attempts), education (improved law enforcement training on the issue of fraud), relations with third countries (cooperation with these countries to combat fraudsters who operate

[61] Report from the Commission based on Article 14 of the Council Framework Decision of 28 May 2001 combating fraud and counterfeiting of non-cash means of payment, Brussels, 30 April 2004, COM (2004) 346 final, 6.

[62] France, Germany, Italy, Ireland and the UK. Finland was late in submitting, but compliant.

[63] Greece, Austria, Netherlands and Luxembourg.

[64] Report from the Commission, Second report based on Article 14 of the Council Framework Decision of 28 May 2001 combating fraud and counterfeiting of non-cash means of payment, Brussels, 20 February 2006, COM (2006) 65 final, 6 f.

from their territories), and assorted other measures.[65] This action plan was updated for the period 2004 to 2007.[66]

(iii) Identity Theft

Identity theft is one of the most potent methods through which the Internet has been utilised for fraudulent purposes. It draws on other types of cybercrime such as hacking, and thrives in an online reality where individuals trustingly submit personal data to make purchases, develop full digital identities, and where social activities that have transferred online demand the sacrifice of personal data as a pre-requisite for full participation. It is this personal data which is the goal of identity theft.

(a) Definition

While there is no clearly established definition of identity theft, it is essentially the fraud of impersonation, and constitutes 'the misappropriation of the identity (such as the name, date of birth, current address or previous addresses) of another person, without his or her knowledge or consent'.[67] It focuses upon an individual's attributed or 'legal' identity, such as name, date and place of birth, parents' names and addresses, and nationality. The UK Home Office defines it as follows: 'Identity Theft occurs when sufficient information about an identity is obtained to facilitate identity fraud, irrespective of whether, in the case of an individual, the victim is alive or dead'.[68] Some consider identity fraud and identity theft as synonymous, while others differentiate identity fraud as a crime directed against institutions (states, banks etc), while identity theft is directed against an individual person.[69] Frequently a differentiation is made whereby identity fraud is characterised by the fact that somebody is tricked to get to their information, whereas identity theft is used in cases where the information is stolen from the victim.[70]

It is important to note in the context of each of these general definitions that identity theft is a preliminary step, used as part of the perpetration of further criminal behaviour. The Home Office describes identity fraud as occurring 'when a false identity or someone else's identity details are used to support unlawful activity, or when someone avoids obligation/liability by falsely claiming that he/

[65] Communication from the Commission on Preventing fraud and counterfeiting of non-cash means of payment, Brussels, 9 February 2001, COM (2001) 11 final, 2 ff.

[66] Communication from the Commission on a new EU Action Plan 2004–2007 to prevent fraud on non-cash means of payment, Brussels, 20 October 2004, COM (2004) 679 final.

[67] MD White and C Fisher, 'Assessing Our Knowledge of Identity Theft: The Challenges to Effective Prevention and Control Efforts' (2008) 19 *Criminal Justice Policy Review* 3.

[68] This is the UK Home Office definition, available at www.identitytheft.org.uk/definition.html.

[69] M McNally and G Newman, *Perspectives on Identity Theft* (Cullompton, Devon, 2008) 2.

[70] C Roberson, *Identity Theft Investigations* (New York, Kaplan, 2008) 4.

she was the victim of identity fraud'.[71] Another prominent scholar calls it, more simply, 'the use of a misappropriated identity in criminal activity, to obtain goods or services by deception'.[72]

(b) Methods

Identity theft can be perpetrated using a variety of methods. There are physical methods such as the stealing of phones, computers, passports, driver's licenses, theft of paper mail. This could involve acts as crude as breaking into a house or raiding the victim's bins. However, the most potent and widespread attacks now involve computer systems. Digital access methods include the use of search engines to get personal data, where one can trawl millions of webpages in a short amount of time. There are insider attacks, where one with legitimate access to information misuses this access. There are outsider attacks, where hacking or spyware is used to obtain data. There are also schemes that employ social techniques, known as 'phishing' – the attempt to acquire personal information through fraud, such as impersonating a trustworthy person or business. The goal of all these attacks is accessing information such as passport numbers, ID numbers, dates of birth, addresses, phone numbers, passwords, and financial account details.

(c) Targets

Identity theft can affect a wide variety of persons, both actual and legal. Four basic categories can be identified: governments, private companies who keep large amounts of data, financial service providers and customers. Their losses can be directly financial through funds extracted from accounts, but for governments, companies and financial service providers there are also more oblique costs, such as that to reputation and trust.

(d) EU Response to Identity Theft?

Particularly bearing in mind this latter concern, about the integrity and reputation of financial system and institutions, how have the European institutions, most especially the EU, responded to safeguard itself and its Member States from the issue of identity theft?

Currently there is no specific offence of identity theft approximated within EU legislation. However, some potential elements of identity theft are caught by other pieces of legislation, such as those on privacy, hacking, fraud, and organised crime.

[71] www.identitytheft.org.uk/definition.html.

[72] M Gercke, 'Internet Related Identity Theft: A Discussion Paper', 22 November 2007, available at www.coe.int/t/dghl/cooperation/economiccrime/cybercrime/cyactivity_events_on_identity_theft/567 port id-d-identity theft paper 22 nov 07.pdf, at 5.

For instance, Directive 95/46/EC protects the rights of individuals to 'privacy with respect to the processing of their personal data', although an exemption is carved out for 'a monitoring, inspection or regulatory function connected, even occasionally, with the exercise of official authority'.[73] Under this Directive, a duty of care is imposed (under Article 17) upon those holding personal data. They must 'implement appropriate technical and organizational measures to protect personal data against . . . unauthorised disclosure or access'. This at least covers the situation where identity theft is facilitated through the negligent conduct of an institution holding an individual's information. Similarly the Framework Decision of 2005 on attacks on information systems renders identity theft criminal if it involved an element of unlawful accessing of information systems (hacking).

The Council of Europe has taken a similar approach. 'Identity theft for fraud' is highlighted in the Committee on Economic Affairs and Development Report 'Europe's Fight Against Economic and Transnational Organised Crime: Progress or Retreat?' However, the Council of Europe's Convention on Cybercrime does not include identity theft as a specific offence. Like the EU regime, the Cybercrime Convention only covers elements that form part of the identity theft. Article 8 addresses computer-related fraud, specifically the 'causing of a loss of property to another, committed intentionally and without right, by any input, alteration, deletion or suppression of computer data, or any interference with the functioning of a computer system, with the fraudulent or dishonest intent of procuring, without right, an economic benefit for oneself or for another'. This clearly covers a substantial aspect of identity theft using computer systems. The Convention also covers illegal access to information systems (Article 2), illegal interception (Article 3), data interference (Article 4), system interference (Article 5), misuse of devices (Article 6), and computer-related forgery (Article 7).

Thus, while there is relevant legislation emanating from both the EU and the Council of Europe, 'neither the Convention on Cybercrime nor the EU framework decision contain a general provision covering any approach to illegally obtain, possess or use identity-related information be internet-related scams'.[74]

(e) A Specific Offence of Identity Theft?

Perhaps unsurprisingly, in the absence of an obligation to do so, most Member States do not yet specifically criminalise identity theft. In the UK, while there have been consultations on whether identity theft should be made a crime, it is only a criminal offence if it can be proved there is some conspiracy to commit a criminal act or fraud, or if such took place. In Italy and France, identity theft will normally

[73] Directive 95/46/EC of the European Parliament and of the Council of 24 October 1995 on the protection of individuals with regard to the processing of personal data and on the free movement of such data [1995] OJ L281/31.

[74] N Mitchison, M Wilikens, L Breitenbach, R Urry and S Portesi, 'Identity Theft: A Discussion Paper', March 2004, available at www.prime-project.eu/community/furtherreading/studies/IDTheftFIN.pdf, at 30.

be criminalised under other provisions such as fraud, information fraud, impersonation, or illegal use and processing of personal data.[75]

Cognisant of this, the EU's fraud prevention expert group in 2007 highlighted that not only is there a vast disparity of penalties applied to identity theft-related crimes across Europe, but that they are likely too low to be properly dissuasive. Their report highlighted a 2002 UK study, which stated that: 'Prosecution of offenders should be pursued more vigorously. One way to ensure this might be through the creation of a new offence of identity theft, which might make successful prosecution both more worthwhile and easier'.

Similarly, in 2007 the Commission itself made steps towards establishing a special offence of identity theft, recognising the substantial links between cybercrime already legislated for, and identity theft.[76] The Commission noted that while this subsequent fraud or theft will be a crime, it may in fact be easier to prosecute identity theft as a standalone offence. In light of this, a recommendation was made that 'EU law enforcement cooperation would be better served were identity theft criminalised in all member states'.[77] A comparative study was launched in July 2007 looking at definitions of identity theft and criminal consequences. Amid broad support for harmonisation of EU criminal law in respect of identity theft, the possibility of EU intervention seems likely.[78]

Despite the presence of broad support for harmonisation that seems to accompany most EU legislative initiatives (at least within the EU), it is not clear that specific legislation on identity theft will necessarily have the desired effect of deterring and decreasing instance of identity theft. As one scholar noted, 'success in the fight against internet-related identity theft is not primarily a question of additional substantive law provisions'.[79] Substantive law provision are inherently reactive, whereas ensuring technological advances in internet security, preventive measures, and cooperation in achieving prevention, is inevitably more vital.

C Terrorism

(i) Introduction

With hindsight, the threat of international terrorism was perhaps the defining feature of the twenty-first century's first decade. On 11 September 2001, the age-old phenomenon of violence and intimidation in pursuit of political ends was given shocking, contemporary expression by the Al Qaeda attacks on New York's Twin Towers. Western countries struggled to re-orient themselves to deal with an

[75] *Ibid.*

[76] See Communication from the Commission to the European Parliament, the Council and the Committee of the Regions – Towards a General Policy on the Fight against Cyber Crime, Brussels, 22 May 2007, COM (2007) 267 final, 8.

[77] *Ibid*, 8.

[78] Fraud Prevention Expert Group, 'Report on Identity Theft/Fraud', Brussels, 22 October 2007, available at http://ec.europa.eu/internal_market/fpeg/docs/id-theft-report_en.pdf.

[79] Gercke, 'Internet Related Identity Theft' (n 72) 32.

ill-defined but potent foe, entering a modern conflict – coined the 'war on terror' – which seemed to somehow subvert traditional ideas of state boundaries, human rights and the rule of law. Against this backdrop, legal frameworks and law enforcement approaches very swiftly transformed, with previously unthinkable laws and measures deemed necessary in order to combat the 'new' threat.

The 'new-ness' of the perceived threat stemmed not only from the apparently amorphous, trans-continental modus operandi of Al Qaeda and affiliates, but was also intertwined with the modern technology that had come to define modern Western culture. Mobile phones and the Internet were key enabling factors for a threat with no real temporal boundaries. Meanwhile, these same tools of communication fed an enduring culture of fear with concentrated, doomsday coverage. Now the negative potential of modern information technology and the Internet seemed all too clear, with worries that an all-pervasive reliance on modern technology could, rather than being a strength, prove a vulnerability.

(ii) Cyber-terrorism

> The more websites, the better it is for us. We must make the internet our tool.[80]

In 2006, *The Economist* magazine reported these words as appearing on a website used by jihadists and Al-Qaeda. They exemplify a popular and intuitive fear, namely that the simultaneous upsurges in international terrorist activity, societal use and reliance upon technology and the internet, and the phenomenon of cybercrime, could together manifest in a growing and potent threat of 'cyber-terrorism'.

This term does not have an accepted definition, but generally refers to 'attacks via the Internet', to access and cause damage to infrastructure, systems, and vital communications. Within this category we would include the use of botnets to undertake large scale targeted attacks, the use of conventional hacking techniques to get into identified strategically important computers, conventional physical attacks launched in conjunction with the aforementioned approaches, and finally, the manipulation of IT systems that control vital interests like railways, airports or the stock market.[81] Sometimes included in the 'cyber-terrorism' category is the 'dissemination of illegal content' such as glorification of terrorism, and distribution of hate speech materials, and also the use of the Internet in non-criminal form, but to serve the logistical ends of terrorism. This could include internal communication, research, planning and analysis.[82]

Thus far, fears of cyber-terrorism attacks have proved unfounded; there is no recorded instance of such an attack by terrorist groups.[83] However, other attacks

[80] 'Terror.com', *The Economist,* 27 April 2006.

[81] Council of Europe's Committee of Experts on Terrorism, *Cyberterrorism – The Use of the Internet for Terrorist Purposes* (Strasbourg, Council of Europe Publishing, 2007) 18.

[82] *Ibid,* 11. See further ch 5.

[83] Though some believe such attacks have taken place, but have not been revealed to the public, see M Gercke, '"Cyberterrorismus" – Aktivitäten terroristischer Organisationen im Internet' (2007) 23 *Computer und Recht* 62, 63.

have shown the potential impact. In 2007, Estonia suffered a huge cyber attack on its information infrastructure, with vandalism of sites and denial of service strikes using botnets. It was the first cyber attack directed at the security of an entire country.[84] While no conclusive proof was ever found, the attack is widely accepted to have come from Russia, with blame being attributed to the Russian government. Although some referred to the Estonia attacks as cyber-terrorism, a state attack cannot be considered terrorism in the conventional sense – the term terrorism normally considered only applies to non-state actors.[85] Likewise, a very different kind of attack took place in 2008 in Australia. A disgruntled former employee, using a computer, gave commands to a sewage system, which saw 800,000 litres of raw sewage spill into local parks and rivers.[86] Neither case can be considered cyber-terrorism, but both illustrate the kind of destruction that could be possible for terrorist groups with the right access or expertise.[87]

(iii) The Basic EU Framework on Terrorism

Post 9/11, the effect on the legal landscapes of Western nations was profound; over a decade on many of the exceptional 'emergency' responses have endured to an apparent state of permanence. The bombings in London and Madrid that followed in 2005 seemed only to galvanise the political will for further strong action domestically, but also, necessarily, on the supranational level. In this regard, the EU had an important role to play. Even prior to the 9/11 attacks, the EU had adopted a plethora of measures focused on the problem of terrorism.[88] Terrorism was frequently considered in the broader context of the fight against organised crime.[89] However, the attack on New York made further, decisive action a necessity, at least politically. This section first of all outlines the key framework decision defining terrorism within the EU, then analyses responses to cyber-terrorism specifically.

[84] J Davis, 'Hackers Take Down the Most Wired Country in Europe' (2007) *Wired Magazine* Issue 15.09.

[85] B Hoffman, *Inside Terrorism*, 2nd edn (New York, Columbia University Press, 2006) 41.

[86] http://csrc.nist.gov/groups/SMA/fisma/ics/documents/Maroochy-Water-Services-Case-Study_report.pdf.

[87] Even if there is no real evidence the danger of cyber-terrorism is an oft-addressed subject; see Council of Europe's Committee of Experts on Terrorism, *Cyberterrorism – The Use of the Internet for Terrorist Purposes* (n 81).

[88] The Council Decision of 3 December 1998 instructing Europol to deal with crimes committed or likely to be committed in the course of terrorist activities against life, limb, personal freedom or property [1999] OJ C26/22; The Council Joint Action 96/610/JHA of 15 October 1996 concerning the creation and maintenance of a Directory of specialised counter-terrorist competences, skills and expertise to facilitate counter-terrorism cooperation between the Member States of the European Union [1996] OJ L273/1; The Council Joint Action 98/428/JHA of 29 June 1998 on the creation of a European Judicial Network [1998] OJ L191/4, with responsibilities in terrorist offences, in particular Article 2; The Council Joint Action 98/733/JHA of 21 December 1998 on making it a criminal offence to participate in a criminal organisation in the Member States of the European Union [1998] OJ L351/1 and the Council Recommendation of 9 December 1999 on cooperation in combating the financing of terrorist groups [1999] OJ C373/1.

[89] While united by a common opposition to government authority, organised crime and terrorism normally have fundamentally different objectives, which renders this grouping unsatisfactory.

(a) Council Framework Decision on Combating Terrorism

The first and most significant post-9/11 legislative step was the Framework Decision of 2002 on combating terrorism.[90] This Framework Decision determined that terrorist offences should be approximated across all EU Member States, and that penalties and sanctions should be uniform and sufficiently serious.[91]

Article 1(1) outlines terrorist acts, namely those aimed at 'seriously intimidating a population', 'unduly compelling', 'seriously destabilising or destroying'. Nine specific acts are outlined, including attacks on life, physical integrity and kidnapping/hostage taking, but also 'causing extensive destruction' to facilities, infrastructure, private property, offences related to weapons, attacks on natural resources, as well as attempts thereof. Despite the wide range of offences specified, Article 1(2) is careful to make clear that it 'shall not have the effect of altering the obligation to respect fundamental rights and fundamental legal principles'. Such a provision is important, with human rights concerns often deemed secondary in comparison to security concerns. It is important to note is that the definition of terrorism the EU adopted is one of the broadest nationally or supranationally. Article 2(1) defines terrorist group as 'a structured group of more than two persons, established over a period of time and acting concert to commit terrorist offences'. This excludes groups randomly formed to immediately commit an offence. Article 2(2) compels Member States to ensure criminalisation for those directing such a terrorist group, and participating in the activities of such a group. The idea of participation is widely construed to include supplying information or material resources, and providing funding, as long as there is knowledge that such participation will contribute to the criminal activities of the group.[92]

Article 4 includes the acts of 'Inciting, aiding or abetting, and attempting' to commit the crimes outlined in Article 1. Article 5 repeats the EU's normal language in regard to penalties, namely that the offences referred to in Articles 1–4 be punishable with 'effective, proportionate and dissuasive criminal penalties'. Further definition is given in Article 4(2), with Member States needing to ensure that the offences mentioned in Article 1(1) and Article 4 are punished by custodial sentences more severe than if the offence was committed without the special terrorist intent stated in Article 1(1). An exception is made where the offences are already the most severe allowed under the Member State legal system.[93]

The Framework Decision had the potential to have a fundamental effect upon national criminal law systems. Prior to 2002, only six states had specifically defined terrorist offences.[94] Other states treated acts of terrorism under common criminal law statutes. Now obligated by the Framework Decision, those states

[90] Council Framework Decision of 13 June 2002 on combating terrorism (2002/475/JHA) [2002] OJ L164/3.

[91] *Ibid*, Recital 6.

[92] *Ibid*, Art 2(b).

[93] *Ibid*, Art 5(2).

[94] Proposal for a Council Framework Decision on combating terrorism, Brussels, 19 September 2001, COM (2001) 521 final, 6 f.

introduced specialised offences, while the six with existent regimes each widened the scope of these offences.[95]

(b) EU Regulations and Cyber-terrorism

As outlined above, the 2002 Framework Decision did not include specific reference to cyber-terrorism. However certain acts in the category could still fall within its ambit.[96] It focuses on the damage caused by the attack, and the intent of the perpetrator. In this way, under Article 1, intentional cybercrime acts 'which, given their nature or context, may seriously damage a country or an international organisation where committed with the aim of: – seriously intimidating a population, or – unduly compelling a Government or international organisation to perform or abstain from performing any act, or – seriously destabilising or destroying the fundamental political, constitutional, economic or social structures of a country or an international organisation' shall be deemed to be terrorist offences.

In particular, it is envisaged that computers could be the method through which 'extensive destruction to a Government or public facility, a transport system, an infrastructure facility, including, an information system' could be caused. The extent of the possible damage to computer infrastructure is highlighted, which would incorporate large-scale virus attacks of denial of service attacks. Minor attacks would not be included, however, and the cybercrime act would need 'terrorist' intent on the part of the perpetrator. In this way, the 'terroristic' elements of the crimes serve as aggravating factors, and Article 5 requires they attract more severe custodial sentences than offences without the terroristic intent.

Further, certain aspects of cyber-terrorism can fall under non-terrorism-focused EU regulations. For example, for terrorism acts involving 'hacking' the Framework Decision on attacks against information systems criminalises the acts of illegally accessing information system (Article 2), illegal interference with systems (Article 3), illegally interfering with data (Article 4), as well as inchoate offences. Certain regulations prohibiting spam, spyware and malicious software could also be relevant for mass denial of service attacks in particular.

As can be seen, while the EU Framework Decision did not prioritise cyber-terrorism, most serious acts of cyber-terrorism would have been covered under the EU Framework Decision as it was in 2002. However, this Framework Decision did not consider the wider potentialities of the Internet in spreading terrorist messages, recruiting, training and planning. Thus, in 2007 a proposal was made to update the 2002 Framework Decision on combating terrorism,[97] focusing on

[95] See further on implementation, ch 5.

[96] See Council of Europe's Committee of Experts on Terrorism, *Cyberterrorism – The use of the Internet for terrorist purposes* (n 81) 55.

[97] Proposal for a Council Framework Decision amending Framework Decision 2002/475/JHA on combating terrorism, Brussels, 6 November 2007, COM (2007) 650 final, 2.

preventing terrorism and addressing the modern modus operandi of terrorism. As stated by the Council:

> The Internet serves . . . as one of the principal boosters of the processes of radicalisation and recruitment and also serves as a source of information on terrorist means and methods, thus functioning as a 'virtual training camp'. The dissemination of terrorist propaganda and terrorist expertise through the Internet complements and enhances off-line indoctrination and training and contributes to the development of a stronger and wider platform of terrorist activists and supporters.[98]

(c) *Framework Decision 2008/919/JHA on Combating Terrorism*

This proposal led to the Council Framework Decision 2008/919/JHA of 28 November 2008, amending Framework Decision 2002/475/JHA on combating terrorism. This Framework Decision serves not to repeal, but rather amend and supplement the 2002 Framework Decision by adding legal order offences focused on the prevention of terrorism – 'offences linked to terrorist activities'.[99] Thus, the two must be read together. The new offences included in the 2008 Framework Decision are largely derived from the 2005 Council of Europe Convention on Prevention of Terrorism.

The three new offences are public provocation to commit a terrorist offence,[100] recruitment for terrorism,[101] and training for terrorism.[102] With the reality of modern communication via the Internet, each of these elements is likely to involve the use of computers. Article 4(1) also makes aiding and abetting these acts a criminal offence, though Article 4(4) leaves the criminalisation of attempt to Member State discretion, and there is no crime of inciting these offences.

It is vital to recognise that these acts are punishable even where no terrorist offence is actually committed. This represents a transition to a preventive paradigm, which has come to exemplify the response to terrorism in a number of Member States following 9/11. The emphasis is upon controlling those who may commit crimes, rather than punishing those who do. Article 2 states that the Framework Decision will not require states to take measures contra fundamental principles of free expression. However, as one scholar critically stated: 'A wide range of conduct could potentially be included within the criminalisation scope

[98] *Ibid.*

[99] Council Framework Decision 2008/919/JHA of 28 November 2008 amending Framework Decision 2002/475/JHA on combating terrorism [2008] OJ L330/21, Art 3(1).

[100] *Ibid,* Art 3(1)(a); public provocation is defined as the distribution, or otherwise making available, of a message to the public, with the intent to incite the commission of one of the offences listed in Art 1(1)(a)–(h) (of the 2002 Framework Decision), where such conduct, whether or not directly advocating terrorist offences, causes a danger that one or more such offences may be committed.

[101] *Ibid,* Art 3(1)(b); recruitment for terrorism is defined as soliciting another person to commit one of the offences listed in Art 1(1)(a)–(h) or in Art 2(2) (of the 2002 Framework Decision).

[102] *Ibid,* Art 3(1)(c); training for terrorism is defined as providing instruction in the making or use of explosives, firearms or other weapons or noxious or hazardous substances, or in other specific methods or techniques, for the purpose of committing one of the offences listed in Art 1(1)(a)–(h), knowing that the skills provided are intended to be used for this purpose.

of the Framework decision, while, on the other hand, the safeguards included in the instrument are drafted in rather general terms and their effect in the implementation process in member states is unclear'.[103] It is important to note that a 'terrorist motivation' must be evidenced, stemming from the link with Article 1 of the 2002 Framework Decision. Regardless, it is broad, subjective, and therefore questionable in terms of legal certainty.

(d) Other Initiatives to Protect Critical Infrastructure

The substantial part of the fear associated with terrorism, and by extension cyberterrorism, is concern over threats to critical infrastructure. A number of non-judicial EU initiatives have sought to safeguard this infrastructure. Council Directive 2008/114/EC on the identification and designation of European critical infrastructures and the assessment of the need to improve their protection was passed in 2008. A proposal on a critical infrastructure warning information network followed,[104] but was later withdrawn.[105]

In 2009, a Communication was made from the Commission, titled 'Protecting Europe from Large Scale Cyber-attacks and Disruptions: Enhancing Preparedness, Security and Resilience'.[106] The Communication cites the 'unprecedented level of sophistication' of attacks, performed for 'profit or political reasons'.[107] It highlights the fact that ICT (information and communications technology) systems, services, networks and infrastructures (in short, ICT infrastructures) form a vital part of the European economy and society, either providing essential goods and services or constituting the underpinning platform of other critical infrastructures. These should be regarded as critical information infrastructures (CIIs).[108] The Communication highlighted that attacks on such CIIs need not necessarily be terrorist in nature, but could also be at risk from foreign governments. The Communication outlines a plan of immediate actions to secure CIIs, focusing on prevention and preparedness. This measure was one of those intended to complement judicial efforts to prosecute offences.[109]

[103] V Mitsilegas, 'The Third Wave of Third Pillar Law: Which Direction for EU Criminal Justice?' (2009) 34 *EL Review* 523, 526.

[104] Proposal for a Council Decision, on a Critical Infrastructure Warning Information Network (CIWIN), Brussels, 27 October 2008, COM (2008) 676 final.

[105] Withdrawal of Obsolete Commission Proposals (2012/C 156/06), List of proposals withdrawn [2012] OJ C156/10.

[106] Communication on Protecting Europe from Large Scale Cyber-attacks and Disruptions: Enhancing Preparedness, Security and Resilience Brussels, 30 March 2009, COM (2009) 149 final.

[107] *Ibid*, 4.

[108] *Ibid*, 2.

[109] See also Council Decision of 12 February 2007 establishing for the period 2007 to 2013, as part of General Programme on Security and Safeguarding Liberties, the Specific Programme 'Prevention, Preparedness and Consequence Management of Terrorism and other Security related Risks' (2007/124/EC) [2007] OJ L58/1.

D Money Laundering in the Online Age

(i) Introduction

The term money laundering may evoke images of infamous 1920s Chicago gangster Al Capone running Chinese laundries as a means to disguise the origins of his ill-gotten prohibition-era gains. However, this age-old criminal process has come a long way since. Nowadays, UNODC estimates between two and five per cent of the world's GDP (800bn to 2 trillion USD) is laundered annually.[110] Despite these developments in the scope of money laundering, the principles remain the same. It is the process through which profits from criminal activities are passed through financial systems to hide their initial criminal origins. 'Dirty money', derived from criminal activity, becomes 'clean money', useable without tracing to its source – hence 'laundering'.

It is, in essence, a process of deceiving authorities as to the actual origin of money. Following laundering, funds can then be used for other, legitimate purposes, without detection. For this reason, it is a vital element of criminal activity; it allows the gains of crime to be used for other purposes without detection.

(ii) Definition

There is no universally accepted formal definition of money laundering. The EC Convention on Laundering, Search and Seizure and Confiscation of the Proceeds from Crime 1990, Article 1 defines it as:

> The conversion or transfer of property, knowing that such property is derived from serious crime, for the purpose of concealing or disguising the illicit origin of the property or of assisting any person who is involved in committing such an offence or offences to evade the legal consequences of his action, and the concealment or disguise of the true nature, source, location, disposition, movement, rights with respect to, or ownership of property, knowing that such property is derived from serious crime.

The UN Global Programme against Money Laundering describes it more simply as 'a process which disguises illegal profits without compromising the criminals who wish to benefit from the proceeds'.

(a) Three-Step Process

Broadly speaking, there are three steps in the money laundering process or 'laundry-cycle': placement, layering and integration.[111] Placement is the changing of bulk cash into less suspicious, portable form by depositing into the financial system. This

[110] www.unodc.org/unodc/en/money-laundering/globalization.html.
[111] www.unodc.org/unodc/en/money-laundering/laundrycycle.html.

more portable form allows the removal of the cash from its illegal place of origin. Layering is the creation of a detailed series of financial transactions, frequently across jurisdictions and made to look legitimate. This process is normally extremely complex in order to increase difficulty in tracing the funds back to illegitimate source. Integration is the use of the laundered funds for normal economic activity.

(b) Effect

Money laundering enables criminals to derive the maximum benefit from their criminal activity. As such, it is a key driver and enabler of criminal behaviour. Its presence can significantly impact the integrity of the banking and finance market, a key currency. At this level, money laundering is a threat to confidence in financial systems and institutions. The International Monetary Fund (IMF) also highlighted the possibility of inexplicable changes in money demand, increased volatility of international capital flow and especially exchange rates.[112] For this reason there have been many international efforts to address the problem on a supranational level.[113]

(iii) The EU and Money Laundering

The potential negative effects of money laundering upon the EU are substantial. As such, it has taken a number of steps to address the problem of money laundering. First, on 3 December 1998 a Joint Action 98/699/JHA was adopted by the Council on money laundering, the identification, tracing, freezing, seizing and confiscation of instrumentalities and the proceeds from crime.[114] Article 1(1) highlights the 1990 Council of Europe Convention on Laundering, Search, Seizure and Confiscation of Proceeds of Crime, specifying that there shall be 'no reservations . . . made or upheld' in regard to Article 2 of the 1990 Convention on offences punishable by imprisonment of a maximum of more than a year, or Article 6, on serious offences (with a minimum of more than six months' detention). Article 1(2) obliges Member States to ensure legislation allows for confiscation of property to the value of such proceeds. Article 1(3) requires Member States to enact legislation and procedures that 'enable it to permit the identification and tracing of suspected proceeds from crime at the request of another

[112] www.imf.org/external/np/ml/2001/eng/021201.htm.

[113] The major international institution in this area is the Financial Action Taskforce (FATF). Its 'Forty Recommendations on Combating Money Laundering and Terrorist Financing' was adopted in 1990. Various UN conventions also address the issue, including the United Nations Convention Against Illicit Traffic in Narcotic Drugs and Psychotropic Substances 1988, the UN Convention on the Suppression of Terrorist Financing of 1999, the UN Convention against Transnational Organised Crime of 2000, and the UN Convention against Corruption of 2003.

[114] Joint Action of 3 December 1998 adopted by the Council, on money laundering, the identification, tracing, freezing, seizing and confiscation of instrumentalities and the proceeds from crime (98/699/JHA) [1998] OJ L333/1.

Member State where there are reasonable grounds to suspect that a criminal offence has been committed'.

Article 2 requires Member States to prepare guides on identifying, tracing, freezing or seizing and confiscating instrumentalities and the proceeds from crime. Article 3 specifies that requests from other Member States shall be given the same priority as those in domestic measures. Article 4 focuses on effective cooperation between those investigating in different Member States. Article 5 provides that states work against asset dissipation including 'such measures as may be necessary to ensure that assets which are the subject of a request from another Member State may be frozen or seized expeditiously so that a later confiscation request is not frustrated'.

The next relevant EU legislation was the Council Framework Decision 2001/500/JHA of 26 June 2001 on money laundering, the identification, tracing, freezing, seizing and confiscation of instrumentalities and the proceeds of crime. This Joint Action served to repeal several articles of the joint action of 1998. Recital 4 'calls for the approximation of criminal law and procedures on money laundering (in particular confiscating funds)' and that 'the scope of criminal activities which constitute principal offences for money laundering should be uniform and sufficiently broad in all Member States'. Recital 6 highlights that 'money laundering is at the very heart of organized crime and should be rooted out wherever it occurs', and that 'concrete steps are taken to trace freeze, seize and confiscate the proceeds of crime'.

The Framework Decision itself first, in Article 1, reasserts the importance of the Articles 2 and 6 of the 1990 Convention, mirroring what was stated in the Joint Action of 1998. Article 2 provides that Member States ensure that offences are punishable 'by deprivation of liberty for a maximum of not less than 4 years'. Article 3 provides that Member States take 'the necessary steps to ensure that its legislation and procedures on the confiscation of the proceeds of crime also allow, at least in cases where these proceeds cannot be seized, for the confiscation of property the value of which corresponds to such proceeds, both in purely domestic proceedings and in proceedings instituted at the request of another Member State, including requests for the enforcement of foreign confiscation orders'. Article 4 repeats the provisions of Article 3 of the 1998 Joint Action, specifying that requests from other Member States shall be given the same priority as those in domestic measures.

(iv) Cyber-laundering

As far back as 1997, concerns were increasing about the possibilities the Internet age offered money laundering opportunities.[115] As with all criminal activity, methods of money laundering have evolved over time. Effective money laundering in any form must be quick, discrete, secure and worldwide in scope. The

[115] 'Next, Cyberlaundering?' *The Economist*, 24th July 1997.

Internet was a perfect vehicle due to its decentralised nature, instant communication potential, and anonymity.

There are now online auctions, online sales, online gambling, and online games. Further, there are always new methods of payment, prepaid payment cards, e-money currencies, paypal accounts, and even mobile phone payments. Virtual worlds with their own, real life valued currency can be used to facilitate money laundering. Such new means of payment are fruitful ground for money laundering, as regulatory regimes and loopholes take time to catch up. Bypassing the established financial sector makes it easier to escape the oversight of financial regulations. As one writer put it, '[c]yberlaundering is the safest way for criminals to launder dirty money if the government cannot reconstruct the transactions of an audit trail'.[116]

The process of cyber-laundering still ordinarily follows the same three stages as identified above. At the placement stage, anonymity is possible, with no in-person transactions required.[117] This circumvents reporting requirements. When layering, all that is needed is a receptacle for funds that allows the setting up of accounts without effective validation of identity. From there, instantaneous online transfer makes tracing almost impossible. At integration, again, the options presented by the internet are almost infinite.

(a) *How to Prevent Cyber-laundering?*

The most important element in preventing cyber-laundering is that preventive technology needs keep pace with the evolution of the Internet and payment methods. Further, as anonymity is a pre-requisite for cyber-laundering, identification checks for new financial instruments are necessary, and financial transactions must be prevented from taking place anonymously. Further, there must be coordination and cooperation between different jurisdictions, to deal with the inherently transnational nature of the issue.

The EU has taken some steps in this direction. Regulation No 1889/2005 of the European Parliament and of the Council of 26 October 2005 on controls of cash entering or leaving the community is the key preventive measure of the European institutions.[118] Recital 2 reasserts that the use of laundered money has negative effects on economic development, and recalls Directive 91/308/EEC of June 1991 on the prevention of the use of the financial system for laundering was a community mechanism to prevent money laundering by monitoring transactions

[116] J Straub, 'The Prevention of E-Money Laundering: Tracking the Elusive Audit Trail' (2002) 25 *Suffolk Transnational Law Review* 515, 522.

[117] S Philippsohn, 'The Dangers of New Technology – Laundering on the Internet' (2001) 5 *Journal of Money Laundering Control* 87.

[118] This falls within the wider aim of the EU to prevent fraudulent use of financial institutions, fearing damage to the bank's reputation; see Directive 2005/60/EC of the European Parliament and of the Council of 26 October 2005 on the prevention of the use of the financial system for the purpose of money laundering and terrorist financing [2005] OJ L309/15, Recital 1.

through credit and financial institutions and certain types of professions. The intention was to supplement this Directive with a control system on cash entering or leaving the EU. Recital 3 identified disparities between different national regimes as 'detrimental to the proper functioning of the internal market' and called for harmonisation to ensure 'equivalent level of control on movements of cash crossing the borders of the community'.

Recital 5 specifies that cash carried in or out of the community area must be subject to 'obligatory declaration'. Customs authorities would be responsible for gathering this information, with only amounts over 10,000 Euros must be declared. Recital 13 highlights the need for penalties for non-declaration in accordance with the Regulation. Article 2(2) defines 'cash' as including monetary instruments such as travellers cheques, negotiable instruments such as 'cheques, promissory notes and money orders' whether in bearer form or in any such form where the title passes upon delivery. Article 3(1) sets out the basic obligation to declare cash of 10,000 Euros or over. Article 3(2) specifies that the declaration must contain details of the declarant, owner of cash, intended recipient, amount and nature of cash provenance and intended use, transport route, means of transport. Under Article 4, cash may be detained in the event of failure to comply with the above provisions. Where the sum of money is lower than 10,000 Euros, but there are 'indications of illegal activities associated with the movement of cash', Article 5(2) allows that details may also be recorded and processed.

The problem of money laundering in general, but in particular cyber-laundering, continues to pose a serious challenge to the EU and its Member States. As such, a recent 2013 proposal has been made by the Commission indicating its intention to strengthen the EU's criminal law response to money laundering. Criminal law harmonisation for this offence was proposed in 2013.[119] However, even with harmonisation of Member State offences and penalties, the imperative to launder ill-gotten gains will endure. New methods, drawing on the Internet, will constantly develop in response to this imperative, with law enforcement always struggling to keep up.

III Harmonisation and General Principles of Criminal Law

A Introduction

The first part of this chapter outlined the EU's approach to the harmonisation of the criminal law of Member States as a method to address issues of common con-

[119] Proposal for a Directive of the European Parliament and the Council on the prevention of the use of the financial system for the purpose of money laundering and terrorist financing, COM/2013/045 final.

cern relating to the 'cybercrime' phenomenon. In this part the concept of harmonisation will be examined in more detail, and consideration will be paid in particular to the current and potential significance for harmonisation efforts in the context of the 'general part' principles of the criminal law. As we have seen above, the EU has thus far focused its harmonisation measures upon the specific rules that define crimes. The true scope of criminalisation in relation to specific crimes part is ultimately determined by the definition of the general concepts of liability such as intent, participation and inchoate offences.[120] As such, the definition of such general principles of liability and its determinative role in the true scope of criminalisation is potentially highly significant to EU criminal law harmonisation efforts. The extent of this significance depends upon the goals and correlative parameters of the EU's harmonisation measures.

B The Concept of Harmonisation

As highlighted in chapters 1 and 2, within the EU legislation and documents, two terms are used to describe the goal of measures concerned with criminal law: approximation and harmonisation. Harmonisation is now the term most commonly used by scholars and practitioners to describe the process and intention of EU criminal law measures. However, despite frequent use the term lacks a clear definition. The term 'approximation' is often used interchangeably with 'harmonisation'. Approximation is a standalone concept within the EU, and is defined as 'progressively adopting measures establishing minimum rules relating to the constituent elements of criminal acts and to penalties'.[121] Its emphasis is minimum regulation and the elimination of norms contra EU standards. However, despite the perception of interchangeability, 'harmonisation' seems to represent a loftier goal for EU criminal law. One scholar describes it as the 'making more similar or alike different justice systems or parts of it' and 'the realization of improvement and harmony with the absence of disparities'.[122] Others emphasise a less intrusive definition, perhaps closer to that of 'approximation' – not the elimination of disparities, but the elimination of friction between the systems.[123]

This lexical uncertainty surrounding perhaps the key tenet of EU criminal law reflects precisely the lack of consensus, underlying tension, and subsequent incoherence as to what the desired ends of EU criminal law are, and the consequent allowable impact upon Member State national legal systems. This is an extremely

[120] In legal systems which distinguish between specific and general parts, the *general part* is made up of the principles and doctrine that apply to the criminal law generally and determine liability for defined crimes: D Brody, J Acker and W Logan, *Criminal Law* (Gathersburg, Aspen Publishers, 2001) 161.

[121] Treaty of the European Union 2002, Art 31(1)(e) TEU.

[122] F Tadic, 'How Harmonious can Harmonisation Be? A Theoretical Approach towards Harmonisation of (Criminal) Law' in Klip and Van der Wilt (eds), *Harmonisation and Harmonising Measures in Criminal Law* (n 7) 8–9.

[123] U Nelles, 'Definitions of Harmonisation' in Klip and Van der Wilt (eds), *Harmonisation and Harmonising Measures in Criminal Law* (n 7) 34.

important issue, which touches on the apparently competing imperatives of some cautious Member States as they prioritise national sovereignty, EU law scholars considering the developments of the field, and even the institutional tendencies of the EU overall. It sets the outwardly constrictive explicit competencies included in the Lisbon Treaty, against the potentially much wider competencies of some of the Treaty's more vaguely constructed provisions. Ultimately, if the goal of the EU is merely approximating 'minimum rules', or 'eliminating friction' then the measures to achieve this will have fewer repercussions for state sovereignty. However, if the explicit or implicit goal or tendency of EU institutions and criminal law is rather the 'elimination of disparities', leading to unification rather than harmonisation, then the implications for national legal systems of Member States will necessarily be far more profound and wide ranging. The differing general part principles of the EU Member State legal systems would be implicated, as something closer to a common EU criminal code would eventually be necessitated.

C The Limits of EU Harmonisation Competence Post-Lisbon: Harmonisation of the General Principles of Criminal Liability?

As outlined above, Article 83 TFEU gives the EU a genuine, explicit competence to approximate the laws of Member States.[124] Article 83(1) TFEU provides that the EU may 'establish minimum rules concerning the definition of criminal offences and sanctions'. Then, Article 83(2) TFEU includes a further 'annex-competence', insofar as the EU may also take harmonisation measures where to do so is necessary 'to ensure the effective implementation of a Union policy in an area which has been subject to harmonisation measures'. Under Article 83 TFEU, the EU may only regulate minimum standards in the allowed areas or in areas already regulated, using compulsory but indirectly effective directives. Further, these directives may extend only to definitions of crimes and penalties. The EU has been notably reticent about attempting to define the general principles of liability.

Criminal law is sometimes divided between *special* and *general* parts;[125]even in systems which do not rely on this distinction, generally applicable concepts, such as intention, nevertheless provide definitions of the principles to be applied in the context of specific crimes.

Whether the EU's criminal law competence *could* include the creation of a 'general part' is not established clearly. Neither Article 83(1) TFEU, nor 83(2) TFEU provide explicitly for the binding definition of general part principles or concepts (attempt, participation etc). As such, there is definitely no explicit competence in

[124] B Hecker, '§ 10 Harmonisierung' in U Sieber, FH Brüner, H Satzeger and B v Heintschel-Heinegg (eds), *Europäisches Strafrecht* (Baden-Baden, Nomos, 2011) para 10 n 32; B Hecker, 'Europäisches Strafrecht post-Lissabon' in K Ambos (ed), *Europäisches Strafrecht post-Lissabon* (Göttingen, Universitätsverlag, 2011) 19–20. See further ch 2.

[125] Common law systems use the terminology 'general principles of law' rather than 'general part'.

this regard. However, a line can be drawn to general principles of national criminal law systems, if to do so is necessary to effectively combat the relevant crimes. As the EU can enact regulation regarding the special part, and the special part cannot generally be considered separate from general part principles, there seems at least an implicit, if slightly tenuous, basis to address these principles under Article 83.[126] In addition, it is clear that the EU would be entitled to define such principles in the context of the specific legislation, if this were necessary in order to enable the harmonisation of the criminal law in the area in question.

As we have seen in the first part of this chapter, the EU's measures have generally extended only to the special part. While each Joint Action or Framework Decision may identify required aspects of the general part with regard to specific crimes, the EU does not define these aspects. Further, the terminology used is inconsistent, and that employed is often already a term of art in the national criminal law of various Member States. As Klip observes, there has been 'no systematic thinking on this at the Union level [. . .] there are lots of lacunae and loose ends'.[127]

D The Effect of Lack of Harmonisation of General Principles

What is the actual effect of this lack of common definition of general part principles between Member States upon the scope of criminalisation? This section considers three key modalities of the general part: intent, participation offences and inchoate offences. The legal systems of four different Member States are assessed: that of Austria, England and Wales, France, Germany. It assesses to what extent the definitions of these general part concepts are divergent between these Member States. From this initial study, implementation of the Framework Decision on attacks against information systems will be scrutinised for the purpose of illustration of the differing scopes of criminalisation.[128]

(i) Intention

Intention constitutes the subjective element of a criminal offence. Criminal justice systems distinguish between different degrees of intent, which affect the level of liability. Union instruments frequently refer broadly to 'intentional conduct'[129]

[126] K Ambos, *Internationales Strafrecht, Strafanwendungsrecht – Völkerstrafrecht – Europäisches Strafrecht – Rechtshilfe*, 3rd edn (Munich, Verlag CH Beck, 2011) 475 fn 74.

[127] Klip, *European Criminal Law* (n 52) 166.

[128] The Member States have until September 2015 to implement the Directive on attacks against information systems.

[129] See, for example, Art 2, para 1 of the Council Framework Decision 2004/757/JHA of 25 October 2004 laying down minimum provisions on the constituent elements of criminal acts and penalties in the field of illicit drug trafficking [2004] OJ L335/8; Council Framework Decision 2004/68/JHA of 22 December 2003 on combating the sexual exploitation of children and child pornography [2004] OJ L13/44; Council Framework Decision 2003/568/JHA of 22 July 2003 on combating corruption in the private sector [2003] OJ L192/54; Arts 2–6 of the Council Framework Decision 2005/222/JHA of 24 February 2005 on attacks against information systems [2005] OJ L69/67.

or acts that have been intentionally committed. Indeed, it seems clear that EU framework decisions criminalise only intentional conduct.[130] However, the meaning of 'intention' is not defined.[131]

Member States with common law systems follow the classical dichotomy;[132] that is, they delineate between the objective (external) and subjective (internal) elements of a crime. England and Wales is an example, where criminal responsibility requires the objective *actus reus* (guilty act) and the concurrent subjective *mens rea* (guilty mind).[133] There are two relevant classes of *mens rea* in England and Wales: intention and recklessness. The relevant class(es) of *mens rea* are specified for each criminal offence.

The meaning of intention has developed through the common law, with two strands evolving: direct and oblique intent.[134] Direct intent is present in relation to a result when either 'it is his purpose to cause it'. The law on oblique intention is less clear. Generally, oblique intent is present where the result was not intended, but the accused 'knows that it would occur in the ordinary course of events if he were to succeed in his purpose of causing some other result'.[135] We can best understand an obliquely intended result as one that is a virtually certain side effect or necessary pre-requisite of the accused's main purpose. Intent is assessed subjectively, without comparison to any 'reasonableness' standard.[136]

Significantly, however, in England and Wales a crime can be committed even where there is no intention to cause a harmful result. The law of 'recklessness' covers the circumstance where an unjustifiable risk was consciously taken by the accused.[137] It can be differentiated from oblique intention through the fact that recklessness concerns foresight of risk, rather than foresight of a virtual certainty. With recklessness, the accused is aware of the potential adverse consequence to his actions, but proceeds anyway, thus creating the risk of harm (if not actually desiring it).

The Computer Misuse Act 1990 is the relevant English law covering the areas set out in the Framework Decision. It specifies that the crimes of unauthorised access to computer material and unauthorised access with intent to commit or facilitate commission of further offences require intent.[138] However, the offence of

[130] Klip, *European Criminal Law* (n 52) 189.

[131] BR Killmann, '§ 11 Systematisierung' in U Sieber, FH Brüner, H Satzeger and B v Heintschel-Heinegg (eds), *Europäisches Strafrecht* (Baden-Baden, Nomos, 2011) para 11 n 18.

[132] Eg England and Wales, Scotland, Ireland.

[133] It is important to note is that the oft-mentioned idea of 'guilty mind' is in fact slightly misleading; mens rea refers to the state of mind required for the crime.

[134] Key cases on intention include *Steane* [1947] 1 All ER 813; *Moloney* [1985] 1 All ER 1025; *Nedrick* [1986] 3 All ER 1.

[135] Law Commission, 'Legislating the Criminal Code: Offences Against the Person and General Principles' (Law Com No 218, 1993) c 14; D Ormerod, *Smith and Hogan's Criminal Law*, 13th edn (Oxford, Oxford University Press, 2011) 115; M Allen, *Textbook on Criminal Law*, 7th edn (Oxford, Oxford University Press, 2003) 64–65.

[136] Criminal Justice Act 1967, s 8.

[137] Ormerod, *Smith and Hogan's Criminal Law* (n 135) 118.

[138] Computer Misuse Act 1990, s 1(a).

impairing operation of computer is also punishable where the accused is reckless as to his acts.[139]

Within the EU, there is a group of civil law countries that also follow the classical dichotomy.[140] France is an example, with a bipartite identification of the subjective *element materiel* and objective *element moral* of a crime. In France intentional acts will be punishable,[141] while if the law prescribes it, so too will negligent behaviour.[142] Dolus eventualis (*dol éventuel*), where the accused is aware of the likely outcome of his action, is normally classified as an act of negligence (*faute d'imprudence*).[143] However, for special assault and homicide offences the French Criminal Code includes two qualified forms of intention, '*préméditation*' or '*dol aggravé*'.[144] Under these definitions, a sentence will be aggravated if the offender has the plan to fulfil the crime and then acts in accordance with his prior plan.[145]

French criminal law regulates system interference under Article 323-1 CP. As this provision does not specify otherwise, this offence incorporates only intentional interference. As defined above, French criminal law appears to envisage a relatively narrow range of acts of system interference that would meet the threshold of being intentional.

By contrast, German criminal law is a tripartite system with a normative conception of culpability that addresses not only intent, but also blameworthiness.[146] The three elements are *Tatbestandsmässigkeit* (the legal description of the offences), *Rechtswidrigkeit* (wrongfulness) and *Schuld* (culpability).[147] The legal description of the offences includes both objective elements (*objektiver Tatbestand*) and subjective elements (*subjektiver Tatbestand*). In the context of *Rechtswidrigkeit*, an assessment is made of whether the offender's act was justified, for example, whether it was carried out in self-defence. *Schuld* meanwhile is a check for any exculpation of the offender.[148]

Broadly speaking, in German criminal law only intentional acts (*vorsätzliche Handlungen*) are punishable as criminal offences. In specific circumstances, where prescribed in the relevant law, negligent behaviour (*fahrlässiges Verhalten*) can also be punishable.[149] Penalties are normally much less in this situation. Overall, intention can be defined as knowledge (*Wissen*) and will (*Wollen*) in relation to all

[139] Computer Misuse Act 1990, s 3.

[140] Examples include France, Italy, Sweden and Greece.

[141] Art 121-3(1) Code Pénal (CP).

[142] Faute d'imprudence, de négligence ou de manquement à une obligation de prudence ou de sécurité prévue par la loi ou le règlement (Art 121-3(3) CP).

[143] R Bernardini, *Droit pénal général, Introduction au droit criminel, Théorie générale de la responsabilité pénale* (Paris, Gualino éditeur, 2003) 393.

[144] See Art 222-13, 222-12, 132-72 CP.

[145] R Bernardini, *Droit pénal général, Introduction au droit criminel* (n 143) 391–92.

[146] Examples of countries with this tripartite system are Germany, Austria, Portugal and Spain.

[147] K Kühl, *Strafrecht Allgemeiner Teil*, 7th edn (Munich, Vahlen, 2012) 7–8.

[148] *Ibid*, 7–8.

[149] § 15 German Criminal Code. However, even where a negligent act is punishable, there is usually a substantial difference in the designated sentence.

physical elements of the offence.[150] More specifically, three basic forms of intention can be identified. First, *Absicht* is defined by the strong will of the delinquent, with the result of the criminal offence being his main goal.[151] Second, *Wissentlichkeit* is defined by the strong knowledge of the offender, with acts committed cognisant of the fact that they will result in the commission of the crime.[152] Third, and most complex, *Eventualvorsatz* (or *dolus eventualis*) covers the situation where the offender considers the commission of the crime is possible, but nonetheless acts in light of this possibility.[153] While the exact definition of *dolus eventualis* is controversial, as a matter of principle an act committed in such a state of mind will be deemed to have been committed intentionally.[154]

Under the German penal code, interference with information systems is regulated in § 202(a)(1) StGB (*Ausspähen von Daten*). Under this law, only intentional acts are punishable (incorporating *dolus eventualis* as defined above). In this context, this requires that the offender must be aware of the possibility that his action will allow him to access protected data, and that he proceeds nonetheless.

Though each of the countries surveyed has a system of criminal law that requires the satisfaction of broadly similar subjective elements, the definitions of these concepts are quite different in each national context. This means that, by extension, the scope of criminal offences also differs in each context. Consider the scope of intention in each of the contexts we have reviewed. The concept of 'recklessness' in England and Wales is more expansive than the German *Vorsatz,* and in some way comparable with *dolus eventualis* and *bewusste Fahrlässigkeit.* Recall that the latter is not enough to constitute intention (*Vorsätzlichkeit*) under the German criminal law. The French approach is even more restrictive, with *dolus eventualis* not constituting intention. As such, this example shows that the different Member States, due to their different understanding of the definition of intention, necessarily treat a range of different acts as intentional system interference. Further, this can also make a difference to the imposed penalties between states, with repercussions for legal certainty throughout the EU.[155]

(ii) Participation

EU law is inconsistent concerning participation offences. Participation is mentioned in Article A of Title II JA 97/154 on Trafficking in Human Beings, Article 4 of Framework Decision 2003/80 on the protection of the environment and Article 1,

[150] G Freund, *Strafrecht Allgemeiner Teil,* 2nd edn (Berlin, Springer, 2009) 280.

[151] K Lackner and K Kühl, *Strafgesetzbuch, Kommentar,* 27th edn (Munich, CH Beck, 2011) para 15 n 20.

[152] Freund, *Strafrecht Allgemeiner Teil* (n 150) 280.

[153] *Ibid,* 281.

[154] Lackner and Kühl, *Strafgesetzbuch, Kommentar* (n 151) para 15 n 28; Kühl, *Strafrecht Allgemeiner Teil* (n 147) 93.

[155] K Tiedemann, 'Grunderfordernisse einer Regelung des Allgemeinen Teils' in K Tiedemann (ed), *Wirtschaftsstrafrecht in der Europäischen Union: Rechtsdogmatik, Rechtsvergleich, Rechtspolitik, Freiburg-Symposium* (Köln, Heymanns, 2002) 20.

paragraph 3 of the Financial Interests Convention.[156] All specify that 'participation in' the offences described should be criminalised as well as the complete offences. None define what is meant by participation.

Reference is frequently made in the EU instruments to aiding and abetting, but these terms are not defined. This is evidenced in Article 3 of Framework Decision 2003/568 on corruption in the private sector, Article 4 of Framework Decision 2002/475 on combating terrorism, Article 2 of Framework Decision 2002/629 on combating trafficking in human beings, Article 4 of Framework Decision 2004/68 on child pornography, and Article 5 of Framework Decision 2005/222 on attacks against information systems. The terminology used can also be inconsistent between EU instruments.[157]

The criminal law of England and Wales differentiates between principal offenders and accessories.[158] Simply put, the principal offender is the perpetrator whose act is the most immediate cause of the *actus reus* element of the crime.[159] The Accessories and Abettors Act of 1861 covers those who 'aid, abet, counsel or procure'. 'Aid' is defined as giving help, support or assistance to the principal. It does not imply a causal connection with the crime, nor a consensus between the aider and the principal.[160] 'Abetting' is the act of encouraging the principal.[161] Generally, the two acts are considered together – 'aid or/ and abet'. The act of abetting is relevant only in conjunction with the act of 'aiding'; it plays no independent role in English criminal law.[162] Closely linked with 'abetting' is also the act of 'counselling', meaning to advise the offender.[163] The act of 'procuring' is often considered alongside 'counselling', meaning to produce by endeavour.[164] 'Counselling and procuring' is sometimes described more simply as encouraging the principal.[165]

Similarly, German criminal law also differentiates between perpetration (*Täterschaft*) and participation (*Teilnahme*). A perpetrator commits the offence, whereas a participant takes part in the crime of another person.[166] Both forms can be further differentiated. The term *Täterschaft* can be defined in three ways. First, the *Unmittelbare Täter* is a person who directly commits a crime alone. He will be seen as the principal (see § 25(1) StGB).[167] Second the *Mittelbare Täter* is a person

[156] Art 2, para 1 of Joint Action of 21 December 1998 adopted by the Council on the basis of Article K.3 of the Treaty on European Union, on making it a criminal offence to participate in a criminal organisation in the Member States of the European Union (98/733/JHA) [1998] OJ L351/1 provides criminalisation of 'conduct of any person consisting in an agreement with one or more persons that an activity should be pursued'. Here, participation is a separate crime.

[157] Killmann, '§ 11 Systematisierung' (n 131) para 11 n 23.

[158] A Ashworth, *Principles of Criminal Law*, 6th edn (Oxford, Oxford University Press, 2009) 404.

[159] Allen, *Textbook on Criminal Law* (n 135) 206.

[160] Ormerod, *Smith and Hogan's Criminal Law* (n 135) 192–93.

[161] *Ibid*, 193.

[162] Ashworth, *Principles of Criminal Law* (n 158) 407.

[163] Ormerod, *Smith and Hogan's Criminal Law* (n 135) 195.

[164] *Ibid.*

[165] Ashworth, *Principles of Criminal Law* (n 158) 413.

[166] Lackner and Kühl, *Strafgesetzbuch, Kommentar* (n 151) Vorbemerkungen zu para 25–para 31 n 28; Kühl, *Strafrecht Allgemeiner Teil* (n 147) 734.

[167] Kühl, *Strafrecht Allgemeiner Teil* (n 147) 747.

who uses another person as a tool (the so-called *Tatmittler*) to commit a crime. This person will be considered the indirect perpetrator (see § 25(1) alternative 2 StGB).[168] Third, the *Mittäter* is a co-offender, relevant where several persons commit a crime together (see § 25(2) StGB). Here, a conscious and intentional interaction of offenders is required. Generally they must plan and execute the crime together.[169]

Two forms of *Teilnahme*, or participation, are contemplated in German criminal law: *Anstiftung* and *Gehilfenschaft*. The term *Anstiftung* translates roughly as 'incitement', though it should not be confused with the common law concept of incitement as an incohate offence. Under § 26 of the German Criminal Code a person is penalised if they instigate a crime committed by another. For this to be the case, it is necessary that the individual, objectively viewed, gave the perpetrator the idea of committing the crime.[170] In terms of the subjective element, it is required that the instigator has a double intention – acting intentionally in relation to his own action, but also in relation to the main crime committed.[171] Instigation requires that the main offence be actually committed or at least attempted.[172] In terms of attempt to instigate a crime, this will only be punishable if a person attempts to instigate another to commit a felony (§ 30(1) StGB). The instigator will be sentenced the same as the offender (§ 26 StGB).

Gehilfenschaft is the German offence of 'aiding and abetting'. Provision § 27(1) StGB defines one who renders aid to an offender to commit an intentional crime as 'abettor'. His contribution to the crime must be 'causal' in nature, meaning that the contribution enabled or reinforced the violation of a legally protected interest.[173] *Gehilfenschaft*, like *Anstiftung*, requires the same double intention. The abettor must intend both his actions in assistance of the main offence, but also the commission of the main offence.[174] Such assistance can be physical or psychological in nature.[175] Once more, the main offence must be committed or at least attempted.[176] Attempted aiding and abetting, however, is not punishable.[177] While the instigator will be sentenced the same as the offender, the nature of the involvement means the sentence has to be mitigated (§ 27(2) StGB).

For the purpose of comparison, another EU Member State, Austria, is particularly interesting. This is because the Austrian legal system follows an entirely

[168] *Ibid*, 749.

[169] Lackner and Kühl, *Strafgesetzbuch, Kommentar* (n 151) para 25 n 9–12; Kühl, *Strafrecht Allgemeiner Teil* (n 147) 780–91.

[170] Kühl, *Strafrecht Allgemeiner Teil* (n 147) 823.

[171] *Ibid*, 834.

[172] Lackner and Kühl, *Strafgesetzbuch, Kommentar* (n 151) para 26 n 7; Kühl, *Strafrecht Allgemeiner Teil* (n 147) 859–60.

[173] Lackner and Kühl, *Strafgesetzbuch, Kommentar* (n 151) para 27 n 2; Kühl, *Strafrecht Allgemeiner Teil* (n 147) 842–43.

[174] Lackner and Kühl, *Strafgesetzbuch, Kommentar* (n 151) para 27 n 7; Kühl, *Strafrecht Allgemeiner Teil* (n 147) 859–60.

[175] Lackner and Kühl, *Strafgesetzbuch, Kommentar* (n 151) para 27 n 4.

[176] *Ibid*, para 27 n 8.

[177] *Ibid*, para 27 n 9.

different conception of criminal participation. Each person who instigates or assists in the execution of a crime is considered a principal (§ 12 Ö-StGB). As such, there is no differentiation between perpetration and participation. Each person involved in the crime is considered a party to the offence.[178] This circumstance, where all persons who made a causal contribution to the crime are perpetrators,[179] is in fact a totally different system with an extensive definition in comparison to the other systems we have reviewed.[180] However, the different systems will not result in as wide disparities in the actual punishment, as the sentence will be matched to the culpability of the respective person in each system. The significance of the difference is dogmatic, rather than in practice.[181]

These considerably different approaches to the regulation of participation in criminal offences make it extremely likely that the scope of criminalisation of aiding and abetting attacks against information systems as required by Article 5 of the Framework Decision and now Article 8 of the Directive will differ substantially across the Member States.

(iii) Attempt

The inchoate offence of 'attempt' is found in a number of EU instruments, such as Title II 1997 Joint Action 97/154 on Trafficking in Human Beings, and Article 5, paragraph 3 of the Framework Decision on attacks against information systems.[182] No specific definition is given, though certain deductions can be made. For instance, Article 4, paragraph 2 of the Framework Decision 2002/475 on combating terrorism suggests that the modality of attempt should not be considered for preparatory offences.[183] Nonetheless, generally the definition of attempt is left to Member States, with a number of different approaches evidenced.

In England and Wales, the Criminal Attempts Act 1981 defines attempt as follows: 'If, with intent to commit an offence to which this section applies, a person does an act which is more than merely preparatory to the commission of the

[178] AE Hollaender and C Mayerhofer, *Grundlagen des österreichischen Strafrechts, Allgemeiner Teil I* (Innsbruck, Studienverlag, 2007) 142

[179] EE Fabrizy, *StGB samt ausgewählten Nebengesetze, Kurzkommentar*, 10th edn (Vienna, Manzsche, 2010) para 12 n 1

[180] W Schöberl, *Die Einheitstäterschaft als europäisches Modell, Die strafrechtliche Beteiligungsregelung in Österreich und den nordischen Ländern* (Vienna, Neuer Wissenschaftlicher Verlag, 2006) 51–52.

[181] T Weigend, 'Mindestanforderungen an ein europaweit geltendes harmonisiertes Strafrecht' in F Zieschang, E Hilgendorf and K Laubenthal (ed), *Strafrecht und Kriminalität in Europa* (Baden-Baden, Nomos, 2003) 77–78.

[182] See for example Art 3(2)(c) and 3(2)(d) of the Council Framework Decision of 29 May 2000 on increasing protection by criminal penalties and other sanctions against counterfeiting in connection with the introduction of the euro (2000/383/JHA) [2000] OJ L140/1; Art 1 of the Council Framework Decision of 13 June 2002 on combating terrorism (2002/475/JHA) [2002] OJ L164/3.

[183] It excludes two stated acts from being criminalised in the attempt modality (attempt to possess weapons and attempt to threaten to commit any of the offences listed in Art 1, para 1(a) to (h)). All excluded offences are preparatory offences. It seems that under Union law attempt and preparatory offences must be regarded as being mutually exclusive; see Klip, *European Criminal Law* (n 52) 193–94.

offence, he is guilty of attempting to commit the offence'.[184] The application of this principle applies to an attempt even where the facts are such that the commission of the offence is impossible.[185] The law also covers the circumstance where the person's intention would not in itself be regarded as amounting to intent to commit an offence, but if the facts of the case had been as he believed them to be, his intention would amount to an offence.[186] In short, even impossible attempts are punishable.[187] Further, a voluntary withdrawal from the commission of the crime will not remove criminal responsibility.[188]

Under German criminal law, 'attempt' requires that the person has made a decision to commit a crime. This means he must fulfil the subjective elements of the offence, particularly intention.[189] *Dolus eventualis* (awareness of the likely outcome of the action) will be sufficient if it also suffices for the completed offence.[190] To satisfy the requisite physical element of the attempt, the offender must have immediately begun the commission of the crime, with an external confirmation of the offender's decision.[191] The action must be regionally and temporally proximate to the execution of the offence.[192] The German law differentiates between the attempt of a crime (*Verbrechen*), which is always punishable, and the attempt of an offence (*Vergehen*), which is only punishable where the criminal code provides.[193] In addition, attempt can be punished with a more minor sentence than the completed crime.[194] It is an optional mitigating circumstance.[195]

The issue of impossibility is more challenging to define, as § 22 and § 23(3) StGB make clear that in general, impossible attempt will be punishable.[196] In contrast to the English law, however, § 23(3) StGB provides that an impossible attempt shall not be punishable if the impossibility stems from a total lack of judgement of the part of the offender. For this to be the case, the offender's conception must misjudge commonly known principles or situations.[197] Once more in contrast to the English law, in Germany voluntary withdrawal (*Rücktritt*) will relieve the individual of criminal responsibility for his behaviour.[198]

Similar to the German concept, Austrian criminal law defines attempt in the following way: An offence is attempted if a person confirms his intention to commit that crime by carrying an action that is forgoing to the execution of the

[184] Criminal Attempts Act 1981, s 1(1).
[185] Criminal Attempts Act 1981, s 1(2).
[186] Criminal Attempts Act 1981, s 1(3).
[187] Allen, *Textbook on Criminal Law* (n 135) 283–85; Ashworth, *Principles of Criminal Law* (n 158) 445–47.
[188] Ormerod, *Smith and Hogan's Criminal Law* (n 135) 423.
[189] Lackner and Kühl, *Strafgesetzbuch, Kommentar* (n 151) para 22 n 2.
[190] Kühl, *Strafrecht Allgemeiner Teil* (n 147) 492.
[191] Lackner and Kühl, *Strafgesetzbuch, Kommentar* (n 151) para 22 n 3.
[192] *Ibid*, para 22 n 4–7.
[193] German Criminal Code, para 23(1).
[194] *Ibid*, para 23(2).
[195] Lackner and Kühl, *Strafgesetzbuch, Kommentar* (n 151) para 23 n 2.
[196] *Ibid*, para 23 n 5.
[197] *Ibid*, para 23 n 8.
[198] German Criminal Code, para 24.

crime.[199] Impossible attempt will not be punishable[200]. This will be the case where for a legal or factual reason there is a priori no chance that the offence can be completed.[201]

Overall, the concepts of attempt are quite similar between the three legal systems analysed.[202] However, some significant differences exist. Impossible attempt will be punishable in some systems, but not in others (eg Austria). Also, voluntary withdrawal will not prevent punishment in the UK, as it will in both Germany and Austria.

EU instruments, if they mention them at all, are extremely inconsistent in relation to general part definitions, in particular for participation and inchoate offences. As such, as we can see above, Member States are accorded full freedom in how they define these specific modalities. Meeting the standard of the EU in this regard seems to require only that each Member State be able to identify an element of the domestic criminal law that corresponds roughly to that identified in the Union instrument. Frequently the same terminology will be used, but with a variety of differing Member State specific definitions. As such, disparities in the effective scope of criminalisation in implementing EU legislation not only exist, but are an unavoidable manifestation of the current approach to EU criminal law. Even where states have closely implemented Union law, behaviour punishable in one EU state will not be punishable in another.

E Implications of Differing Scopes of Criminalisation

That certain behaviour punishable in one EU state will not be punishable in another, even following EU harmonisation measures, is a natural by-product of the current form and scope of EU criminal law. Currently, even in so-called 'harmonised' areas, only what we can label harmonisation *de minimis* is really possible. The differing general principles of liability are one reason why this is the case. The implications of this divergence for EU criminal law depend entirely upon the rationales underpinning the EU harmonisation measures.

It seems clear that successful harmonisation of the criminal laws of the Member States would require that the general principles of liability be more clearly defined. One way of achieving this would be for the specific pieces of legislation to set out definitions of concepts such as intention or aiding and abetting specifically for that piece of legislation. This approach would not necessarily improve harmonisation,

[199] Austrian Criminal Code, para 15(2).

[200] *Ibid*, para 15(3).

[201] Fabrizy, *StGB samt ausgewählten Nebengesetze, Kurzkommentar* (n 179) para 15 n 20; H Fuchs, *Österreichisches Strafrecht. Allgemeiner Teil I: Grundlagen und Lehre von der Straftat*, 7th edn (Vienna, Springer 2008) 254–57.

[202] It's important to note, however, that there are also concepts in other Member States which have different (more objective than subjective) approaches; see M Cancio, 'Überlegungen zu einer gemeineuropäischen Regelung des Versuchs' in K Tiedemann (ed), *Wirtschaftsstrafrecht in der Europäischen Union: Rechtsdogmatik, Rechtsvergleich, Rechtspolitik, Freiburg-Symposium* (Köln, Heymanns, 2002) 169 ff.

however, as the Member States would still be able to increase the scope of criminalisation in their jurisdiction, such as by criminalising the reckless commission of offences or by continuing to class *dolus eventulis* as intention, even if intention were not so defined in the EU legislation. The approach might have the advantage of facilitating the assessment of implementation of the provisions and of the true extent of harmonisation.

The same issues apply to the creation of a general part applicable to all EU offences: Member States would be able to extend the scope of criminalisation beyond the provisions set out in the EU instruments. Only the harmonisation of the general part of the criminal laws of the Member States would result in total harmonisation; it seems extremely unlikely, though, that this would be welcomed or accepted by the Member States.

Conclusions

I Criminalisation

A Extent of EU Criminal Law

The introduction of the Treaty of Lisbon has led some to declare a new era of EU criminal law, with the provisions of Article 83 TFEU fleshing out and attempting for the first time to explain the harmonisation purposes of the substantive criminal law.[1] However, while Article 83 TFEU clearly represents a significant breakthrough for EU criminal law competence, it is important to note that the extent of the competence is still limited in four ways.

First, competence under Article 83 TFEU is limited in terms of the nature of the crimes to which measures may be applied. The competence in Article 83(1) TFEU applies only to 'areas of particularly serious crime with a cross-border dimension resulting from the nature or impact of such offences or from a special need to combat them on a common basis'.[2] This seemingly presents two basic limitations, one geographical (the requirement of 'a cross-border dimension'), and one relating to severity (the requirement that the crimes be 'particularly serious').

Second, the competence set out in Article 83 TFEU is limited by subject area. Article 83(1) TFEU prescribes limited areas as open for EU harmonisation measures: 'terrorism, trafficking in human beings and sexual exploitation of women and children, illicit drug trafficking, illicit arms trafficking, money laundering, corruption, counterfeiting of means of payment, computer crime and organized crime'. Article 83(2) TFEU is limited to areas that have previously been subject to harmonisation measures.

Third, the EU is limited in what type of measures it may take. Under Article 83 TFEU, the EU can only use directives to harmonise laws. Unlike regulations, directives possess an inherent flexibility, as they must be transposed into domestic legal systems by the Member States themselves. This gives Member States substantial discretion in relation to implementation – they are bound only as to the impact of their approaches. Thus viewed, the directive as a legislative mechanism

[1] N Long, 'Towards a European Criminal Code' (2011) *European Institute of Public Administration Scope* 49, 50.

[2] Art 83(1) TFEU.

affords states some latitude in contemplation of their distinctive national systems, while focusing on ensuring the application of EU provisions.

Fourth, and perhaps most importantly, EU harmonisation competence is limited to the basic definition of criminal conduct and the requirement of sanctions. Essentially, the EU may outline types of behaviour it wishes to see criminalised in the Member States, and minimum sanctions for these forms of behaviour. In turn, Member States are obliged to introduce these certain norms and concepts in to their domestic legal systems, but are not required to do more than this.[3] The EU only identifies the end to be achieved; Member States have control over the means of implementation.[4]

It is clear that the EU does not currently have its own 'system' of criminal law. Neither the framework decisions, nor the directives can in themselves be seen to constitute EU substantive criminal law; instead they place obligations on each Member State to ensure that the stipulated conduct is criminalised within its jurisdiction. In other words, the provisions are not directly applicable, but can only be relied upon by prosecuting authorities or individuals if they have been implemented in the domestic law of a Member State. This point may seem to be something of a technicality, but it is in fact of major importance. The EU does not (yet, at least) have bodies capable of enforcing the application of the criminal law provisions set out in its legislation. There is no court with the jurisdiction to try individuals for violating these provisions, no prosecution authorities and no police force. There cannot thus be said to be a European criminal justice system as such.

B The Creation of Criminal Law: Lessons from the Information Society

The overview of the regulatory approach of the EU in the context of the information society demonstrates that the criminal law is not at the forefront of its concerns. Indeed the EU's approach displays a certain degree of uncertainty as to the proper role of the criminal law. The principal concern of the EU is orientated towards creating regulation which promotes the proper functioning of the internal market;[5] the criminal law has the potential to be of use in this regard, but equally it could have the opposite effect, for instance, if restrictive obligations are placed on internet service providers (ISPs). Despite the essentially secondary nature of the criminal law in the broader context of the EU's regulation of the information society, the EU regulation has, as we have seen, had a considerable impact on the criminal laws of the Member States in this field. In view of this it is crucial that the EU takes seriously the process of criminalisation.

[3] I Topa, 'Where do we Stand with Harmonisation of Substantive Criminal law in the EU? Remarks on the Changes Introduced by the Lisbon Treaty' (2012) 4 *Silesian Journal of Legal Studies* 89, 92.

[4] Art 288 TFEU.

[5] See further ch 3.

Clarity about the reasons underpinning the criminal law response of the EU is of crucial importance. An important pre-requisite to the EU's ability to create criminal law is the prospect of the Member States achieving some sort of agreement on the need for, and the limits of, such criminalisation. As we have seen, this has not always been simple. In the context of intellectual property rights, widespread public scepticism about the potential for the imposition of user liability for illegal downloading or streaming and for censorship of the Internet led to a total breakdown of the Commission's attempts to develop an EU approach to the matter.[6] Even in relation to 'serious crime', difficulties in determining the scope of criminalisation have emerged. In the context of offences involving racism, it took almost a decade to reach agreement on even very basic definitions of conduct and early indications suggest that implementation has been patchy.[7]

The EU's approach to the regulation of the information society exemplifies the perennial dichotomy that lies at the core of the EU criminal law project – between 'the quest for meaningful harmonisation, on the one hand, and the respect for state sovereignty and national diversity, on the other'.[8] Differences between the Member States may not simply constitute minor annoyances which serve as a barrier to greater cooperation across the EU, but may be attributable to the fact that criminal law is essentially a political matter and that any attempt to regulate it must deal with the relationship between the state and its citizens.[9] Criminal law is a fundament of state sovereignty. Criminal measures are a key form of state control of citizen's behaviour, and the criminal law's effectiveness depends upon an element of democratic legitimacy – the acceptance and endorsement of the populace. As the German Constitutional Court has stated:

> [D]emocratic self-determination is affected in an especially sensitive manner by provisions of criminal law and criminal procedure, the corresponding basic powers in the treaties must be interpreted strictly [. . .] and their use requires particular justification.[10]

Such considerations ought to lie at the heart of the EU's approach to criminal law, with subsidiarity and proportionality as bedrock principles intended to ensure it. Generally these considerations mean criminal law measures should be determined at the state level, unless there is a special reason for this process to take place at the EU level.

The EU has done very little to explain the need for criminal law. In the Framework Decision on racism and xenophobia, for instance, it is stated that 'racism and xenophobia constitute a threat against groups of persons which are the

[6] See further ch 4.
[7] See further ch 5.
[8] V Mitsilegas, 'The Third Wave of Third Pillar Law: Which Direction for EU Criminal Justice?' (2009) 34 *EL Rev* 523, 536.
[9] See RA Duff, L Farmer, SE Marshall, M Renzo and V Tadros, *The Boundaries of the Criminal Law* (Oxford, Oxford University Press 2010) 7.
[10] German Constitutional Court, 2 BvE 2/08 of 30 June 2009, para 358.

target of such behaviour',[11] but there is no explanation of the nature of the threat or any evidence cited in support of the use of the criminal law in tackling it. This type of explanation is insufficient to justify a criminal law response, even in the context of serious crime.

The EU's disregard for setting out the case for criminal law may be explained by the fact that until recently its principal focus has been on serious crime. It could be argued that if there is clear consensus on illegality, there is no need to expressly explain why the conduct should be criminalised. But there seems to be some tension between this position and the arguments provided by the Commission for EU legislation. This is well-illustrated by the provisions on content regulation.[12] On the one hand, it is frequently stated that there is a common consensus that certain content is illegal,[13] but on the other hand, the rationale for EU legislation is often based on the importance, in the information and communications technology environment, of avoiding loopholes or 'safe-havens' for criminal activities.[14] If the need for EU criminal law provisions on content regulation is justified by the existence of different standards in the various Member States, then this would suggest that there is no common consensus as to the need for, or the scope of, criminal law provisions in the areas identified. Alternatively, if there is already a common consensus about the extent of content regulation through the criminal law, then this would seem to negate the need for EU legislative action. The suggestion that it is only the 'exact definition' of the offence which 'varies from country to country'[15] does not help in this regard; the extent of the variation, and with it the potential expansion of the field of criminalisation, remains unclear. Either way there is a clear contradiction in the reasoning which makes it all the more important that the need for, and scope of, any proposed criminal laws be carefully assessed.

In view of the difficulties encountered setting the boundaries of criminalisation and the competence set out in Article 83(2) TFEU it seems likely that the EU will have to do more in the future to justify the need for a criminal law response.

[11] Council Framework Decision 2008/913/JHA of 28 November 2008 on combating certain forms and expressions of racism and xenophobia by means of criminal law [2008] OJ L328/55, Recital 5.

[12] See further ch 5.

[13] Communication of the Commission to the European Parliament, the Council, the Economic and Social Committee and the Committee of the Regions, Illegal and Harmful Content on the Internet, Brussels, 16 October 1996, COM (1996) 487.

[14] *Ibid*, at 3.a: 'Where certain acts are punishable under the criminal law of one Member State, but not in another, practical difficulties of enforcing the law may arise'; see too Commission, Green Paper on the protection of minors and human dignity in audiovisual and information services, Brussels, 16 October 1996, COM (1996) 483 final, at 2: 'As the definition of offences varies from one country to another, all reprehensible acts are not necessarily punishable in all Member States'.

[15] *Ibid*.

II Harmonisation

A Defining Harmonisation

Harmonisation is a term which is widely used yet ill-defined. Identifying the rationale of EU harmonisation requires a brief examination of the development of harmonisation competence. Looking back to the situation prior to the Lisbon Treaty, the competence for criminal law measures at the EU level stemmed from Article 31 EU. Article 31(1)(c) EU provided that common action on judicial cooperation should encompass measures 'ensuring compatibility of the rules applicable in the Member States, as may be necessary to improve such cooperation'. This provision did not seek to eliminate differences, but rather ensure that there were no legal obstacles to the cooperation sought between Member States. Article 31(1)(e) EU provided for the progressive adoption of 'measures establishing minimum rules relating to the constituent elements of criminal acts and to penalties in the fields of organized crime, terrorism and illicit drug trafficking'. By mentioning 'common minimum rules' for the limited number of matters listed, this provision alluded indirectly to what has since become widely known as 'approximation' or 'harmonisation'. The purpose of these measures was to facilitate cooperation.[16]

The genesis of EU competence in criminal law is therefore not one based on the rationale of harmonisation, but rather on cooperation. This idea has developed, and the concepts of what is now known as approximation or harmonisation cannot be understood without reference to the partnering concept of mutual recognition, which has been called 'the motor of the European integration in criminal law in recent years'.[17] Mutual recognition is given a clear founding in the Lisbon Treaty; Article 61(3) TFEU stating that: 'the Union shall endeavour to ensure a high level of security through the mutual recognition of judgments in criminal matters and, if necessary, through the approximation of criminal laws'. If approximation and mutual recognition seem to be treated as separate concepts to 'ensure a high level of security' under Article 61(3) TFEU, Article 82(1) TFEU seems to treat them more as corollary parts. It states 'judicial cooperation in criminal matters in the Union shall be based on the principle of mutual recognition of judgments and judicial decisions and shall include the approximation of the laws and regulations of the Member States'. Here, approximation is required insofar as it is necessary for mutual recognition in criminal matters – it facilitates the functioning of mutual recognition within the Union.[18]

[16] See futher ch 1.

[17] V Mitsilegas, 'The Constitutional Implications of Mutual Recognition in Criminal Matters in the EU' (2006) 43 *CMLR* 1277, 1277.

[18] M Fletcher, R Loof and B Gilmore, *EU Criminal Law and Justice* (Edward Elgar, Cheltenham, 2008) 37.

Mutual recognition is a form of criminal law integration that is endorsed strongly by sceptical Member States on the basis that is does not entail substantial changes in domestic substantive criminal law.[19] Recall that national differences are an important part of Article 67(1) TFEU, which states that the EU will establish an area of freedom, security and justice as regards to fundamental rights 'and the different legal systems and traditions of member states'. This provision, which sets up the legal foundation for EU minimum-standard setting in criminal procedure under Article 82(2) TFEU, reveals the intention of the Member States not to furnish the EU with unlimited competence. As such, EU legislation does not have the effect of requiring Member States to alter key elements of domestic criminal law.[20] This corresponds to EU criminal law *de minimis*, as represented through the Lisbon Treaty's limited explicit competencies. In this conception, differences such as those in the context of the general principles of liability are vital; representing the protection of fundamental aspects of domestic legal systems, with the resulting discrepancies in criminalisation inherent in the limited integration goals consented to by Member States.

B Reasons for Harmonisation

(i) Cross-border Cooperation and the Information Society

One of the main reasons referred to by the EU for harmonisation is the cross-border dimension which has been highlighted by advances in information and communications technology. Differences in the criminal laws of the Member States are often referred to as providing criminals with an advantage, by allowing them to choose the Member State with the most lenient laws or simply by making the prosecution and investigation of crime more complicated.[21] There are, however, two clear problems with this approach: first, there is little consideration given to explaining the cross-border element of the various crimes, and second, if a matter is truly transnational, then criminals are likely to find safe havens outside the EU.

These problems are well-illustrated by the EU legislation concerning content regulation. Child pornography offences or offences involving racism do not necessarily have much of a cross-border dimension and the various pieces of legislation do little to explain the cross-border element.[22] Only the potential for such

[19] Mitsilegas, 'The Third Wave of Third Pillar Law' (n 8) 545.

[20] See also A Klip, *European Criminal Law: an Integrative Approach* (Cambridge, Intersentia, 2009) 156.

[21] See eg A Weyembergh, 'Approximation of the Criminal Law, the Constitutional Treaty and the Hague Programme' (2005) 42 *CMLR* 1567, 1579; A Bernardi, 'Opportunité de l'harmonisation' in M Delmas-Marty, G Giudicelli-Delage and F Lambert-Abdelgawad (eds), *L'harmonisation des sanctions pénales en Europe* (Paris, Société de legislation compare, 2003) 461.

[22] According to Turner, none of the policy documents on racism and xenophobia make much of the significant transnational dimension of crime, see JI Turner, 'The Expressive Dimension of EU Criminal Law' (2012) 60 *American Journal of Comparative Law* 555, 568–70.

material to be disseminated via the Internet or other audio-visual media lends such offences something of a 'cross-border' dimension. But even in this context there is recognition of the necessary limitations of EU action, not least because many of the websites that host unlawful content are outside of the EU.[23] By invoking the Internet or audio-visual media platforms, the EU institutions are provided with a cross-border justification and are then able to argue for a broader approach on the basis of the coherence of the criminal law: It would be problematic for various types of online content to be criminalised, if the same content would be considered legal if it were to appear in print. The consequence of this type of argument though is that information networks are used not just as an excuse to impose stricter regulation, but also to justify broader EU criminal law regulation despite the lack of a cross-border element.[24]

(ii) Effective Implementation of EU Policy

Clearly the rationale for harmonisation now goes beyond mere cooperation. The goal is consistent protection of the legally protected interests across the EU, and hence the effective implementation or enforcement of EU policies.[25] This harmonisation is intended to serve the creation of an area of freedom justice and security, equal legal protection throughout the EU and thereby to assist in the fight against crime. Article 67(3) TFEU outlines instruments that can be used to ensure the area of freedom, justice and security exists, but is limited insofar as 'approximation of criminal laws is restricted by condition of necessity'.

This corresponds with the effectiveness criteria of Article 83(2) TFEU, which allows harmonisation when necessary for effective implementation of a Union policy already subject to harmonisation.[26] The concepts of necessity and effectiveness can be viewed as underpinning principles of EU criminal law, yet their meaning in tandem is not clear.[27] Could, for instance, the harmonisation of the general part principles of the criminal law be deemed 'necessary' in future? Currently, in pursuit of the goal of effectiveness, it is left to Member States to identify, define and

[23] See eg Commission Proposal for a Framework Decision on Racism and Xenophobia, Brussels, 28 November 2001, COM (2001) 664 final, at 5

[24] Communication of the Commission to the European Parliament, the Council, the Economic and Social Committee and the Committee of the Regions, Illegal and Harmful Content on the Internet, Brussels, 16 October 1996, COM (1996) 487, at 5.a: '*One general conclusion is that any regulatory action intended to protect minors should not take the form of an unconditional prohibition of using the Internet to distribute certain content that is available freely in other media. Another conclusion is that existing rules on content regulation need to be examined to see whether they* can be applied by analogy, and that the most restrictive rules should not be applied simply because of the Internet's wide potential reach' (emphasis in the original).

[25] B Hecker, 'Europäisches Strafrecht post-Lissabon' in K Ambos (ed), *Europäisches Strafrecht post-Lissabon* (Göttingen, Universitätsverlag, 2011) 19.

[26] Art 83(2) TFEU.

[27] On effectiveness as a constitutional principle, see E Herlin-Karnell, *The Constitutional Dimension of European Criminal Law* (Oxford, Hart, 2012).

utilise the general principles of liability that allow it to meet this EU obligation.[28] In short, 'effectiveness' relies on the general principles of liability applicable in the different criminal law systems of Member States.[29] As the scope of criminalisation can vary quite substantially between Member States, the minimum standard set differs depending on the general part principles state by state.[30] The key question is exactly how much harmonisation is 'necessary' to achieve the 'effective' implementation of EU policies?

It is not clear that the current harmonisation *de minimis* (with a very low level of harmonisation achieved) has actually been effective. Indeed, the result of the application of the EU regulation in the context of content regulation and privacy might be characterised as implementation without harmonisation. Wayembergh describes the current situation thus:

> Even as regards substantive criminal law, only some of its aspects have been approximated. The level of sanctions have been tackled but, despite certain developments, rather vaguely. Most efforts have concerned the definition of certain types of offences. However, numerous articles of framework decisions concerned are restricted in the sense that they grant to the Member States a possibility to derogate from the obligation contained therein. In that respect, one can speak of harmonization 'en trompe l'oeil'.[31]

It is by no means certain that vague definitions of criminal conduct are sufficient to achieve anything approaching the standardisation of individual crimes. In this context the failure to provide any definition of frequently cited legal principles such as 'intention', 'attempt' or 'aiding and abetting' is particularly noticeable.[32] In view of this it seems extremely unlikely, even in the event of the widespread correct implementation of framework decisions and directives, that the criminalised conduct will be standardised across the continent. The Commission recognised this when it wrote in one of its implementation reports that the legal systems of the Member States 'vary greatly' and that 'in many cases legal concepts and expressions cannot always be easily compared to one another'.[33] This is a serious matter as it calls into question the genuineness of the goal of 'approximation'[34] and threatens to jeopardise both the internal coherence of the criminal laws of the

[28] See further ch 7.

[29] BR Killmann, '§ 11 Systematisierung' in U Sieber, FH Brüner, H Satzeger and B v Heintschel-Heinegg (eds), *Europäisches Strafrecht* (Baden-Baden, Nomos, 2011) para 11 n 24; see also Explanatory Report on the Convention on the protection of the European Communities' financial interests [1997] OJ C191/1, 'For "participation", "instigation" and "attempt", the definitions in national criminal law apply'.

[30] Case C 28/99 *Criminal proceedings against Jean Verdonck, Ronald Everaert and Edith de Baedts* [2001] ECR I-03399.

[31] A Weyembergh, 'The Functions of Approximation of Penal legislation Within the European Union' (2005) 12 *Maastricht Journal of European and Comparative Law* 149, 152.

[32] See further ch 7.

[33] Report from the Commission to the Council and the European Parliament, Based on Article 10 of the Council Framework Decision of 19 July 2002 on combating trafficking in human beings, Brussels, 02 May 2006, COM (2006) 187 final, 6.

[34] See also K Nuotio, 'Harmonisation of Criminal Sanctions in the European Union – Criminal Law Science Fiction' in EJ Husabø and A Strandbakken (eds), *Harmonization of Criminal Law in Europe*, (Antwerp, Intersenia, 2005), 79, 96 et seq.

Member States and any notion of consistency in relation to the EU provisions impacting on the criminal law. This has led some scholars to conclude that the effectiveness criteria actually requires a more complete harmonisation and that it is 'questionable whether these goals are met with instruments introducing a low degree of harmonisation or legal certainty'.[35]

This perspective does not consider that the criteria of effectiveness could be interpreted as limiting the use of criminal law only to where it will affect conduct. It could also mean that it should only be used where criminal law is the most effective way of controlling conduct. It is undefined in EU criminal doctrine, meaning it is not clear what constitutes effectiveness in the EU context. However, what is clear is that there exists an assumption that the presence of criminal law in and of itself is a guarantor of the required effectiveness.[36] As one scholar has succinctly put it, 'there is an over-reliance on the magic of the criminal law'.[37] The EU's approach focuses on extensive criminalisation, based on a subjective element, aiming primarily at prevention. [38] It does this through obligating Member States to create new criminal offences, or to extend the boundaries of criminal conduct in domestic law in line with the definition of a framework decision or directive. As these definitions of criminal conduct agreed at the EU level are generally more expansive, this means a greater scope of acts will be punishable within Member States.[39]

However, as Mitsilegas has written, amid this focus on increased harmonisation and extensive criminalisation there is a 'danger of marginalizing the examination of whether criminal law is actually the most appropriate form of addressing the issues at stake'.[40] This prevailing approach emphasises the significance of EU legislation when there are a number of other reasons why harmonisation measures may not have been effective. Most importantly, effectiveness of EU criminal law in pursuit of EU policies also relies upon the actual implementation of the harmonised rules at the Member State level. As one prominent scholar states: 'One cannot forget what the rationale of harmonisation is: it is not about making all national criminal law systems alike, it is about using them consistently'.[41]

This consistent use depends upon the priorities and capacities of the police, prosecution and judiciary across Member States. Unfortunately, there is a lack of scientific analysis of the adoption and actual effects of harmonisation measures. As one scholar states, 'Rarely, if ever, cross-national horizontal analysis has ever been conducted in order to understand the approaches of the different legal systems in

[35] Mitsilegas, 'The Third Wave of Third Pillar Law' (n 8) 537.

[36] An example is the Court of Justice case C-176/03 *Commission v Council* [2005] ECR I-07879.

[37] E Herlin-Karnell, 'What Principles Drive (or Should Drive) European Criminal Law?' (2010) 11 *German Law Journal* 1115, 1123.

[38] Mitsilegas, 'The Third Wave of Third Pillar Law' (n 8) 536.

[39] M Borgers, 'Functions and Aims of Harmonisation after the Lisbon Treaty. a European Perspective' in C Fijnaut and J Ouwerkerk (eds), *The Future of Police and Judicial Cooperation in the EU* (Leiden, Nijhoff, 2010).

[40] Mitsilegas, 'The Third Wave of Third Pillar Law' (n 8) 537.

[41] Borgers, 'Functions and Aims of Harmonisation' (n 39) 354.

relation to a specific crime'.[42] Among sceptical Member States, there have been calls for more rigorous analysis. For example, the UK House of Commons has expressed the view that the EU must base criminal law harmonisation on statistical evidence of the added value of such harmonisation.[43] While the Commission conducts evaluations as specified in many framework decisions, they are based upon information submitted by Member States, are frequently delayed, and do not include sufficient information to allow for proper assessment of effectiveness. This lack of rigorous analysis betrays an implicit assumption that seems to exist at the heart of EU criminal law; that fewer differences between laws will mean more effective cooperation[44] and more effective implementation of EU policies. As such, it is an assumption ever in favour of increased harmonisation for increased effectiveness. Harmonisation developments driven by this assumption can only ever move the corpus closer to unification.

Perhaps naturally, this has led some to question what is driving the push for further integration and harmonisation. As one author writes: '[T]he question remains as to what extent concerns for the citizens are genuinely driving this agenda and to what degree such an agenda is driven by other aspirations such as the establishment of an autonomous EU system of criminal law'.[45]

C The End of Harmonisation?

In general, the momentum of a harmonisation process will always be towards increasing convergence, which, if unfettered, will lead to complete unification of the involved legal systems. Perhaps correspondingly, the tendency of a nation state will generally be towards safeguarding, rather than sacrificing, sovereignty. As such, the EU's institutional impulse to integration and greater harmonisation (as shown by the increasing scope of harmonisation and lack of critical analysis of the actual results of this harmonisation) confronts a state impulse to maintaining sovereignty (evidenced by the relatively narrow construction of explicit competencies agreed under the Lisbon treaty). As we have seen, the explicit competence set out in the Lisbon Treaty in Article 83 TFEU is still significantly limited in scope – indeed it can be argued that in reality Article 83 TFEU in its entirety represents no substantial modification of EU competence in substantive criminal law,[46] as it is limited to the

[42] F Calderoni, *Organized Crime Legislation in the European Union: Harmonization and Approximation of Criminal Law, National Legislations and the EU Framework Decision on the Fight Against Organized Crime* (Berlin, Springer, 2010) 19.

[43] House of Commons Home Affairs Committee, Justice and Home Affairs Issues at European Union Level, Third Report of Sessions 2006–07, vol 1 (London, 2007).

[44] Topa, 'Where do we Stand with Harmonisation of Substantive Criminal Law in the EU' (n 3) 90.

[45] E Herlin-Karnell, 'EU Criminal Law Relocated Recent Developments' (2011) *Uppsala Faculty of Law Working Paper* 6b, 10.

[46] Though it nonetheless still represents a progression compared to pre-Lisbon, as Member States are now obliged to implement the European rules. J Vogel, 'Strafgesetzgebungskompetenzen der Europäischen Union' in K Ambos (ed), *Europäisches Strafrecht post-Lissabon*, 14 (Göttingen, Universitätsverlag, 2011) 44.

listed areas under Article 83(1) TFEU,[47] or those already subject to harmonisation measures in the context of Article 83(2) TFEU.[48]

Member States are also provided with a safeguard, with Article 83(3) TFEU offering a so-called 'emergency brake' relating to measures concerned with criminal procedure and substantive law, where in the opinion of the Member State the draft legislation 'would affect fundamental aspects of its criminal justice system'. This situation allows a suspension of ordinary legislative procedure, whereby unwilling Member States, even in the minority, can opt out of a legal instrument while allowing other states to proceed. It has already been used, with Protocol No 21 (Ireland and the United Kingdom) and Protocol No 22 (Denmark) to the Lisbon Treaty. These states were able to use the provision to opt out of the area of Freedom, Justice and Security and will be bound only if they express will to join.[49] The emergency brake allows Member States to express concern at weakening state sovereignty in relation to EU criminal law. Yet it also creates a situation of increased complexity in relation to achieving harmonisation goals, with a lack of uniformity between Member States. Also, it can be viewed as a way for other Member States to form areas of enhanced cooperation, ahead of those more concerned with sovereignty implications. Ultimately the ramifications of the 'emergency brake' are not yet clear, but its further application or otherwise will definitely be controversial regardless.

Viewed from this perspective, some have concluded that the Lisbon Treaty sends the message 'that the aspirations to unify the criminal law systems of the Member States have been moderated and that the Member States are first and foremost responsible for the substance of their criminal laws'.[50] In this vein, do the limitations of the Lisbon Treaty and Article 83 TFEU represent the terminal moment of EU criminal law, the triumph of the conservative approach of states over the harmonising impulse of the EU?

The architecture of the Lisbon Treaty and the history of the development of competencies of the EU militate strongly against this conclusion. Within the Lisbon Treaty there is clearly the potential for further development of EU criminal law competency. First, the broadly worded Article 325 TFEU has been interpreted by some as giving the EU a further competence to issue directly applicable

[47] Though controversy remains over whether the list of named criminal law areas is conclusive, or whether other domains could be added. At the very least, for new areas to be harmonised, it would seem they would have to be particularly serious, have a cross-border dimension, and require unanimity in the Council. In favour of the conclusive character of the list, see B Hecker, *Europäisches Strafrecht*, 4th edn (Berlin, Springer, 2012) para 11 n 4; C Safferling, *Internationales Strafrecht, Strafanwendungsrecht – Völkerstrafrecht – Europäisches Strafrecht* (Berlin, Springer, 2011) 413; for a different view, see K Ambos, *Internationales Strafrecht, Strafanwendungsrecht – Völkerstrafrecht – Europäisches Strafrecht – Rechtshilfe*, 3rd edn (Munich, Verlag CH Beck, 2011) 472.

[48] Art 83(2) TFEU can be seen more as a formal sanctioning of the ECJ judgments in the *Environmental Protection* (Case C-176/03 *Commission v Council*, ECR [2005] I-7879) and *Ship Source Pollution* (C-440/05 *Commission v Council*, ECR [2007] I-9097) cases, than as an innovative competence.

[49] Topa, 'Where do we Stand with Harmonisation of Substantive Criminal Law in the EU' (n 3) 94.

[50] Borgers, 'Functions and Aims of Harmonisation' (n 39) 354.

criminal provisions.[51] Article 325 (1) TFEU states that: 'The Union and the Member States shall counter fraud and any other illegal activities affecting the financial interests of the Union through measures to be taken in accordance with this Article, which shall act as a deterrent and be such as to afford effective protection in the Member States'. The view that this Article could provide a further criminal law competence seems founded on two factors. First, the reservation included in the former treaty is conspicuous by its absence. TEU counterpart Article 280 (4) TFEU limited competence by providing that 'these measures shall not concern the application of national criminal law or the national administration of justice'.[52] Further, the mention of the word 'deterrent', and also 'afford effective protection' seem reminiscent of EU criminal law competency. If this perspective is correct, then the language of Article 325 TFEU would seem to allow for a broader competency than under Article 83 TFEU, as it mentions only 'measures', rather than 'minimum rules' as in Article 83(1) TFEU.[53]

Second, substantial questions remain concerning the establishment of other elements such as a European Public Prosecutor's office (EPPO). There is considerable uncertainty about how this office would or could function, if established under Article 86 TFEU by the Member States. Its competence would be for crimes threatening the financial interests of the EU, but it could also be expanded to include other serious crimes with a cross border dimension, should the European Council and Parliament so wish. The main question is whether the EPPO would act on the basis of national criminal law systems, or those of its own definition. If it is the former, no central body of law would be required, bar a short procedural code ensuring coordination with national bodies. However, if it is the latter, a more substantial common legislative effort would be necessitated, which would necessarily entail even greater integration.[54] As such, some authors see a forthcoming breakthrough towards a 'proper' European criminal law system, which could contain supranational penal provisions and be enforced through the

[51] An argument is also made by some scholars on the interpretation of the implied power clause Art 352. It allows the EU to legislate to achieve a treaty objective where no other provision gives a basis for action. Previously this only related to the common market, but TFEU expanded it to include almost any objective of the Treaty. Two Declarations appended to the Treaty limit Art 352 somewhat, but even so, the provision is significantly broader than it was before the Treaty of Lisbon. See Treaty of Lisbon amending the Treaty on European Union and the Treaty Establishing the European Community, Declarations 41 and 42, 13 December 13 [2007] OJ C306/1.

[52] B Hecker, '§ 10 Harmonisierung' in in U Sieber, FH Brüner, H Satzeger and B v Heintschel-Heinegg (eds), *Europäisches Strafrecht* (Baden-Baden, Nomos, 2011) para 10 n 26; Ambos, *Internationales Strafrecht, Strafanwendungsrecht – Völkerstrafrecht – Europäisches Strafrecht – Rechtshilfe* (n 47) 388; Hecker, *Europäisches Strafrecht* (n 47) § 4 n 82; H Satzger, *Internationales und Europäisches Strafrecht, Strafanwendungsrecht – Europäisches Straf- und Strafverfahrensrecht – Völkerstrafrecht*, 4th edn (Baden-Baden, Nomos, 2010) § 8 N 24; Vogel, 'Strafgesetzgebungskompetenzen der Europäischen Union' (n 46) 48; Safferling, *Internationales Strafrecht, Strafanwendungsrecht – Völkerstrafrecht – Europäisches Strafrecht* (n 47) 409.

[53] Safferling, *Internationales Strafrecht, Strafanwendungsrecht – Völkerstrafrecht – Europäisches Strafrecht* (n 47) 409.

[54] Long, 'Towards a European Criminal Code' (n 1) 51.

European public prosecutor.[55] This would follow on from former European codification initiatives such as the Green Paper[56] on criminal-law protection of the financial interests of the Community and the establishment of a European Prosecutor[57] or the Corpus Juris 2000.[58]

III Europeanisation

This overview of the development of EU criminal law with relevance for the information society demonstrates that it has not followed a pre-determined plan or blueprint. What can be said with certainty is that there is certainly no wide support at the level of the Member States for more harmonisation. Indeed, there is a clear and overt resistance among Member States to further communitarisation.[59] The Lisbon Treaty reflects this caution. Article 83 TFEU, while a significant watershed insofar as it creates explicit EU criminal law competence, nonetheless shows that 'the relevance of the national legal order in both international and European environment is undisputed'.[60]

However, it is important to consider the development of the corpus of EU criminal law competence to this point. It has evolved slowly, in light of political exigencies and real world imperatives, and, importantly, often contra the stated intentions of states. This so-called 'expressive dimension'[61] of EU criminal law could be considered to be a euphemism for the EU acting outside its statutory competence, beyond what states have authorised. There can be little doubt that the EU's involvement in the criminal law has a considerable symbolic dimension. By marking out various types of conduct as violating EU law, it is can be seen to be 'expressing and defining its own political identity' thereby building the 'supranational demos which it is repeatedly said to lack and which is seen by many as a prerequisite to genuine legitimacy'.[62] It would seem, however, that there has been little consideration given to the need for criminal laws as opposed to other forms of regulation. In this regard, generalised assumptions that criminal laws are desirable and useful do not provide a substantial enough basis for the introduction of criminal law.

[55] Hecker, '§ 10 Harmonisierung' (n 52) para10 n 26; Hecker, 'Europäisches Strafrecht post-Lissabon' (n 25) 27; Satzger, *Internationales und Europäisches Strafrecht, Strafanwendungsrecht – Europäisches Straf- und Strafverfahrensrecht – Völkerstrafrecht* (n 52) para 8 n 25–7.

[56] http://ec.europa.eu/anti_fraud/documents/fwk-green-paper-corpus/corpus_juris_en.pdf.

[57] Green Paper on criminal-law protection of the financial interests of the Community and the establishment of a European Prosecutor, Brussels, 11 December 2001, COM (2001) 715 final.

[58] Hecker, *Europäisches Strafrecht* (n 47) para 14 n 47 f; Safferling, *Internationales Strafrecht, Strafanwendungsrecht – Völkerstrafrecht – Europäisches Strafrecht* (n 47) 438–41.

[59] Mitsilegas, 'The Third Wave of Third Pillar EU Criminal Law' (n 8) 356.

[60] Topa, 'Where do we Stand with Harmonisation of Substantive Criminal Law in the EU' (n 3) 97.

[61] As one writer put it, 'The EU's action in such cases is better explained by a different motivation – to reaffirm the Union's core values and to strengthen its political identity. This is the expressive dimension of EU criminal law': Turner, 'The Expressive Dimension of EU Criminal Law' (n 22) 359.

[62] Turner, 'The Expressive Dimension of EU Criminal Law' (n 22) 372–573.

This illustrates the underlying reality of EU criminal law – its existence is owed in large part to what has been called 'competence creep'.[63] As we consider the future development of EU criminal law, we should recall, as one writer correctly put it, 'just three decades ago, most observers of the European Union (and its predecessor, the European Community) would have dismissed the notion of EU criminal law as fanciful'.[64] Now built on the firmer foundation of the Lisbon Treaty, it seems unlikely this ever-developing road to EU criminal law can be paved in any direction other than towards increased harmonisation.

[63] M Pollack, 'Creeping Competence: The Expanding Agenda of the European Community' (1994) 14 *Journal of Public Policy* 95.

[64] Turner, 'The Expressive Dimension of EU Criminal Law' (n 22) 358.

Annex

Table of Prohibited Conduct and Sentences

Framework Decision	Criminal offence	Article	Maximum sentence
Council Framework Decision of 29 May 2000 on **increasing protection by criminal penalties and other sanctions against counterfeiting in connection with the introduction of the euro** (2000/383/JHA) [2000] OJ L140/1	The fraudulent making or altering of currency, whatever means are employed.	Art 3(1)(a)	Imprisonment, the maximum being not less than eight years.
	The fraudulent uttering of counterfeit currency.	Art 3(1)(b)	Effective, proportionate and dissuasive criminal penalties.
	The import, export, transport, receiving, or obtaining of counterfeit currency with a view to uttering the same and with knowledge that it is counterfeit.	Art 3(1)(c)	Effective, proportionate and dissuasive criminal penalties.
	The fraudulent making, receiving, obtaining or possession of: – instruments, articles, computer pro-grams and any other means peculiarly adapted for the counterfeiting or altering of currency, or – holograms or other components of currency which serve to protect against counterfeiting.	Art 3(1)(d)	Effective, proportionate and dissuasive criminal penalties.
	Participating in or instigating: the fraudulent making or altering of currency, whatever means are employed; the fraudulent uttering of counterfeit currency; the import, export, transport, receiving, or obtaining of counterfeit currency with a view to uttering the same and with knowledge that it is counterfeit; or the fraudulent making, receiving, obtaining or possession of:	Art 2	Effective, proportionate and dissuasive criminal penalties.

Table (*cont.*)

Framework Decision	Criminal offence	Article	Maximum sentence
Council Framework Decision of 29 May 2000 on **increasing protection by criminal penalties and other sanctions against counterfeiting in connection with the introduction of the euro** (2000/383/JHA) [2000] OJ L140/1 (*cont.*)	– instruments, articles, computer pro-grams and any other means peculiarly adapted for the counterfeiting or altering of currency; or – holograms or other components of currency which serve to protect against counterfeiting.		
	Attempting the fraudulent making or altering of currency, whatever means are employed; the fraudulent uttering of counterfeit currency; the import, export, transport, receiving, or obtaining of counterfeit currency with a view to uttering the same and with knowledge that it is counterfeit.	Art 2	Effective, proportionate and dissuasive criminal penalties.
Council Framework Decision 2001/413/JHA of 28 May 2001 **on combating fraud and counterfeiting of non-cash means of payment** [2001] OJ L149/1	The intentional theft or other unlawful appropriation of a payment instrument, at least in respect of credit cards, other cards issued by financial institutions, travellers cheques, eurocheques, other cheques and bills of exchange.	Art 2(a)	Effective, proportionate and dissuasive criminal penalties.
	The intentional counterfeiting or falsification of a payment instrument in order for it to be used fraudulently, at least in respect of credit cards, other cards issued by financial institutions, travellers cheques, eurocheques, other cheques and bills of exchange.	Art 2(b)	Effective, proportionate and dissuasive criminal penalties.

Framework Decision	Criminal offence	Article	Maximum sentence
Council Framework Decision 2001/413/JHA of 28 May 2001 **on combating fraud and counterfeiting of non-cash means of payment** [2001] OJ L149/1 (*cont.*)	The intentional receiving, obtaining, transporting, sale or transfer to another person or possession of a stolen or otherwise unlawfully appropriated, or of a counterfeited or falsified payment instrument in order for it to be used fraudulently, at least in respect of credit cards, other cards issued by financial institutions, travellers cheques, eurocheques, other cheques and bills of exchange.	Art 2(c)	Effective, proportionate and dissuasive criminal penalties.
	The intentional fraudulent use of a stolen or otherwise unlawfully appropriated, or of a counterfeited or falsified payment instrument, at least in respect of credit cards, other cards issued by financial institutions, travellers cheques, eurocheques, other cheques and bills of exchange.	Art 2(d)	Effective, proportionate and dissuasive criminal penalties.
	The intentional performing or causing a transfer of money or monetary value and thereby causing an unauthorised loss of property for another person, with the intention of procuring an unauthorised economic benefit for the person committing the offence or for a third party, by: – without right introducing, altering, deleting or suppressing computer data, in particular identification data; or – without right interfering with the functioning of a computer programme or system.	Art 3	Effective, proportionate and dissuasive criminal penalties.

Table (*cont.*)

Framework Decision	Criminal offence	Article	Maximum sentence
Council Framework Decision 2001/413/JHA of 28 May 2001 **on combating fraud and counterfeiting of non-cash means of payment** [2001] OJ L149/1 (*cont.*)	The intentional fraudulent making, receiving, obtaining, sale or transfer to another person or possession of: – instruments, articles, computer programmes and any other means peculiarly adapted for the commission of any of the offences described under Art 2(b); – computer programmes, the purpose of which is the commission of any of the offences described under Art 3.	Art 4	Effective, proportionate and dissuasive criminal penalties.
	Participating in or instigating the theft or other unlawful appropriation of a payment instrument; counterfeiting or falsification of a payment instrument in order for it to be used fraudulently; receiving, obtaining, transporting, sale or transfer to another person or possession of a stolen or otherwise unlawfully appropriated, or of a counterfeited or falsified payment instrument in order for it to be used fraudulently; the fraudulent use of a stolen or otherwise unlawfully appropriated, or of a counterfeited or falsified payment instrument; the intentional performing or causing a transfer of money or monetary value and thereby causing an unauthorised loss of property for another person, with the intention of procuring an unauthorised economic benefit for the person committing the offence or for a third party, by:	Art 5	Effective, proportionate and dissuasive criminal penalties.

Framework Decision	Criminal offence	Article	Maximum sentence
Council Framework Decision 2001/413/JHA of 28 May 2001 **on combating fraud and counterfeiting of non-cash means of payment** [2001] OJ L149/1 (*cont.*)	– without right introducing, altering, deleting or suppressing computer data, in particular identification data; or – without right interfering with the functioning of a computer programme or system; – the intentional fraudulent making, receiving, obtaining, sale or transfer to another person or possession of: – instruments, articles, computer programmes and any other means peculiarly adapted for the commission of any of the offences described under Art 2(b); – computer programmes the purpose of which is the commission of any of the offences described under Art 3.		
	Attempting the theft or other unlawful appropriation of a payment instrument; the counterfeiting or falsification of a payment instrument in order for it to be used fraudulently, the fraudulent use of a stolen or otherwise unlawfully appropriated, or of a counterfeited or falsified payment instrument; the performing or causing a transfer of money or monetary value and thereby causing an unauthorised loss of property for another person, with the intention of procuring an unauthorised economic benefit for the person committing the offence or for a third party, by:	Art 6	Effective, proportionate and dissuasive criminal penalties.

Table (*cont.*)

Framework Decision	Criminal offence	Article	Maximum sentence
Council Framework Decision 2001/413/JHA (*cont.*)	– without right introducing, altering, deleting or suppressing computer data, in particular identification data; or – without right interfering with the functioning of a computer programme or system.		
Council Framework Decision of 26 June 2001 on **money laundering, the identification, tracing, freezing, seizing and confiscation of instrumentalities and the proceeds of crime** (2001/500/JHA) [2001] OJ L182/1	The intentional conversion or transfer of property, knowing that such property is proceeds, for the purpose of concealing or disguising the illicit origin of the property or of assisting any person who is involved in the commission of the predicate offence to evade the legal consequences of his actions, providing the offence is punishable by deprivation of liberty or a detention order for a maximum of more than one year or, as regards those states which have a minimum threshold for offences in their legal system, offences punishable by deprivation of liberty or a detention order for a minimum of more than six months.	Art 1(b)	Derivation of liberty for a maximum of not less than four years, Art 2.
	The intentional concealment or disguise of the true nature, source, location, disposition, movement, rights with respect to, or ownership of, property, knowing that such property is proceeds; and, subject to its constitutional principles and the basic concepts of its legal system, providing the offence is punishable by deprivation of liberty or a detention order for a maximum of more than one	Art 1(b)	Deprivation of liberty for a maximum of not less than four years, Art 2.

Framework Decision	Criminal offence	Article	Maximum sentence
Council Framework Decision of 26 June 2001 on **money laundering, the identification, tracing, freezing, seizing and confiscation of instrumentalities and the proceeds of crime** (2001/500/ JHA) [2001] OJ L182/1 (*cont.*)	as regards those states which have a minimum threshold for offences in their legal system, offences punishable by deprivation of liberty or a detention order for a minimum of more than six months.		
	The intentional acquisition, possession or use of property, knowing, at the time of receipt, that such property was proceeds, providing the offence is punishable by deprivation of liberty or a detention order for a maximum of more than one year or, as regards those states which have a minimum threshold for offences in their legal system, offences punishable by deprivation of liberty or a detention order for a minimum of more than six months.	Art 1(b)	Deprivation of liberty for a maximum of not less than four years, Art 2.
	The intentional participation in, association or conspiracy to commit, attempts to commit and aiding, abetting, facilitating and counselling the commission of any of the offences established in accordance with this article, providing the offence is punishable by deprivation of liberty or a detention order for a maximum of more than one year or, as regards those states which have a minimum threshold for offences in their legal system, offences punishable by deprivation of liberty or a detention order for a minimum of more than six months.	Art 1(b)	Deprivation of liberty for a maximum of not less than four years, Art 2.

Table (*cont.*)

Framework Decision	Criminal offence	Article	Maximum sentence
Council Framework Decision 2002/475/JHA of 13 June 2002 **on combating terrorism** [2002] OJ L164/3 As amended by Council Framework Decision 2008/919/JHA of 28 November 2008 amending Framework Decision 2002/475/JHA on combating terrorism [2008] OJ L330/21	1. The intentional acts referred to below in points (a) to (i), as defined as offences under national law, which, given their nature or context, may seriously damage a country or an international organisation where committed with the aim of: – seriously intimidating a population; or – unduly compelling a government or international organisation to perform or abstain from performing any act; or – seriously destabilising or destroying the fundamental political, constitutional, economic or social structures of a country or an international organisation, shall be deemed to be terrorist offences: (a) attacks upon a person's life which may cause death; (b) attacks upon the physical integrity of a person; (c) kidnapping or hostage taking; (d) causing extensive destruction to a government or public facility, a transport system, an infrastructure facility, including an information system, a fixed platform located on the continental shelf, a public place or private property likely to endanger human life or result in major economic loss;	Art 1(1)	Punishable by custodial sentences heavier than those imposable under national law for such offences in the absence of the special intent required pursuant to Art 1(1), save where the sentences imposable are already the maximum possible sentences under national law.

Framework Decision	Criminal offence	Article	Maximum sentence
Council Framework Decision 2002/475/JHA of 13 June 2002 **on combating terrorism** [2002] OJ L164/3 As amended by Council Framework Decision 2008/919/JHA of 28 November 2008 amending Framework Decision 2002/475/JHA on combating terrorism [2008] OJ L330/21 (*cont.*)	(e) seizure of aircraft, ships or other means of public or goods transport; (f) manufacture, possession, acquisition, transport, supply or use of weapons, explosives or of nuclear, biological or chemical weapons, as well as research into, and development of, biological and chemical weapons; (g) release of dangerous substances, or causing fires, floods or explosions, the effect of which is to endanger human life; (h) interfering with or disrupting the supply of water, power or any other fundamental natural resource the effect of which is to endanger human life; (i) threatening to commit any of the acts listed in (a) to (h). 2. This Framework Decision shall not have the effect of altering the obligation to respect fundamental rights and fundamental legal principles as enshrined in Art 6 of the Treaty on European Union.		
	Intentionally directing a terrorist group (defined as: a structured group of more than two persons, established over a period of time and acting in concert to commit terrorist offences; 'Structured group' shall mean a group that is not randomly formed for the immediate commission of an offence and that does not need to have formally defined roles for its members, continuity of its membership or a developed structure).	Art 2(2)(a)	Custodial sentences, with a maximum sentence of not less than 15 years. For the act referred to in Art 1(1)(i), the maximum sentence shall not be less than eight years.

Table (*cont.*)

Framework Decision	Criminal offence	Article	Maximum sentence
Council Framework Decision 2002/475/JHA of 13 June 2002 **on combating terrorism** [2002] OJ L164/3 As amended by Council Framework Decision 2008/919/JHA of 28 November 2008 amending Framework Decision 2002/475/JHA on combating terrorism [2008] OJ L330/21 (*cont.*)	Intentionally participating in the activities of a terrorist group, including by supplying information or material resources, or by funding its activities in any way, with knowledge of the fact that such participation will contribute to the criminal activities of the terrorist group.	Art 2(2)(b)	A maximum sentence of not less than eight years.
	Public provocation to commit a terrorist offence, irrespective of whether a terrorist offence is actually committed.	Art 3(2)(a)	Punishable by effective, proportionate and dissuasive criminal penalties.
	Recruitment for terrorism, irrespective of whether a terrorist offence is actually committed.	Art 3(2)(b)	Punishable by effective, proportionate and dissuasive criminal penalties.
	Training for terrorism, irrespective of whether a terrorist offence is actually committed.	Art 3(2)(c)	Punishable by effective, proportionate and dissuasive criminal penalties.
	Aggravated theft with a view to committing one of the acts listed in Art 1(1), irrespective of whether a terrorist offence is actually committed.	Art 3(2)(d)	Punishable by effective, proportionate and dissuasive criminal penalties.
	Extortion with a view to the perpetration of one of the acts listed in Art 1(1), irrespective of whether a terrorist offence is actually committed.	Art 3(2)(e)	Punishable by effective, proportionate and dissuasive criminal penalties.
	Drawing up false administrative documents with a view to committing one of the acts listed in Art 1(1)(a) to (h) and Art 2(2)(b), irrespective of whether a terrorist offence is actually committed.	Art 3(2)(f)	Punishable by effective, proportionate and dissuasive criminal penalties.

Framework Decision	Criminal offence	Article	Maximum sentence
Council Framework Decision 2002/475/JHA of 13 June 2002 **on combating terrorism** [2002] OJ L164/3 As amended by Council Framework Decision 2008/919/JHA of 28 November 2008 amending Framework Decision 2002/475/JHA on combating terrorism [2008] OJ L330/21 (*cont.*)	Aiding or abetting an offence referred to in Art 1(1), or Arts 2 or 3.	Art 4(1)	Punishable by custodial sentences heavier than those imposable under national law for such offences in the absence of the special intent required pursuant to Art 1(1), save where the sentences imposable are already the maximum possible sentences under national law.
	Inciting an offence referred to in Art 1(1), or Arts 2 or 3.	Art 4(2)	
	Attempting to commit an offence referred to in Art 1(1) and Art 3(2)(d) to (f), with the exception of possession as provided for in Art 1(1)(f) and the offence referred to in Art 1(1)(i).	Art 4(3)	Punishable by custodial sentences heavier than those imposable under national law for such offences in the absence of the special intent required pursuant to Art 1(1), save where the sentences imposable are already the maximum possible sentences under national law.
	Attempting to commit an offence referred to in Art 3(2)(b) and (c).	Art 4(4)	Punishable by custodial sentences heavier than those imposable under national law for such offences in the absence of the special intent required pursuant to Art 1(1), save where the sentences imposable are already the maximum possible sentences under national law.

Table (*cont.*)

Framework Decision	Criminal offence	Article	Maximum sentence
Council Framework Decision of 28 November 2002 on **the strengthening of the penal framework to prevent the facilitation of unauthorised entry, transit and residence** (2002/946/ JHA) [2002] OJ L328/1	Intentionally assisting a person who is not a national of a Member State to enter, or transit across, the territory of a Member State in breach of the laws of the state concerned on the entry or transit of aliens.[1]	Art 1(1)	Effective, proportionate and dissuasive criminal penalties. When committed for financial gain, punishable by custodial sentences with a maximum sentence of not less than eight years where they are committed in any of the following circumstances: – the offence was committed as an activity of a criminal organisation as defined in Joint Action 98/733/JHA(8); – the offence was committed while endangering the lives of the persons who are the subject of the offence.
	Intentionally assisting, for financial gain, a person who is not a national of a Member state to reside within the territory of a Member State in breach of the laws of the state concerned on the residence of aliens.	Art 1(1)	Effective, proportionate and dissuasive criminal penalties.
	Instigating a person to intentionally assisting another person who is not a national of a Member State to enter, or transit across, the territory of a Member State in breach of the laws of the State concerned on the entry or transit of aliens; or instigating a person to intentionally assisting, for financial gain, another person who is not a national of a Member State to reside within the territory of a Member State in breach of the laws of the state concerned on the residence of aliens.	Art 1(1)	Effective, proportionate and dissuasive criminal penalties. When committed for financial gain, punishable by custodial sentences with a maximum sentence of not less than eight years where they are committed in any of the following circumstances:

[1] Council Directive 2002/90/EC of 28 November 2002 defining the facilitation of unauthorised entry, transit and residence [2002] OJ L328/17.

Framework Decision	Criminal offence	Article	Maximum sentence
Council Framework Decision of 28 November 2002 on **the strengthening of the penal framework to prevent the facilitation of unauthorised entry, transit and residence** (2002/946/ JHA) [2002] OJ L328/1 (*cont.*)			– the offence was committed as an activity of a criminal organisation as defined in Joint Action 98/733/JHA(8); – the offence was committed while endangering the lives of the persons who are the subject of the offence.
	Attempting to intentionally assist another person who is not a national of a Member State to enter, or transit across, the territory of a Member State in breach of the laws of the state concerned on the entry or transit of aliens; or attempting to intentionally assist, for financial gain, another person who is not a national of a Member State to reside within the territory of a Member State in breach of the laws of the state concerned on the residence of aliens.	Art 1(1)	Effective, proportionate and dissuasive criminal penalties.
	Acting as an accomplice to a person who intentionally assists another person who is not a national of a Member State to enter, or transit across, the territory of a Member State in breach of the laws of the state concerned on the entry or transit of aliens; or Acting as an accomplice to a person who intentionally assists, for financial gain, another person who is not a national of a Member State to reside within the territory of a Member State in breach of the laws of the state concerned on the residence of aliens.	Art 1(1)	Effective, proportio nate and dissuasive criminal penalties.

Table (*cont.*)

Framework Decision	Criminal offence	Article	Maximum sentence
Council Framework Decision of 22 July 2003 on **combating corruption in the private sector** (2003/568/JHA) [2003] OJ L192/54	Promising, offering or giving, directly or through an intermediary, to a person who in any capacity directs or works for a private-sector entity an undue advantage of any kind for that person or for a third party, in order that that person should perform or refrain from performing any act, in breach of that person's duties – assuming that this is carried out intentionally and in the course of business activities.	Art 2(1)(a)	Maximum penalty of at least one to three years' imprisonment.
	Directly or through an intermediary, requesting or receiving an undue advantage of any kind, for oneself or for a third party, while in any capacity directing or working for a private-sector entity, in order to perform or refrain from performing any act, in breach of one's duties – assuming that this is carried out intentionally and in the course of business activities.	Art 2(1)(b)	Maximum penalty of at least one to three years' imprisonment.
	Instigating or aiding and abetting the conduct referred to in Art 2 above.	Art 3	Punishable by effective, proportionate and dissuasive criminal penalties.
Council Framework Decision 2004/757/JHA of 25 October 2004 **laying down minimum provisions on the constituent elements of criminal acts and penalties in the field of illicit drug trafficking** [2004] OJ L335/8	The intentional production, manufacture, extraction, preparation, offering, offering for sale, distribution, sale, delivery on any terms whatsoever, brokerage, dispatch, dispatch in transit, transport, importation or exportation of drugs, when committed without right and unless committed exclusively for personal consumption as defined by national law.	Art 2(1)(a)	Punishable by one to three years' imprisonment. Punishable by criminal penalties of a maximum of at least between five and 10 years' imprisonment if: (a) the offence involves large quantities of drugs; (b) the offence either involves those drugs which cause the most harm to health, or has resulted in significant damage to the health of a number of persons.

Framework Decision	Criminal offence	Article	Maximum sentence
Council Framework Decision 2004/757/JHA of 25 October 2004 **laying down minimum provisions on the constituent elements of criminal acts and penalties in the field of illicit drug trafficking** [2004] OJ L335/8 (*cont.*)	The intentional cultivation of opium poppy, coca bush or cannabis plant, when committed without right and unless committed exclusively for personal consumption as defined by national law.	Art 2(1)(b)	Punishable by one to three years' imprisonment. Punishable by criminal penalties of a maximum of at least between five and 10 years' imprisonment if: (a) the offence involves large quantities of drugs; (b) the offence either involves those drugs which cause the most harm to health, or has resulted in significant damage to the health of a number of persons.
	The intentional possession or purchase of drugs with a view to conducting one of the activities listed in (a), when committed without right and unless committed exclusively for personal consumption as defined by national law.	Art 2(1)(c)	Punishable by one to three years' imprisonment. Punishable by criminal penalties of a maximum of at least between five and 10 years' imprisonment if: (a) the offence involves large quantities of drugs; (b) the offence either involves those drugs which cause the most harm to health, or has resulted in significant damage to the health of a number of persons.

Table (*cont.*)

Framework Decision	Criminal offence	Article	Maximum sentence
Council Framework Decision 2004/757/JHA of 25 October 2004 **laying down minimum provisions on the constituent elements of criminal acts and penalties in the field of illicit drug trafficking** [2004] OJ L335/8 (*cont.*)	The intentional manufacture, transport or distribution of precursors, knowing that they are to be used in or for the illicit production or manufacture of drugs, when committed without right and unless committed exclusively for personal consumption as defined by national law.	Art 2(1)(d)	Criminal penalties of a maximum of at least between one and three years' imprisonment. Each Member State shall take the necessary measures to ensure that the offences referred to in Art 2(1)(d) are punishable by criminal penalties of a maximum of at least between five and 10 years of deprivation of liberty, where the offence was committed within the framework of a criminal organisation as defined in Joint Action 98/733/JHA and the precursors are intended to be used in or for the production or manufacture of drugs under the circumstances referred to in paragraphs 2(a) or (b).
	Inciting, aiding and abetting or attempting one of the offences referred to in Art 2.	Art 3(1)	
Council Framework Decision 2008/841/JHA of 24 October 2008 **on the fight against organised crime** [2008] OJ L300/42	Conduct by any person who with intent and with knowledge of either the aim and general activity of the criminal organisation or its intention to commit the offences in question, actively takes part in the organisation's criminal activities, including the provision of information or material means, the recruitment of new members, and all forms of financing of its activities,	Art 2(a) Art 2(b)	Maximum term of imprisonment of at least between two and five years. Same maximum term of imprisonment as the offence at which the agreement is aimed or a maximum term of imprisonment of at least between two and five years.

Framework Decision	Criminal offence	Article	Maximum sentence
Council Framework Decision 2008/841/JHA of 24 October 2008 **on the fight against organised crime** [2008] OJ L300/42 (*cont.*)	knowing that such participation will contribute to the achievement of the organisation's criminal activities, and/ or; conduct by any person consisting in an agreement with one or more persons that an activity should be pursued, which if carried out, would amount to the commission of offences punishable by deprivation of liberty or a detention order of a maximum of at least four years or a more serious penalty to obtain financial or other material benefit, even if that person does not take part in the actual execution of the activity.		
Directive 2008/99/EC of the European Parliament and of the Council of 19 November 2008 on **the protection of the environment through the criminal law** [2008] OJ L328/28	The unlawful and intentional or at least serious negligent discharge, emission or introduction of a quantity of materials or ionising radiation into air, soil or water, which causes or is likely to cause death or serious injury to any person or substantial damage to the quality of air, the quality of soil or the quality of water, or to animals or plants.	Art 3(a)	Punishable by effective, proportionate and dissuasive criminal penalties.
	The unlawful and intentional or at least serious negligent collection, transport, recovery or disposal of waste, including the supervision of such operations and the aftercare of disposal sites, and including action taken as a dealer or a broker (waste management), which causes or is likely to cause death or serious injury to any person or substantial damage to the quality of air, the quality of soil or the quality of water, or to animals or plants.	Art 3(b)	Punishable by effective, proportionate and dissuasive criminal penalties.

Table (*cont.*)

Framework Decision	Criminal offence	Article	Maximum sentence
Directive 2008/99/EC of the European Parliament and of the Council of 19 November 2008 on **the protection of the environment through the criminal law** [2008] OJ L328/28 (*cont.*)	The unlawful and intentional or at least serious negligent shipment of waste, where this activity falls within the scope of Art 2(35) of Regulation (EC) No 1013/2006 of the European Parliament and of the Council of 14 June 2006 on shipments of waste and is undertaken in a non-negligible quantity, whether executed in a single shipment or in several shipments which appear to be linked.	Art 3(c)	Punishable by effective, proportionate and dissuasive criminal penalties.
	The unlawful and intentional or at least serious negligent operation of a plant in which a dangerous activity is carried out or in which dangerous substances or preparations are stored or used and which, outside the plant, causes or is likely to cause death or serious injury to any person or substantial damage to the quality of air, the quality of soil or the quality of water, or to animals or plants.	Art 3(d)	Punishable by effective, proportionate and dissuasive criminal penalties.
	The unlawful and intentional or at least serious negligent production, processing, handling, use, holding, storage, transport, import, export or disposal of nuclear materials or other hazardous radioactive substances which causes or is likely to cause death or serious injury to any person or substantial damage to the quality of air, the quality of soil or the quality of water, or to animals or plants.	Art 3(e)	Punishable by effective, proportionate and dissuasive criminal penalties.

Framework Decision	Criminal offence	Article	Maximum sentence
Directive 2008/99/EC of the European Parliament and of the Council of 19 November 2008 on **the protection of the environment through the criminal law** [2008] OJ L328/28 (*cont.*)	The unlawful and intentional or at least serious negligent killing, destruction, possession or taking of specimens of protected wild fauna or flora species, except for cases where the conduct concerns a negligible quantity of such specimens and has a negligible impact on the conservation status of the species.	Art 3(f)	Punishable by effective, proportionate and dissuasive criminal penalties.
	The unlawful and intentional or at least serious negligent trading in specimens of protected wild fauna or flora species or parts or derivatives thereof, except for cases where the conduct concerns a negligible quantity of such specimens and has a negligible impact on the conservation status of the species.	Art 3(g)	Punishable by effective, proportionate and dissuasive criminal penalties.
	Any conduct which causes the significant deterioration of a habitat within a protected site, when unlawful and committed intentionally or with at least serious negligence.	Art 3(h)	Punishable by effective, proportionate and dissuasive criminal penalties.
	The unlawful and intentional or at least serious negligent production, importation, exportation, placing on the market or use of ozone-depleting substances.	Art 3(i)	Punishable by effective, proportionate and dissuasive criminal penalties.
	Inciting, aiding and abetting the intentional conduct referred to in Art 3.	Art 4	Punishable by effective, proportionate and dissuasive criminal penalties.

Table (*cont.*)

Framework Decision	Criminal offence	Article	Maximum sentence
Council Framework Decision 2008/913/JHA of 28 November 2008 on **combating certain forms and expressions of racism and xenophobia by means of criminal law** [2008] OJ L328/55	Publicly inciting to violence or hatred directed against a group of persons or a member of such a group defined by reference to race, colour, religion, descent or national or ethnic origin.	Art 1(1)(a)	Maximum of at least between one and three years' imprisonment.
	Committing an act referred to in point 1(1)(a) by public dissemination or distribution of tracts, pictures or other material.	Art 1(1)(b)	Maximum of at least between one and three years' imprisonment.
	Publicly condoning, denying or grossly trivialising crimes of genocide, crimes against humanity and war crimes as defined in Arts 6, 7 and 8 of the Statute of the International Criminal Court, directed against a group of persons or a member of such a group defined by reference to race, colour, religion, descent or national or ethnic origins when the conduct carried out is likely to incite violence or racial hatred against such a group or a member of such a group.	Art 1(1)(c)	Maximum of at least between one and three years' imprisonment.
	Publicly condoning, denying or trivialising the crimes defined in Art 6 of the Charter of the International Military Tribunal appended to the London Agreement of 8 April 1945, directed against a group defined by reference to race, colour, religion, descent or national or ethnic origin when the conduct is carried out in a manner likely to incite violence or hatred against such a group or a member of such a group.	Art 1(1)(d)	Maximum of at least between one and three years' imprisonment.
	Instigating the conduct referred to in Art 1(1)(c).	Art 2(1)	Effective, proportionate and dissuasive criminal penalties.

Framework Decision	Criminal offence	Article	Maximum sentence
Council Framework Decision 2008/913/JHA of 28 November 2008 on **combating certain forms and expressions of racism and xenophobia by means of criminal law** [2008] OJ L328/55 (*cont.*)	Aiding and abetting the conduct referred to in Art 1.	Art 2(2)	Effective, proportionate and dissuasive criminal penalties.
Directive 2009/52/EC of the European Parliament and of the Council of 18 June 2009 **providing for minimum standards on sanctions and measures against employers of illegally staying third-country nationals** [2009] OJ L168/24	The employment of illegally staying third-country nationals when committed intentionally, in each of the following circumstances as defined by national law: (a) the infringement continues or is persistently repeated; (b) the infringement is in respect of the simultaneous employment of a significant number of illegally staying third-country nationals; (c) the infringement is accompanied by particularly exploitative working conditions; (d) the infringement is committed by an employer who, while not having been charged with or convicted of an offence established pursuant to Framework Decision 2002/629/JHA, uses work or services exacted from an illegally staying thirdcountry national with the knowledge that he or she is a victim of trafficking in human beings; (e) the infringement relates to the illegal employment of a minor.	Art 9(1)	Punishable by effective, proportionate and dissuasive criminal penalties.

Table (*cont.*)

Framework Decision	Criminal offence	Article	Maximum sentence
Directive 2009/123/EC of 21 October 2009 amending Directive 2005/35/EC on **ship-source pollution and on the introduction of penalties for infringements** [2009] OJ L280/52	Infringements within the meaning of Arts 4 and 5.	Art 5a(1)	Punishable by effective, proportionate and dissuasive penalties.
	Repeated minor cases that do not individually but in conjunction result in deterioration in the quality of water.	Art 5a(3)	Punishable by effective, proportionate and dissuasive penalties.
	Inciting, or aiding and abetting an offence committed with intent and referred to in Art 5a(1) and (3).	Art 5b	Punishable by effective, proportionate and dissuasive penalties.
Directive 2011/36/EU of the European Parliament and of the Council of 5 April 2011 on **preventing and combatting trafficking in human beings and protecting its victims**, and replacing Council Framework Decision 2002/629/JHA [2011] OJ L101/1	The intentional recruitment, transportation, transfer, harbouring or reception of persons, including the exchange or transfer of control over those persons, by means of the threat or use of force or other forms of coercion, of abduction, of fraud, of deception, of the abuse of power or of a position of vulnerability or of the giving or receiving of payments or benefits to achieve the consent of a person having control over another person, for the purpose of exploitation.	Art 2(1)	Punishable by a maximum penalty of at least five years' imprisonment. Or punishable by a maximum penalty of at least 10 years' imprisonment where that offence: (a) was committed against a victim who was particularly vulnerable, which, in the context of this Directive, shall include at least child victims; (b) was committed within the framework of a criminal organisation within the meaning of Council Framework Decision 2008/841/JHA of 24 October 2008 on the fight against organised crime;

Framework Decision	Criminal offence	Article	Maximum sentence
Directive 2011/36/ EU of the European Parliament and of the Council of 5 April 2011 on **preventing and combatting trafficking in human beings and protecting its victims**, and replacing Council Framework Decision 2002/629/ JHA [2011] OJ L101/1 (*cont.*)			(c) deliberately or by gross negligence endangered the life of the victim; or (d) was committed by use of serious violence or has caused particularly serious harm to the victim.
	Inciting, aiding and abetting or attempting to commit an offence referred to in Art 2.	Art 3	Punishable by effective, proportionate and dissuasive penalties, which may entail surrender.
Directive 2011/92/ EU of the European Parliament and of the Council of 13 December 2011 on **combating the sexual abuse and sexual exploitation of children and child pornography**, and replacing Council Framework Decision 2004/68/ JHA [2011] OJ L335/1	Intentionally causing, for sexual purposes, a child who has not reached the age of sexual consent to witness sexual activities, even without having to participate.	Art 3(2)	Punishable by a maximum term of imprisonment of at least one year.[2]

[2] But see Art 9: 'In so far as the following circumstances do not already form part of the constituent elements of the offences referred to in Articles 3 to 7, Member States shall take the necessary measures to ensure that the following circumstances may, in accordance with the relevant provisions of national law, be regarded as aggravating circumstances, in relation to the relevant offences referred to in Articles 3 to 7:

(a) the offence was committed against a child in a particularly vulnerable situation, such as a child with a mental or physical disability, in a situation of dependence or in a state of physical or mental incapacity;
(b) the offence was committed by a member of the child's family, a person cohabiting with the child or a person who has abused a recognised position of trust or authority;
(c) the offence was committed by several persons acting together;
(d) the offence was committed within the framework of a criminal organisation within the meaning of Council Framework Decision 2008/841/JHA of 24 October 2008 on the fight against organised crime;
(e) the offender has previously been convicted of offences of the same nature;
(f) the offender has deliberately or recklessly endangered the life of the child; or
(g) the offence involved serious violence or caused serious harm to the child'.

Table (*cont.*)

Framework Decision	Criminal offence	Article	Maximum sentence
Directive 2011/92/EU of the European Parliament and of the Council of 13 December 2011 on **combating the sexual abuse and sexual exploitation of children and child pornography**, and replacing Council Framework Decision 2004/68/JHA [2011] OJ L335/1 (*cont.*)	Intentionally causing, for sexual purposes, a child who has not reached the age of sexual consent to witness sexual abuse, even without having to participate.	Art 3(3)	Punishable by a maximum term of imprisonment of at least two years.
	Intentionally engaging in sexual activities with a child who has not reached the age of sexual consent.	Art 3(4)	Punishable by a maximum term of imprisonment of at least five years.
	Intentionally engaging in sexual activities with a child, where abuse is made of a recognised position of trust, authority or influence over the child	Art 3(5)(i)	Punishable by a maximum term of imprisonment of at least eight years if the child has not reached the age of sexual consent, and of at least three years of imprisonment, if the child is over that age.
	Intentionally engaging in sexual activities with a child, where abuse is made of a particularly vulnerable situation of the child, in particular because of a mental or physical disability or a situation of dependence.	Art 3(5)(ii)	Punishable by a maximum term of imprisonment of at least eight years if the child has not reached the age of sexual consent and of at least three years' imprisonment if the child is over that age.
	Intentionally engaging in sexual activities with a child, where use is made of coercion, force or threats.	Art 3(5)(iii)	Punishable by a maximum term of imprisonment of at least 10 years if the child has not reached the age of sexual consent and of at least five years' imprisonment if the child is over that age.

Framework Decision	Criminal offence	Article	Maximum sentence
Directive 2011/92/EU of the European Parliament and of the Council of 13 December 2011 on **combating the sexual abuse and sexual exploitation of children and child pornography**, and replacing Council Framework Decision 2004/68/JHA [2011] OJ L335/1 (*cont.*)	Intentionally coercing, forcing or threatening a child into sexual activities with a third party.	Art 3(6)	Punishable by a maximum term of imprisonment of at least 10 years if the child has not reached the age of sexual consent and of at least five years' imprisonment if the child is over that age.
	Intentionally causing or recruiting a child to participate in pornographic performances, or profiting from or otherwise exploiting a child for such purposes.	Art 4(2)	Punishable by a maximum term of imprisonment of at least five years if the child has not reached the age of sexual consent and of at least two years' imprisonment if the child is over that age.
	Intentionally coercing or forcing a child to participate in pornographic performances, or threatening a child for such purposes.	Art 4(3)	Punishable by a maximum term of imprisonment of at least eight years if the child has not reached the age of sexual consent and of at least five years' imprisonment if the child is over that age.
	Intentionally and knowingly attending pornographic performances involving the participation of a child.	Art 4(4)	Punishable by a maximum term of imprisonment of at least two years if the child has not reached the age of sexual consent and of at least one year of imprisonment if the child is over that age.

Table (*cont.*)

Framework Decision	Criminal offence	Article	Maximum sentence
Directive 2011/92/EU of the European Parliament and of the Council of 13 December 2011 on **combating the sexual abuse and sexual exploitation of children and child pornography**, and replacing Council Framework Decision 2004/68/JHA [2011] OJ L335/1 (*cont.*)	Intentionally causing or recruiting a child to participate in child prostitution, or profiting from or otherwise exploiting a child for such purposes.	Art 4(5)	Punishable by a maximum term of imprisonment of at least eight years if the child has not reached the age of sexual consent and of at least five years' imprisonment if the child is over that age.
	Intentionally coercing or forcing a child into child prostitution, or threatening a child for such purposes	Art 4(6)	Punishable by a maximum term of imprisonment of at least 10 years if the child has not reached the age of sexual consent and of at least five years' imprisonment if the child is over that age.
	Intentionally engaging in sexual activities with a child, where recourse is made to child prostitution.	Art 4(7)	Punishable by a maximum term of imprisonment of at least five years if the child has not reached the age of sexual consent and of at least two years' imprisonment if the child is over that age.
	The intentional and unlawful acquisition or possession of child pornography.	Art 5(2)	Punishable by a maximum term of imprisonment of at least one year.
	Intentionally, unlawfully and knowingly obtaining access, by means of information and communication technology, to child pornography.	Art 5(3)	Punishable by a maximum term of imprisonment of at least one year.
	The intentional and unlawful distribution, dissemination or transmission of child pornography.	Art 5(4)	Punishable by a maximum term of imprisonment of at least two years.

Framework Decision	Criminal offence	Article	Maximum sentence
Directive 2011/92/EU of the European Parliament and of the Council of 13 December 2011 on **combating the sexual abuse and sexual exploitation of children and child pornography**, and replacing Council Framework Decision 2004/68/JHA [2011] OJ L335/1 (*cont.*)	The intentional and unlawful offering, supplying or making available child pornography.	Art 5(5)	Punishable by a maximum term of imprisonment of at least two years.
	The intentional and unlawful production of child pornography.	Art 5(6)	Punishable by a maximum term of imprisonment of at least three years.
	The intentional proposal, by means of information and communication technology, by an adult to meet a child who has not reached the age of sexual consent, for the purpose of committing any of the offences referred to in Art 3(4) and Art 5(6), where that proposal was followed by material acts leading to such a meeting	Art 6(1)	Punishable by a maximum term of imprisonment of at least one year.
	Inciting or aiding and abetting to commit any of the offences referred to in Arts 3 to 6.	Art 7(1)	
Directive 2013/40/EU of the European Parliament and of the Council of 12 August 2013 on **attacks against information systems** and replacing Council Framework Decision 2005/222/JHA [2013] OJ L218/8	The intentionally committed access without right, to the whole or to any part of an information system, where committed by infringing a security measure, at least for cases which are not minor.	Art 3	Punishable by effective, proportionate and dissuasive criminal penalties (a maximum term of imprisonment of at least two years, at least for cases which are not minor).

Table (*cont.*)

Framework Decision	Criminal offence	Article	Maximum sentence
Directive 2013/40/EU of the European Parliament and of the Council of 12 August 2013 on **attacks against information systems** and replacing Council Framework Decision 2005/222/JHA [2013] OJ L218/8 (*cont.*)	Seriously hindering or interrupting the functioning of an information system by inputting computer data, by transmitting, damaging, deleting, deteriorating, altering or suppressing such data, or by rendering such data inaccessible, intentionally and without right, is punishable as a criminal offence, at least for cases which are not minor.	Art 4	Punishable by effective, proportionate and dissuasive criminal penalties (a maximum term of imprisonment of at least two years, at least for cases which are not minor).[3]
	Deleting, damaging, deteriorating, altering or suppressing computer data on an information system, or rendering such data inaccessible, intentionally and without right, is punishable as a criminal offence, at least for cases which are not minor.	Art 5	Punishable by effective, proportionate and dissuasive criminal penalties (a maximum term of imprisonment of at least two years, at least for cases which are not minor).
	Intercepting, by technical means, non-public transmissions of computer data to, from or within an information system, including electromagnetic emissions from an information system carrying such computer data, intentionally and without right, is punishable as a criminal offence, at least for cases which are not minor.	Art 6	Punishable by effective, proportionate and dissuasive criminal penalties (a maximum term of imprisonment of at least two years, at least for cases which are not minor).

[3] Member States shall take the necessary measures to ensure that the offences referred to in Arts 4 and 5, when committed intentionally, are punishable by a maximum term of imprisonment of at least three years where a significant number of information systems have been affected through the use of a tool, referred to in Art 7, designed or adapted primarily for that purpose.

Member States shall take the necessary measures to ensure that offences referred to in Arts 4 and 5 are punishable by a maximum term of imprisonment of at least five years where:

(a) they are committed within the framework of a criminal organisation, as defined in Framework Decision 2008/841/JHA, irrespective of the penalty provided for therein;
(b) they cause serious damage; or
(c) they are committed against a critical infrastructure information system.

Member States shall take the necessary measures to ensure that when the offences referred to in Arts 4 and 5 are committed by misusing the personal data of another person, with the aim of gaining the trust of a third party, thereby causing prejudice to the rightful identity owner, this may, in accordance with national law, be regarded as aggravating circumstances, unless those circumstances are already covered by another offence, punishable under national law.

Framework Decision	Criminal offence	Article	Maximum sentence
Directive 2013/40/EU of the European Parliament and of the Council of 12 August 2013 on **attacks against information systems** and replacing Council Framework Decision 2005/222/JHA [2013] OJ L218/8 (*cont.*)	The intentional production, sale, procurement for use, import, distribution or otherwise making available, of one of the following tools, without right and with the intention that it be used to commit any of the offences referred to in Arts 3 to 6, is punishable as a criminal offence, at least for cases which are not minor: (a) a computer programme, designed or adapted primarily for the purpose of committing any of the offences referred to in Arts 3 to 6; (b) a computer password, access code, or similar data by which the whole or any part of an information system is capable of being accessed.	Art 7	Punishable by effective, proportionate and dissuasive criminal penalties (a maximum term of imprisonment of at least two years, at least for cases which are not minor).
	Incitement, or aiding and abetting, to commit an offence referred to in Arts 3 to 7.	Art 8(1)	Punishable by effective, proportionate and dissuasive criminal penalties
	Attempt to commit an offence referred to in Arts 4 and 5	Art 8(2)	Punishable by effective, proportionate and dissuasive criminal penalties.

BIBLIOGRAPHY

Ackermann, JB, '§ 23 Immaterialgüterstrafrecht' in JB Ackermann and G Heine (ed), *Wirtschaftsstrafrecht der Schweiz. Hand- und Studienbuch* (Bern, Stämpfli Verlag, 2013)

Agarwal, N, 'Evaluating IRPED2: The Wrong Answer to Counterfeiting and Piracy' (2010) 27 *Wisconsin International Law Journal* 790

Akindemowo, E, 'The Pervasive Influence of Anti-Terrorist Financing Policy: Post 9/11 Non-Bank Electronic Money Issuance' (2004) 19 *JIBLR* 289

Albors-Llorens, A, 'Changes in the Jurisdiction of the European Court of Justice after the Treaty of Amsterdam' (1998) 35 *CMLR* 1273

Alegre, S and Leaf, M, 'Criminal Law and Fundamental Rights in the European Union: Moving Towards Closer Cooperation' (2003) *European Human Rights Law Review* 326

——, *European Arrest Warrant* (London, Justice, 2003)

Allen, M, *Textbook on Criminal Law*, 7th edn (Oxford, Oxford University Press, 2003)

Allhutter, D, '"Illegale und schädigende Internetinhalte": Pornografie und Grundrechte im Policy Framing der Europäischen Union' (2004) 4 *Österreichische Zeitschrift für Politikwissenschaft* 423

Altenhain, K, 'Europäisches Herkunftslandprinzip und nationales Strafanwendungsrecht' in F Zieschang, E Hilgendorf and K Laubenthal (eds), *Strafrecht und Kriminalität in Europa* (Baden-Baden, Nomos, 2003) 107–26

Ambos, K, *Internationales Strafrecht, Strafanwendungsrecht – Völkerstrafrecht – Europäisches Strafrecht – Rechtshilfe*, 3rd edn (Munich, Verlag CH Beck, 2011)

Apps, KM, 'Case C-176/03, Commission v Council: "Pillars Askew: Criminal Law EC-Style"' (2006) 12 *Columbia Journal of European Law* 625

Arnull, A, 'Taming the Beast? The Treaty of Amsterdam and the Court of Justice' in D O'Keefe and P Twomey (eds), *Legal Issues of the Amsterdam Treaty* (Oxford, Hart, 2007) 153–92

——, *The European Union and its Court of Justice* (Oxford, Oxford University Press, 2006)

Arnull, A, Dashwood, A, Dougan, M, Ross, M, Spaventa, E and Wyatt, D, *Wyatt and Dashwood's European Union Law*, 6th edn (London, Sweet & Maxwell, 2011)

Arthur, C, 'LulzSec 'Hackers Jailed for String of Sophisticated Cyber-attacks', *The Guardian*, 16 May 2013

Ashworth, A, *Principles of Criminal Law*, 6th edn (Oxford, Oxford University Press, 2009)

Asp, P, 'Mutual Recognition and the Development of Criminal Law Cooperation within Europe' in EJ Husabø and A Strandbakken (eds), *Harmonisation of Criminal Law in Europe* (Antwerpen, Intersentia, 2005) 23–40

Bambauer, DE, 'Orwell's Armchair' (2012) 79 *University of Chicago Law Review* 863

Baker, E and Harding, C, 'From Past Imperfect to Future Perfect? A Longitudinal Study of the Third Pillar' (2009) 34 *EL Rev* 25

Baraliuc, I, Depreeuw, S and Gutwirth, S, 'Copyright Enforcement in the Digital Age: A post-ACTA View on the Balancing of Fundamental Rights' (2013) 21 *Int J Law Info Tech* 93

Barendt, E, 'Incitement to, and Glorification of, Terrorism' in I Hare and J Weinstein (eds), *Extreme Speech and Democracy* (Oxford, Oxford University Press, 2009) 445–62

Barnum, DG, 'Indirect Incitement and Freedom of Speech in Anglo-American Law' (2006) *European Human Rights Law Review* 258

Beer, J, *Die Convention on Cybercrime und österreichisches Strafrecht* (Linz, Trauner Verlag, 2005)

Belavusau, U, 'A Dernier Cri from Strasbourg: An Ever Formidable Challenge of Hate Speech' (2010) 16 *European Public Law* 373

Bernardi, A, 'Opportunité de l'harmonisation' in M Delmas-Marty, G Giudicelli-Delage and E Lambert-Abdelgawad (eds), *L'harmonisation des sanctions pénales en Europe* (Paris, Société de legislation compare, 2003) 451–63

Bernardini, R, *Droit pénal général, Introduction au droit criminel, Théorie générale de la responsabilité pénale* (Paris, Gualino éditeur, 2003)

Bitton, M, 'Rethinking the Anti-Counterfeiting Trade Agreement's Criminal Copyright Enforcement Measures' (2012) 102 *Journal of Criminal Law and Criminology* 37

Blaauw, E, Sheridan, L and Winkel, FW, 'Designing Anti-stalking Legislation on the Basis of Victims' Experiences and Psychopathology' (2002) 9 *Psychiatry, Psychology and Law* 136

Blakeney, M, *Intellectual Property Enforcement, A Commentary on the Anti-Counterfeiting Trade Agreement (ACTA)* (Cheltenham, Edward Elgar, 2012)

Blocher, W and Walter, MM, 'Computer Program Directive' in MM Walter and S Von Lewinski (ed), *European Copyright Law. A Commentary* (Oxford, Oxford University Press, 2010)

Bocij, P, 'Victims of Cyberstalking: An Exploratory Study of Harassment Perpetrated via the Internet' (2003) *First Monday* 8

Böllinger, L, 'Die EU-Kommission und die Sexualmoral' (2006) 2 *Hanse Law Review* 5

Borgers, M, 'Functions and Aims of Harmonisation after the Lisbon Treaty. A European Perspective' in C Fijnaut and J Ouwerkerk (eds), *The Future of Police and Judicial Cooperation in the EU* (Leiden, Nijhoff, 2010) 347–56

Böse, M, 'Die Zuständigkeit der Europäsichen Gemeinschaft für das Strafrecht: Zugleich Besprechung von EuGH, Urteil vom 13.9.2005' (2006) 153 *Goltdammers Archiv für Strafrecht* 211

Boyne, SM, 'Free Speech, Terrorism, and European Security: Defining and Defending the Political Community' (2010) 30 *Pace Law Review* 417

Brindle, P and Guelar, F, 'About the New Money Laundering EU Directive: Legal Analysis (2004) 25 *ICCLR* 125

Brodowski, D, 'Strafrechtsrelevante Entwicklungen in der Europäischen Union – ein Überblick' (2011) *Zeitschrift für Internationale Strafrechtsdogmatik* 940

Brody, D, Acker, J and Logan, W, *Criminal Law* (Gathersburg, Aspen Publishers, 2001)

Butler, M, 'Spam – the Meat of the Problem' (2003) 19 *Computer Law & Security Review* 388

Calderoni, F, *Organized Crime Legislation in the European Union: Harmonization and Approximation of Criminal Law, National Legislations and the EU Framework Decision on the Fight Against Organized Crime* (Berlin, Springer, 2010)

Calliess, C and Ruffert-Suhr, M, *EUV/AEUV, Das Verfassungsrecht der Europäischen Union mit Europäischer Grundrechtecharta. Kommentar*, 4th edn (Munich, Beck, 2011)

Cancio, M, 'Überlegungen zu einer gemeineuropäischen Regelung des Versuchs' in K Tiedemann (ed), *Wirtschaftsstrafrecht in der Europäischen Union: Rechtsdogmatik, Rechtsvergleich, Rechtspolitik, Freiburg-Symposium* (Köln, Heymanns, 2002) 169–81

Chehani Ekaratne, S, 'Redundant Restriction: The UK's offence of Glorifying Terrorism' (2010) 23 *Harvard Human Rights Journal* 205

Christodoulou-Varotsi, I, 'Recent Developments in the EC Legal Framework on Ship-Source Pollution: The Ambivalence of the EC's Penal Approach' (2006) 33 *Transportation Law Journal* 371

Clough, J, *Principles of Cybercrime* (Cambridge, Cambridge University Press, 2010)

Cohen-Almagor, R, 'Freedom of Expression, Internet Responsibility, and Business Ethics: The Yahoo! Saga and Its Implications' (2011) 106 *Journal of Business Ethics* 1

Cook, T, *EU Intellectual Property Law* (Oxford, Oxford University Press, 2010)

Corstens, G and Pradel, J, *European Criminal Law* (The Hague, Kluwer Law International, 2002)

Coulson, N and Hutchinson, AEJ, 'Should Access to the Internet be a Fundamental Right?' (2010) 12 *E-Commerce Law and Policy* 12

Council of Europe's Committee of Experts on Terrorism, *Cyberterrorism – The Use of the Internet for terrorist purposes* (Strasbourg, Council of Europe Publishing, 2007)

Craig, P and de Búrca, G, *EU Law*, 5th edn (Oxford, Oxford University Press, 2011)

D'Erme, R, Geiger, C, Grosse Ruse-Khan, H, Heinze, C, Jaeger, T, Matulionyte, R and Metzger, A, 'The Impact of the Anti-Counterfeiting Trade Agreement on the Legal Framework for IP Enforcement in the European Union' in C Geiger (ed), *Constructing European Intellectual Property. Achievements and New Perspectives* (Cheltenham, Edward Elgar, 2013) 394--408

Dashwood, A, 'The Principle of Direct Effect in European Community Law' (1978) 16 *JCMS* 229

Davis, J, 'Hackers Take Down the Most Wired Country in Europe' (2007) 15(09) *Wired Magazine*

Delmas-Marty, M, 'The European Union and Penal Law' (1998) 4 *European Law Journal* 87

Delmas-Marty, M and Vervaele, J, *The Implementation of the Corpus Juris in the Member States*, vol 1 (Antwerp, Intersenia, 2000)

Dionysopoulos, G, *Werbung mittels elektronischer Post, Cookies und Location Based Services: der neue Rechtsrahmen: eine komparative Betrachtung der elektonischen Werbung in der EU und eine Analyse der Umsetzung der Datenschutzrichtlinie für elektronische Kommunikation (RL 2002/58/EG) am Beispiel Deutschland* (Munich, Utz, 2005)

Dolata, U, 'Das Internet und die Transformation der Musikindustrie, Rekonstruktion und Erklärung eines unkontrollierbaren Wandels' (2008)18 *BJS* 354

Douglas-Scott, S, 'The Rule of Law in the European Union – Putting the Security into the Area of Freedom, Security and Justice' (2004) 29 *EL Rev* 219

Dreier, T, 'Satellite and Cable Directive' in MM Walter and S Von Lewinski (ed), *European Copyright Law. A Commentary* (Oxford, Oxford University Press, 2010)

Duff, RA, Farmer, L, Marshall, SE, Renzo, M and Tadros, V, *The Boundaries of the Criminal Law* (Oxford, Oxford University Press 2010)

Eckes, C, Fahey, E and Kanetake, M, 'International, European, and US Perspectives on the Negotiation and Adoption of the Anti-Counterfeiting Trade Agreement (ACTA)' (2012) 20 *Currents: International Trade Law Journal* 20

Editorial, 'Implementation of Money Laundering Framework Decision Still Has Some Way to Go' (2004) 143 *EU Focus* 10

Edwards, L, 'Articles 6-7, ECD: Privacy and Communications Directive 2002' in L Edwards (ed), *The New Legal Framework for E-Commerce in Europe* (Oxford, Hart, 2005) 31–66

——, 'United Kingdom' in PJ Kozyris (ed), *Regulating Internet Abuses: Invasion of Privacy* (Alphen aan den Rijn, Kluwer Law International, 2007) 177–202

Ege, G and Muggli, S, 'Safer Internet Programm und andere Massnahmen der EU zum

Jugendschutz im Internet und in den neuen Medien' in C Schwarzenegger and R Nägeli (eds), *Viertes Zürcher Präventionsforum: Illegale und schädliche Inhalte im Internet und in den neuen Medien – Prävention und Jugenschutz* (Zurich, Schulthess, 2012) 137–87

Eigel, C, 'Internal Security in an Open Market: The European Union Addresses the Need for Community Gun Control' (1995) 18 *British International & Comparative Law Review* 429

European Scrutiny Committee, 11th Report, Session 2006–07 (London, 2007)

European Union Committee of the House of Lords, *The Criminal Law Competence of the European Community*, 42nd Report of Session 2005–06 (London, The Stationary Office, 2006)

——, *The EU Drugs Strategy*, 26th Report (London, 2012)

Fabrizy, EE, *StGB samt ausgewählten Nebengesetze, Kurzkommentar*, 10th edn (Vienna, Manzsche, 2010)

Ferenczi, T, 'La Cour de justice est accusée d›outrepasser ses compétences', *Le Monde*, 13 January 2006

Ferola, L, 'Anti-Bribery Measures in the European Union: A Comparison with the Italian Legal Order' (2000) 28 *International Journal of Legal Information* 512

Fletcher, M, 'Extending "Indirect Effect' to the Third Pillar: The Significance of Pupino' (2005) 30 *EL Rev* 862

——, 'Some Developments to the ne bis in idem Principle in the European Union: Criminal Proceedings Against Hüseyn Gözütok and Klaus Brügge' (2003) 66 *Modern Law Review* 769

Fletcher, M, Loof, R and Gilmore, B, *EU Criminal Law and Justice* (Edward Elgar, Cheltenham, 2008)

Frank, T, '"You've got (Spam-)Mail" – Zur Strafbarkeit von E-Mail-Werbung' (2004) *Computer und Recht* 123

Freund, G, *Strafrecht Allgemeiner Teil*, 2nd edn (Berlin, Springer, 2009)

Fritzemeyer, W and Law, A, 'The CAN-SPAM Act-Analysed from a European Perspective' (2005) 11 *Computer and Telecommunications Law Review* 81

Fuchs, H, *Österreichisches Strafrecht. Allgemeiner Teil I: Grundlagen und Lehre von der Straftat*, 7th edn (Vienna, Springer 2008)

Fuller, L, *The Morality of Law* (New Haven, Yale University Press, 1963)

Funk, A, Zeifang, G, Johnson, D and Spessard, R, 'Unsolicited Commercial Emails in the Jurisdictions of Germany and the USA: Some Thoughts on the New Anti-Spam Laws in Consideration of the Interests of the Parties Involved in Email Traffic' (2004) 5 *Computer Law Review International* 138

Gärditz, KF and Gusy, C, 'Zur Wirkung europäischer Rahmenbeschlüsse im innerstaatlichen Recht: Zugleich Besprechung von EuGH, Urteil vom 16.6.2005' (2006) 153 *Goltdammers Archiv für Strafrecht* 225

Garman, JJ, 'The European Union Combats Racism and Xenophobia by Forbidding Expression: An Analysis of the Framework Decision' (2008) 39 *University of Toledo Law Review* 843

Garrie, D, Armstrong, M and Blakley, A, 'Voice Over Internet Protocol: Reality v. Legal Fiction' (2005) 52 *Fed Law* 38

Gassner, S, 'Das Herkunftslandprinzip nach der E-Commerce-Richtlinie' in O Pläckinger, D Duursma and G Helm (eds), *Aktuelle Entwicklungen im Internet-Recht* (Vienna, NWV, 2002) 27–35

Geiger, Ch, 'Of ACTA, "Pirates" and Organized Criminality – How "Criminal" Should the Enforcement of Intellectual Property Be?'(2010) 46 *ILC* 631

——,'The Anti-Counterfeiting Trade Agreement and Criminal Enforcement of Intellectual Property: What Consequences for the European Union?' in J Rosen (ed), *Intellectual Property Rights at the Crossroads of Trade* (Cheltenham, Edward Elgar, 2012) 167–81

——,'The Construction of Intellectual Property in the European Union: Searching for Coherence' in C Geiger (ed), *Constructing European Intellectual Property: Achievements and New Perspectives* (Cheltenham, Edward Elgar, 2013) 5–23

——,'Weakening Multilateralism in Intellectual Property Lawmaking: a European Perspective on ACTA' (2012) 3 *The WIPO Journal* 166

Gercke, M, '"Cyberterrorismus" – Aktivitäten terroristischer Organisationen im Internet' (2007) *Computer und Recht* 62

——,'Der Rahmenbeschluss über Angriffe auf Informationssysteme' (2005) *Computer und Recht* 468

——,'Die Entwicklung des Internetstrafrechts im Jahr 2005' (2006) 50 *Zeitschrift für Urheber- und Medienrecht* 284

——,'Europe's Legal Approaches to Cybercrime' (2009) 10 *ERA Forum* 409.

Gercke, M, and Brunst, PW, *Praxishandbuch Internetstrafrecht* (Stuttgart, Kohlhammer, 2009)

Gerwehr, S and Daly, S, 'Al-Qaida: Terrorist Selection and Recruitment' in D Kamien (ed) *The McGraw-Hill Homeland Security Handbood* (New York, McGraw-Hill, 2006)

Gibson, J, 'The Directive Proposal on Criminal Sanctions' in Ch Geiger (ed), *Criminal Enforcement of Intellectual Property. A Handbook of Contemporary Research* (Cheltenham, Edward Elgar, 2012) 245–68

Gillespie, AA, 'The Sexual Offences Act 2003: Tinkering with "Child Pornography"' (2004) *Criminal Law Review* 361

Gless, S, *Internationales Strafrecht* (Basel, Helbing Lichtenhahn, 2011)

Goldstein, P and Hugenholtz, B, *International Copyright. Principles, Law and Practice* (Oxford, Oxford University Press, 2013)

Green, SP, 'Moral Ambiguity in White Collar Criminal Law' (2004) 18 *Notre Dame Journal of Law, Ethics and Public Policy* 501

Gronau, N, *Europäisches Urheberrecht Weiterer Harmonisierungsbedarf oder ein einheitliches Europäisches Urheberrechtsgesetz?* (Hamburg, Diplomica Verlag, 2010)

Gross, MJ, 'The Silent War', *Vanity Fair*, July 2013

Grosse Ruse-Khan, H, 'Criminal Enforcement and International IP Law' in Ch Geiger (ed), *Criminal Enforcement of Intellectual Property. A Handbook of Contemporary Research* (Cheltenham, Edward Elgar, 2012) 171–90

Guillaume, G, 'Terrorism and International Law' (2004) 53 *International and Comparative Law Quarterly* 537

Harding, C, 'The Identity of European Law: Mapping Out the European Legal Space' (2000) 6 *European Law Journal* 128

Harlow, C, *Accountability in the European Union* (Oxford, Oxford University Press, 2002)

Harris, D, O'Boyle, M, Warbrick, C, Bates, E and Buckley, C, *Harris, O'Boyle & Warbrick Law of the European Convention on Human Rights*, 2nd edn (Oxford, Oxford University Press, 2009)

Hayes, J, 'Cookie Law: A Hostage to Fortune?' (September 2012) *Engineering & Technology* 67

Hecker, B, *Europäsiches Strafrecht*, 4th edn (Berlin, Springer, 2012)

——,'Europäisches Strafrecht post-Lissabon' in Kai Ambos (ed), *Europäisches Strafrecht post-Lissabon* (Göttingen, Universitätsverlag, 2011) 13–28

——,'§ 10 Harmonisierung' in U Sieber, FH Brüner, H Satzeger and B v Heintschel-Heinegg (eds), *Europäisches Strafrecht* (Baden-Baden, Nomos, 2011) 252–71

Hedemann-Robinson, M, 'The EU and Environmental Crime: The Impact of the ECJ's Judgment on Framework Decision 2005/667 on Ship Source Pollution' (2008) 20 *Journal of Environmental Law* 279

Hefendehl, R, 'Europäischer Umweltschutz: Demokratiespritze für Europa oder Brüsseler Putsch' (2006) 4 *Zeitschrift für Internationale Strafrechtsdogmatik* 161

Heffermann, A, *Telekommunikationsrecht, Liberalisierung und Wettbewerb* (Vienna, Verlag Österreich, 2002)

Henn, J, 'Targeting Transnational Content Regulation' (2003) 21 *Boston University International Law Journal* 157

Herlin-Karnell, E, 'Commission v Council: Some Reflections on Criminal Law in the First Pillar' (2007) 13 *European Public Law* 69

——, *The Constitutional Dimension of European Criminal Law* (Oxford, Hart, 2012)

——, 'EU Competence after Lisbon' in A Biondi, P Eeckhout and S Ripley (eds), *EU Law after Lisbon* (Oxford, Oxford University Press, 2012) 331–46

——, 'EU Criminal Law Relocated Recent Developments' (2011) *Uppsala Faculty of Law Working Paper* 6b

——, 'The Lisbon Treaty and the Area of Criminal Law and Justice' (2008) 3 *European Policy Analysis* 1

——, 'Subsidiarity in the Area of EU Justice and Home Affairs – A Lost Cause?' (2009) 15 *European Law Journal* 351

——, 'What Principles Drive (or Should Drive) European Criminal Law?' (2010) 11 *German Law Journal* 1115

de Hert, P, 'Division of Competences between National and European Levels with regard to Justice and Home Affairs' in J Apap (ed), *Justice and Home Affairs in the EU: Liberty and Security Issues after Enlargement* (Cheltenham, Edward Elgar, 2004) 61–113

de Hert, P and Kloza, D, 'Internet (access) as a New Fundamental Right: Inflating the Current Rights Framework? (2012) *European Journal of Law and Technology* 3

Hesse, C, 'The Rise of Intellectual Property, 700 b.c.–a.d. 2000: An Idea in the Balance' (2002) *Daedalus* 26

Hildebrandt, M, 'European Criminal Law and European Identity, (2007) 1 *Criminal Law and Philosophy* 57

Hilgendorf, E ,'Tendenzen und Probleme einer Harmonisierung des Internetstrafrechts auf Europäischer Ebene' in C Schwarzenegger, O Arter and F Jörg (eds), *Internet-Recht und Strafrecht* (Berne, Stämpfli, 2005) 257–98

Hinarejos, A 'Integration in Criminal Matters and the Role of the Court of Justice' (2011) 36 *EL Rev* 420

Hoeren, T, 'Germany' in PJ Kozyris (ed), *Regulating Internet Abuses: Invasion of Privacy* (Alphen aan den Rijn, Kluwer Law International, 2007) 57–71

Hoffman, B, *Inside Terrorism*, 2nd edn (New York, Columbia University Press, 2006)

Hollaender, AE and Mayerhofer, C, *Grundlagen des österreichischen Strafrechts, Allgemeiner Teil I* (Innsbruck, Studienverlag, 2007)

House of Commons European Scrutiny Committee, *The UK's Block Opt-Out of pre-Lisbon Criminal Law and policing Measures*, 21st Report of Session 2013–14, HC 683 (London, 2013)

——, 12th Report of Session 2012–13 (London, 2012)

Howit, D, 'Pornography and the Paedophile: Is it Criminogenic?' (1995) 68 *British Journal of Medical Psychology* 15

Hunt, A, 'Criminal Prohibitions on Direct and Indirect Encouragement of Terrorism' (2007) *Criminal Law Review* 441

Jacobs, F, 'The Lisbon Treaty and the Court of Justice' in A Biondi, P Eeckhout and S Ripley (eds), *EU Law after Lisbon* (Oxford, Oxford University Press, 2012) 197–212

Jaeger, M, 'Les rapports entre le droit communautaire et le droit pénal: l'institution d'une communauté de droit' (2004) 84 *Revue de Droit Pénal et de Criminologie* 1099

Jancic, D, 'The European Political Order and Internet Piracy: Accidental or Paradigmatic Constitution-Shaping' (2010) 6 *European Constitutional Law Review* 430

Jareborg, N, 'Criminalization as Last Resort (*Ultima Ratio*)' (2004) 2 *Ohio State Journal of Criminal Law* 521

Jenness, V, 'The Hate Crime Canon and Beyond: A Critical Assessment' (2001) 12 *Law and Critique* 279

de Jesus Butler, I, 'Ensuring Compliance with the Charter of Fundamental Rights in Legislative Drafting: The Practice of the European Commission' (2012) 37 *EL Rev* 397

Kaiafa-Gband, M, 'The Development towards Harmonization with Criminal Law in the European Union – A Citizen's Perspective' (2001) 9 *European Journal of Crime, Criminal Law and Criminal Justice* 239

——,'The Importance of Core Principles of Substantive Criminal Law for a European Criminal Policy Respecting Fundamental Rights and the Rule of Law' (2011) 1 *European Criminal Law Review* 7

——,'The Prevention of Terrorism and the Criminal Law of Pre-Preventive Enforcement: New Criminal Acts for the Fight against Terrorism in the European Union' (in Greek) (2009) *Poinika Chronika* 385

Karaganis, J and Renkema, L, 'Copy Culture in the US and Germany' (2013) *The American Assembly* 30

Kierkegaard, SM, 'Here Comes the Cybernators' (2006) 22 *Computer Law and Security Report* 381

——,'Taking a Sledgehammer to Crack the Nut: The EU Enforcement Directive' (2005) 21 *Computer Law & Security Review* 494

——,'To Block or not to Block – European Child Porno Law in Question' (2011) 27 *Computer Law & Security Review* 573

Killmann, BR, '§10 Systematisierung' in U Sieber, FH Brüner, H Satzeger and B v Heintschel-Heinegg (eds), *Europäisches Strafrecht* (Baden-Baden, Nomos, 2011) 252–71

——,'§ 11 Systematisierung' in U Sieber, FH Brüner, H Satzeger and B v Heintschel-Heinegg (eds), *Europäisches Strafrecht* (Baden-Baden, Nomos, 2011) 272–80

Kiska, R, 'Hate Speech: A Comparison between the European Court of Human Rights and the United States Supreme Court Jurisprudence' (2012) 25 *Regent University Law Review* 107

Klip, A, *European Criminal Law: An Integrative Approach* (Cambridge, Intersentia, 2009)

——, *European Criminal Law*, 2nd edn (Cambridge, Intersentia, 2012)

Klip, A and Van der Wilt, H (eds), *Harmonisation and Harmonising Measures in Criminal Law*, vol 186 (The Royal Academy of Arts and Science, Amsterdam, 2002)

Kortlander, J, 'Is Filtering the New Silver Bullet in the Fight against Child Pornography on the Internet? A Legal Study into the Experiences of Australia and Germany' (2011) 17 *Computer and Telecommunications Law Review* 199

Kozyris, PJ, 'General Report' in PJ Kozyris (ed), *Regulating Internet Abuses: Invasion of Privacy* (Alphen aan den Rijn, Kluwer Law International, 2007) 1–26

Kreutzer, T, 'Auf dem Weg zu einem Urheberrecht für das 21. Jahrhundert. Ideen für eine zukünftige Regulierung kreativer Güter' (2012) 92 *Wirtschaftsdienst* 701

Kudlich, H, 'Herkunftslandprinzip und internationales Strafrecht' (2004) *HRRS* 282

Kühl, K, *Strafrecht Allgemeiner Teil*, 7th edn (Munich, Vahlen, 2012)

Kur, A and Dreier, T, *European Intellectual Property Law* (Cheltenham, Edward Elgar, 2013)

Lackner, K and Kühl, K, *Strafgesetzbuch, Kommentar*, 27th edn (Munich, CH Beck, 2011)

Ladenburger, C, 'Police and Criminal Law in the Treaty of Lisbon' (2008) 4 *European Constitutional Law Review* 20

Lehti, M and Aromaa, K 'Trafficking for Sexual Exploitation' (2006) 34 *Crime and Justice* 133

Leme, LP, 'The Council Directive on Control of the Acquisition and Possession of Weapons and its Categorization of Firearms: A Rational Approach to Public Safety?' (1996) 37 *Harvard International Law Journal* 568

Lenaerts, K and Jadoul, L, 'Quelle contribution de la Cour de justice des Communautés européennes au développement de l'espace de liberté, de sécurité et de justice?' in G de Kerchove and A Weyembergh (eds), *L'espace pénal européen: enjeux et perspectives* (Bruxelles, Editions de l'Université de Bruxelles, 2002) 199–222

Lessig, L, *Code and Other Laws of Cyberspace* (New York, Basic Books, 1999)

von Lewinski, S, 'Database Directive' in MM Walter and S Von Lewinski (ed), *European Copyright Law. A Commentary* (Oxford, Oxford University Press, 2010)

——,'Rental and Lending Rights Directive' in MM Walter and S von Lewinski (eds), *European Copyright Law: A Commentary* (Oxford, Oxford University Press, 2010)

—— and Walter, MM, 'Information Society Directive' in MM Walter and S Von Lewinski (ed), *European Copyright Law. A Commentary* (Oxford, Oxford University Press, 2010)

Lim Saw, C and Leong, SHS, 'Defining Criminal Liability for Primary Acts of Copyright Infringement – the Singapore Experience' (2008) *Journal of Business Law* 304

Lloyd, IJ, *Information Technology Law*, 6th edn (Oxford, Oxford University Press, 2011)

Long, N, 'Towards a European Criminal Code' (2011) *European Institute of Public Administration Scope* 49

Lowe, V, 'The Law of Unintended Consequences – A Perspective on the Draft Directive on Criminal Measures to Enforce Intellectual Property Rights' (2006) 163 *Criminal Lawyer* 3

Mac Sithigh, D, 'Regulating the Medium: Reactions to Network Neutrality in the European Union and Canada' (2011) 14 *Journal of Internet Law* 3

Manta, ID, 'The Puzzle of Criminal Sanctions for Intellectual Property Infringement' (2011) 24 *Harvard Journal of Law and Technology* 469

Masuda, Y, *The Information Society as post-Industrial Society* (Bethesda, World Future Society, 1981)

McNally, M and Newman, G, *Perspectives on Identity Theft* (Cullompton, Devon, 2008)

McStay, A, 'I Consent: An Analysis of the Cookie Directive and its Implications for UK Behavioural Advertising' (2012) 15 *New Media and Society* 596

Merati-Kashani, J, *Der Datenschutz im E-Commerce – Die rechtliche Bewertung der Erstellung von Nutzerprofilen durch Cookies* (Munich, Beck, 2005)

Meuwese, A, *Impact Assessment in EU Lawmaking* (The Hague, Kluwer Law, 2008)

Millar, G, 'The European Protection of Freedom of Expression; Reflections On Some Recent Restrictive Trends', available at www-ircm.u-strasbg.fr/seminaire_oct2008/docs/Millar_Trends_in_the_Recent_Case-Law.pdf, at 1

Mineshima, D, 'The Rule of Law and EU Expansion' (2002) 24 *Liverpool Law Review* 73

Mitsilegas, V, *EU Criminal Law* (Oxford, Hart, 2009)

——,'The Competence Question: The European Community and Criminal Law' in E Guild and F Geyer (eds), *Security versus Justice: Police and Judicial Cooperation in the European Union* (Aldershot, Ashgate, 2008) 153–70

——,'The Constitutional Implications of Mutual Recognition in Criminal Matters in the EU' (2006) 43 *CMLR* 1277

——,'The Third Wave Third Pillar Law: Which Direction for EU Criminal Justice?' (2009) 34 *EL Rev* 523

Modena Group on Stalking, 'Protecting Women from the New Crime of Stalking: A Comparison of Legislative Approaches Within the European Union. Final report' (2007) *University of Modena and Reggio Emilia for the European Commission*

Mogel, V, *Europäisches Urheberrecht* (Vienna, Verlag Österreich, 2001)

Moran, LJ 'Affairs of the Heart: Hate Crime and the Politics of Crime Control' (2001) 12 *Law and Critique* 331

Mosteshar, S, *European Community Telecommunications Regulation* (London, Graham & Trotman, 1993)

Möwes, B and Meider, AK, *Die Revision der EG-Fernsehrichtlinie* (Berlin, Berliner Wissenschafts-Verlag, 2008)

Munro, VE, 'A Comparative Study of Responses to the Trafficking of Women for Prostitution' (2006) 46 *British Journal of Criminology* 318, 330

Mutchler, A, 'CAN-SPAM versus the European Union E-Privacy Directive: Does Either Provide a Solution to the Problem of Spam' (2010) *43 Suffolk UL Rev* 957

Naylor, RT, '"Marlboro Men" Review of M Naím, Illicit: How Smugglers, Traffickers and Copycats are Hijacking the Global Economy' (2007) 29 *London Review of Books* 37

Nelles, U, 'Definitions of Harmonisation' in A Klip and H Van der Wilt (eds), *Harmonisation and Harmonising Measures in Criminal Law. Vol. 186* (The Royal Academy of Arts and Science, Amsterdam, 2002) 31–43

Nevin, C, 'Surveillance Over Europe' (Summer 2009) *Economist Intelligent Life Magazine*

Nihoul, P and Rodford, P, *EU Electronic Communications Law, Competition and Regulation in the European Telecommunications Market*, 2nd edn, (Oxford, Oxford University Press, 2011)

Nöding, T, *Das neue europäische Telekommunikationsrecht und die Konvergenz der Übertragungswege* (Berlin, Tenea, 2004)

Nolan, M, 'Law Reform, beyond Mere Opinion Polling and Penal Populism' in A Norrie et al (eds), *Regulating Device* (Oxford, Hart, 2009) 165–84

Norberg, PA, Horne, DA and Horne, D, 'Standing in the Footprint: Including the Self in the Privacy Debate and Policy Development' (2009) 43 *Journal of Consumer Affairs* 495

Nuotio, K, 'Harmonisation of Criminal Sanctions in the European Union – Criminal Law Science Fiction' in EJ Husab and A Strandbakken (eds), *Harmonization of Criminal Law in Europe*, (Antwerp, Intersenia, 2005) 79–101

——,'Terrorism as a Catalyst for the Emergence, Harmonisation and Reform of Criminal Law' (2006) 4 *Journal of International Criminal Justice* 998

Obokata, T, 'EU Council Framework Decision on Combating Trafficking in Human Beings: A Critical Appraisal' (2003) 40 *CMLR* 917

——,'"Trafficking" and "Smuggling" of Human Beings in Europe: Protection of Individual Rights or State Interests?' (2001) 5 *Web Journal of Current Legal Interests* 1

Ormerod, D, *Smith and Hogan's Criminal Law*, 13th edn (Oxford, Oxford University Press, 2011)

Peers, S, 'EU Criminal Law and the Treaty of Lisbon' (2008) 33 *EL Rev* 507

Peers, S, *EU Justice and Home Affairs Law*, 3rd edn (Oxford, Oxford University Press, 2011)
——, 'Finally "Fit for Purpose"? The Treaty of Lisbon and the End of the Third Pillar Order' (2008) *YEL* 47
——, 'Mutual Recognition and Criminal Law in the European Union: Has the Council got it Wrong?' (2004) 41 *CMLR* 5
——, 'Salvation Outside the Church: Judicial Protection in the Third Pillar After the Pupino and Segi Judgments' (2007) 44 *CMLR* 883
——, 'The European Community's Criminal Law Competence: The Plot Thickens' (2008) 33 *EL Rev* 399
——, 'The European Union and Substantive Criminal Law: Reinventing the Wheel?' (2002) 33 *Netherlands Yearbook of International Law* 47
——, 'The Mother of All Opt-Outs? The UK's Possible Opt-Out from Prior Third Pillar Measures in June 2014' (2012) *Statewatch Analysis* 168
——, 'The Opt-Out that Fell to Earth: The British and Polish Protocol Concerning the EU Charter of Fundamental Rights' (2012) 12 *Human Rights Law Review* 375
Philippsohn, S, 'The Dangers of New Technology—Laundering on the Internet' (2001) 5 *Journal of Money Laundering Control* 87
Pichinot, C, *Konvergenz der Medien in Europa im Spannungsfeld von E-Commerce- und Fernsehrichtlinie* (Göttingen, Cuvillier Verlag, 2005)
Pohl, T, 'Verfassungsvertrag durch Richterspruch. Die Entscheidung des EuGH zu Kompetenzen der Gemeinschaft im Umweltstrafrecht' (2006) *ZIS* 213
Pollack, M, 'Creeping Competence: The Expanding Agenda of the European Community' (1994) *Journal of Public Policy* 95
Porat, MU, 'Global Implications of the Information Society' (1978) 28 *Journal of Communication* 28 (1978) 70
Posadas, A, 'Combating Corruption under International Law' (2000) 10 *Duke Journal of Comparative and International Law* 345
Prechal, S, 'Direct Effect, Indirect Effect, Supremacy and the Evolving Constitution of the European Union', in Bernard (ed), *The Fundamentals of EU Law Revisited: Assessing the Impact of the Constitutional Debate* (Oxford, Oxford University Press, 2007) 35–70
Proulx, J, Perrault, C and Ouimet, M, 'Pathways in the Offending Process of Extrafamilial Sexual Child Molesters' (1999) *11 Journal of Research and Treatment* 117
Purcell, R, Pathe, M and Mullen, PE, 'Stalking: Defining and Prosecuting a new Category of Offending' (2004) 27 *International Journal of law and Psychiatry* 157
Ray, L and Smith, D, 'Racist Offenders and the Politics of 'Hate Crime' (2001) 12 *Law and Critique* 203
Reed, R and Murdoch, J, *Human Rights Law in Scotland*, 3rd edn (London, Bloomsbury, 2011)
Reinbothe, J, 'Die Entwicklung des EU-Richtlinienentwurfs zum Urheberrecht im Kontext mit den internationalen Konventionen' in H Prütting et al (ed), *Die Entwicklung des Urheberrechts im europäischen Rahmen* (Munich, CH Beck'sche Verlagsbuchhandlung, 1999) 1–11
Reindl-Krauskopf, S, *Computerstrafrecht im Überblick*, 2nd edn (Vienna, Facultas, 2009)
Roberson, C, *Identity Theft Investigations* (New York, Kaplan, 2008)
Safferling, C, *Internationales Strafrecht, Strafanwendungsrecht – Völkerstrafrecht – Europäisches Strafrecht* (Berlin, Springer, 2011)
Sanchez-Hermosilla, F, 'Neues Strafrecht für den Kampf gegen Computerkriminalität' (2003) *Computer und Recht* 774

Satzger, H, *Internationales und europäisches Strafrecht. Strafanwendungsrecht. Europäisches Straf- und Strafverfahrensrecht. Völkerstrafrecht*, 6th edn (Baden-Baden, Nomos, 2013)

——,'Strafrechtliche Providerhaftung' in P W Heermann and A Ohly (ed), *Verantwortlichkeit im Netz: Wer haftet wofür?* (Stuttgart, Richard Boorberg Verlag, 2003) 161–80

Satzger, H, and Pohl, T, 'The German Constitutional Court and the European Arrest Warrant: Cryptic Signals from Karlsruhe' (2006) 4 *Journal of International Criminal Justice* 686

Sauter, W, 'EU Regulation for the Convergence of Media, Telecommunications, and Information Technology: Arguments for a Constitutional Approach?' (1998) 1 *ZERP-Diskussionspapier* 1

——,'The Consultation on EU regulation for Convergence' (1999) 10 *Util Law Rev* 3

Savin, A, *EU Internet Law* (Cheltenham, Edward Elgar Publishing, 2013)

Schloetter, AL, 'The Acquis Communautaire in the Area of Copyright and Related Rights: Economic Rights' in TE Synodinou (ed), *Codification of European Copyright Law Challenges and Perspectives* (Alphen aan den Rijn, Kulwer Law International, 2012) 115–32

Schöberl, W, *Die Einheitstäterschaft als europäisches Modell, Die strafrechtliche Beteiligungsregelung in Österreich und den nordischen Ländern* (Vienna, Neuer Wissenschaftlicher Verlag, 2006)

Schuh, D, *Computerstrafrecht im Rechtsvergleich – Deutschland, Österreich, Schweiz* (Berlin, Duncker & Humblot, 2011)

Schwarzenegger, Ch, 'Die Internationalisierung des Wirtschaftsstrafrechts und die schweizerische Kriminalpolitik: Cyberkriminalität und das neue Urheberstrafrecht' (2008) 127 ZSR II 399–503

——,'Hyperlinks und Suchmaschinen aus strafrechtlicher Sicht' in O Plöckinger, D Duursma and M Mayrhofer (ed), *Internet-Recht. Beiträge zum Zivil- und Wirtschaftsprivatrecht, Öffentlichen Recht, Strafrecht* (Vienna, NWV, 2004) 395–434

Sieber, U, 'Instruments of International Law: Against Terrorist Use of the Internet' in M Wade and A Maljevic (eds), *A War on Terror?: The European Stance on a New Threat* (New York, Springer, 2010)

——,'Memorandum on a Model European Penal Code' (1998/99) 1 *European Journal of Law Reform* 445–71

——,'§ 24 Computerkriminalität' in U Sieber, FH Brüner, H Satzeger and B v Heintschel-Heinegg (eds), *Europäisches Strafrecht* (Baden-Baden, Nomos, 2011) 393–421

Skinner, S, 'The Third Pillar Treaty Provisions on Police Cooperation: Has the EU Bitten off More than it Can Chew?' (2002) 8 *Columbia Journal of European Law* 203

Sottiaux, S, 'Leroy v France: Apology of Terrorism and the Malaise of the European Court of Human Rights' Free Speech Jurisprudence' (2009) *European Human Rights Law Review* 415

Spencer, JR, 'Opting out of EU Criminal Justice?' (2012) 7 *Archbold Review* 6

Spindler, G, 'Das Gesetz zum elektronischen Geschäftsverkehr – Verantwortlichkeit der Diensteanbieter und Herkunftslandprinzip' (2002) 55 *NJW* 926

——,'Herkunftslandprinzip und Kollisionsrecht – Binnenmarktintegration ohne Harmonisierung: Die Folgen der Richtlinie im elektronischen Geschäftsverkehr für das Kollisionsrecht' (2002) *RabelsZ* 633

Staiger, I, 'Trafficking in Children for the Purposes of Sexual Exploitation in the EU: The Council Framework Decision of 19 July 2002 on combating trafficking in human beings and its implementation into German law' (2005) 13 *European Journal of Crime, Criminal Law and Criminal Justice* 603

Stefanou, C, White, S and Xanthaki, H, *OLAF at the Crossroads – Action against EU fraud* (Oxford, Hart, 2011)

Steiner, J, 'Direct Applicability in EEC law – A Chameleon Concept' (1982) 98 *LQR* 229

——, Woods, L and Twigg-Flesner, C, *EU Law*, 10th edn (Oxford, Oxford University Press, 2009)

Stevens, T, 'New Media and Counter-Narrative Strategies' in: EJAM Kessels (ed), *Countering Violent Extremist Narratives,* National Coordinator for Counterterrorism, July 2010

Straub, J, 'The Prevention of E-Money Laundering: Tracking the Elusive Audit Trail' (2002) 25 *Suffolk Transnational Law Review* 515

Stromdale, C, 'Regulating Online Content: A Global View' (2007) 13 *Computer and Telecommunications Law Review* 173

Sugden, P, 'How Long is a Piece of String? The Meaning of "Commerical Scale" in Copyright Piracy', (2009) 31 *European Intellectual Property Review* 202

Suhr, O, 'Strafrechtsharmonisierung in der Europäischen Union: Neue Grenzziehungen und zusätzliche Kontrollaufträge' (2008) *ZEuS* 57

Tadić, F, 'How Harmonious can Harmonisation Be? A Theoretical Approach towards Harmonisation of (Criminal) Law' in A Klip and H Van der Wilt (eds), *Harmonisation and Harmonising Measures in Criminal Law. Vol. 186* (The Royal Academy of Arts and Science, Amsterdam, 2002) 1–23

Taylor, M and Quayle, E, *Child Pornography: An Internet Crime* (Hove, Brunner-Routledge, 2003)

Thürauf, A, 'Cookie Opt-in in Grossbritannien – Zukunft der Cookies?' (2012) 1 *Zeitschrift für Datenschutz* 24

Tiedemann, K, 'Grunderfordernisse einer Regelung des Allgemeinen Teils' in K Tiedemann (ed), *Wirtschaftsstrafrecht in der Europäischen Union : Rechtsdogmatik, Rechtsvergleich, Rechtspolitik, Freiburg-Symposium* (Köln, Heymanns, 2002) 3–22

time.lex, Study on activities undertaken to address threats that undermine confidence in the Information Society, such as spam, spyware and malicious software SMART 2008/0013 (Brussels, 2009)

Timofeeva, YA, 'Hate Speech Online: Restricted or Protected? Comparisons of Regulations in the United States and Germany' (2003) 12 *Journal of Transnational Law and Policy* 262

Tjaden, P and Thoennes, N, 'Stalking in America: Findings from the National Violence Against Women Survey' (1998) *National Institute of Justice and Centers for Disease Control and Prevention Research in Brief*

Topa, I, 'Where do we Stand with Harmonisation of Substantive Criminal law in the EU? Remarks on the Changes Introduced by the Lisbon Treaty' (2012) 4 *Silesian Journal of Legal Studies* 89

Trechsel, S, *Human Rights in Criminal Proceedings* (Oxford, Oxford University Press, 2005)

Tritton, G et al, *Intellectual Property in Europe* (London, Sweet & Maxwell, 2008)

Turano, L, 'Spain: Banning Political Parties as a Response to Basque Terrorism' (2003) 1 *International Journal of Constitutional Law* 730

Turner, JI, 'The Expressive Dimension of EU Criminal Law' (2012) 60 *American Journal of Comparative Law* 555

Ungerer, H and Costello, N, *Telekommunikation in Europa, Freie Wahl für den Benutzer im europäischen Binnenmarkt des Jahres 1992: Eine Herausforderung für die Europäische Gemeinschaft* (Brussells, Kommission der Europäischen Gemeinschaften, 1989)

Unger, R, *Law in Modern Society: Towards a Criticism of Social Theory* (New York, Free Press, 1976)

The United Kingdom Parliament Select Committee on European Scrutiny, *Democracy and Accountability in the EU and the Role of National Parliaments*, 33rd Report (London, 2002)
Urpmann-Wittzack, R, 'Das Anti-Counterfeiting Trade Agreement (ACTA) als Prüfstein für die Demokratie in Europa' (2011) 49 *Archiv des Völkerrechts* 105
Van Dijk, J, *The Network Society*, 2nd edn (London, Sage, 2006)
Vaver, D, *Some Aspects of the TRIPS Agreement: Copyright Enforcement and Dispute Settlement* (Oxford, 2000)
Verbiest, T, 'France' in PJ Kozyris (ed), *Regulating Internet Abuses: Invasion of Privacy* (Alphen aan den Rijn, Kluwer Law International, 2007) 45–56
——, 'Loi pour la Confiance Dans l'Economie Numerique: Examen du Nouveau Regime du Commerce Electronique' (2005) *Acta Universitatis Lucian Blaga* 160
Verdussen, M, *Contours et enjeux du droit constitutionnel pénal* (Brussels, Bruyant, 1995) 695
Vermeulen, G, 'Where Do We Currently Stand with Harmonisation in Europe?' in A Klip and H Van der Wilt (eds), *Harmonisation and Harmonising Measures in Criminal Law* (Amsterdam, Royal Netherlands Academy of Science, 2002) 65–76
Vogel, J, 'Strafgesetzgebungskompetenzen der Europäischen Union' in K Ambos (ed), *Europäisches Strafrecht post-Lissabon* (Göttingen, Universitätsverlag Göttingen, 2011) 41–56
Wall, D, 'Digital Realism and the Governance of Spam as a Cybercrime' (2005) 10 *European Journal of Criminal Law Policy and Research* 309
Walter, MM, 'Term Directive' in MM Walter and S Von Lewinski (ed), *European Copyright Law: A Commentary* (Oxford, Oxford University Press, 2010)
Walter, MM and Goebel, D, 'Enforcement Directive' in MM Walter and S Von Lewinski (ed), *European Copyright Law. A Commentary* (Oxford, Oxford University Press, 2010)
Wasmeier, M and Thwaites, N, 'The Battle of the Pillars: Does the European Community Have the Power to Approximate National Criminal Laws?' (2004) 29 *EL Rev* 613
Weenink, H, 'The Legal Framework for the Protection of the Euro against Counterfeiting' (2004) 19 *JIBLR* 276
Weigend, T, 'Mindestanforderungen an ein europaweit geltendes harmonisiertes Strafrecht' in F Zieschang, E Hilgendorf and K Laubenthal (ed), *Strafrecht und Kriminalität in Europa* (Baden-Baden, Nomos, 2003) 57–80
Weitendorf, S, *Die interne Betrugsbekämpfung in den Europäischen Gemeinschaften durch das Europäische Amt für Betrugsbekämpfung (OLAF)* (Hamburg, Lit, 2007)
Weyembergh, A, 'Approximation of Criminal Laws, the Constitutional Treaty and the Hague Programme' (2005) 42 *CMLR* 1567
——, 'The Functions of Approximation of Penal legislation Within the European Union' (2005) 12 *Maastricht Journal of European and Comparative Law* 149
White, MD and Fisher, C, 'Assessing Our Knowledge of Identity Theft: The Challenges to Effective Prevention and Control Efforts' (2008) 19 *Criminal Justice Policy Review* 3
White, S, 'Harmonisation of Criminal Law under the First Pillar' (2006) 31 *EL Rev* 81
Williams, KL, Howell, T, Cooper, BS, Yuille, JC and Paulhus, DL, 'Deviant Sexual Thoughts and Behaviours: the Roles of Personality and Pornography Use' (May 2004) Department of Psychology, University of British Columbia. Part of Presentation at the Annual Conference of the American Psychological Society, Chicago, IL
Williams, KS, 'Child Pornography Law: Does it Protect Children?' (2004) 26 *Journal of Social Welfare and Family Law* 245
Wyatt, D et al, *Wyatt and Dashwood, European Union Law* (London, Sweet & Maxwell, 2006)

van den Wyngaert, C, 'Eurojust and the European Public Prosecutor in the Corpus Juris Model: Water and Fire?' in N Walker (ed), *Europe's Area of Freedom, Justice and Security* (Oxford, Oxford University Press, 2004) 201–39

INDEX